ORANGE PLANET

2

HARUKA FUKUSHIMA

Translated and adapted by Kaya Laterman
Lettered by North Market Street Graphics

DEL
REY

BALLANTINE BOOKS • NEW YORK

Orange Planet volume 2 is a work of fiction. Names, characters, places, and incidents are the products of the author's imagination or are used fictitiously. Any resemblance to actual events, locales, or persons, living or dead, is entirely coincidental.

A Del Rey Manga/Kodansha Trade Paperback Original

Published in the United States by Del Rey Books, an imprint of The Random House Publishing Group, a division of Random House, Inc., New York.

Publication rights arranged through Kodansha Ltd.

First published in Japan in 2006 by Kodansha Ltd., Tokyo

ISBN 978-0-345-51339-7

Printed in the United States of America

www.delreymanga.com

9 8 7 6 5 4 3 2 1

Translator/Adapter: Kaya Laterman
Lettering: North Market Street Graphics

Contents

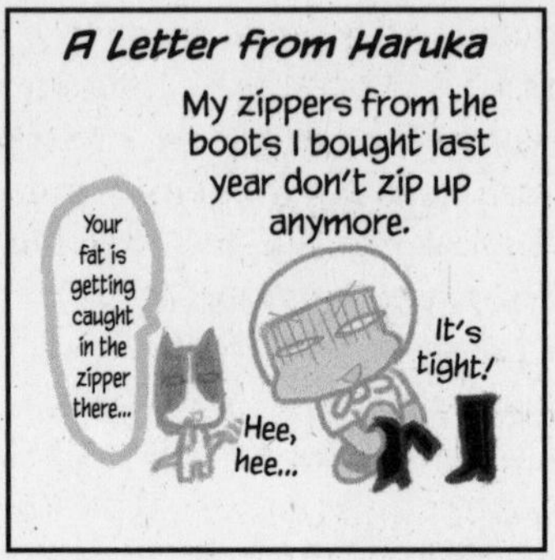
A Letter from Haruka
My zippers from the boots I bought last year don't zip up anymore.
It's tight!
Your fat is getting caught in the zipper there...
Hee, hee...

Honorifics Explained

Throughout the Del Rey Manga books, you will find Japanese honorifics left intact in the translations. For those not familiar with how the Japanese use honorifics and, more important, how they differ from American honorifics, we present this brief overview.

Politeness has always been a critical facet of Japanese culture. Ever since the feudal era, when Japan was a highly stratified society, use of honorifics—which can be defined as polite speech that indicates relationship or status—has played an essential role in the Japanese language. When addressing someone in Japanese, an honorific usually takes the form of a suffix attached to one's name (example: "Asuna-san"), is used as a title at the end of one's name, or appears in place of the name itself (example: "Negi-sensei," or simply "Sensei!").

Honorifics can be expressions of respect or endearment. In the context of manga and anime, honorifics give insight into the nature of the relationship between characters. Many English translations leave out these important honorifics and therefore distort the feel of the original Japanese. Because Japanese honorifics contain nuances that English honorifics lack, it is our policy at Del Rey not to translate them. Here, instead, is a guide to some of the honorifics you may encounter in Del Rey Manga.

-san: This is the most common honorific and is equivalent to Mr., Miss, Ms., or Mrs. It is the all-purpose honorific and can be used in any situation where politeness is required.

-sama: This is one level higher than "-san" and is used to confer great respect.

-dono: This comes from the word "tono," which means "lord." It is an even higher level than "-sama" and confers utmost respect.

-kun: This suffix is used at the end of boys' names to express familiarity or endearment. It is also sometimes used by men among friends, or when addressing someone younger or of a lower station.

-chan: This is used to express endearment, mostly toward girls. It is also used for little boys, pets, and even among lovers. It gives a sense of childish cuteness.

Bozu: This is an informal way to refer to a boy, similar to the English terms "kid" and "squirt."

Sempai/Senpai: This title suggests that the addressee is one's senior in a group or organization. It is most often used in a school setting, where underclassmen refer to their upperclassmen as "sempai." It can also be used in the workplace, such as when a newer employee addresses an employee who has seniority in the company.

Kohai: This is the opposite of "sempai" and is used toward underclassmen in school or newcomers in the workplace. It connotes that the addressee is of a lower station.

Sensei: Literally meaning "one who has come before," this title is used for teachers, doctors, or masters of any profession or art.

-[blank]: This is usually forgotten in these lists, but it is perhaps the most significant difference between Japanese and English. The lack of honorific means that the speaker has permission to address the person in a very intimate way. Usually, only family, spouses, or very close friends have this kind of permission. Known as *yobisute*, it can be gratifying when someone who has earned the intimacy starts to call one by one's name without an honorific. But when that intimacy hasn't been earned, it can be very insulting.

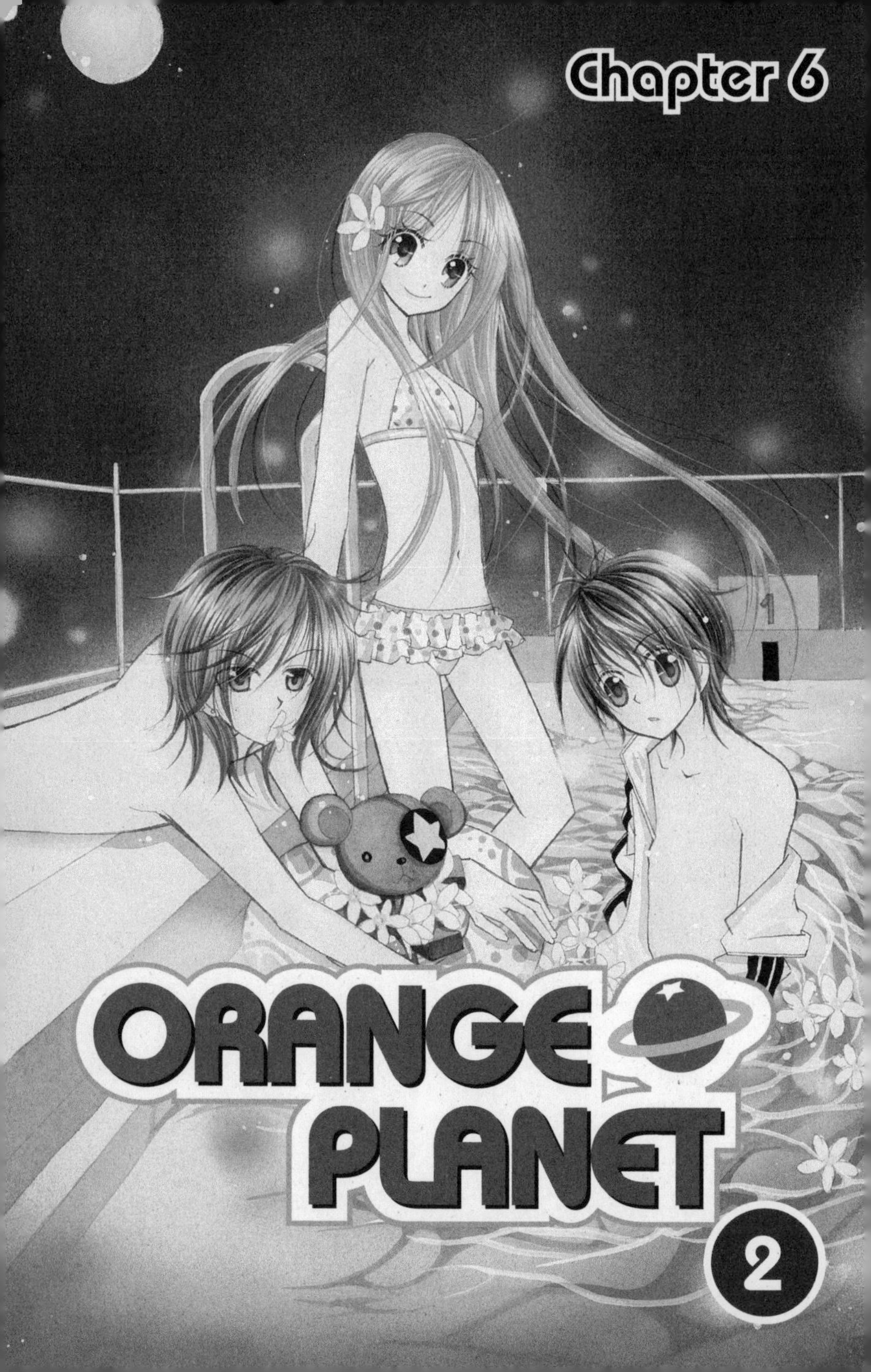
Chapter 6
ORANGE PLANET
2

Orange Planet
The Story Thus Far...

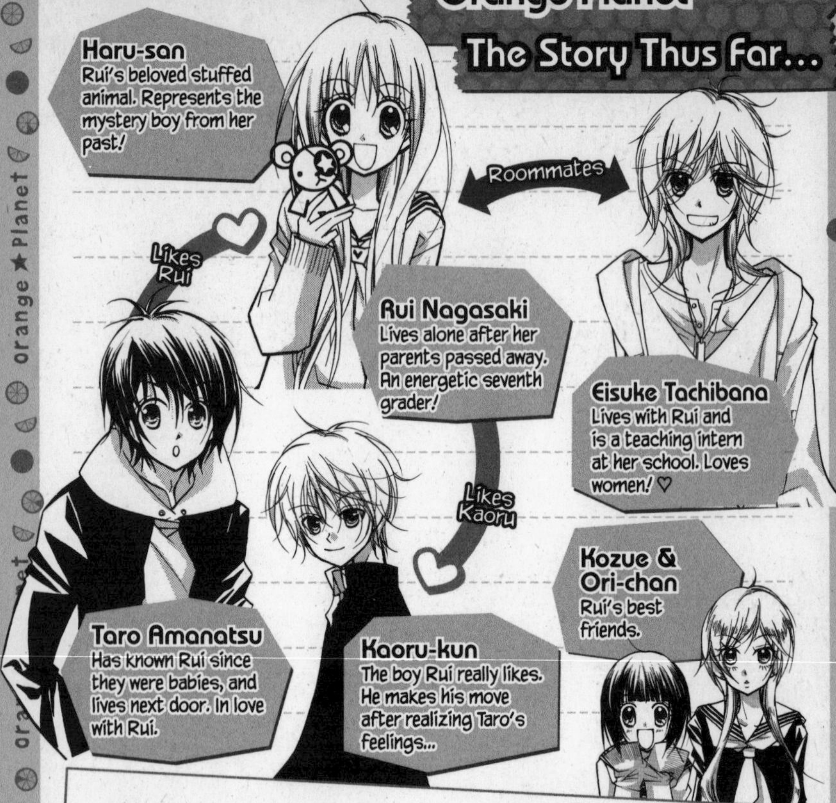
Haru-san
Rui's beloved stuffed animal. Represents the mystery boy from her past!
Roommates
Likes Rui
Rui Nagasaki
Lives alone after her parents passed away. An energetic seventh grader!
Eisuke Tachibana
Lives with Rui and is a teaching intern at her school. Loves women! ♡
Likes Kaoru
Kozue & Ori-chan
Rui's best friends.
Taro Amanatsu
Has known Rui since they were babies, and lives next door. In love with Rui.
Kaoru-kun
The boy Rui really likes. He makes his move after realizing Taro's feelings...

☆ After her parents passed away, Rui was on her own. Unable to forget the boy who lifted her spirits during her parents' funeral, she began to write letters to a stuffed animal, but never received a reply.

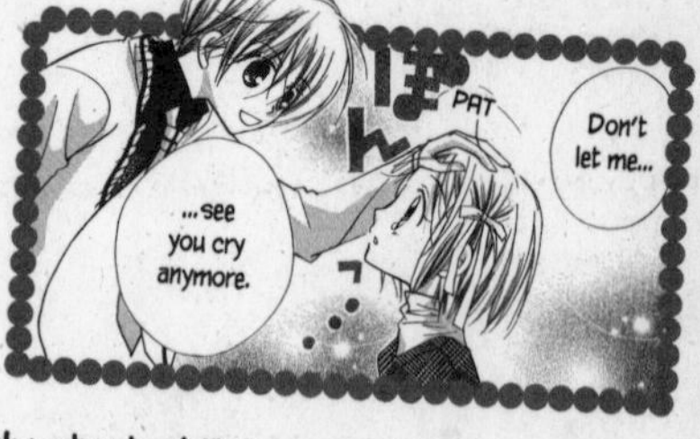
PAT
Don't let me...
...see you cry anymore.

☆ Then one day, Rui got a roommate!! The man who suddenly started living with her turned out to be a teaching intern at her school!! They started secretly living together and...?!

☆ In the meantime, Taro couldn't stop thinking about Rui. But Rui really likes Kaoru. A bizarre love triangle was formed... Kaoru acts like he's interested in Rui, but who does he really like?!

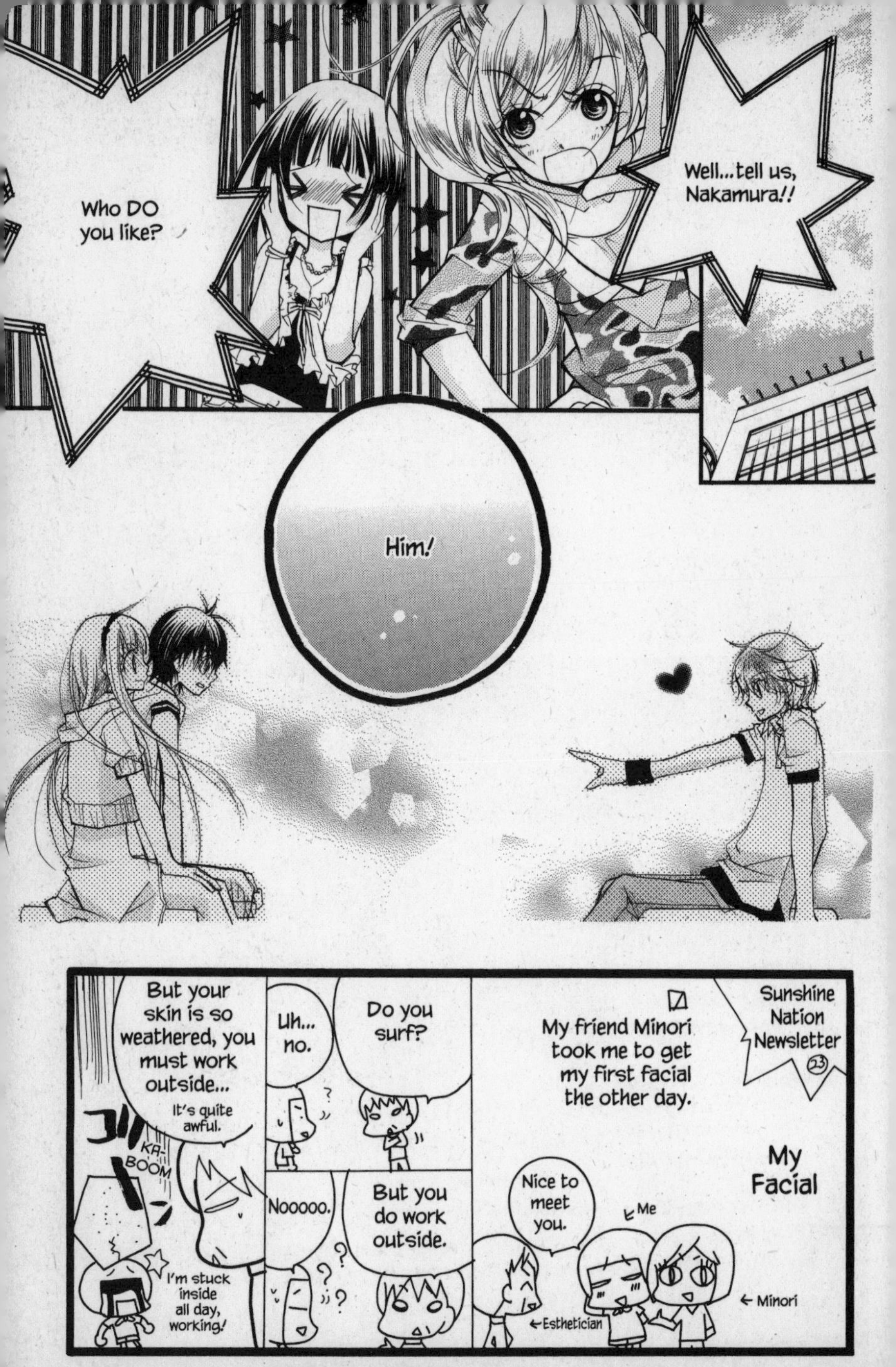
Well...tell us, Nakamura!!
Who DO you like?
Him!
Sunshine Nation Newsletter 23
My Facial
My friend Minori took me to get my first facial the other day.
Nice to meet you.
Me
Minori
Esthetician
Do you surf?
Uh... no.
But you do work outside.
Nooooo.
But your skin is so weathered, you must work outside...
It's quite awful.
KA-BOOM
I'm stuck inside all day, working!

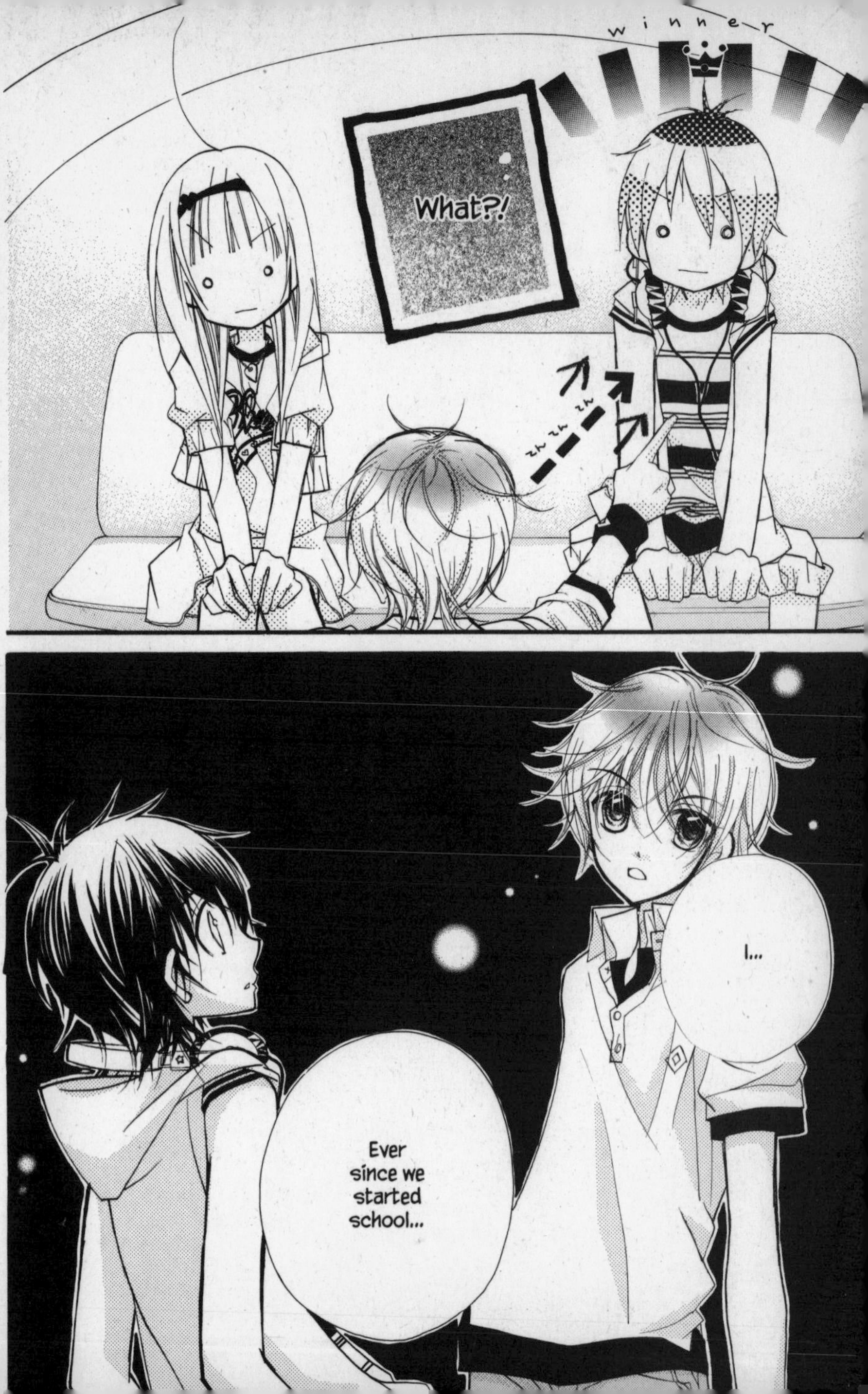
winner
What?!
I...
Ever since we started school...

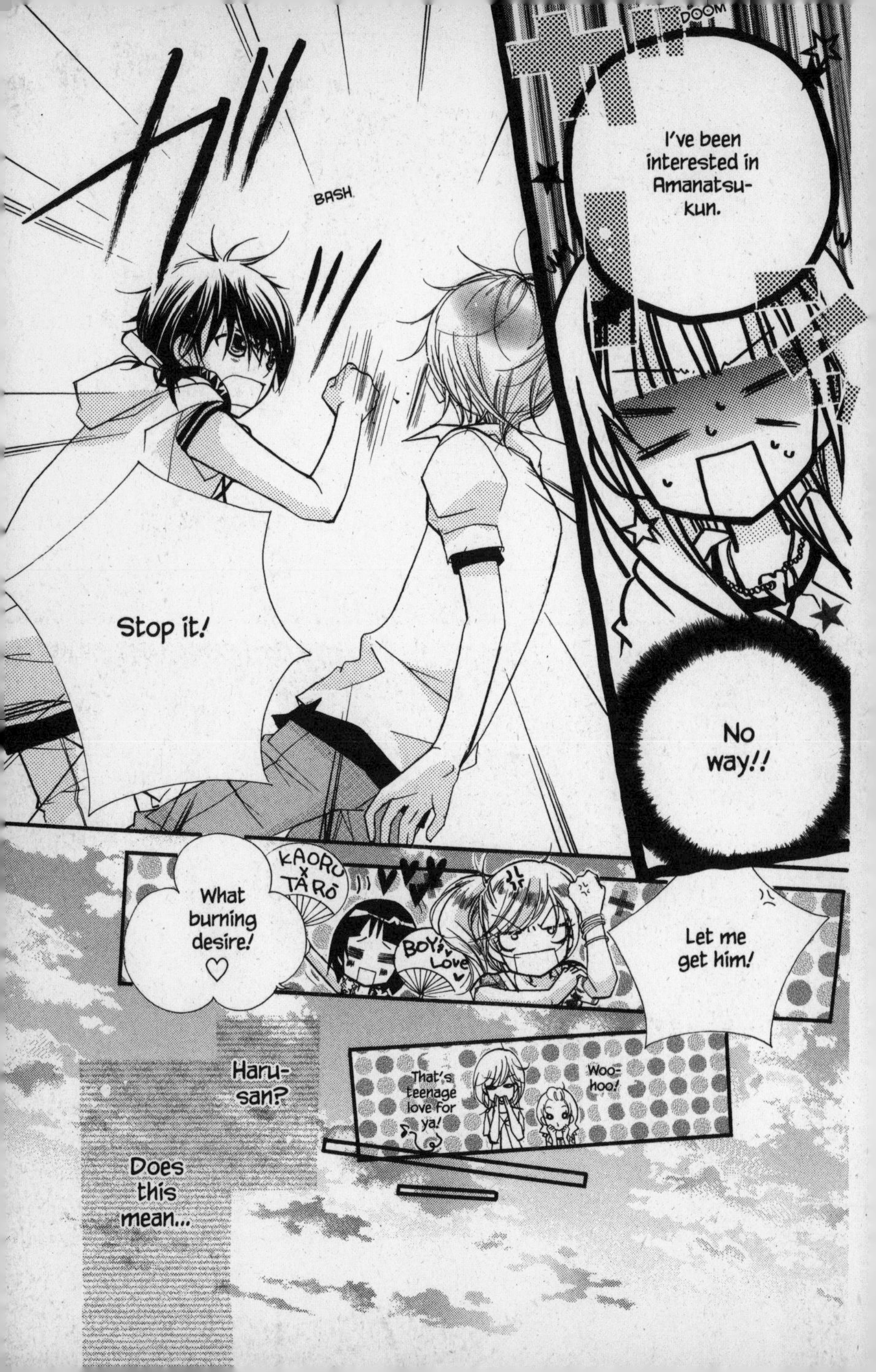
DOOM
I've been interested in Amanatsu-kun.
No way!!
BASH
Stop it!
Let me get him!
KAORU x TĀRŌ
BOYS LOVE
What burning desire! ♡
Woo-hoo!
That's teenage love for ya!
Haru-san?
Does this mean...

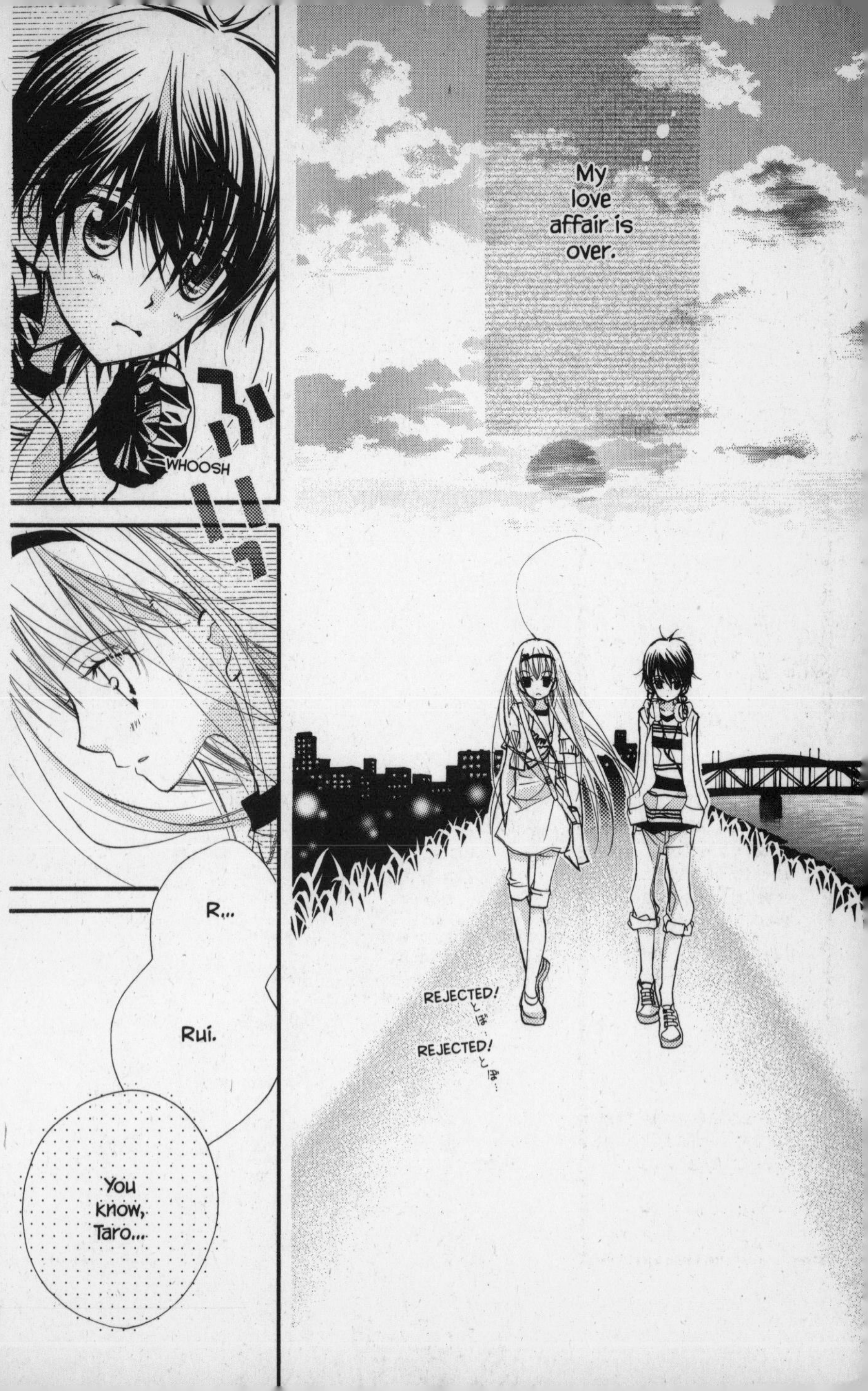

My love affair is over.
REJECTED! とぼ…
REJECTED! とぼ…
WHOOSH
R...
Rui.
You know, Taro...

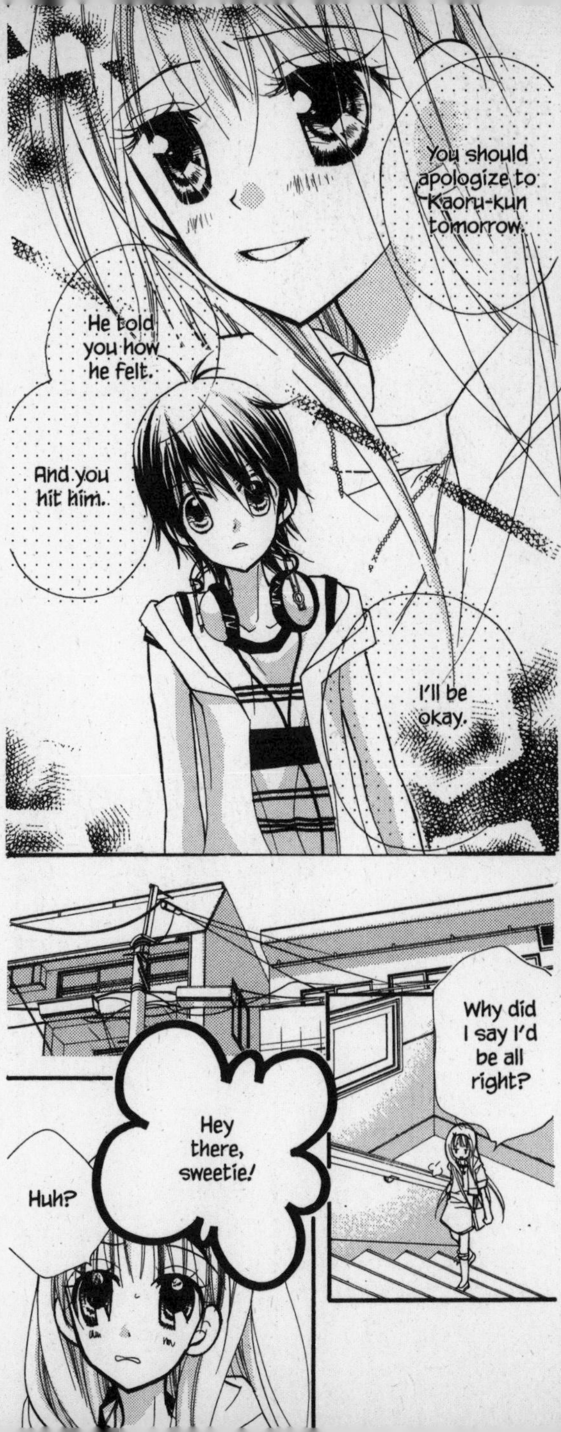

You should apologize to Kaoru-kun tomorrow.
He told you how he felt.
And you hit him.
I'll be okay.
Why did I say I'd be all right?
Hey there, sweetie!
Huh?

ONE

☐ How is everyone? I'm...

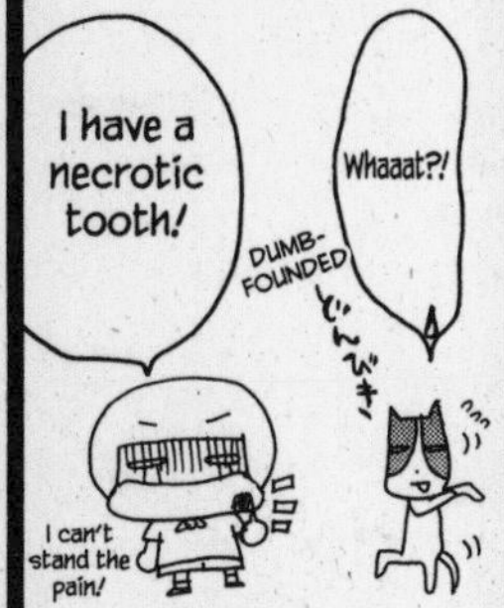

I have a necrotic tooth!
Whaaat?!
DUMB-FOUNDED
I can't stand the pain!

Ahhhhh!

What's a necrotic tooth? I'm too scared to find out. What if my teeth start to crumble?

I'm turning into an old lady!

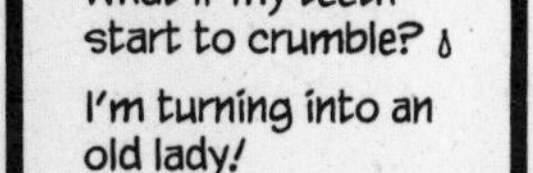

POUND!
POUND!
POUND!

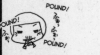

☐ So I ended up getting my teeth filled like the old lady that I am...

Thanks in advance!

← On to PART TWO

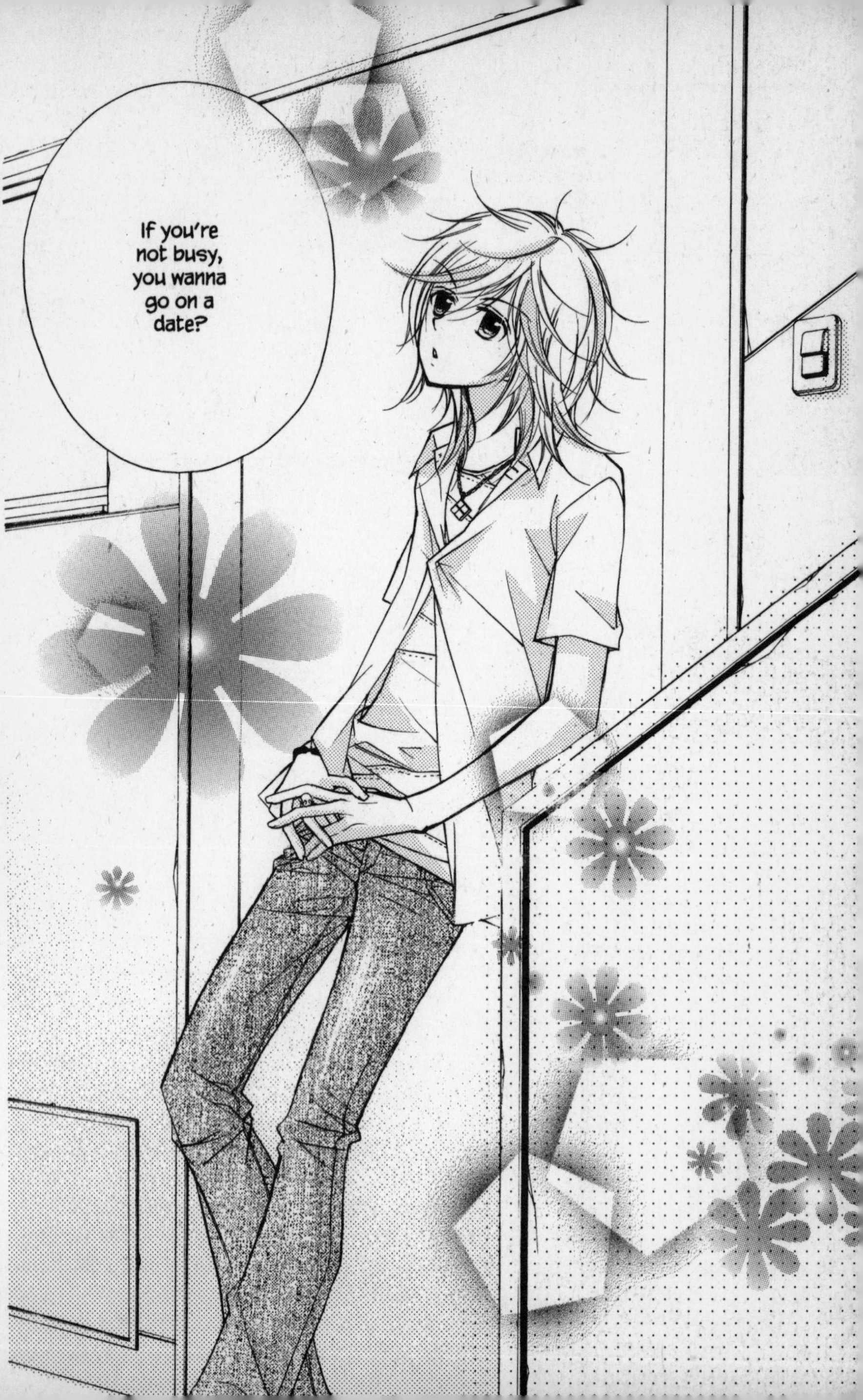
If you're not busy, you wanna go on a date?

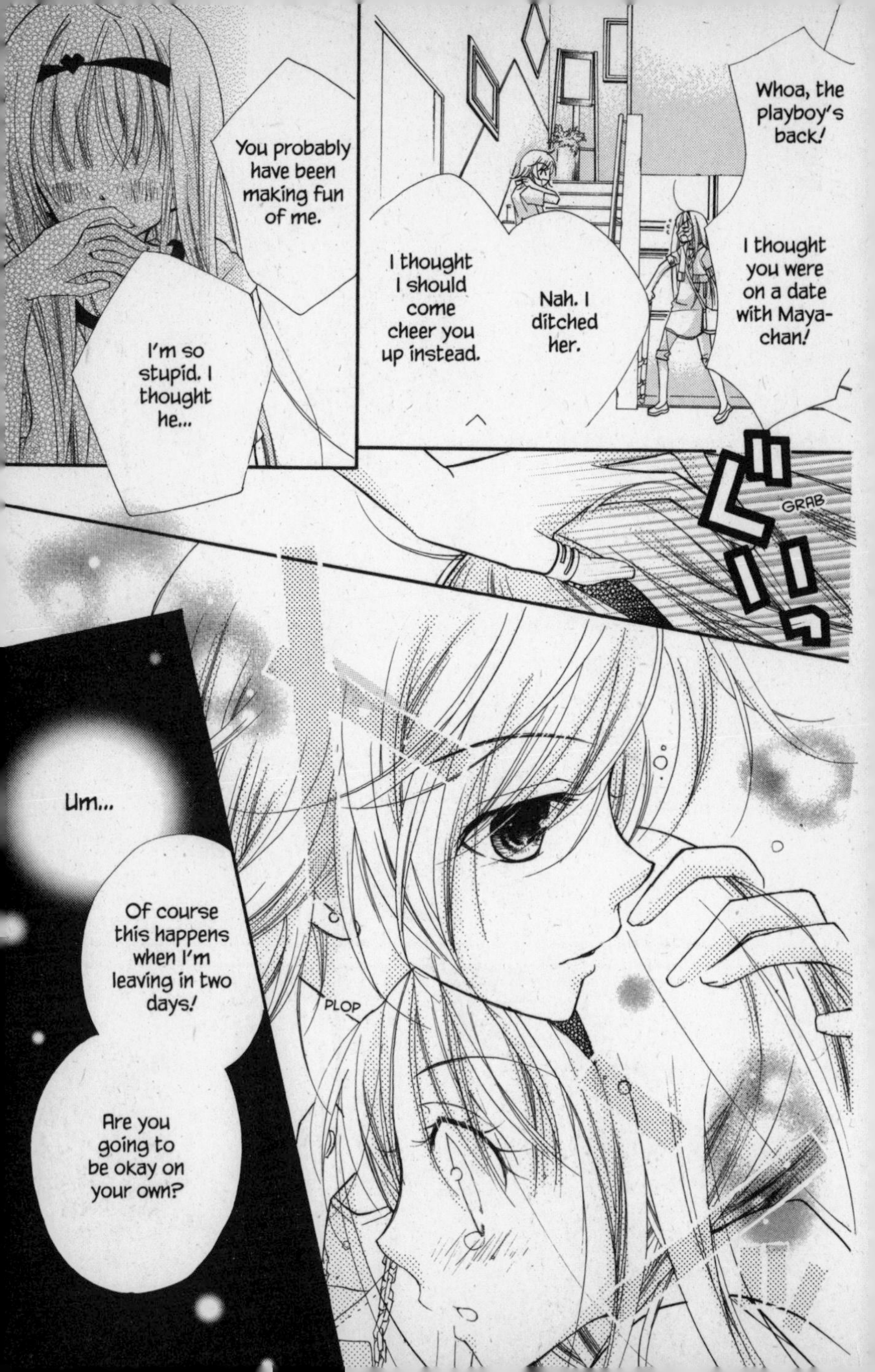
Whoa, the playboy's back!
I thought you were on a date with Maya-chan!
Nah. I ditched her.
I thought I should come cheer you up instead.
You probably have been making fun of me.
I'm so stupid. I thought he...
GRAB
PLOP
Um...
Of course this happens when I'm leaving in two days!
Are you going to be okay on your own?

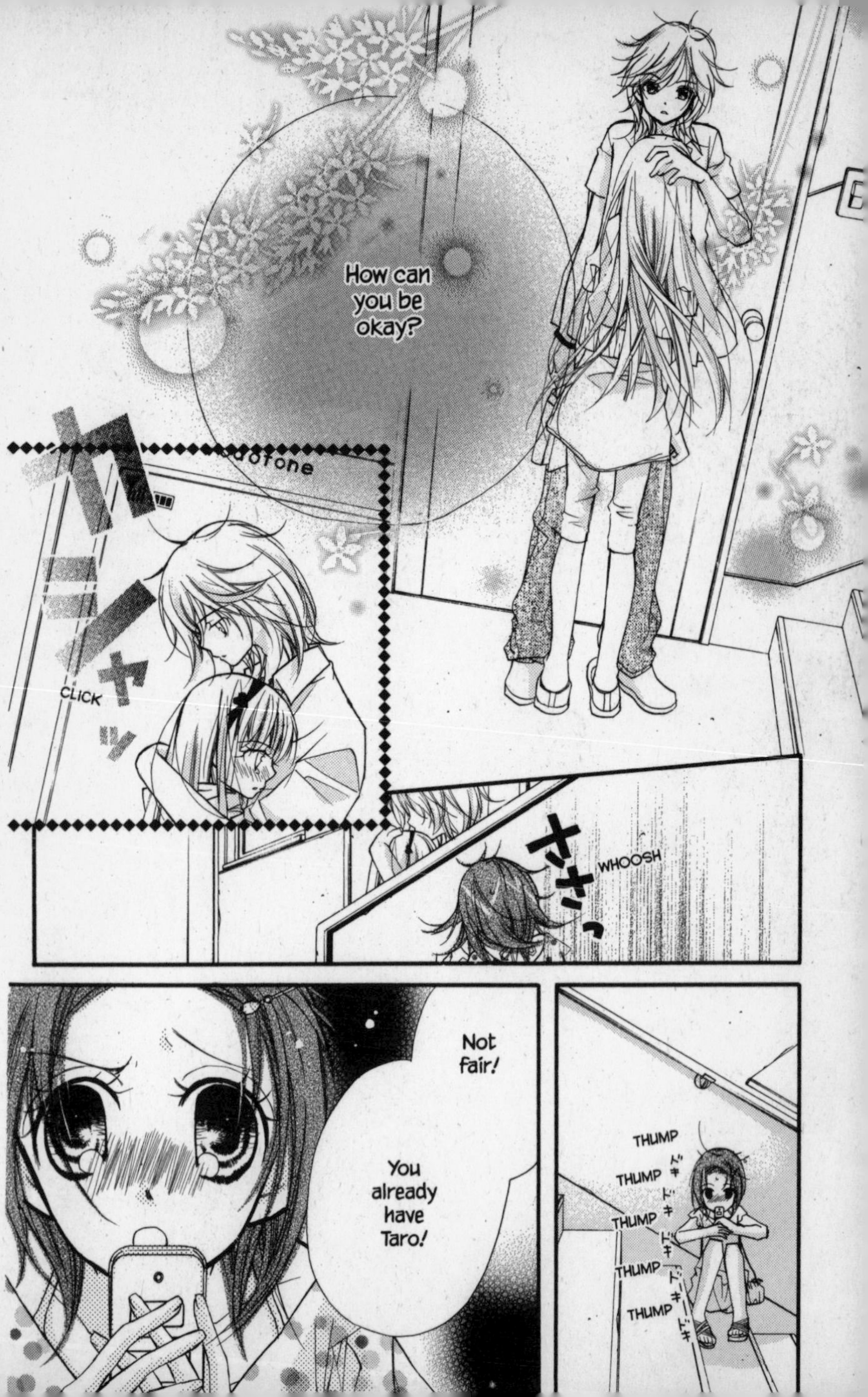

How can you be okay?
odafone
カチャッ
CLICK
ささっ
WHOOSH
THUMP
THUMP
THUMP
THUMP
THUMP
ドキ
ドキ
ドキ
ドキ
ドキ
Not fair!
You already have Taro!

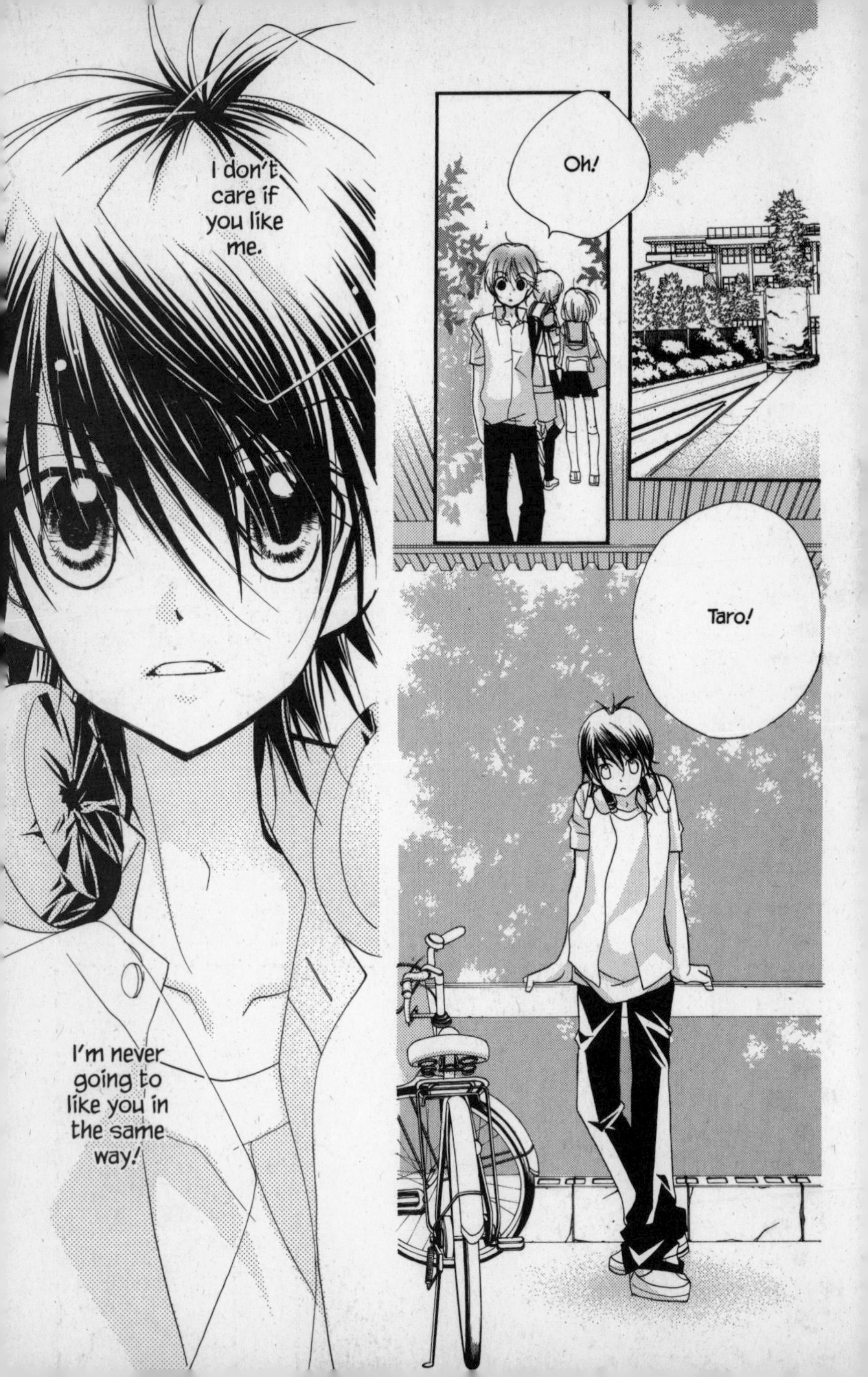
Oh!
Taro!
I don't care if you like me.
I'm never going to like you in the same way!

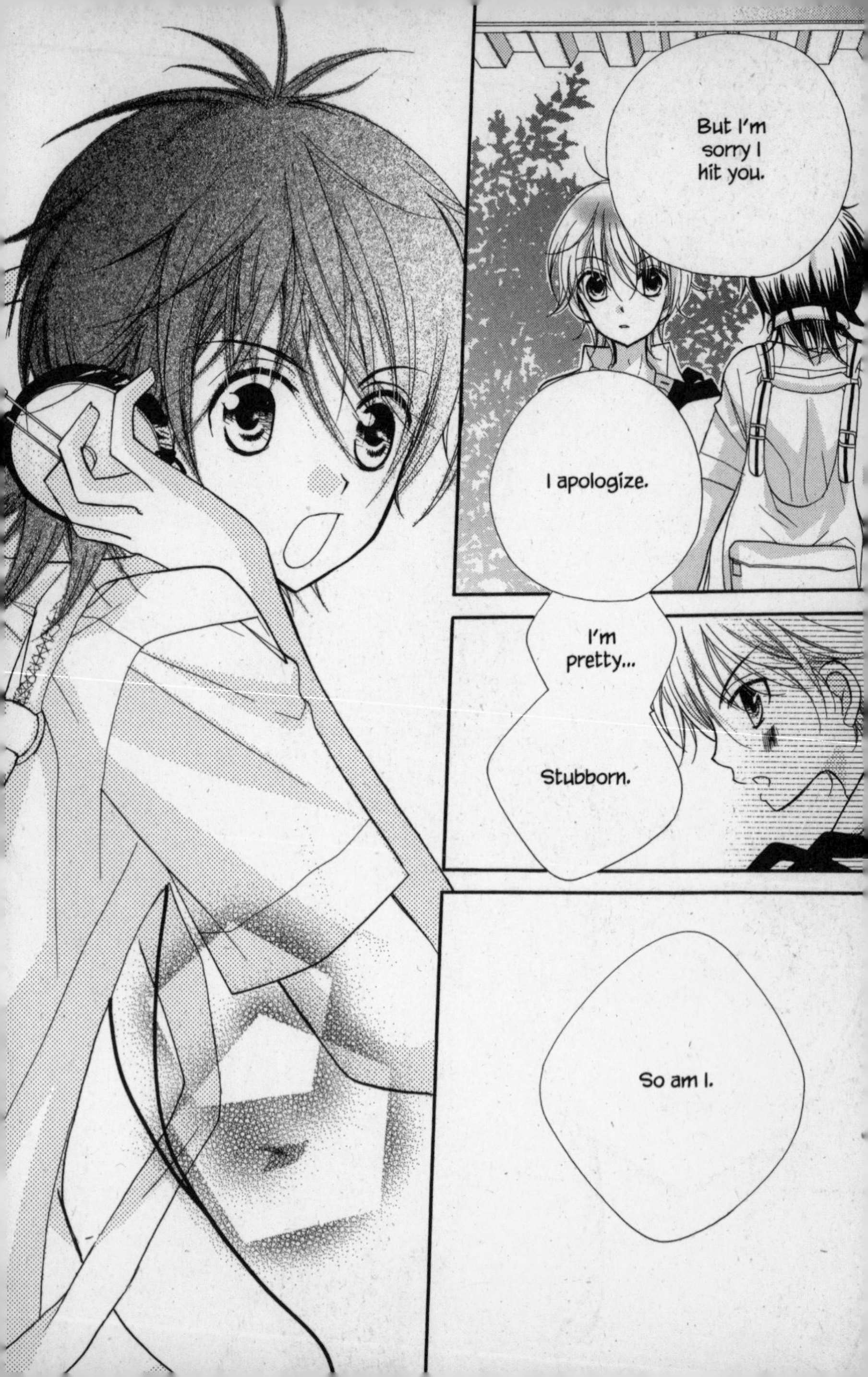
But I'm sorry I hit you.
I apologize.
I'm pretty...
Stubborn.
So am I.

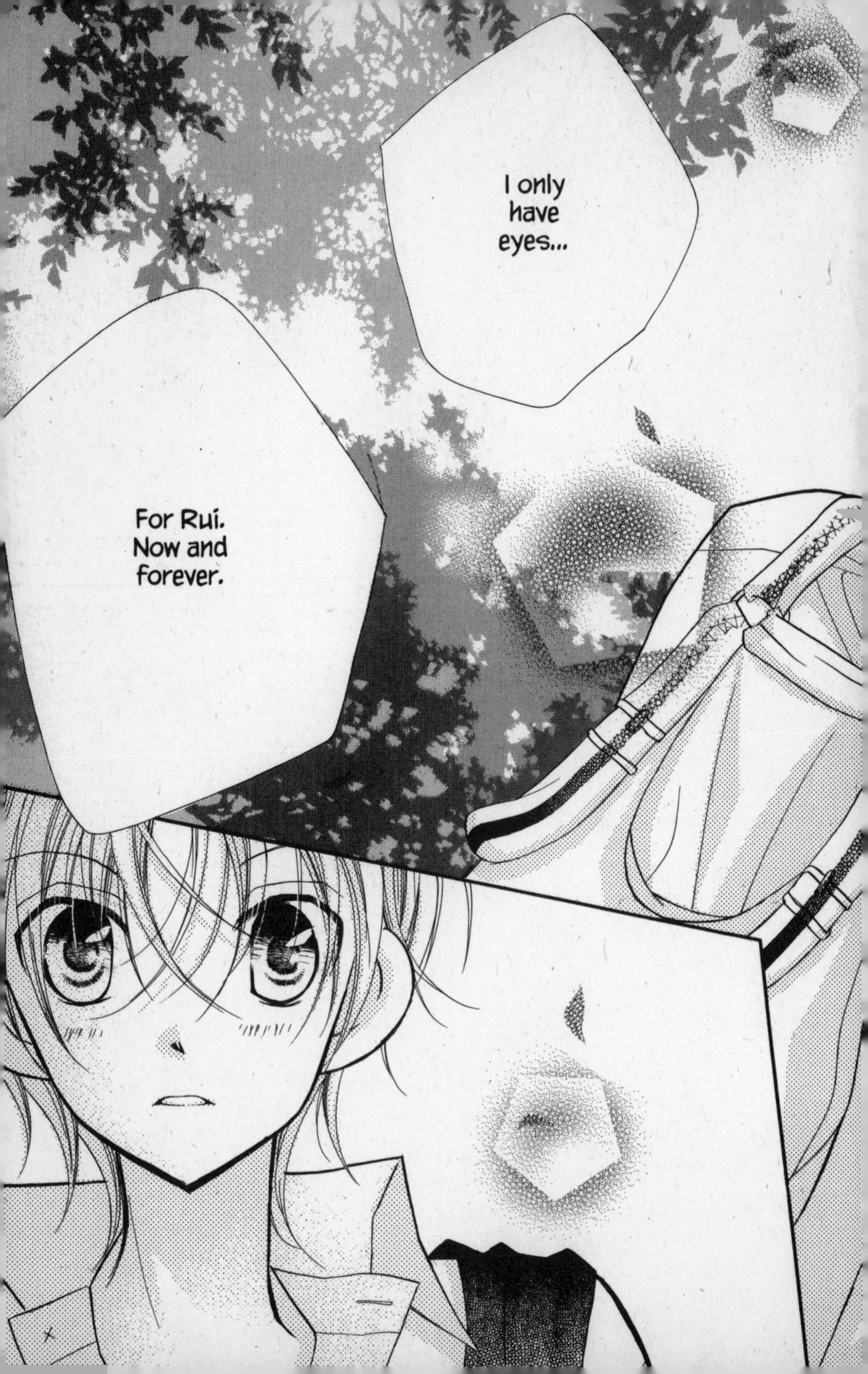
I only have eyes...
For Rui. Now and forever.

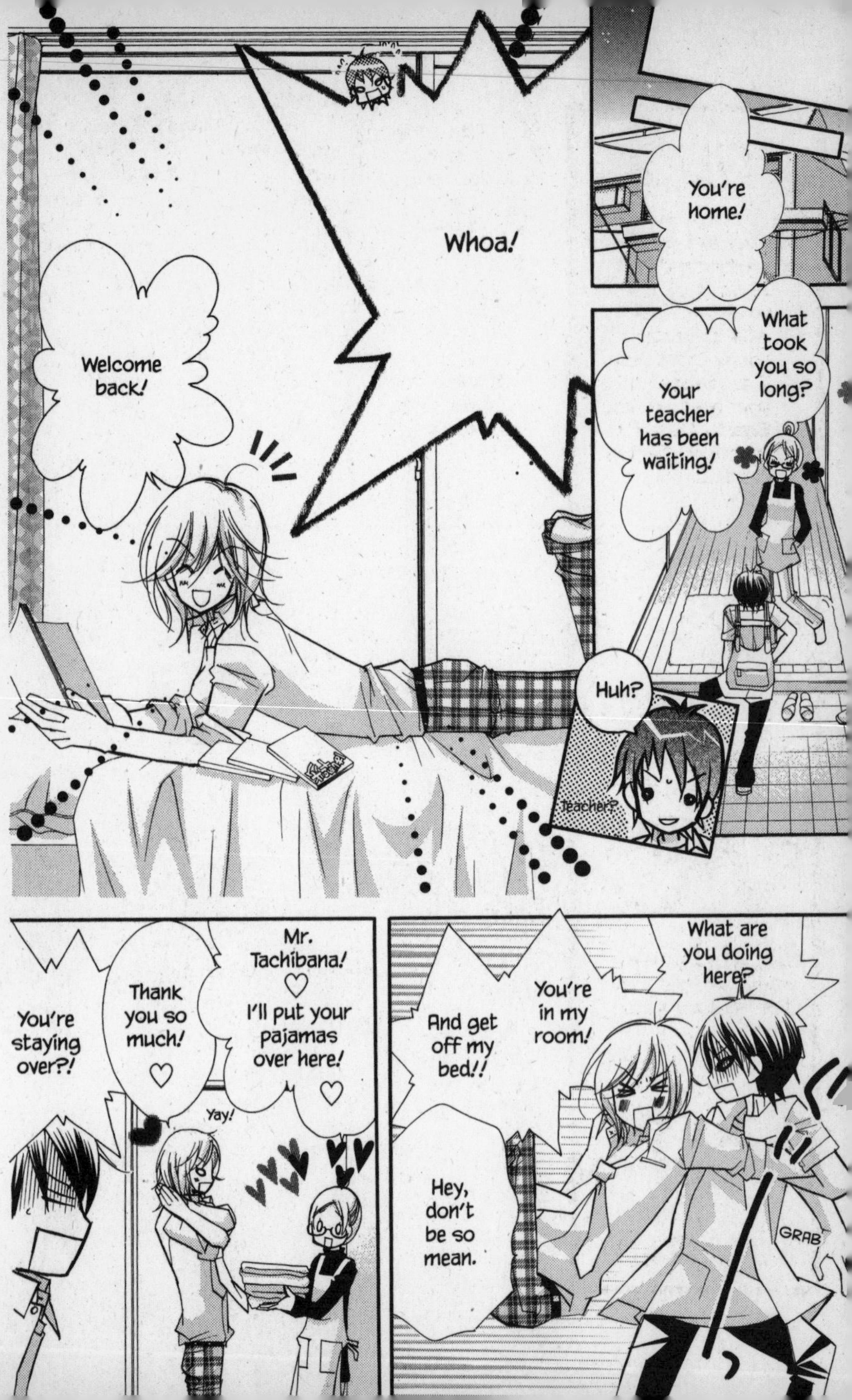
You're home!
What took you so long?
Your teacher has been waiting!
Huh?
Teacher?
Whoa!
Welcome back!
What are you doing here?
You're in my room!
And get off my bed!!
Hey, don't be so mean.
GRAB
Mr. Tachibana! ♡
I'll put your pajamas over here! ♡
Thank you so much! ♡
Yay!
You're staying over?!

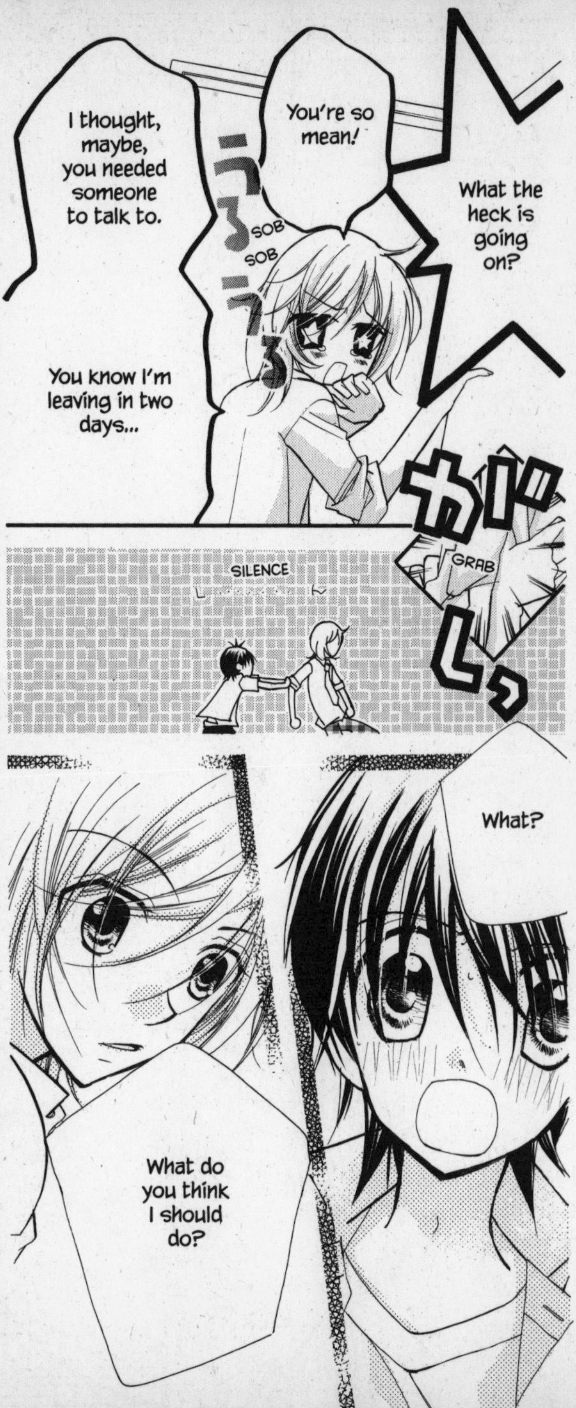
You're so mean!
What the heck is going on?
I thought, maybe, you needed someone to talk to.
SOB
SOB
You know I'm leaving in two days...
GRAB
SILENCE
What?
What do you think I should do?

TWO

☑ When *Orange Planet 1* was published, I asked all of you to tell me which male character you liked the best. Thanks for all of your great replies. Shortly thereafter, my editor, Zushee, decided...

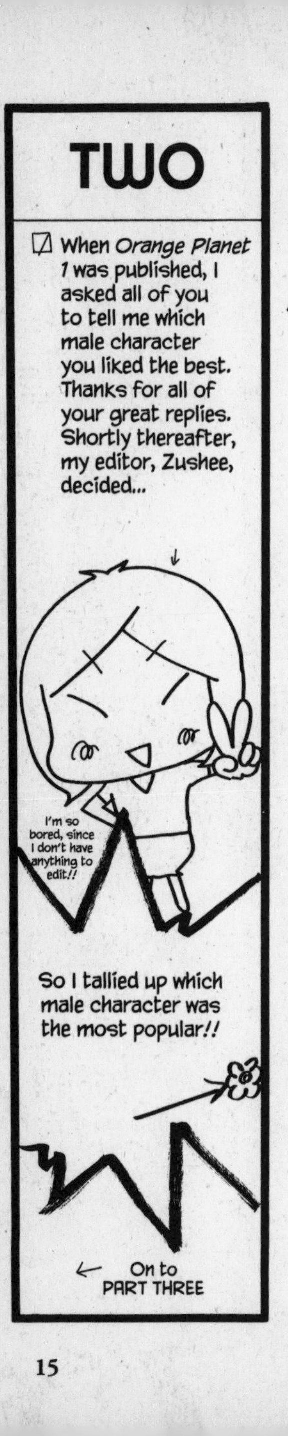
I'm so bored, since I don't have anything to edit!!

So I tallied up which male character was the most popular!!

On to PART THREE

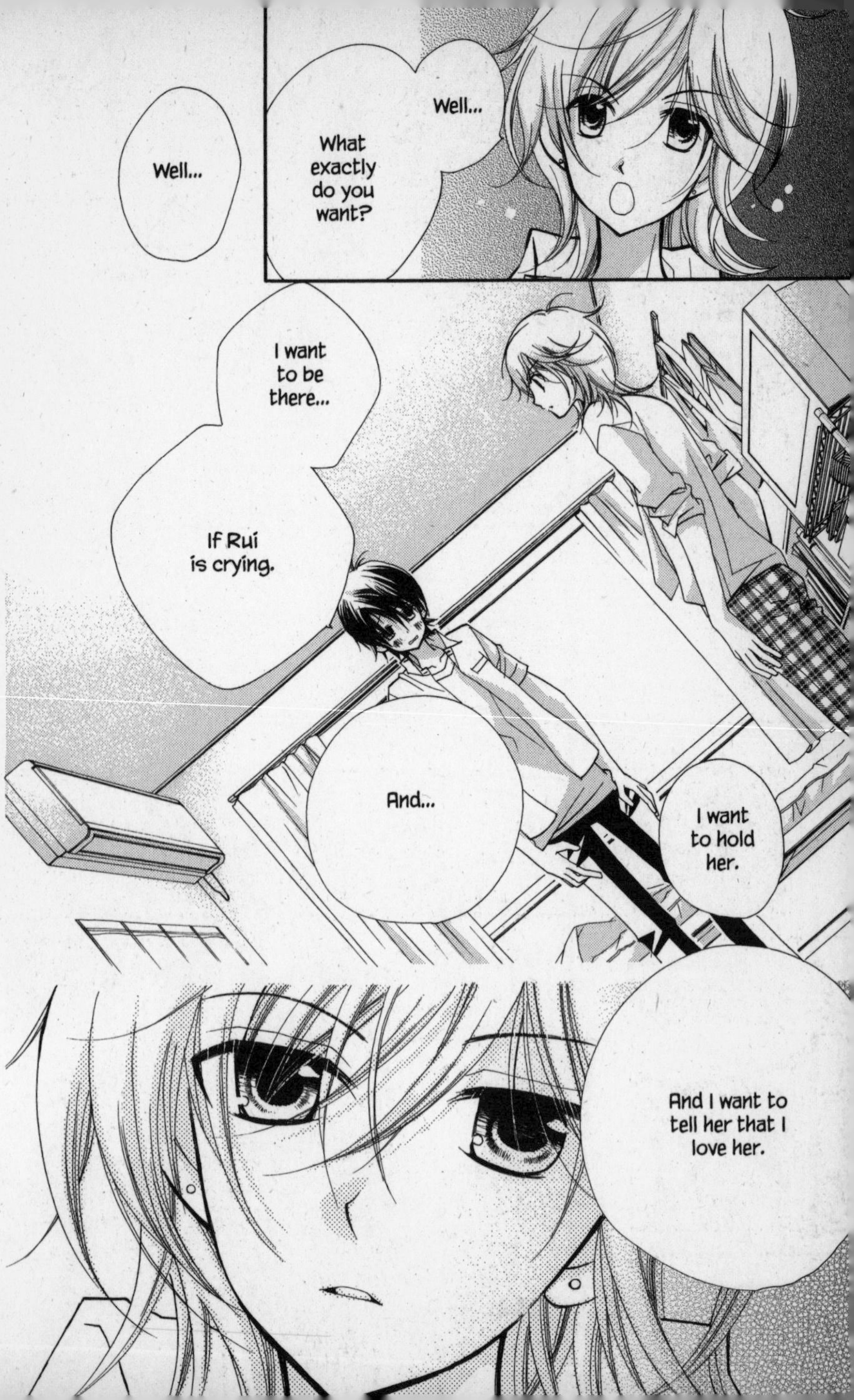
Well...
What exactly do you want?
Well...
I want to be there...
If Rui is crying.
And...
I want to hold her.
And I want to tell her that I love her.

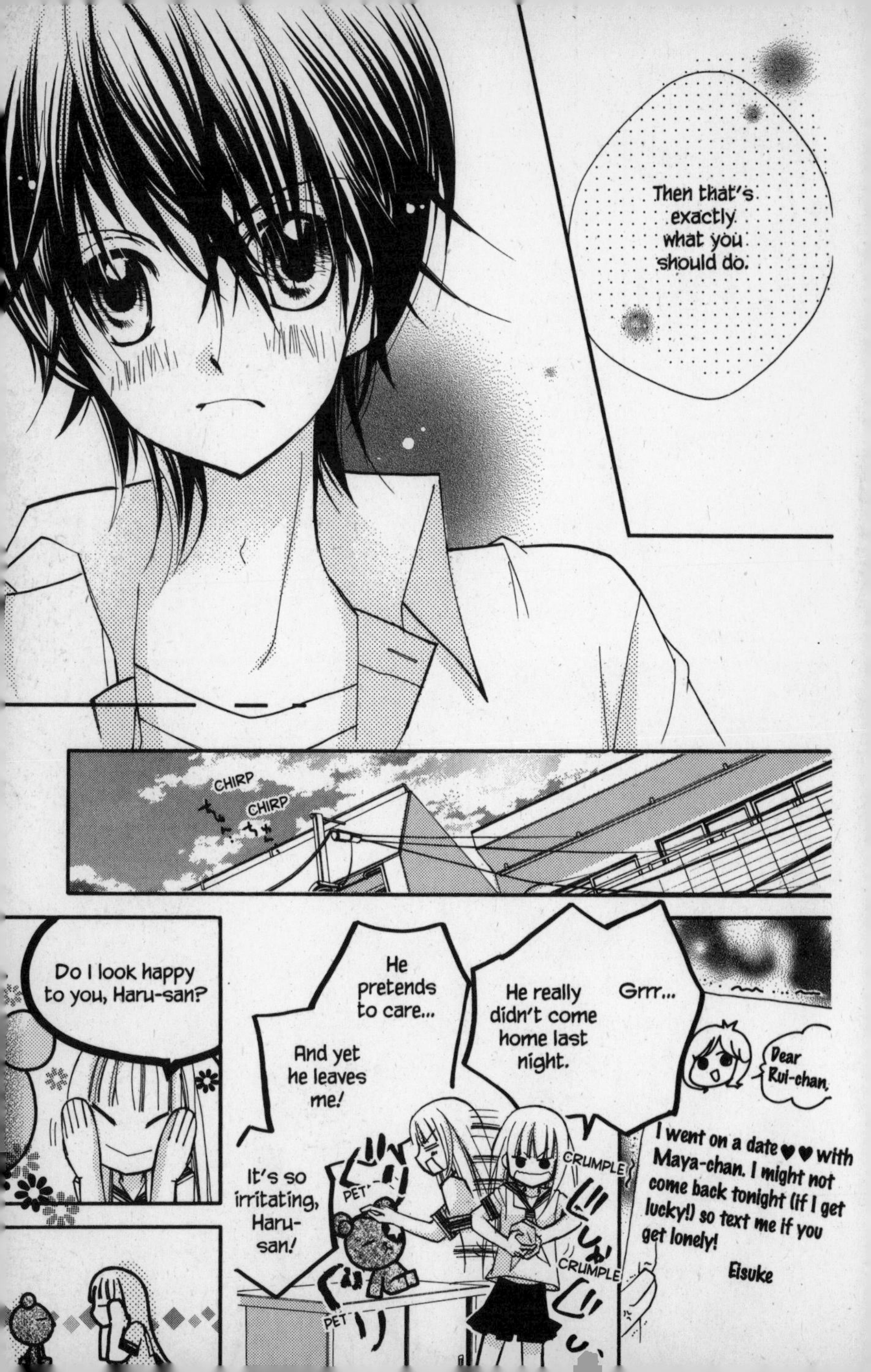

Then that's exactly what you should do.
CHIRP
CHIRP
Dear Rui-chan,
I went on a date ♥ ♥ with Maya-chan. I might not come back tonight (if I get lucky!) so text me if you get lonely!
Eisuke
Grrr...
He really didn't come home last night.
He pretends to care...
And yet he leaves me!
CRUMPLE
CRUMPLE
It's so irritating, Haru-san!
PET
PET
Do I look happy to you, Haru-san?

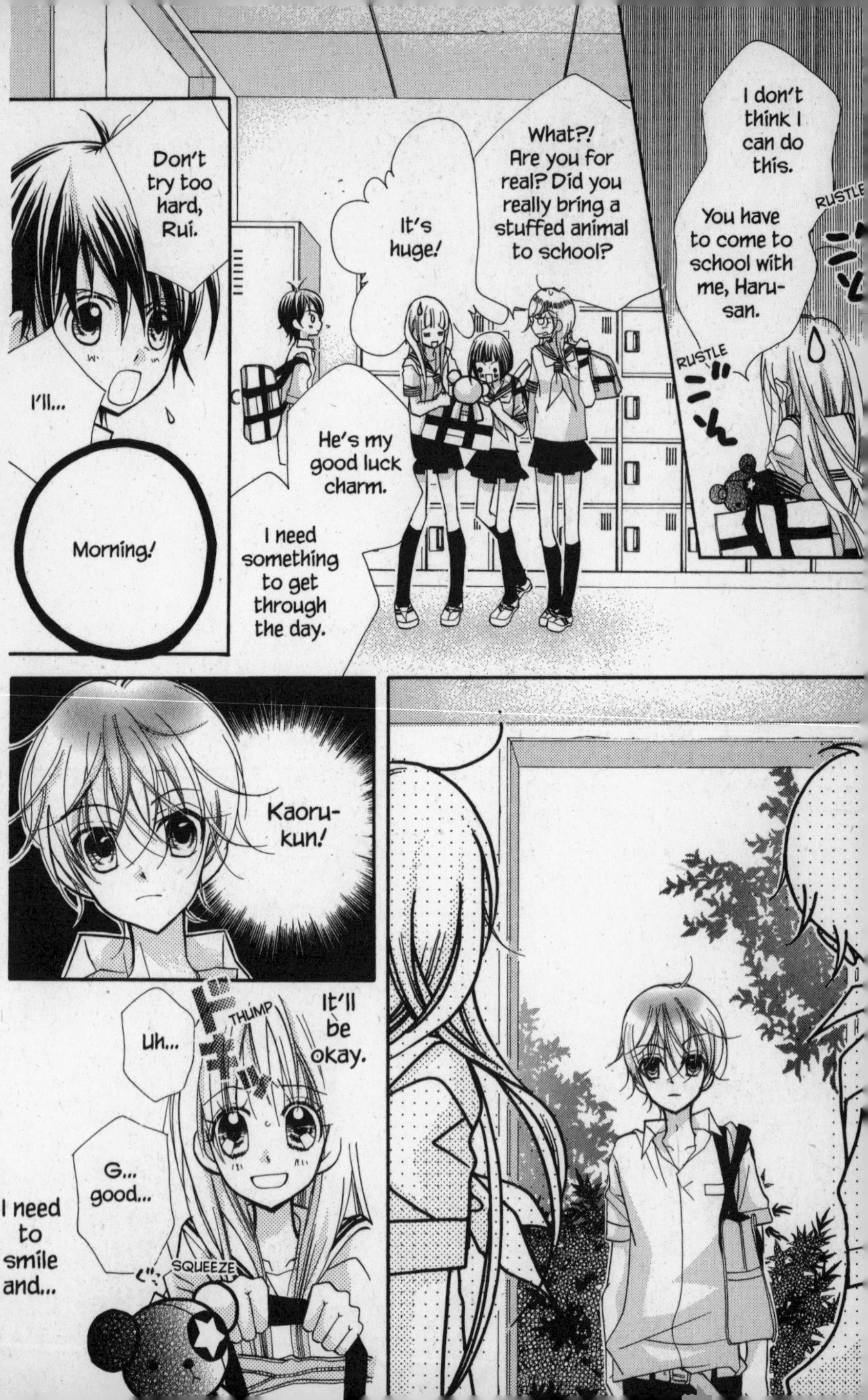
I don't think I can do this.
You have to come to school with me, Haru-san.
RUSTLE
RUSTLE
What?! Are you for real? Did you really bring a stuffed animal to school?
It's huge!
He's my good luck charm.
I need something to get through the day.
Don't try too hard, Rui.
I'll...
Morning!
Kaoru-kun!
It'll be okay.
THUMP
Uh...
G... good...
I need to smile and...
SQUEEZE

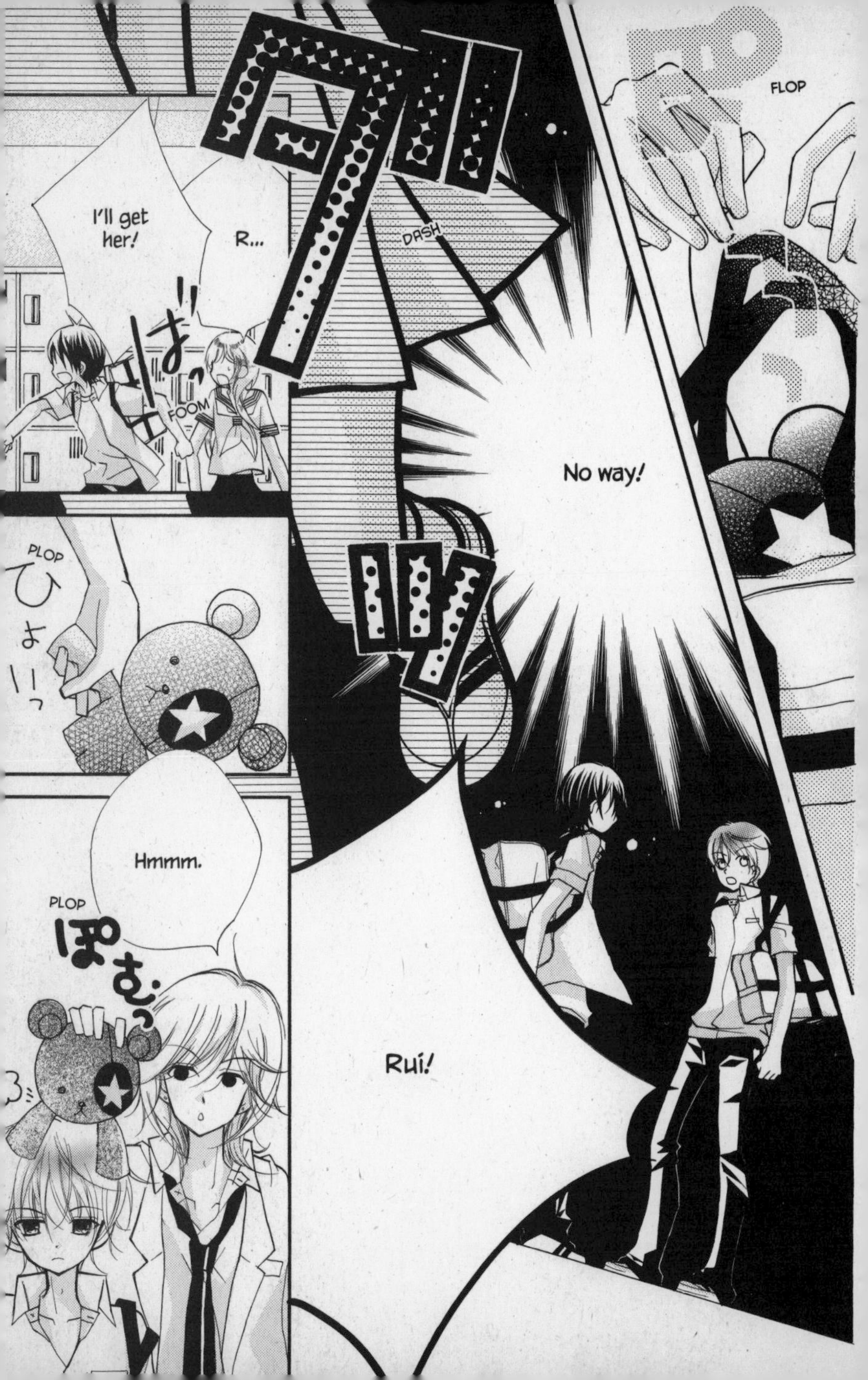
FLOP
DASH
No way!
Rui!
R...
I'll get her!
ばっ
FOOM
PLOP
ひょいっ
Hmmm.
PLOP
ぽむっ

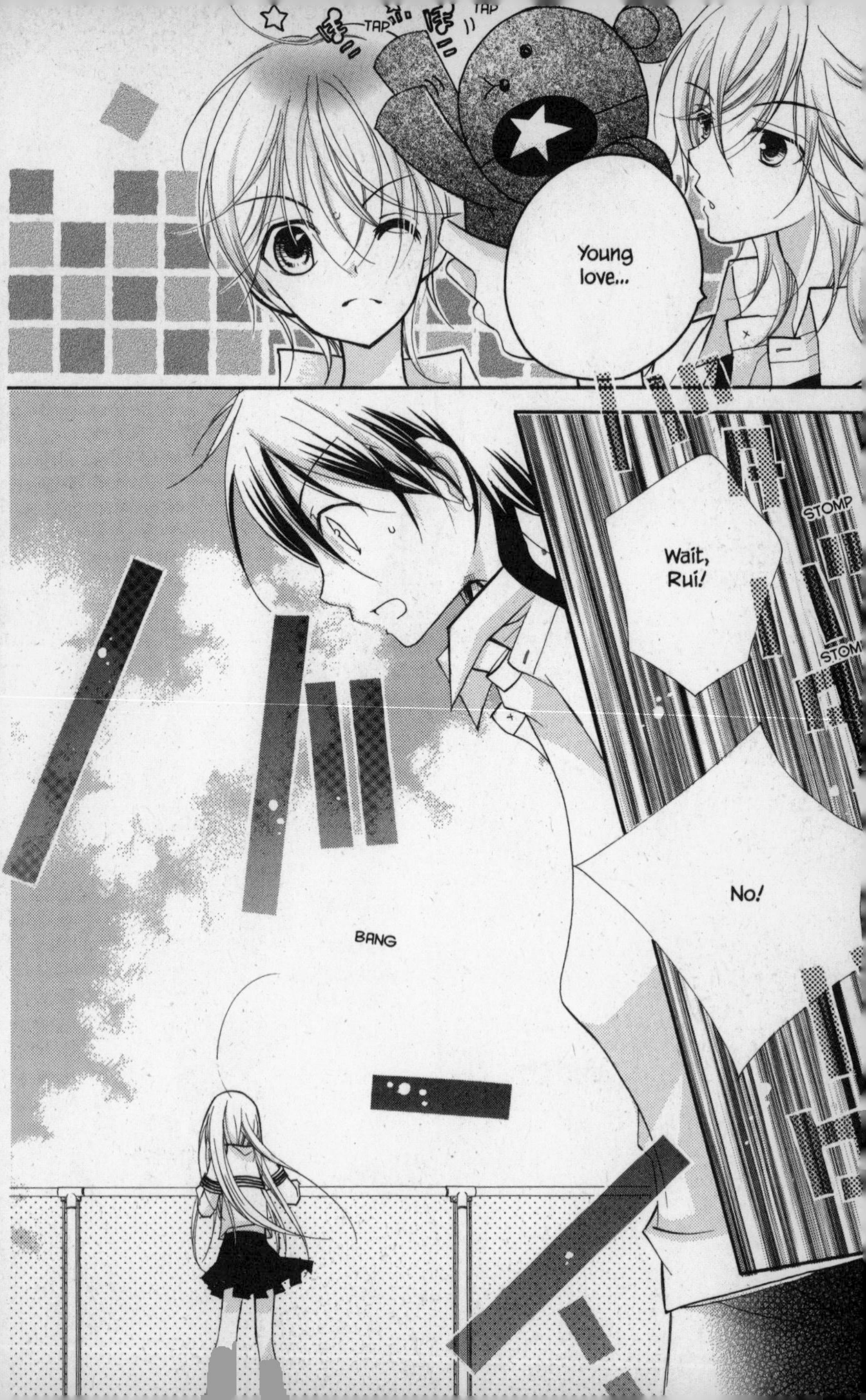
TAP
TAP
Young love...
STOMP
STOMP
Wait, Rui!
No!
BANG

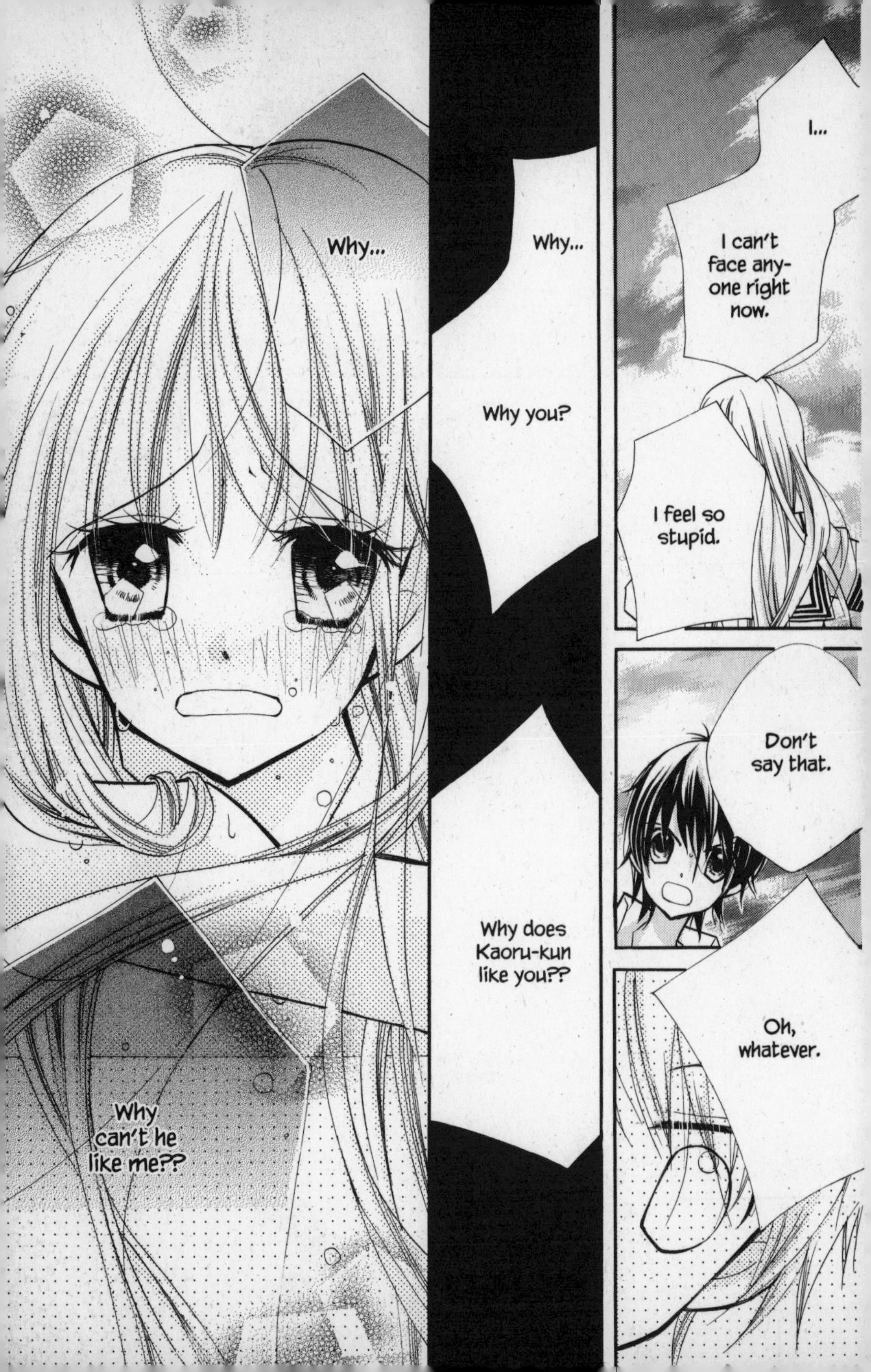
I...
I can't face any-one right now.
I feel so stupid.
Don't say that.
Oh, whatever.
Why...
Why you?
Why does Kaoru-kun like you??
Why...
Why can't he like me??

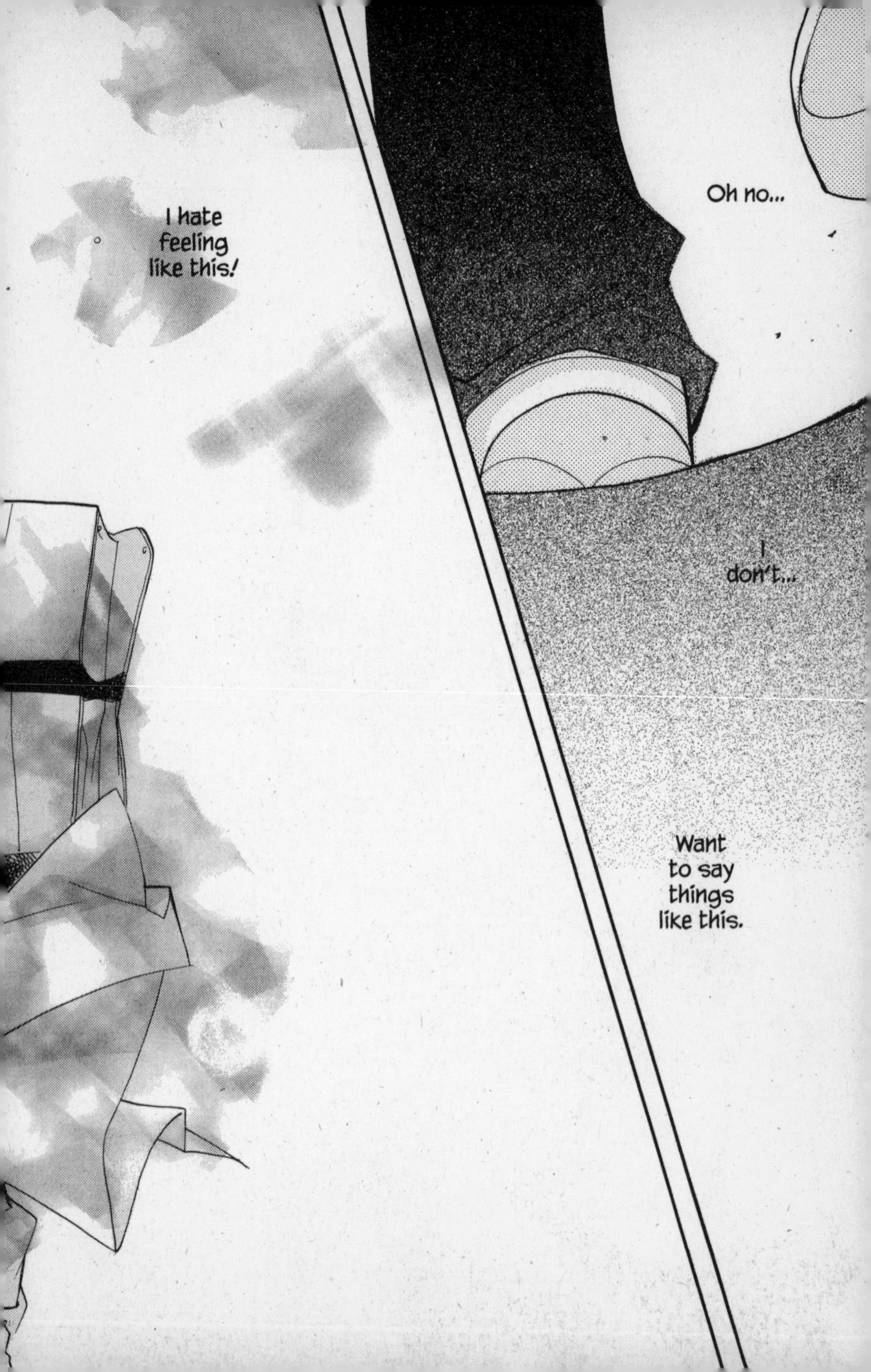
Oh no...
I don't...
Want to say things like this.
I hate feeling like this!

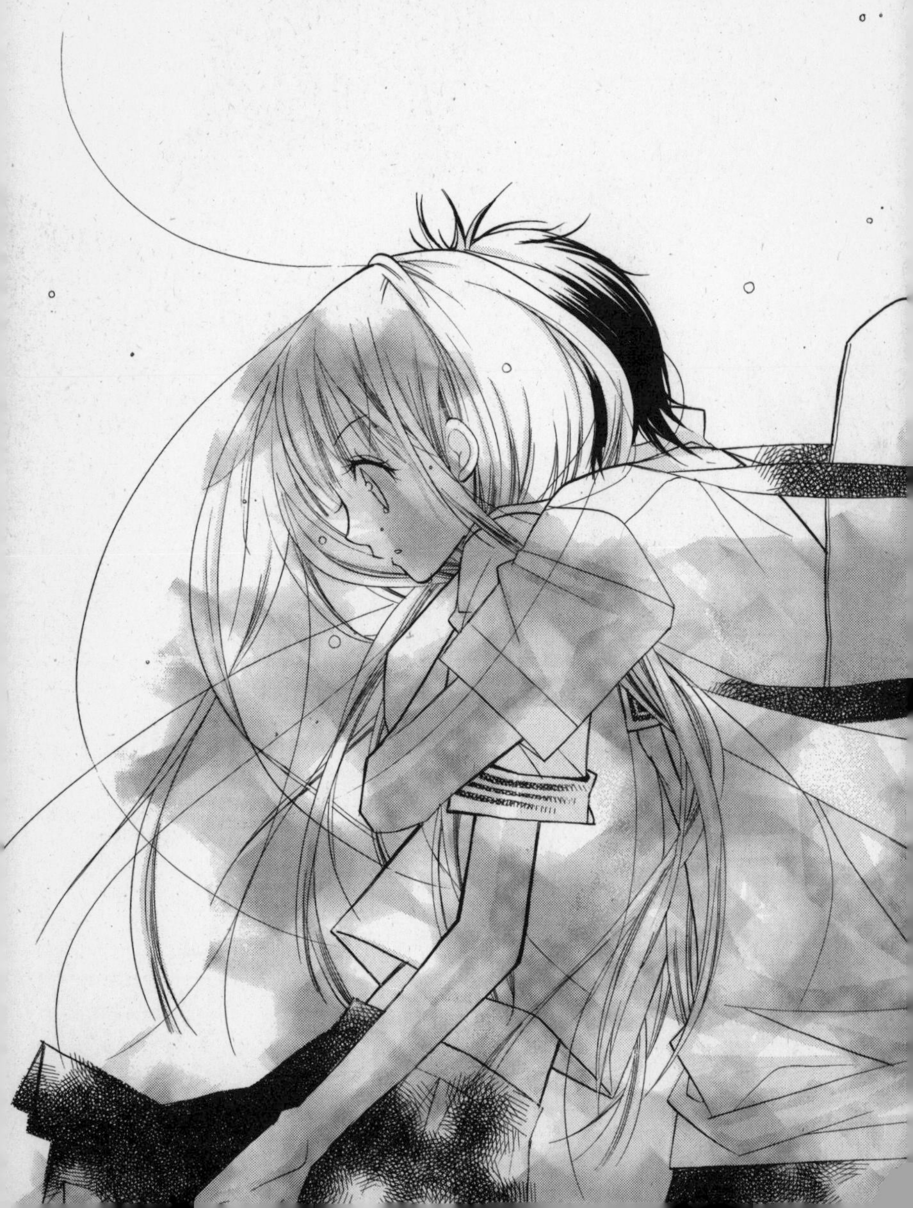

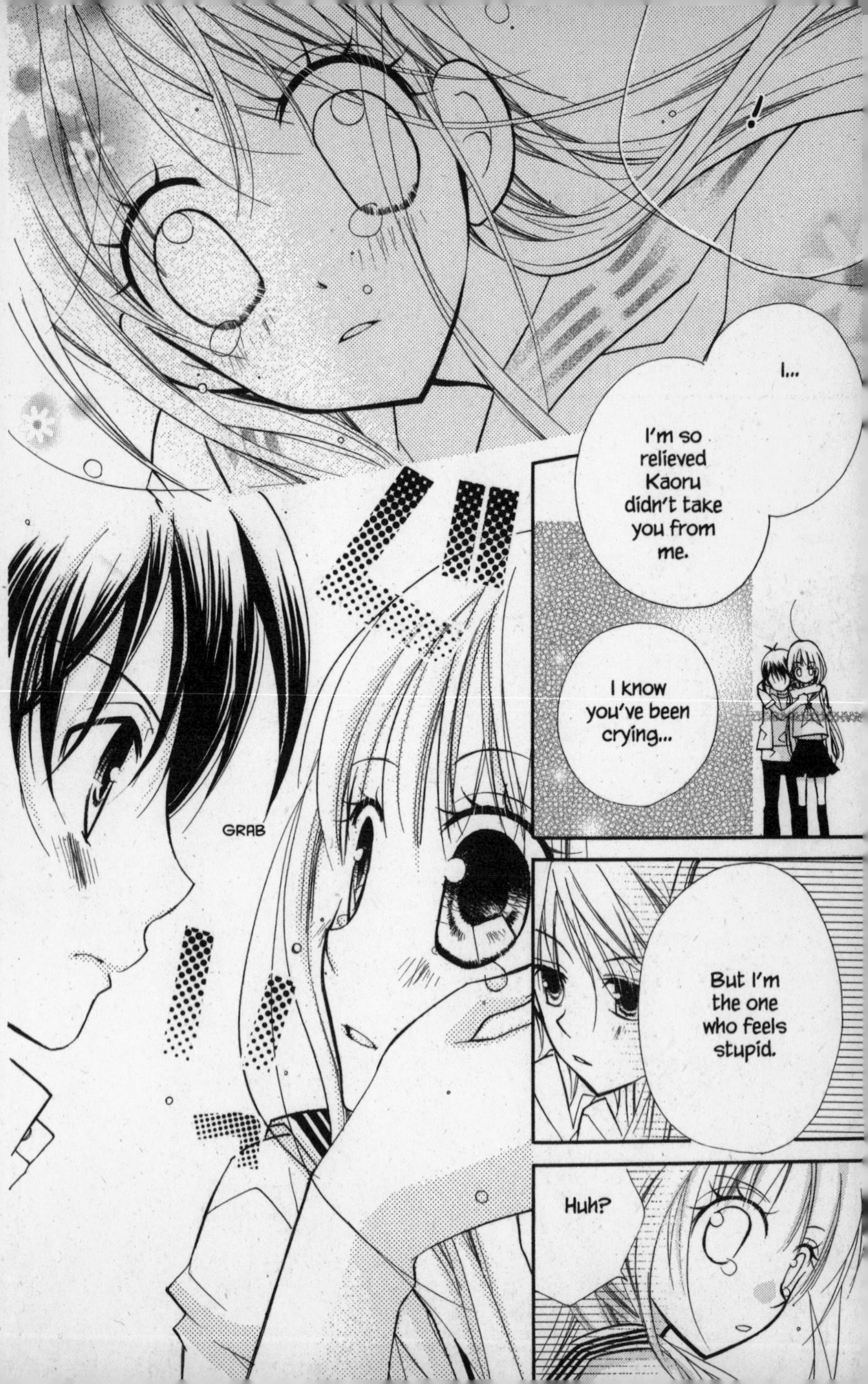
!
I...
I'm so relieved Kaoru didn't take you from me.
I know you've been crying...
GRAB
But I'm the one who feels stupid.
Huh?

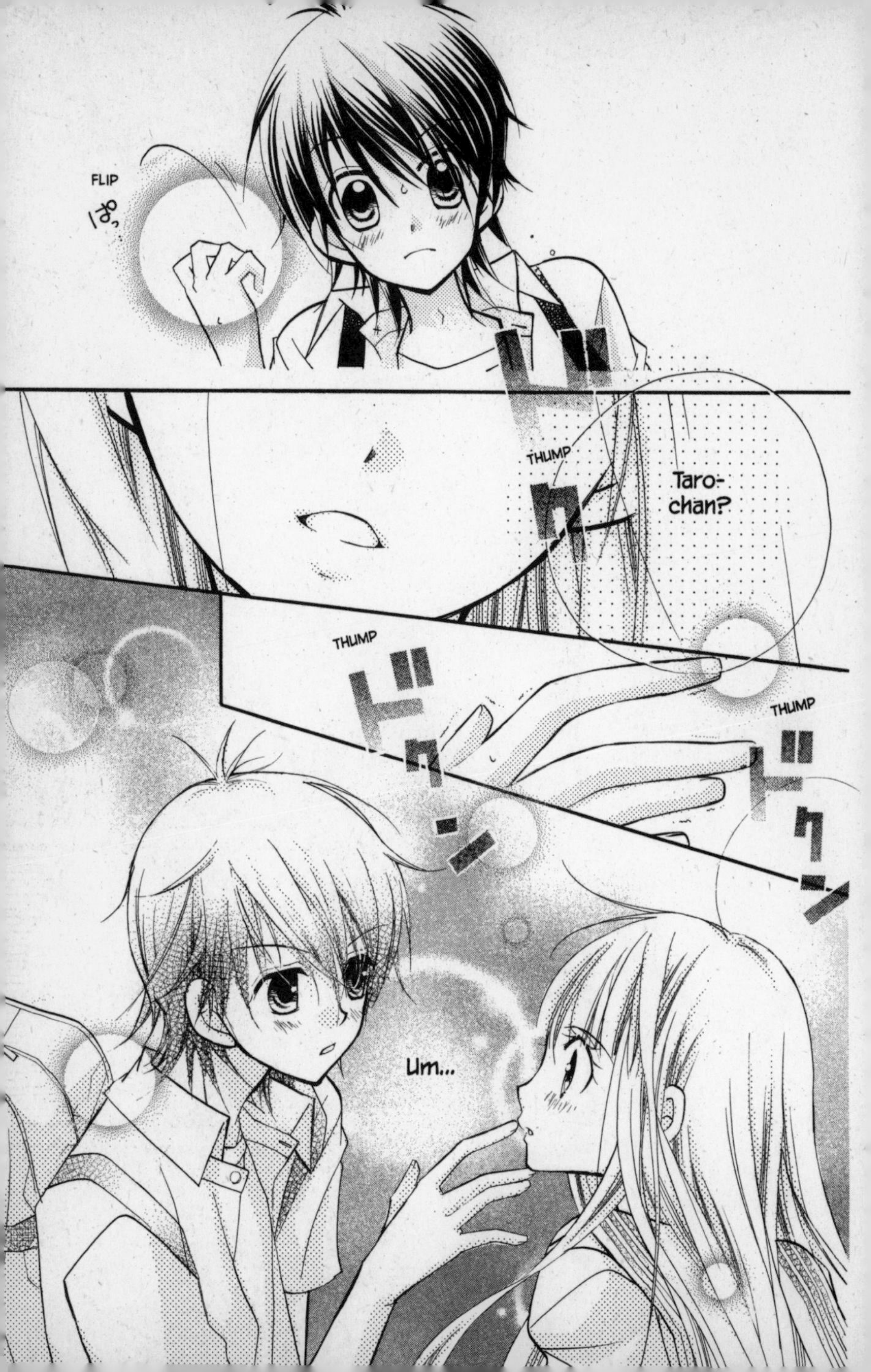
FLIP
ぱっ
THUMP
Taro-chan?
THUMP
ドクン
THUMP
ドクン
Um...

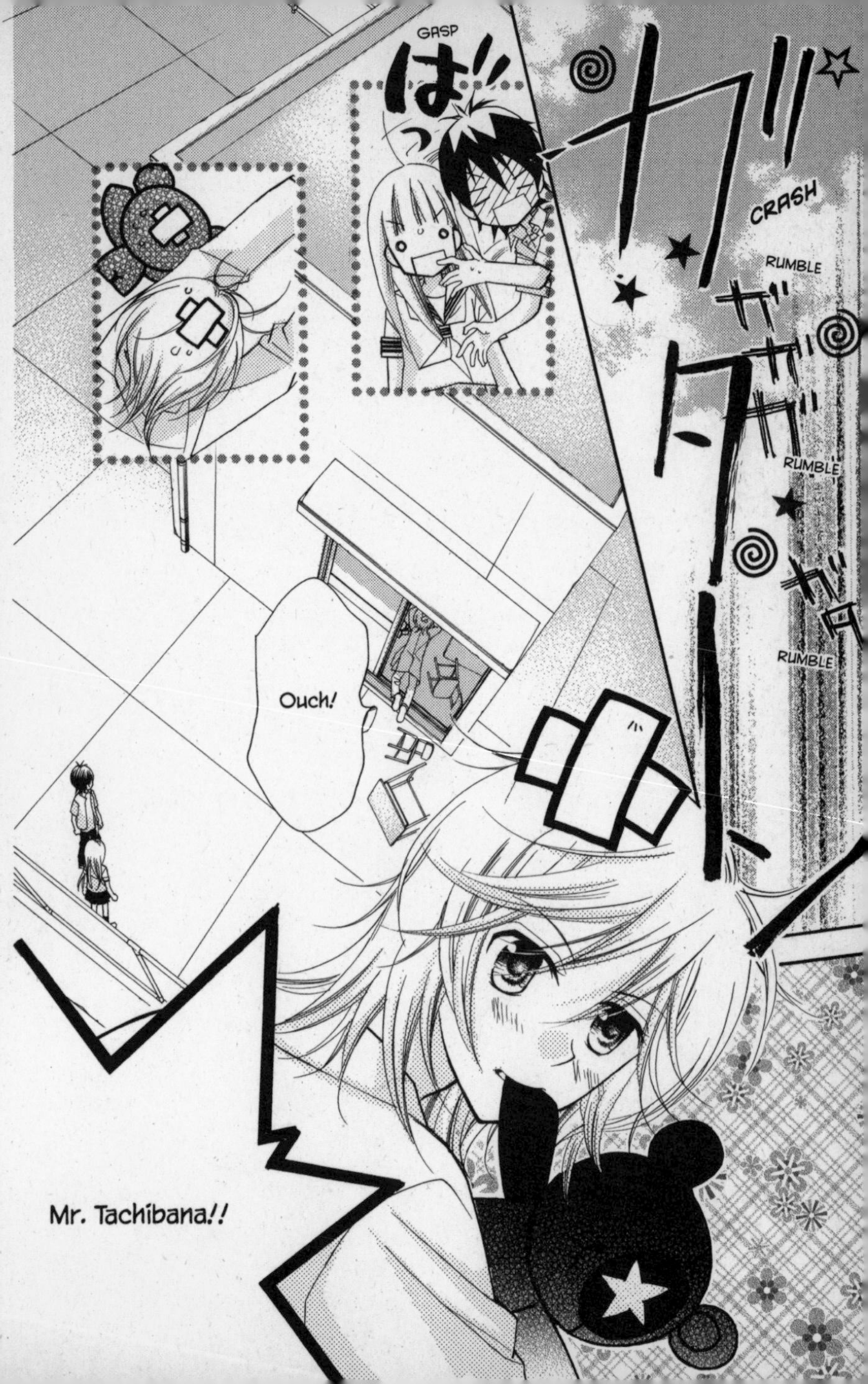

CRASH
RUMBLE
RUMBLE
RUMBLE
GASP
はっ
Ouch!
Mr. Tachibana!!

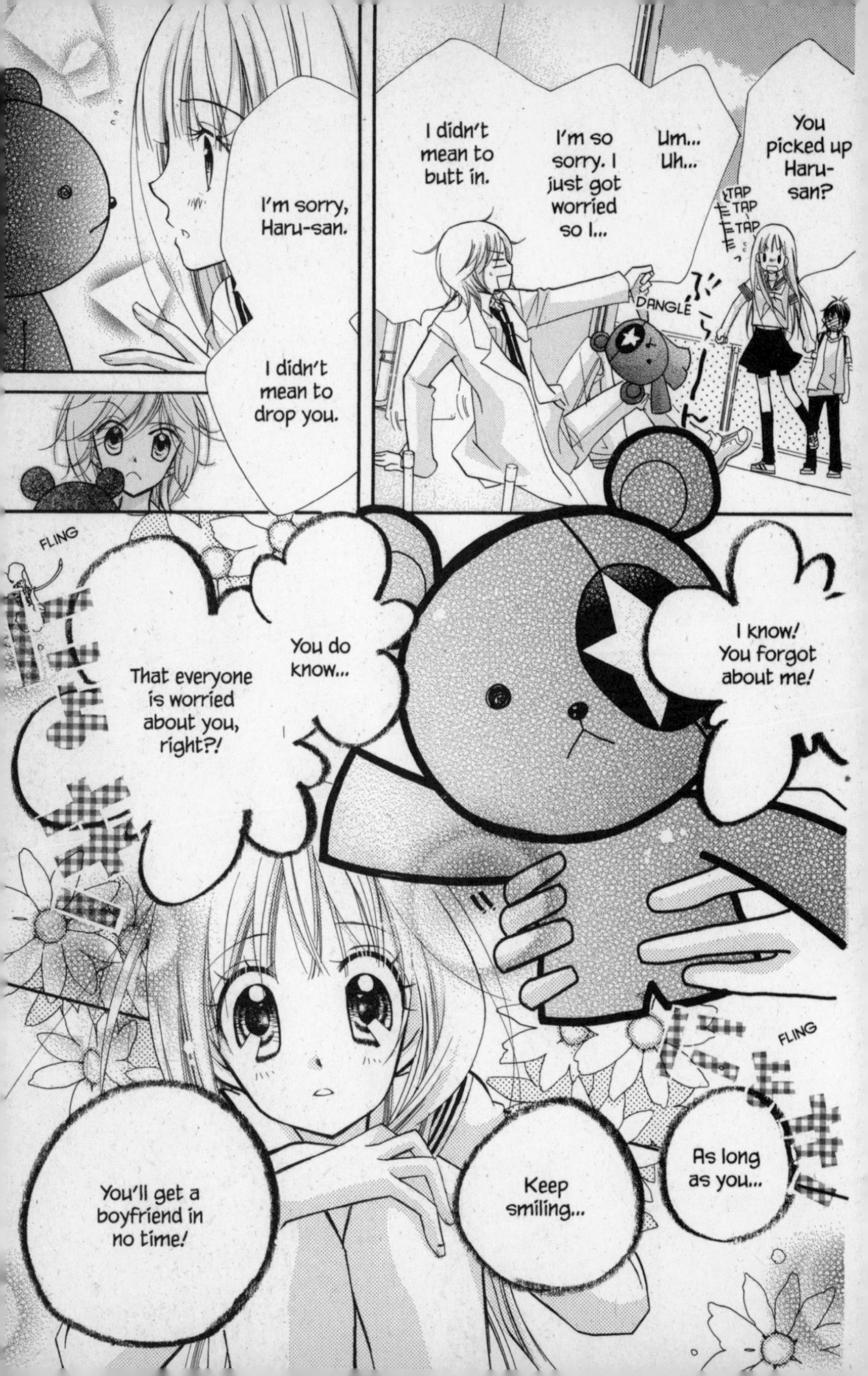
You picked up Haru-san?
TAP TAP TAP
Um... Uh...
I'm so sorry. I just got worried so I...
I didn't mean to butt in.
DANGLE
I'm sorry, Haru-san.
I didn't mean to drop you.
I know! You forgot about me!
You do know...
That everyone is worried about you, right?!
FLING
FLING
As long as you...
Keep smiling...
You'll get a boyfriend in no time!

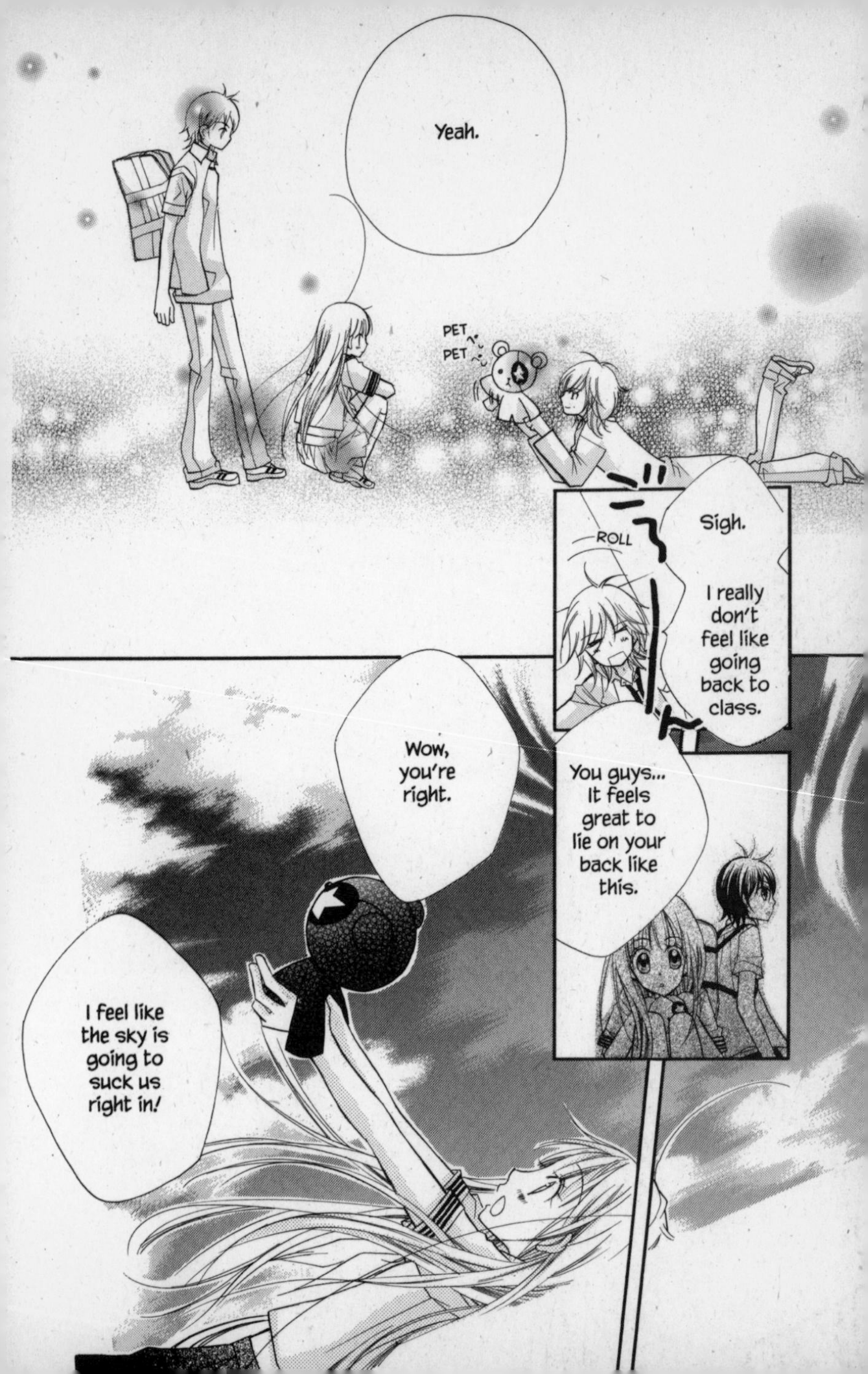
Yeah.
PET PET
ROLL
Sigh.
I really don't feel like going back to class.
You guys... It feels great to lie on your back like this.
Wow, you're right.
I feel like the sky is going to suck us right in!

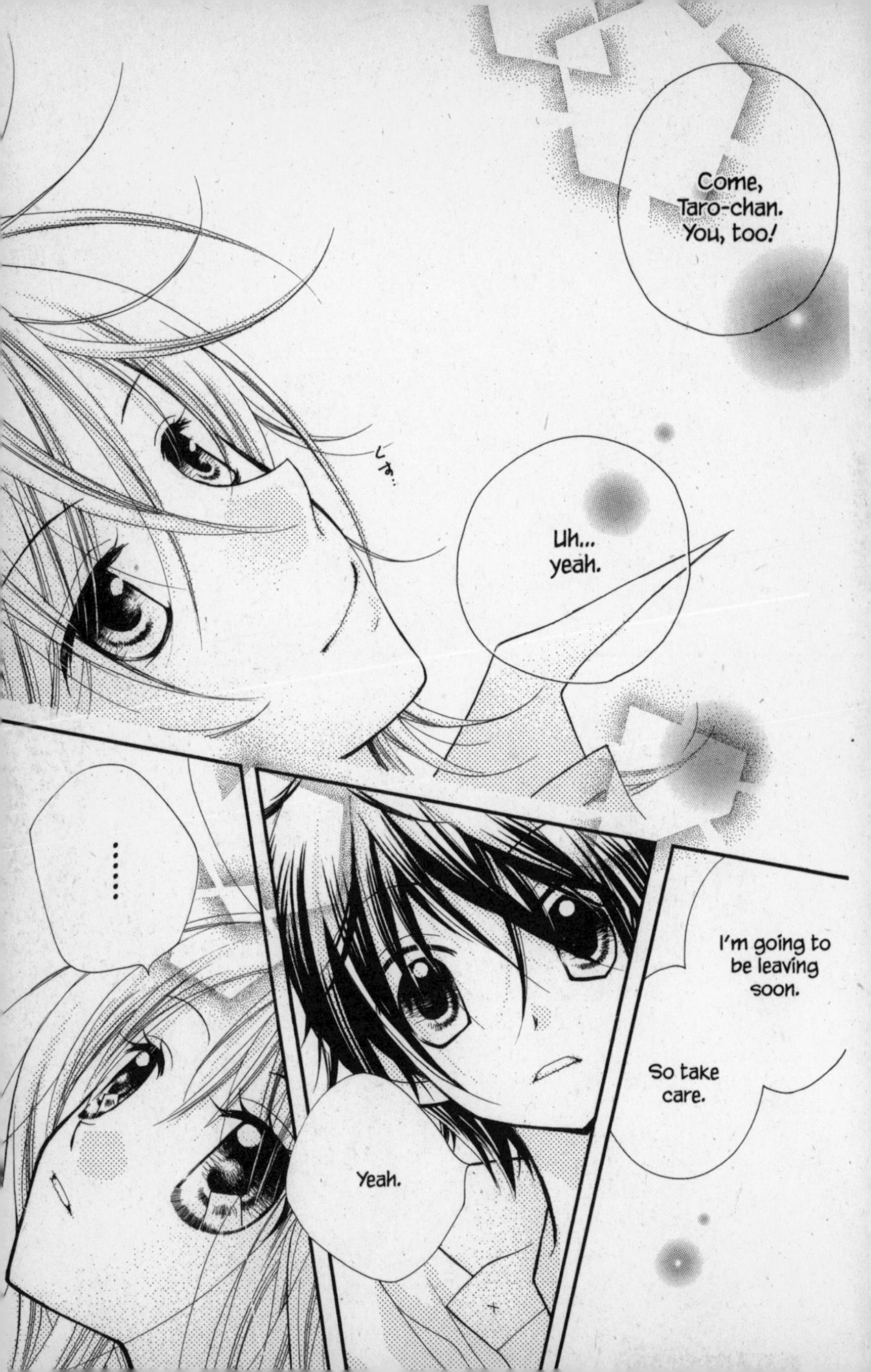
Come, Taro-chan. You, too!
ぐす…
Uh... yeah.
I'm going to be leaving soon.
So take care.
Yeah.
......

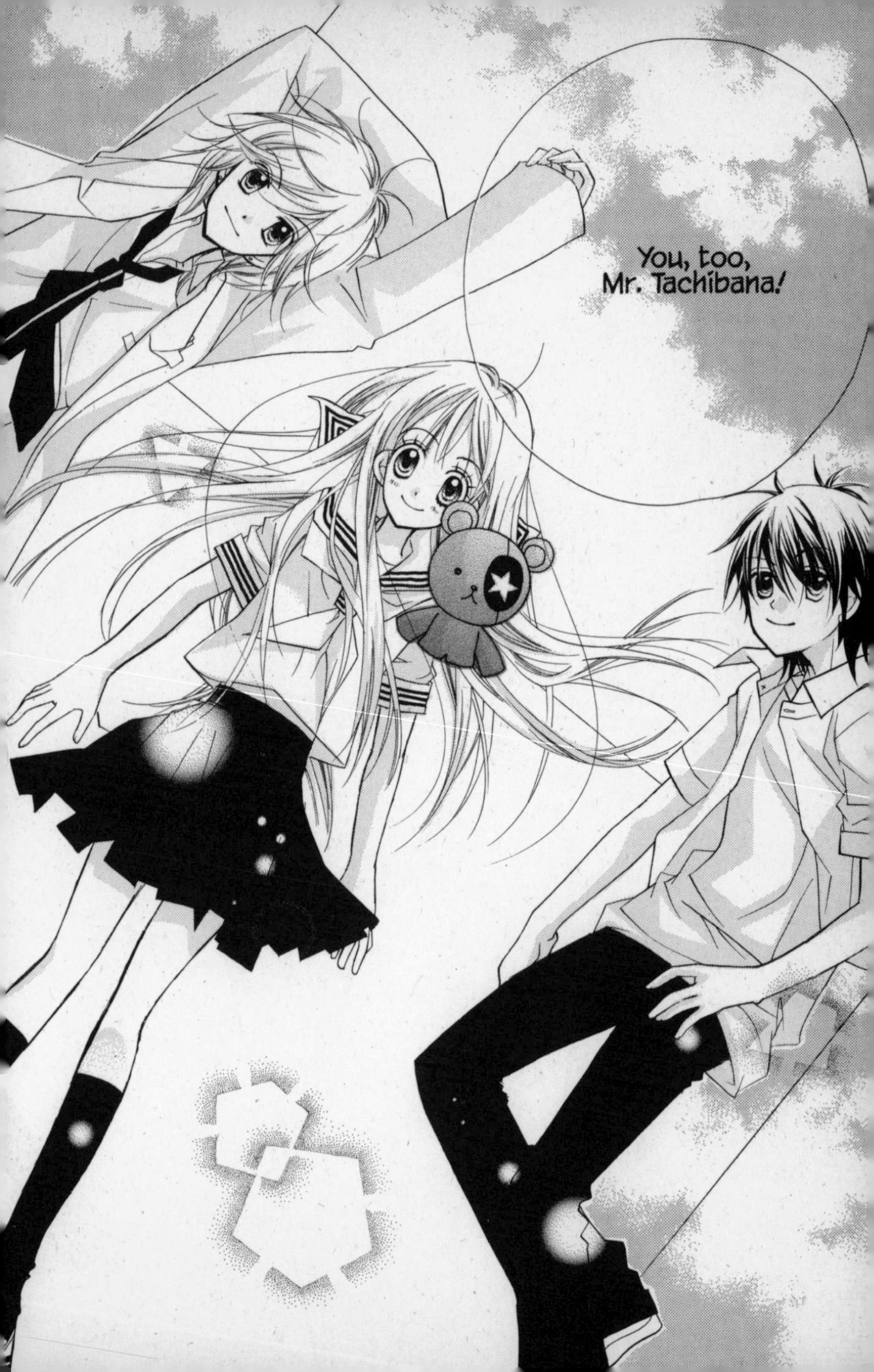
You, too, Mr. Tachibana!

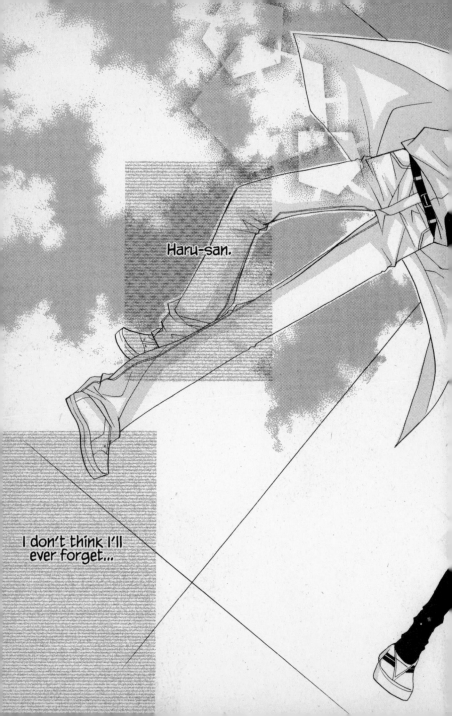

Haru-san.

I don't think I'll ever forget...

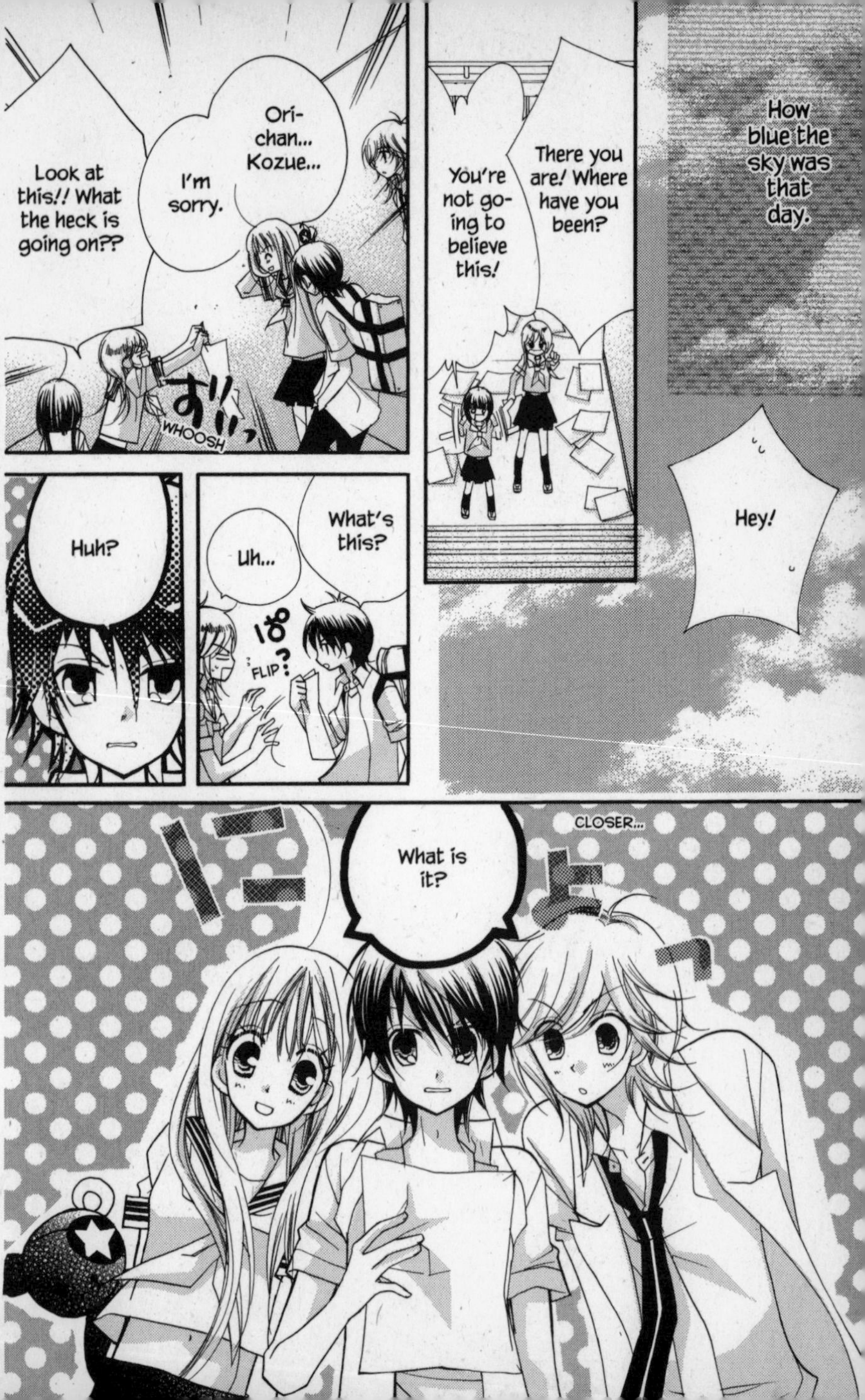
How blue the sky was that day.
Hey!
There you are! Where have you been?
You're not go-ing to believe this!
Ori-chan... Kozue...
I'm sorry.
Look at this!! What the heck is going on??
すり!!っ
WHOOSH
What's this?
Uh...
ぱ
FLIP
Huh?
CLOSER...
What is it?

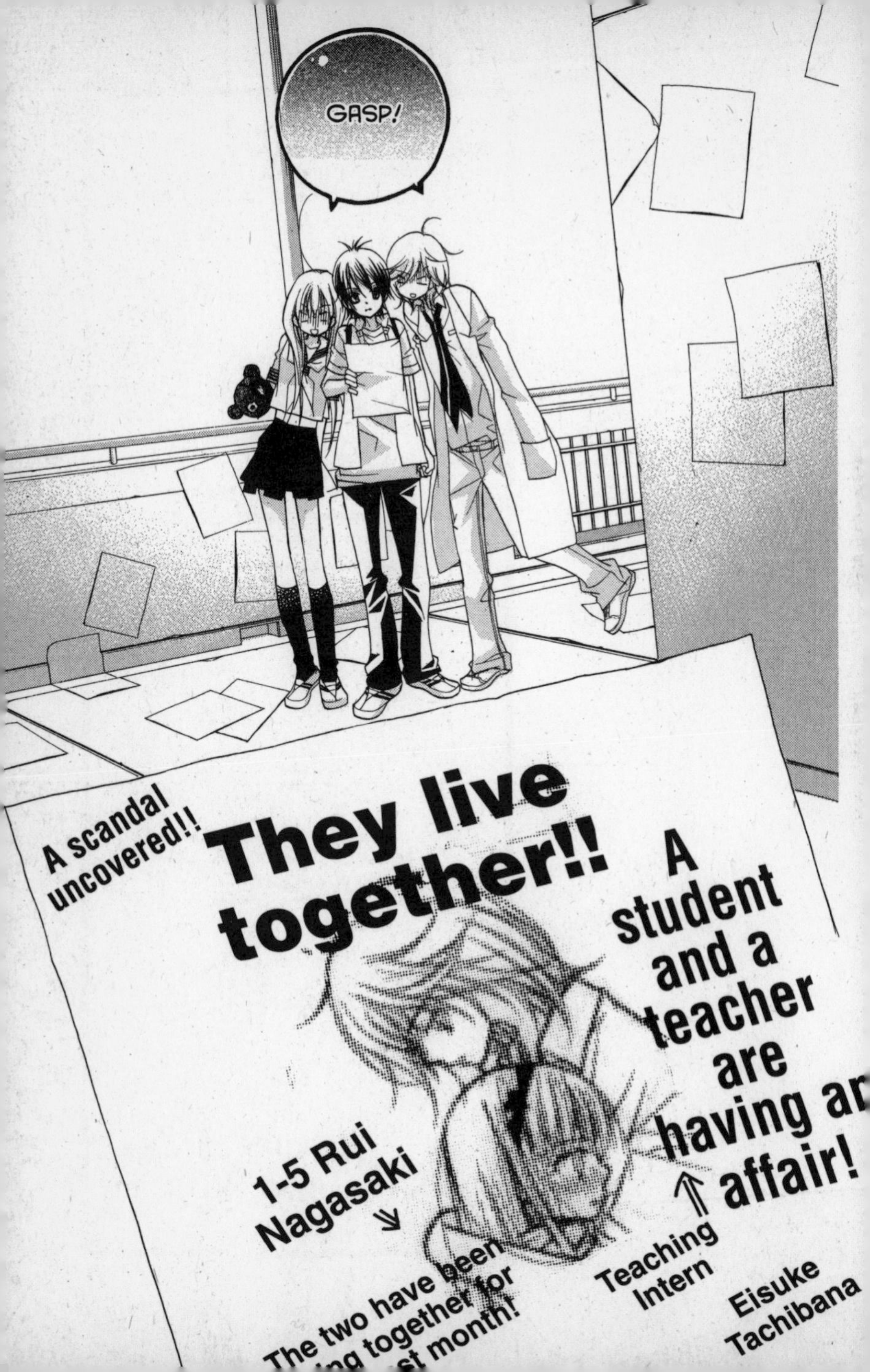
GASP!
They live together!!
A scandal uncovered!!
A student and a teacher are having an affair!
1-5 Rui Nagasaki
Teaching Intern
Eisuke Tachibana
The two have been
ing together for
st month!

Hello!

Yo!

I'm the dog.
I'm Haruka.

☑ I cannot tell you how totally, wholly grateful I am and how totally, wholly thankful I am to everyone reading *Orange Planet 2!*

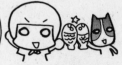

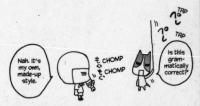

TAP
TAP
Is this grammatically correct?
CHOMP CHOMP
Nah. It's my own, made-up style.

☑ I changed my drawing style, as well as the story line just a bit, so you may end up liking different characters more than before. I hope this is a welcome change...

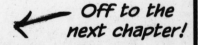

← *Off to the next chapter!*

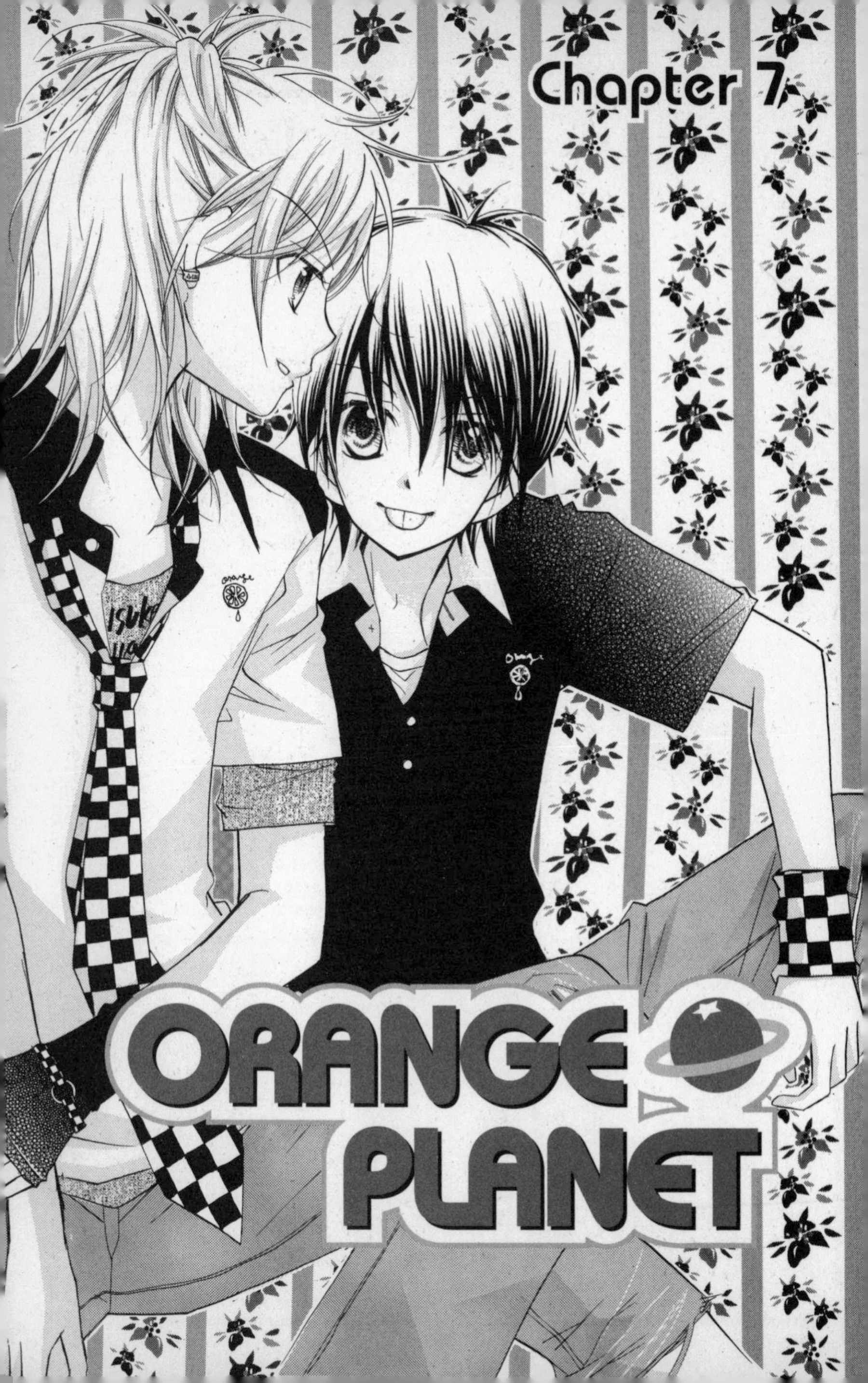
Chapter 7
ORANGE PLANET

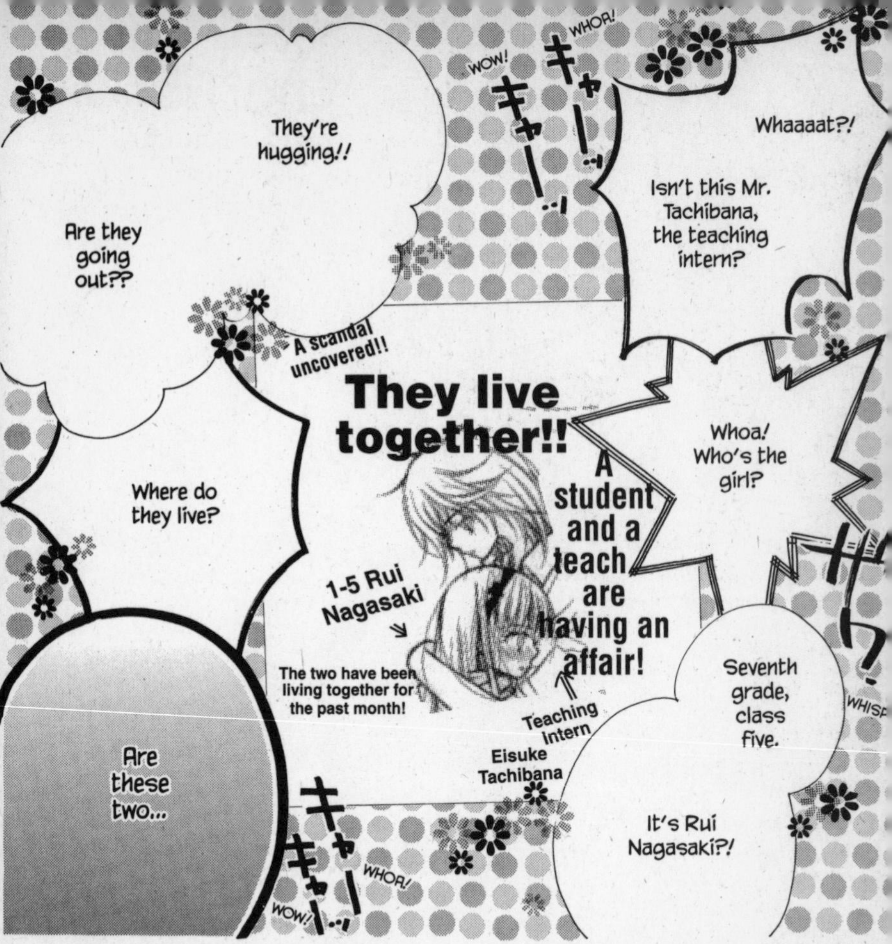
WHOA!
WOW!
Whaaaat?!
Isn't this Mr. Tachibana, the teaching intern?
Whoa! Who's the girl?
Seventh grade, class five.
It's Rui Nagasaki?!
A scandal uncovered!!
They live together!!
A student and a teach are having an affair!
1-5 Rui Nagasaki
The two have been living together for the past month!
Teaching intern
Eisuke Tachibana
They're hugging!!
Are they going out??
Where do they live?
Are these two...
WHOA!
WOW!

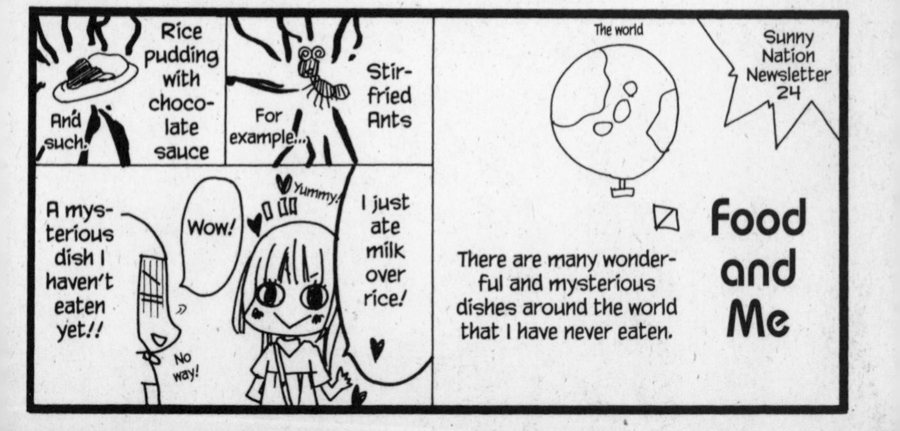
Sunny Nation Newsletter 24
Food and Me
The world
There are many wonderful and mysterious dishes around the world that I have never eaten.
Stir-fried Ants
For example...
Rice pudding with chocolate sauce
And such.
I just ate milk over rice!
Yummy!
Wow!
A mysterious dish I haven't eaten yet!!
No way!

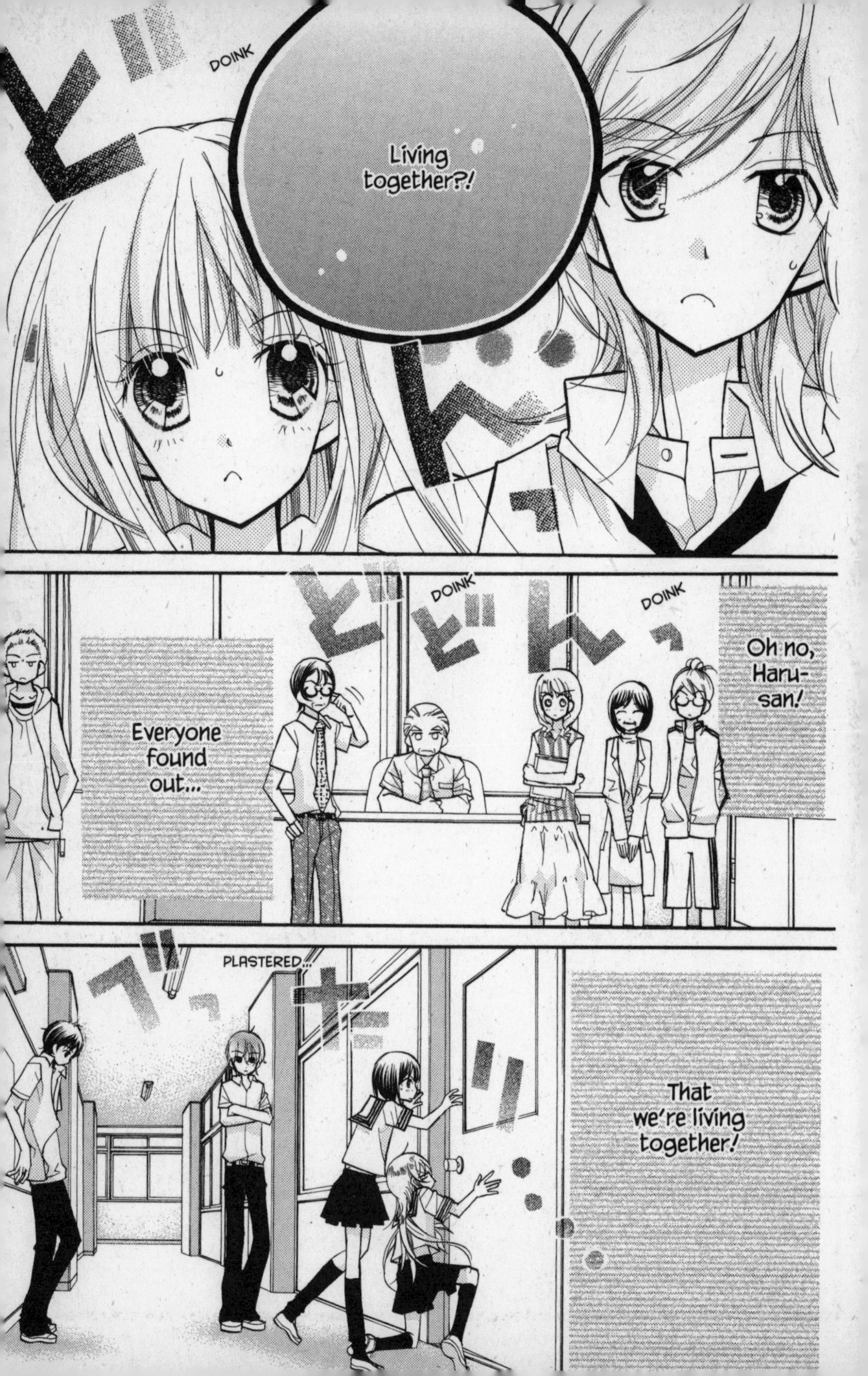
Living together?!
DOINK
Oh no, Haru-san!
DOINK
DOINK
Everyone found out...
That we're living together!
PLASTERED...

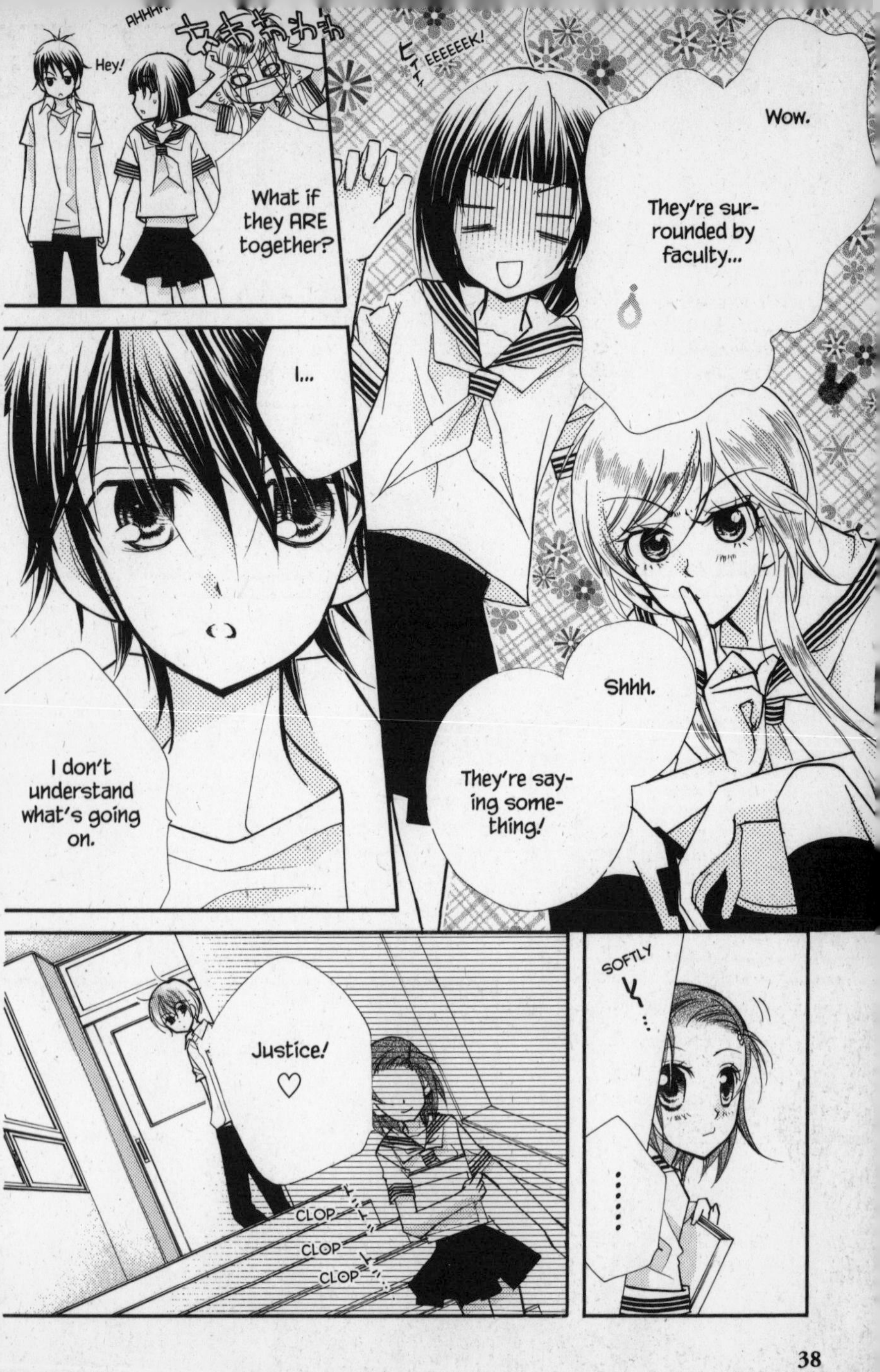
EEEEEEK!
Wow.
They're surrounded by faculty...
Shhh.
They're saying something!
AHHHH
Hey!
What if they ARE together?
I...
I don't understand what's going on.
SOFTLY
......
Justice! ♡
CLOP
CLOP
CLOP

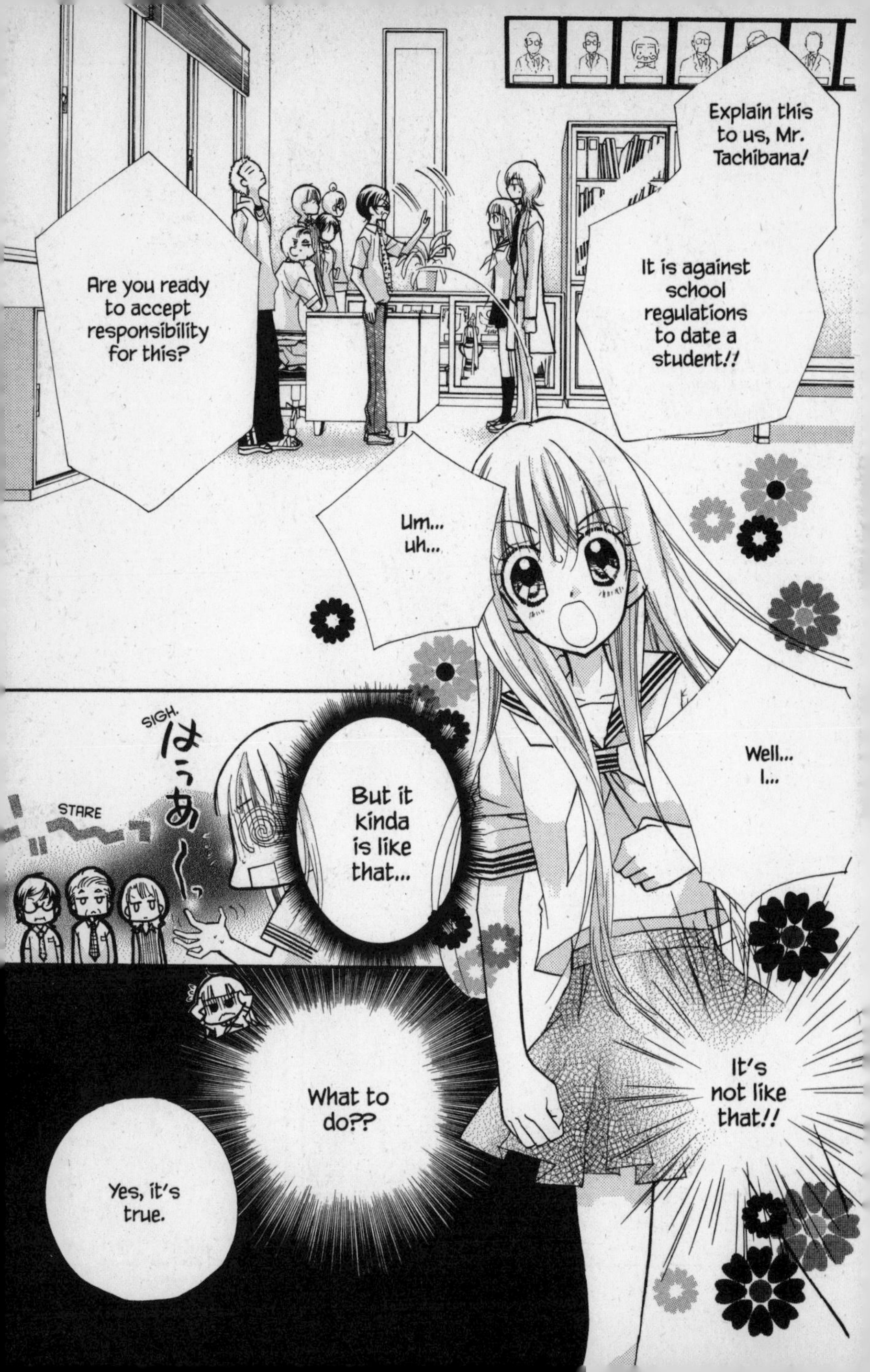
Explain this to us, Mr. Tachibana!
It is against school regulations to date a student!!
Are you ready to accept responsibility for this?
Um... uh...
Well... I...
It's not like that!!
But it kinda is like that...
SIGH.
はぁあ〜っ
STARE
What to do??
Yes, it's true.

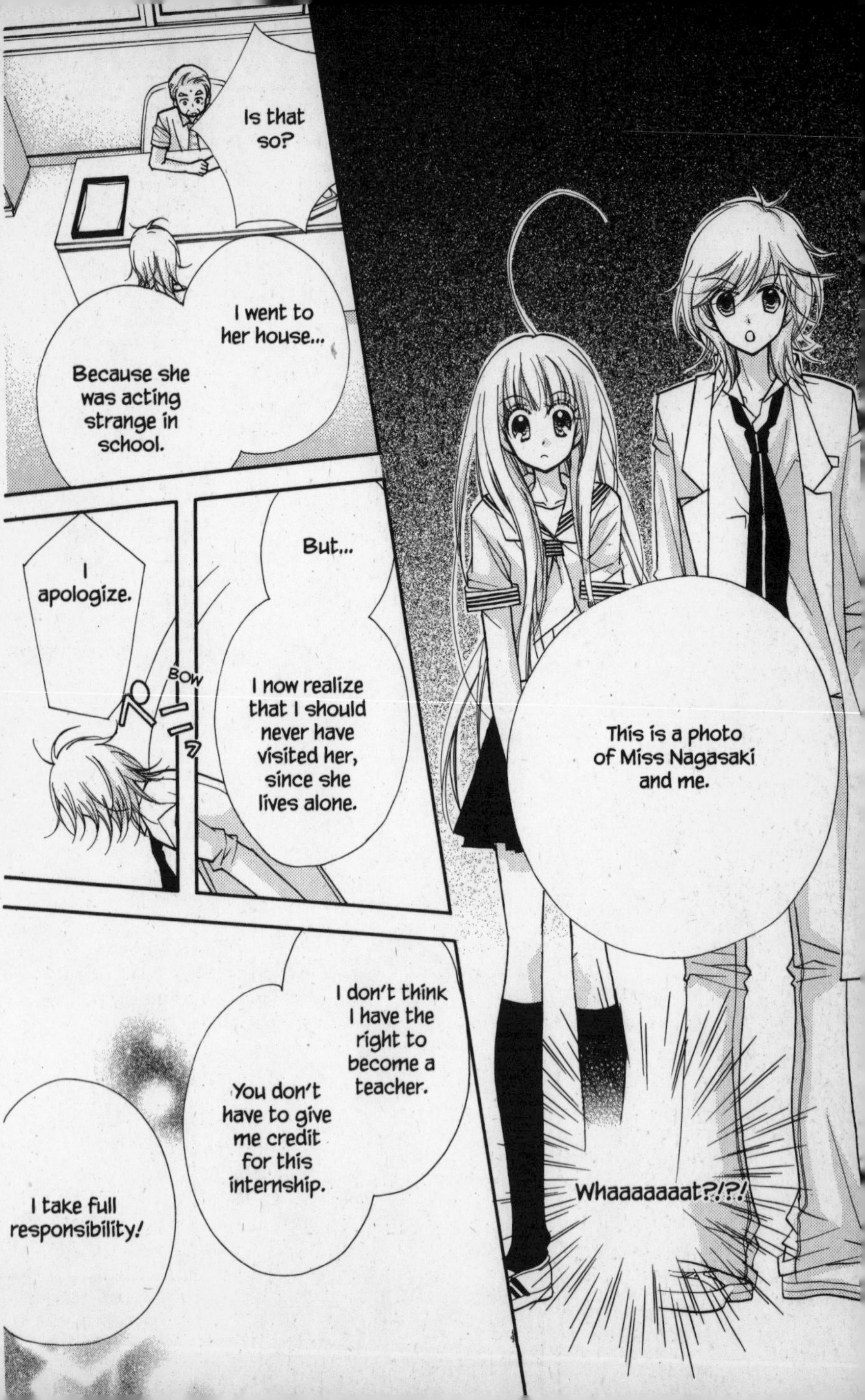
This is a photo of Miss Nagasaki and me.
Whaaaaaaat?!?!
Is that so?
I went to her house...
Because she was acting strange in school.
But...
I now realize that I should never have visited her, since she lives alone.
BOW
I apologize.
I don't think I have the right to become a teacher.
You don't have to give me credit for this internship.
I take full responsibility!

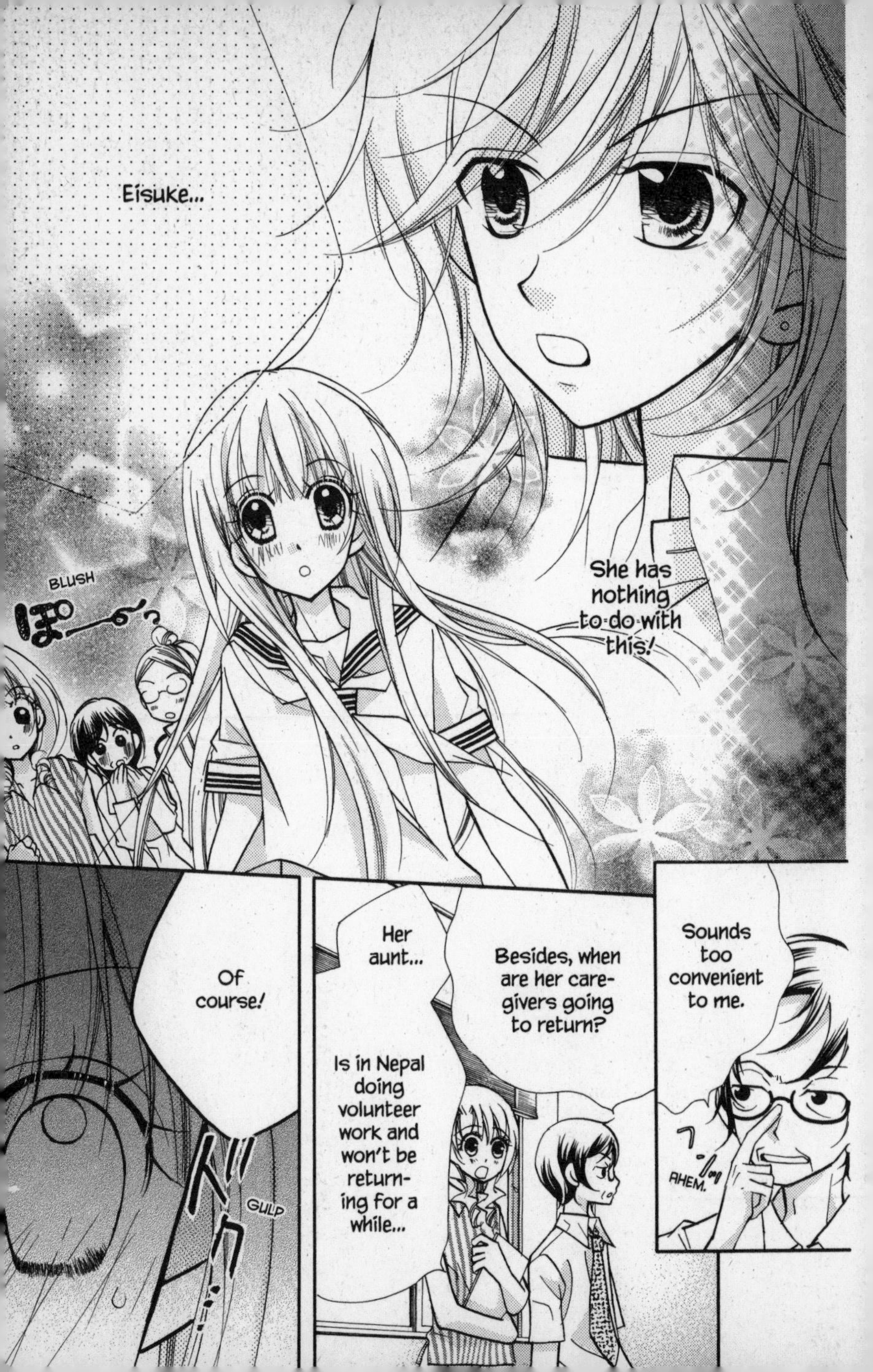

She has nothing to do with this!
Eisuke...
BLUSH
ぽ〜
Sounds too convenient to me.
AHEM.
Besides, when are her care-givers going to return?
Her aunt...
Is in Nepal doing volunteer work and won't be returning for a while...
Of course!
GULP

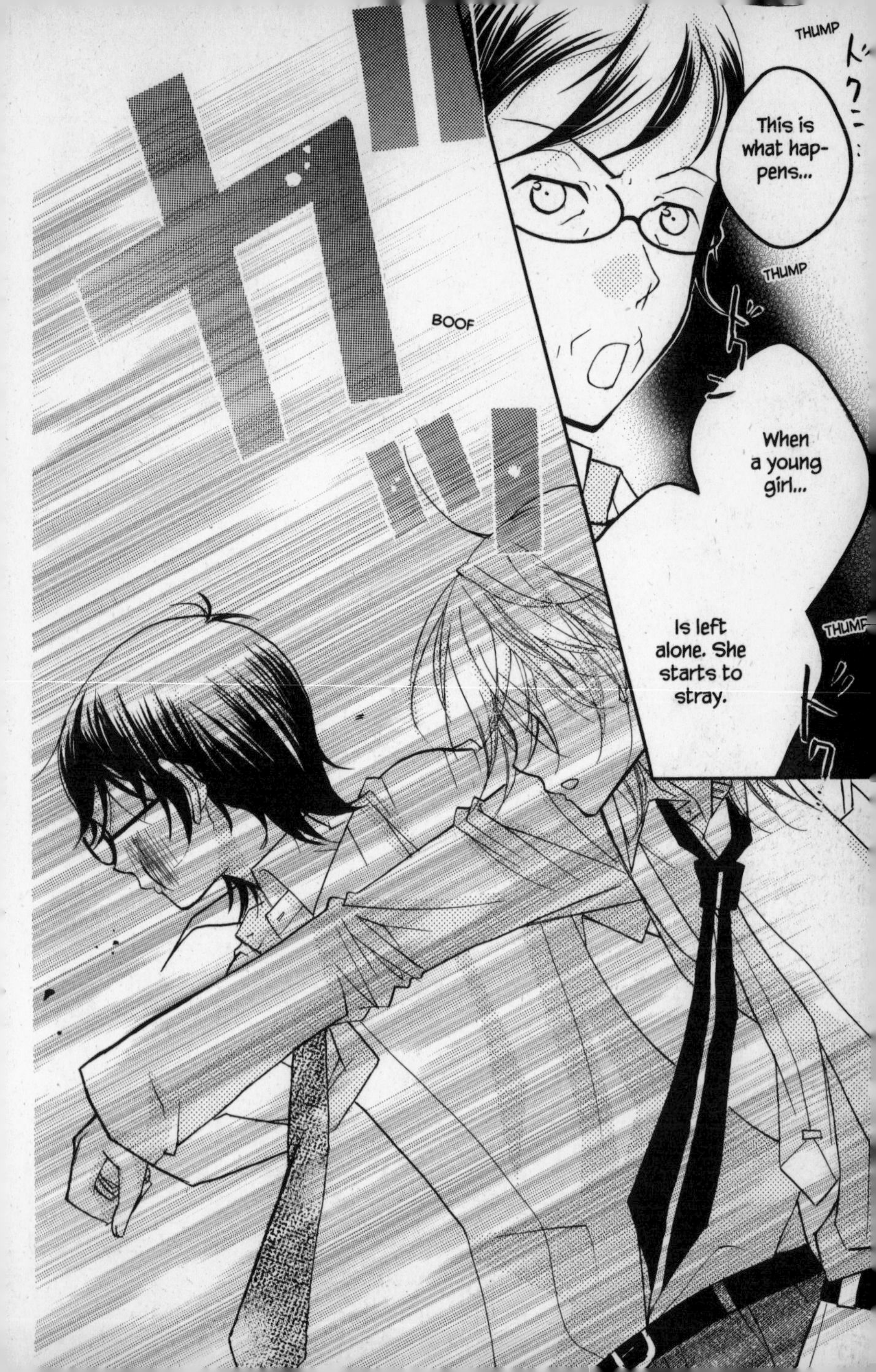
THUMP
This is what hap-pens...
THUMP
When a young girl...
THUMP
Is left alone. She starts to stray.
BOOF

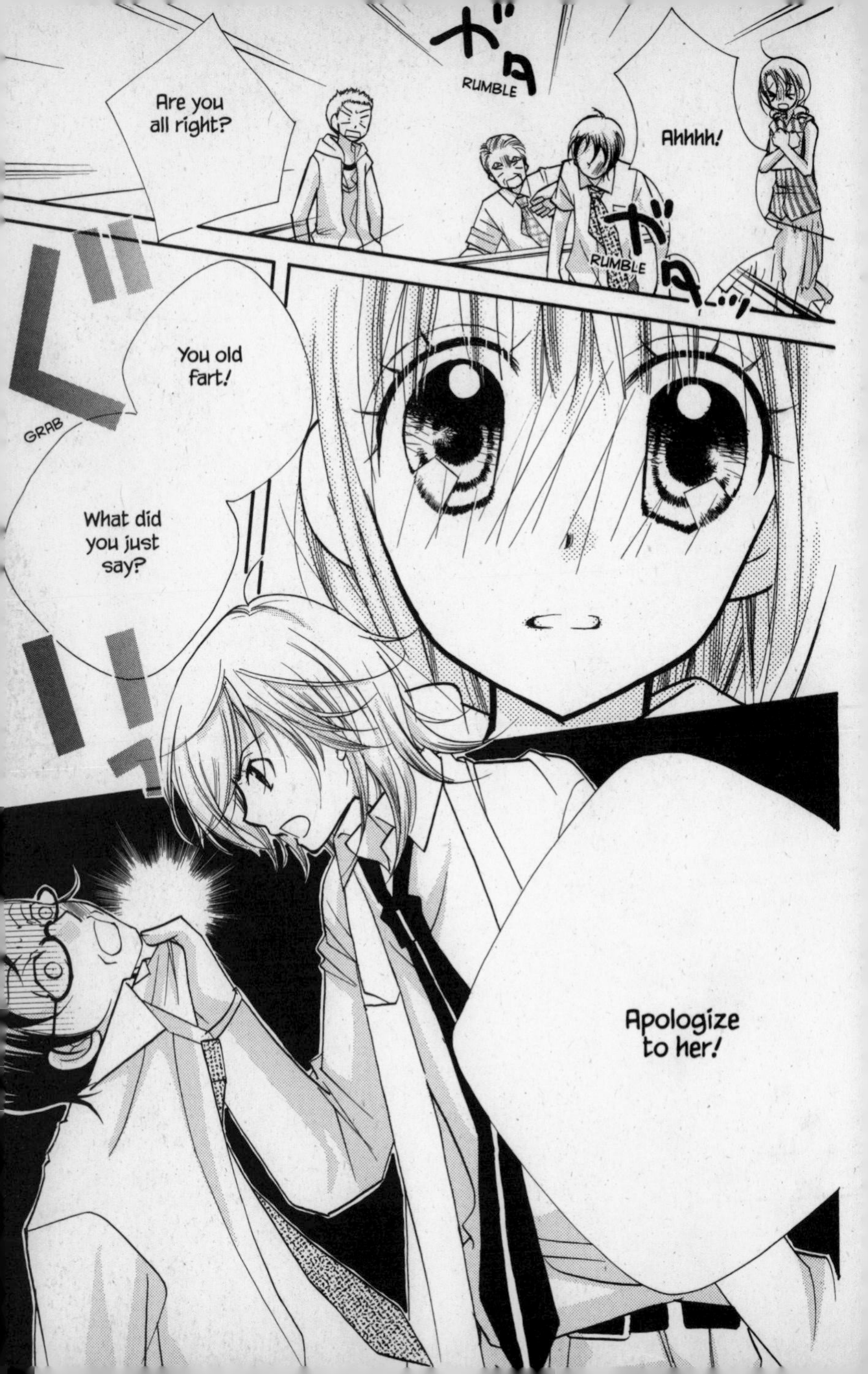
Ahhhh!
RUMBLE
RUMBLE
Are you all right?
You old fart!
GRAB
Apologize to her!
What did you just say?

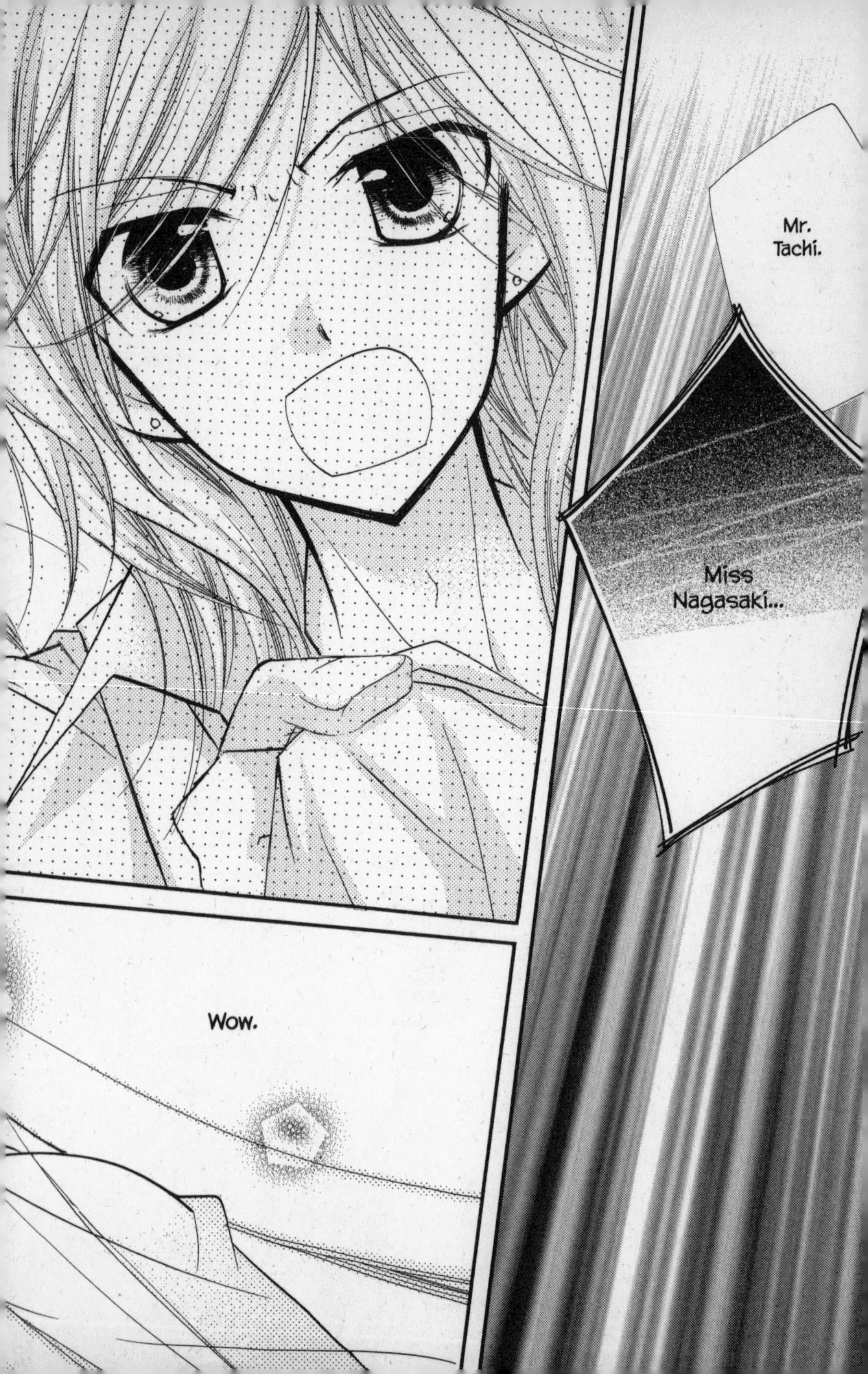
Mr. Tachi.
Miss Nagasaki...
Wow.

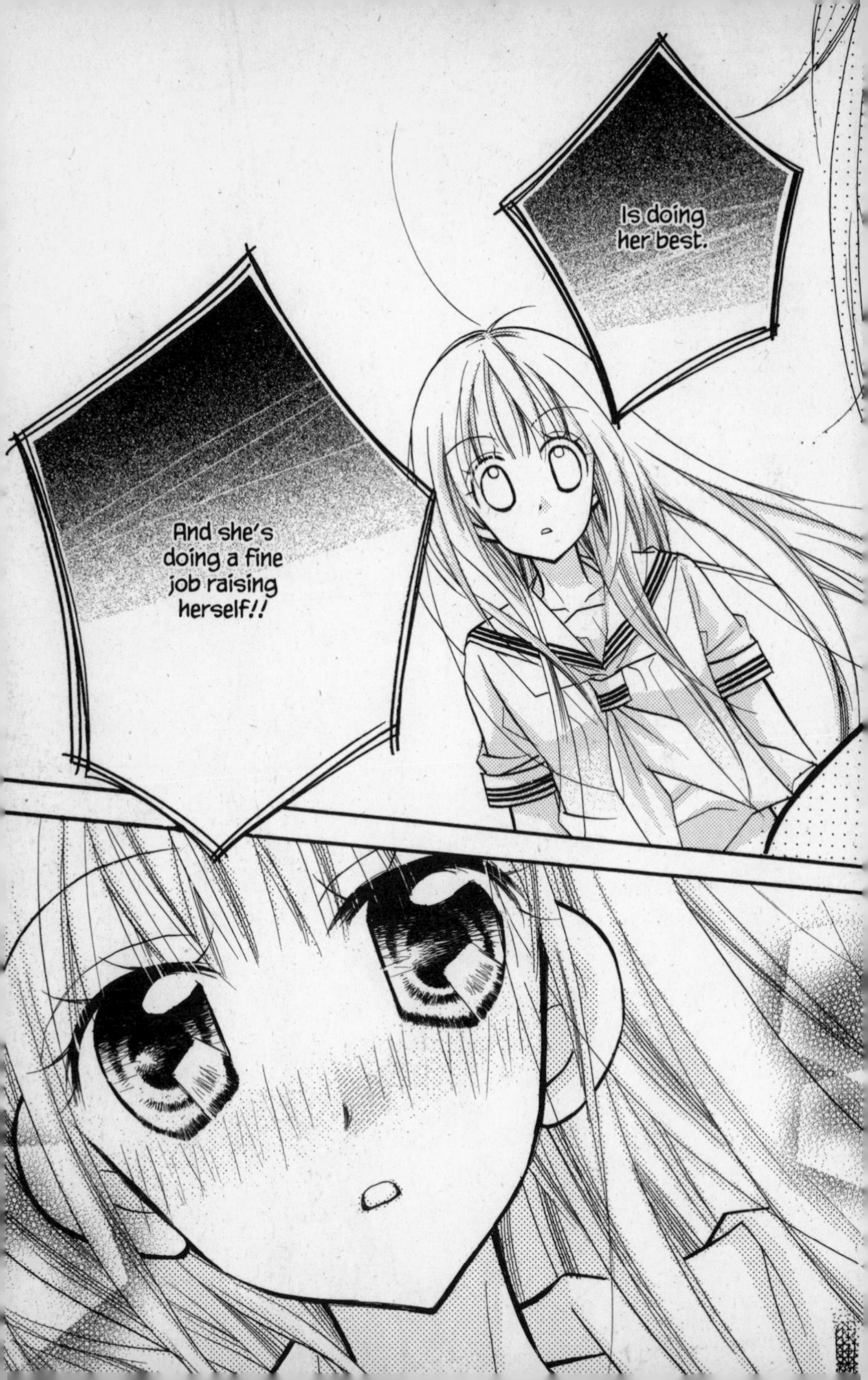
Is doing her best.
And she's doing a fine job raising herself!!

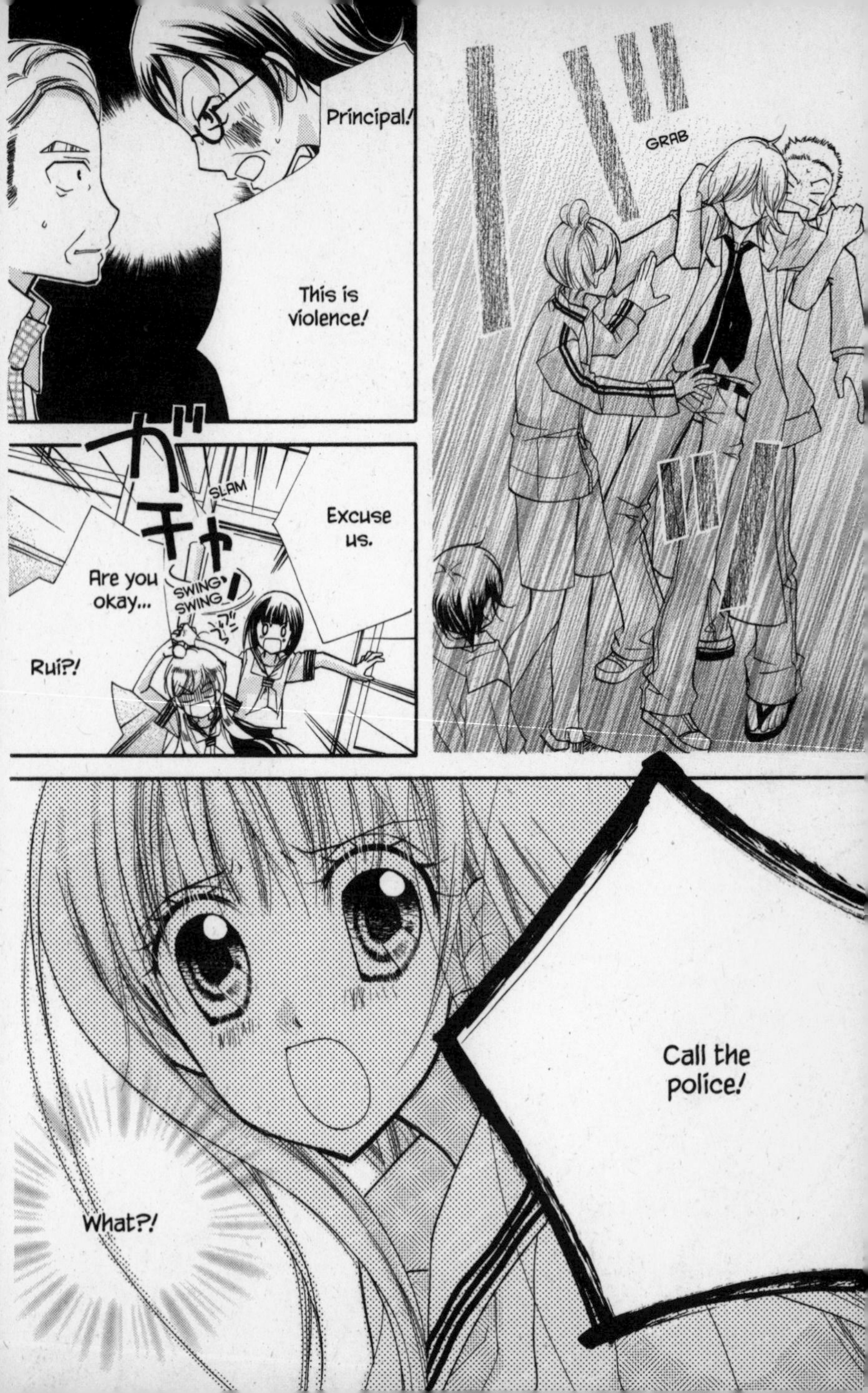
GRAB
Principal!
This is violence!
ガチャ
SLAM
Excuse us.
SWING SWING
Are you okay...
Rui?!
Call the police!
What?!

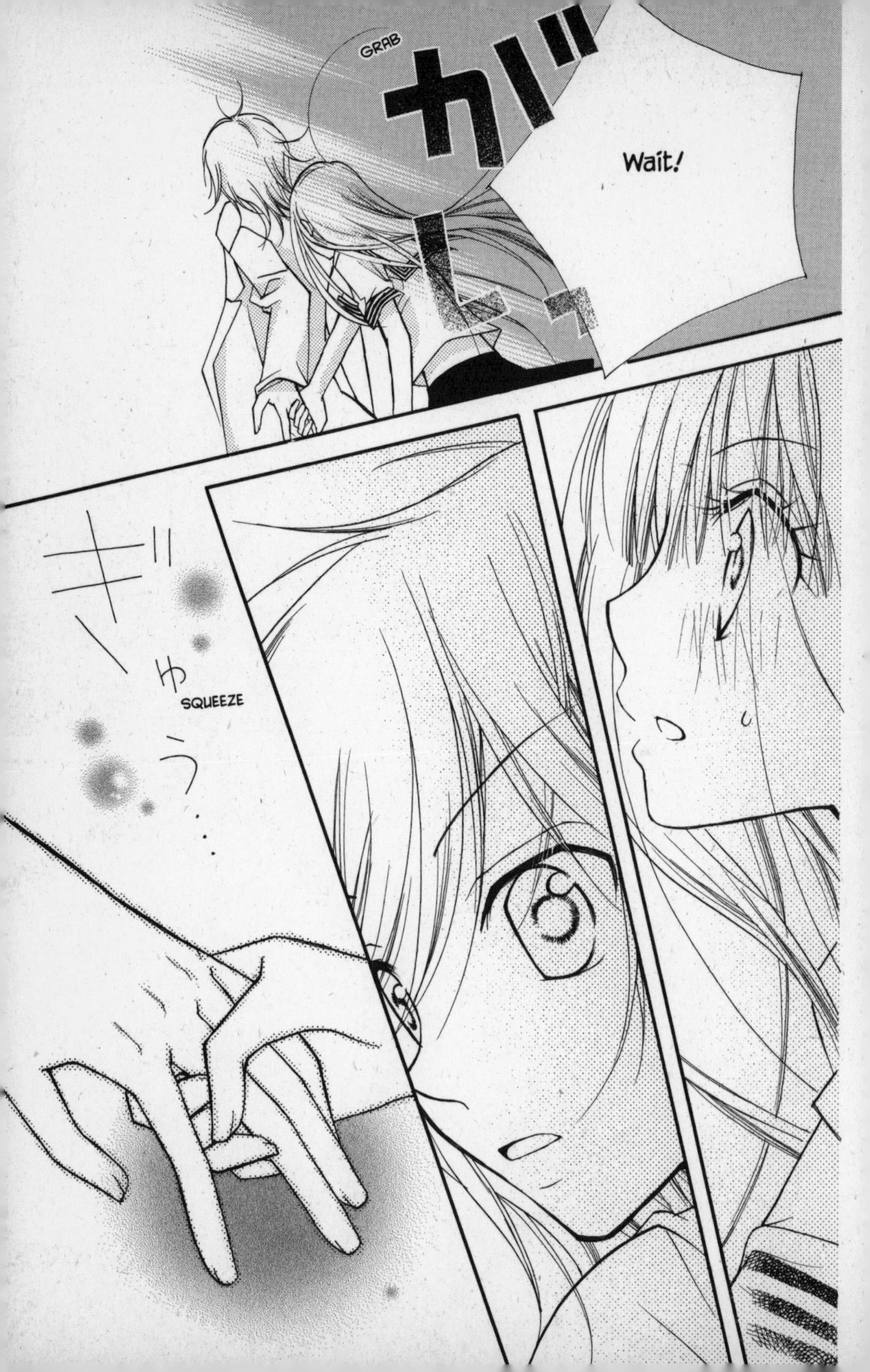
Wait!
GRAB
SQUEEZE

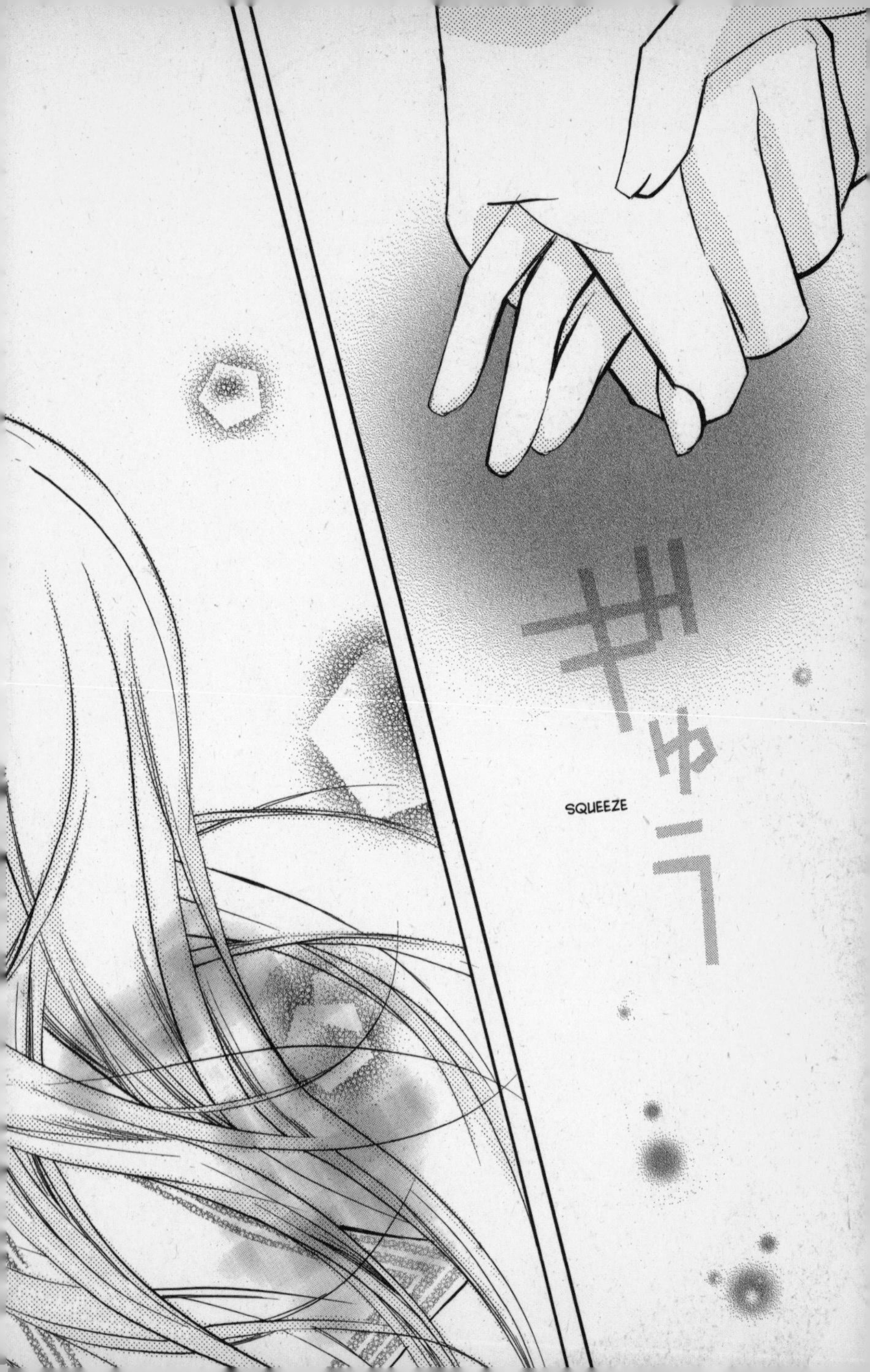
ぎゅう
SQUEEZE

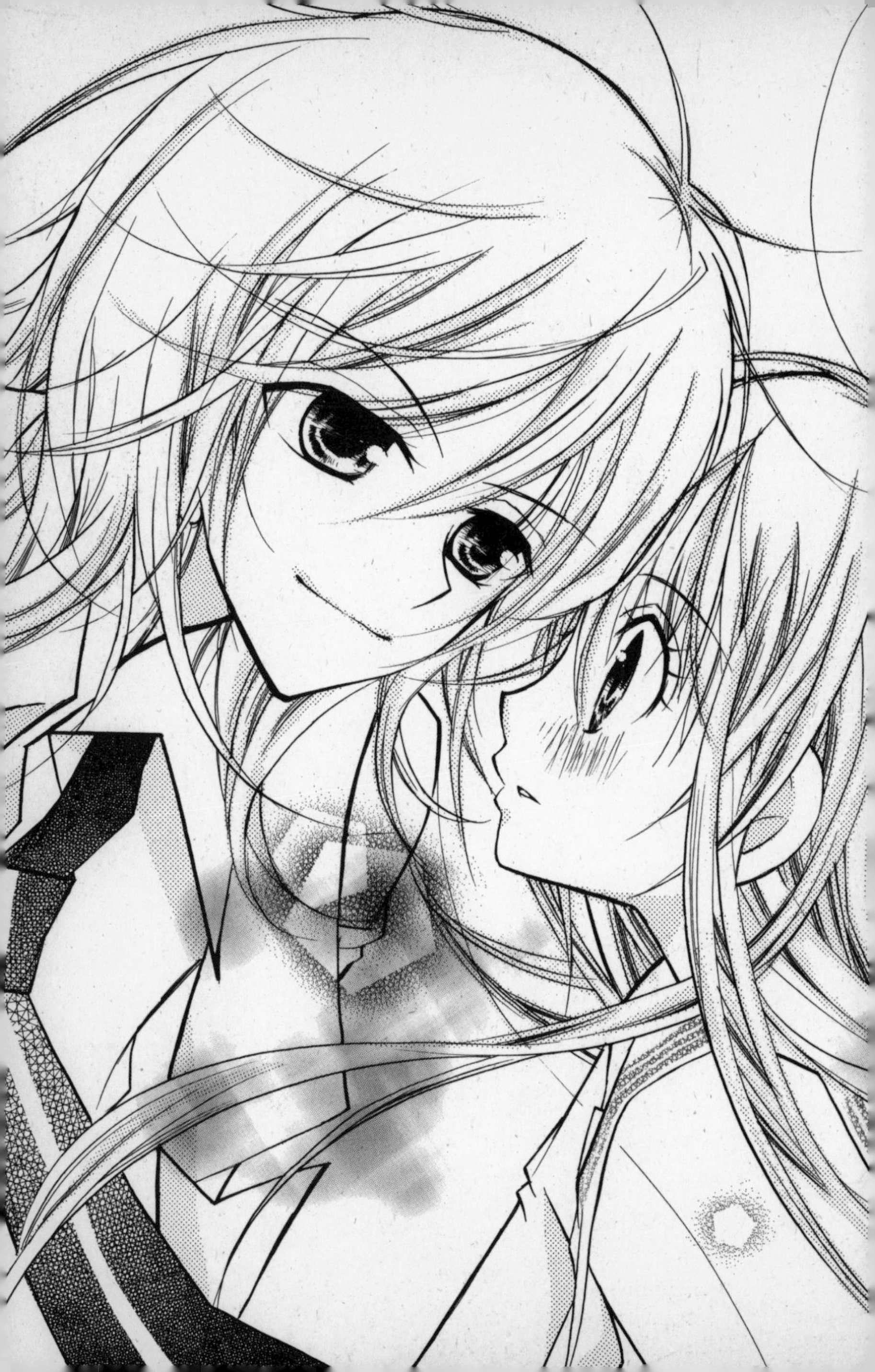

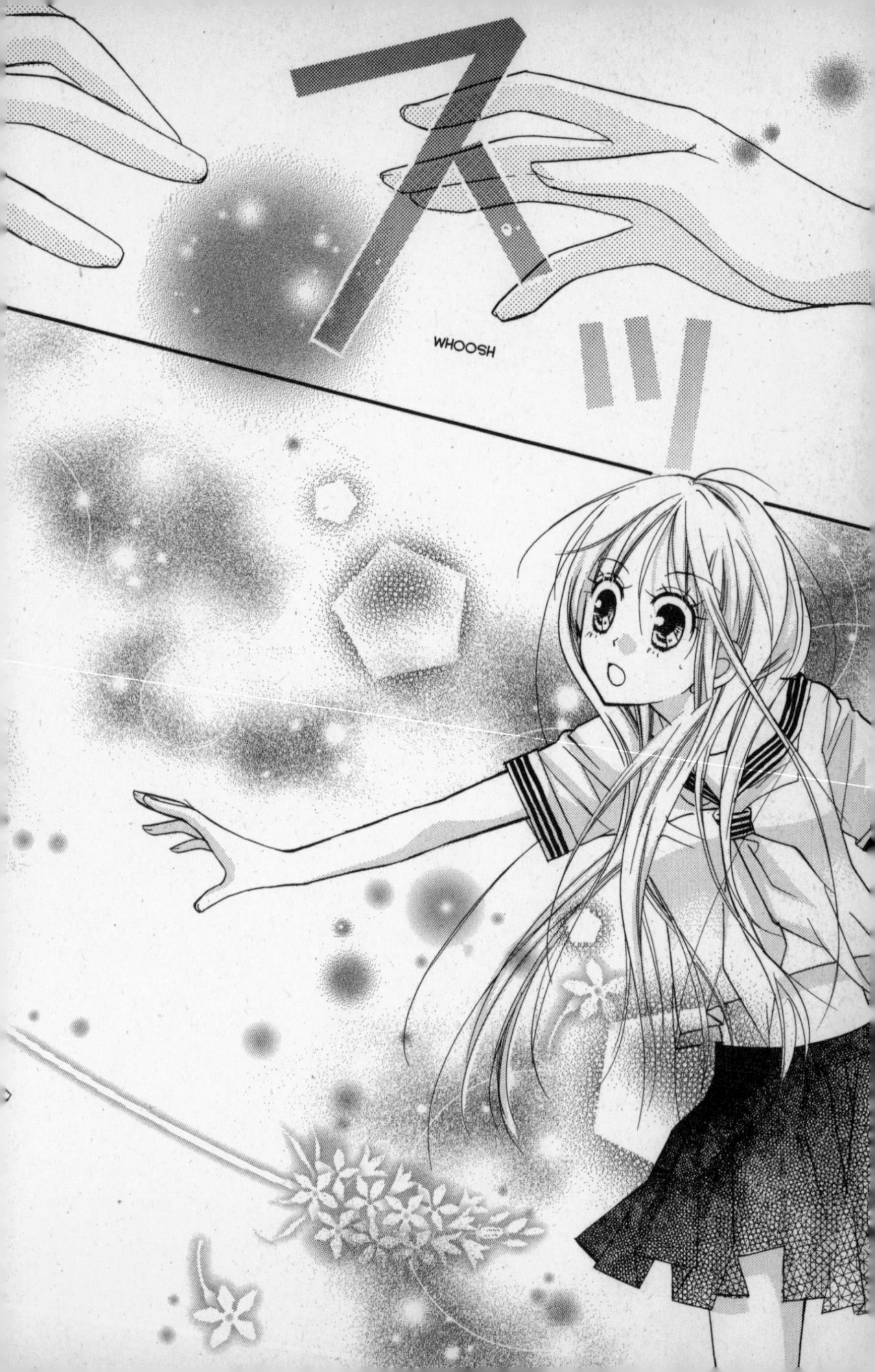
WHOOSH

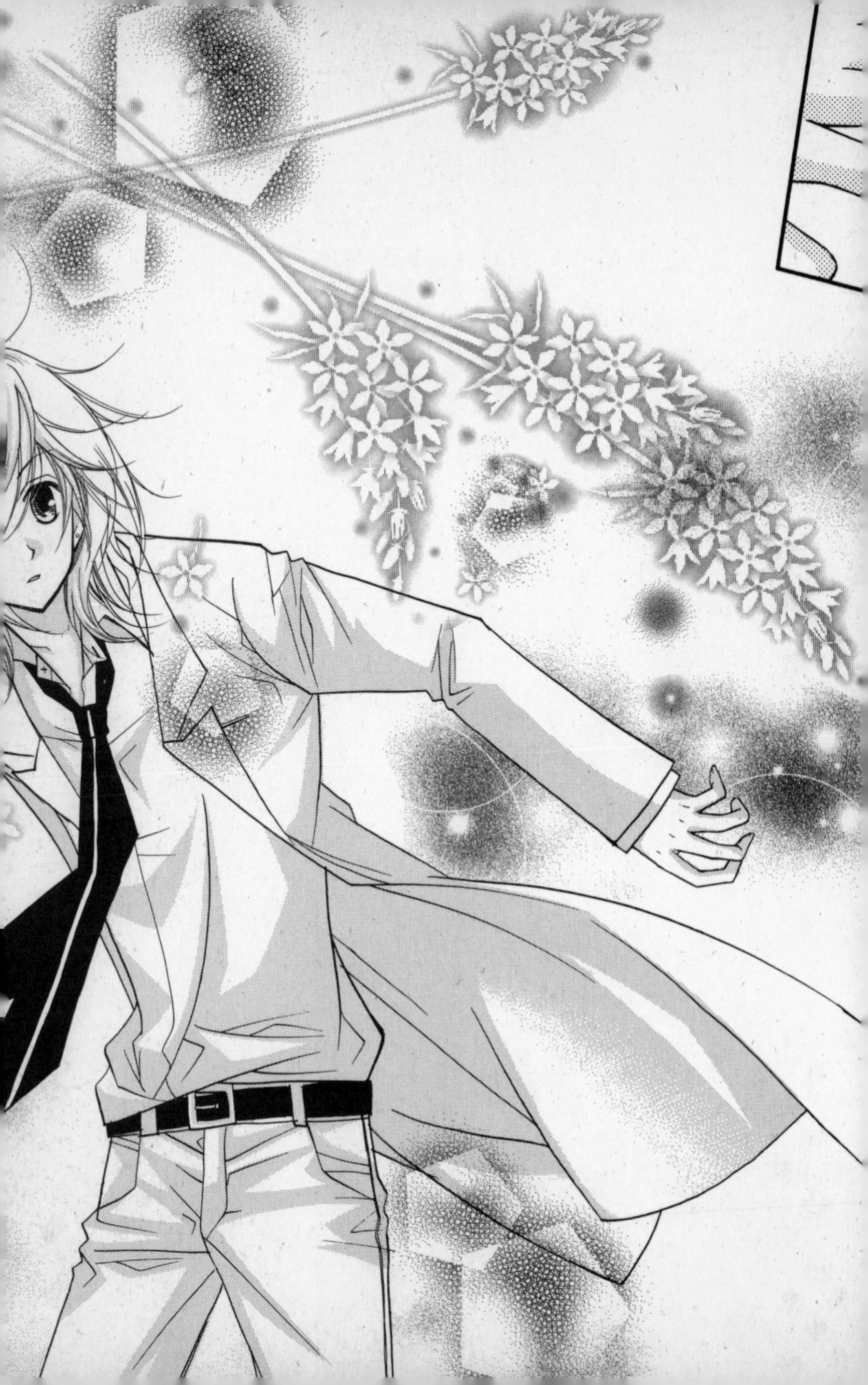

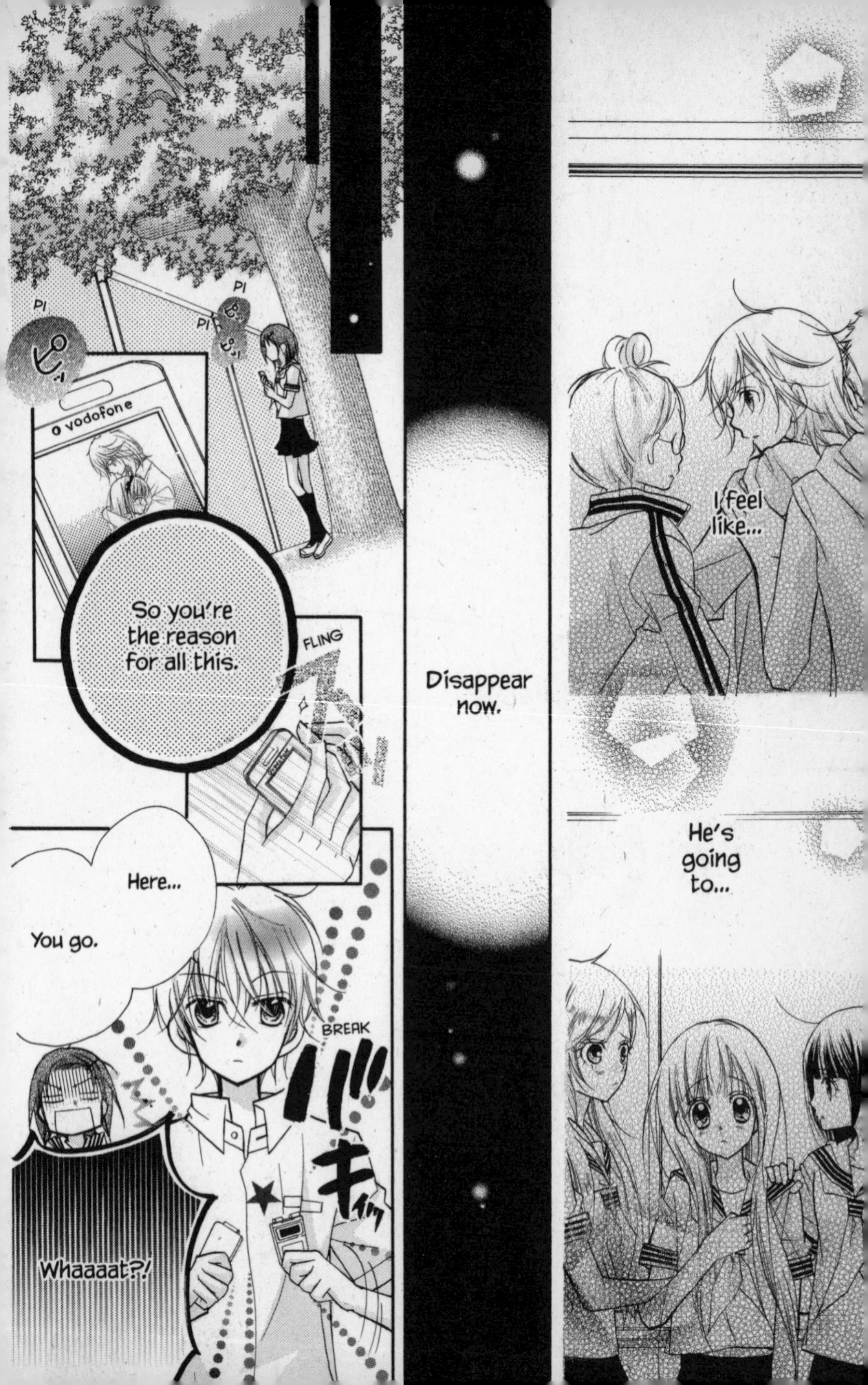

I feel like...
He's going to...
Disappear now.
PI
PI
PI
o vodofone
So you're the reason for all this.
FLING
Here...
You go.
BREAK
Whaaaat?!

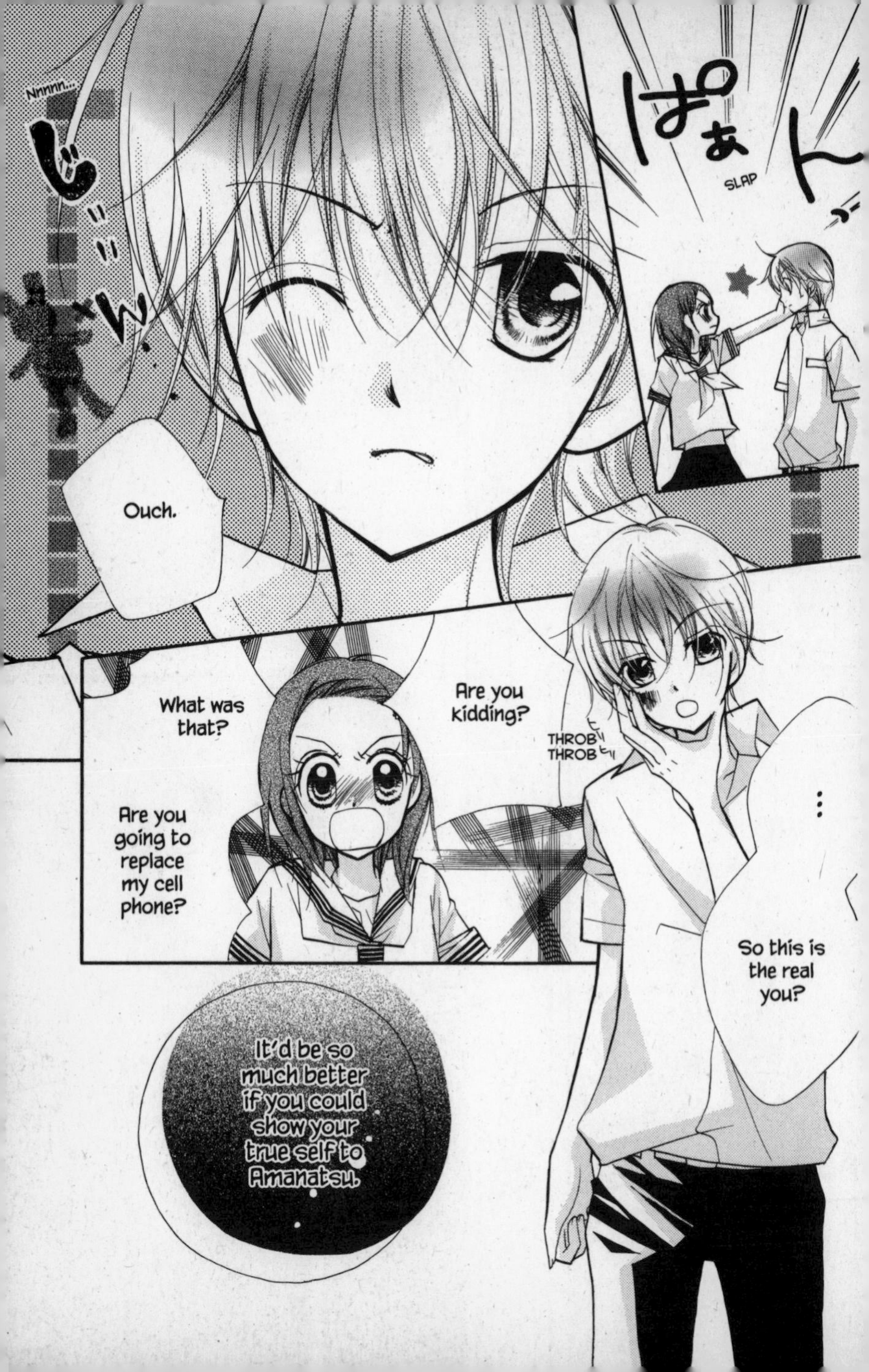

ぱぁ~ん
SLAP
Nnnnn...
Ouch.
THROB THROB
...
So this is the real you?
What was that?
Are you kidding?
Are you going to replace my cell phone?
It'd be so much better if you could show your true self to Amanatsu.

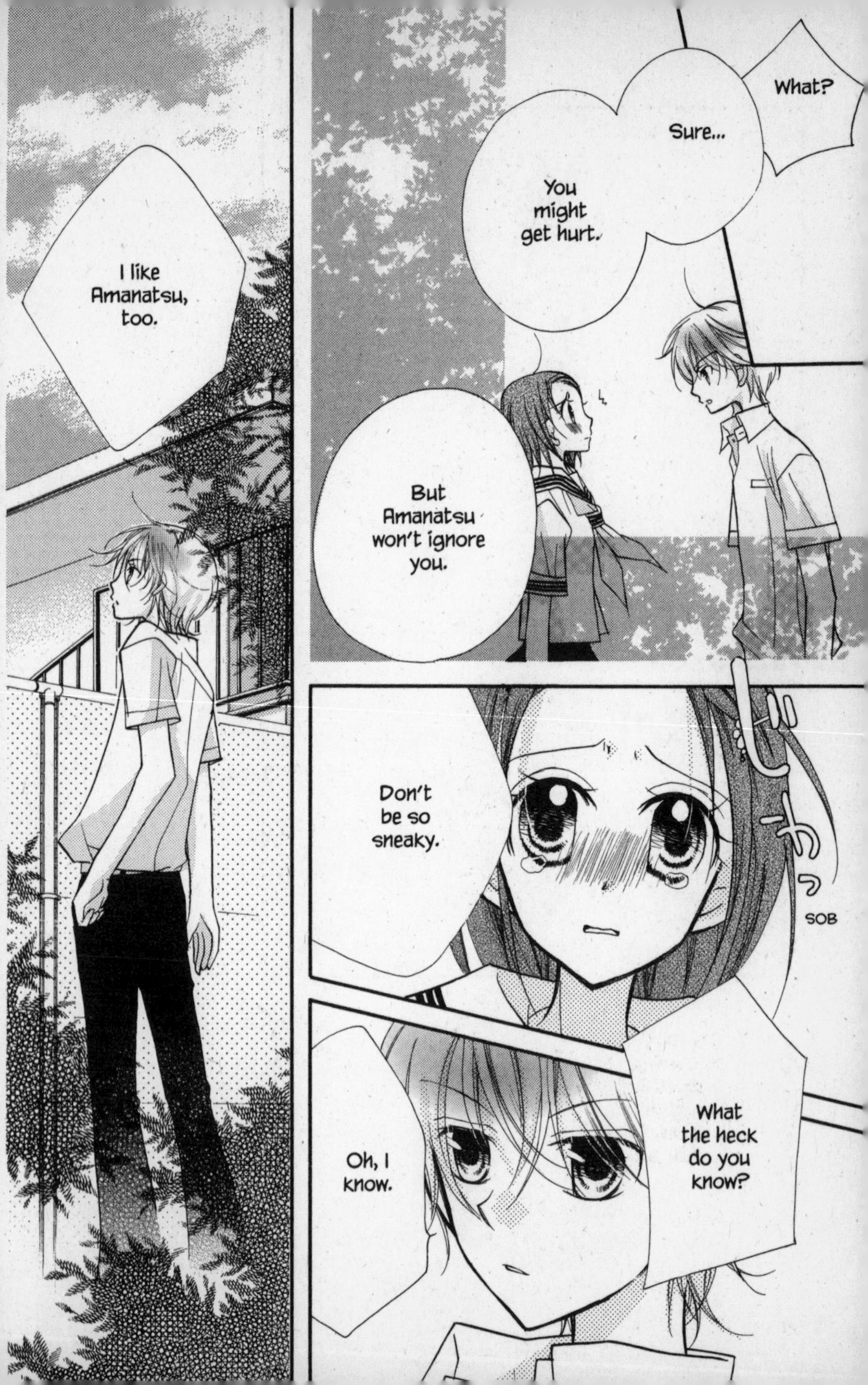
What?
Sure...
You might get hurt.
But Amanatsu won't ignore you.
Don't be so sneaky.
SOB
What the heck do you know?
Oh, I know.
I like Amanatsu, too.

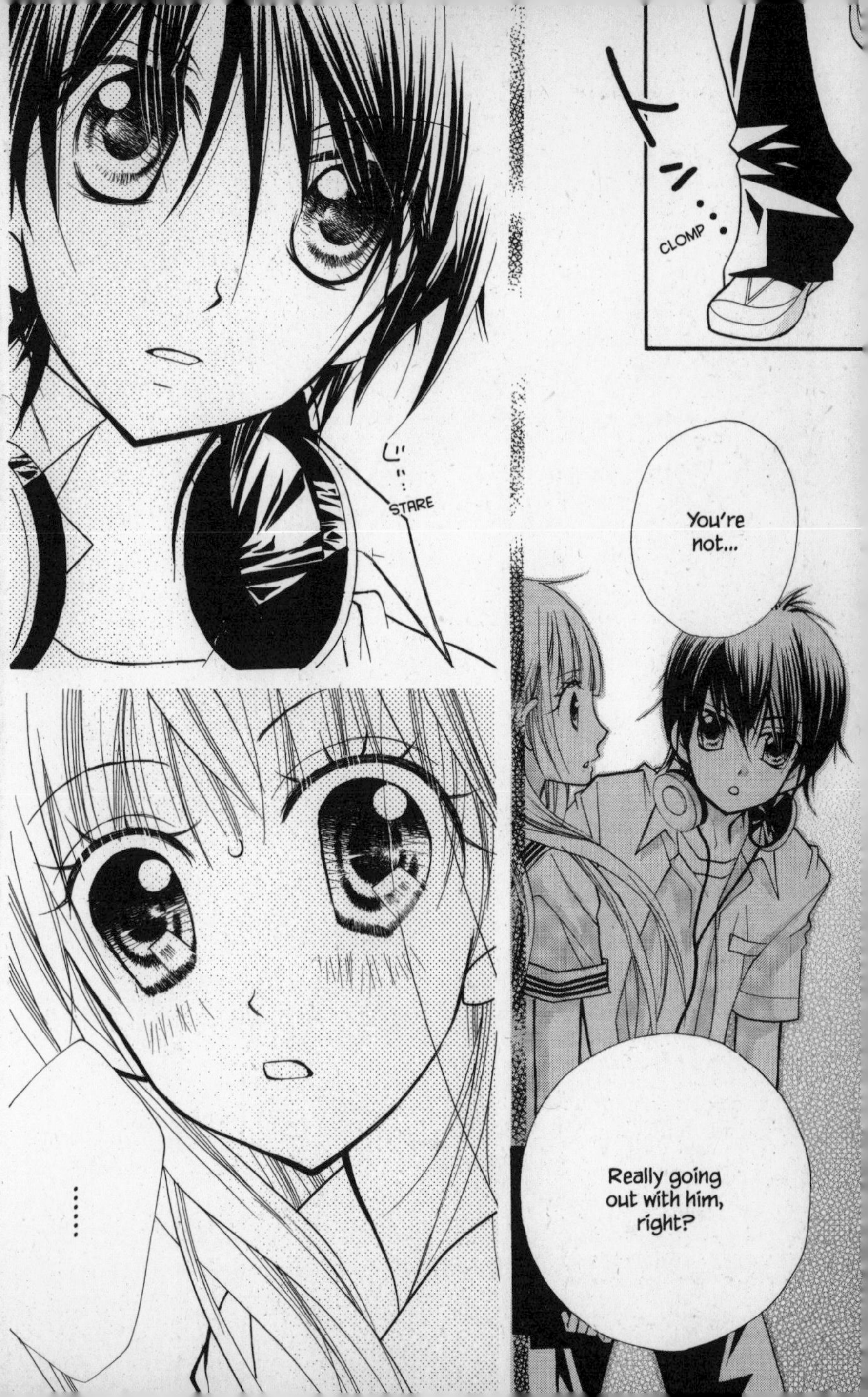
CLOMP
You're not...
Really going out with him, right?
STARE
......

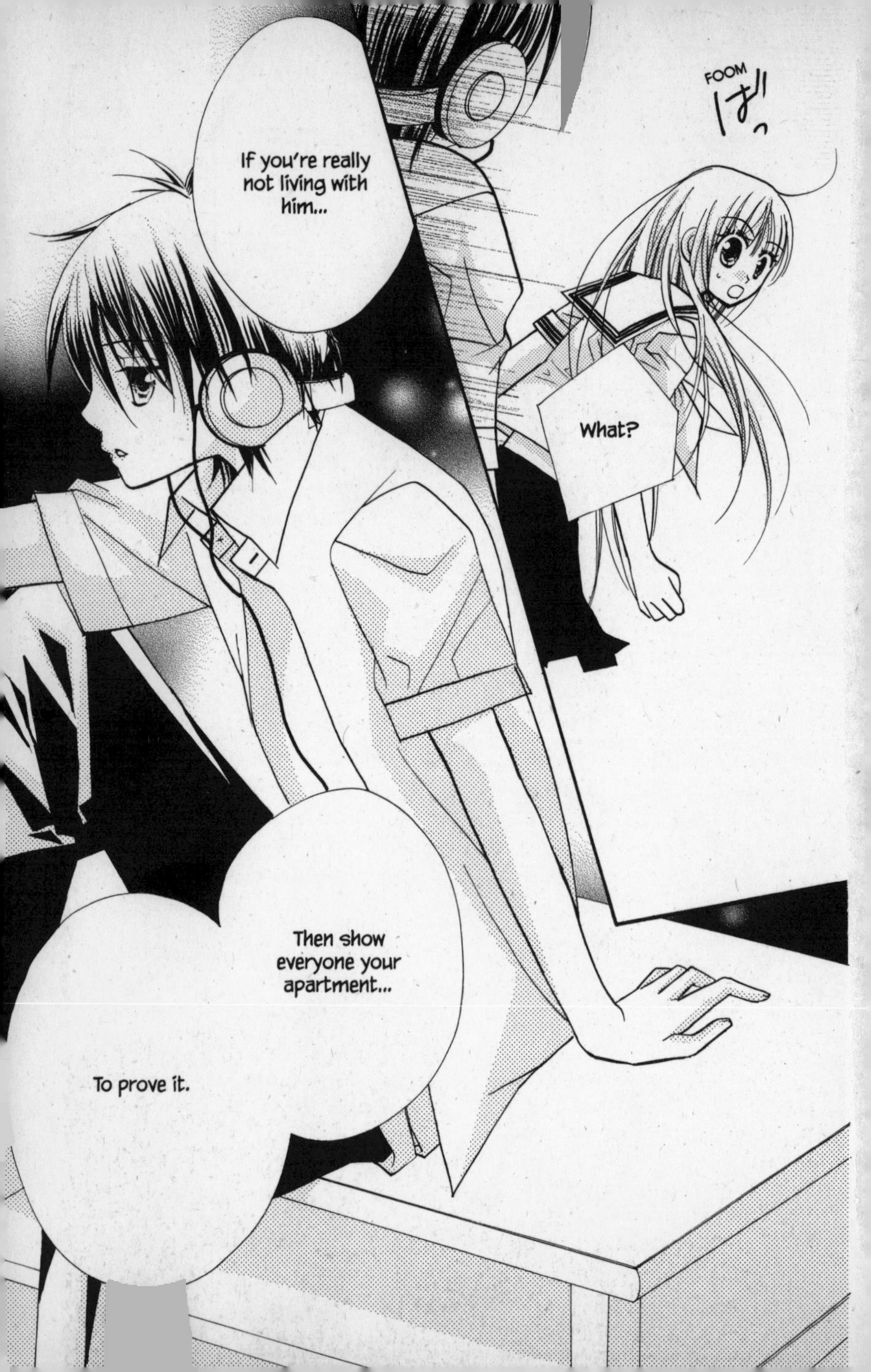
FOOM
ぱっ
What?
If you're really not living with him...
Then show everyone your apartment...
To prove it.

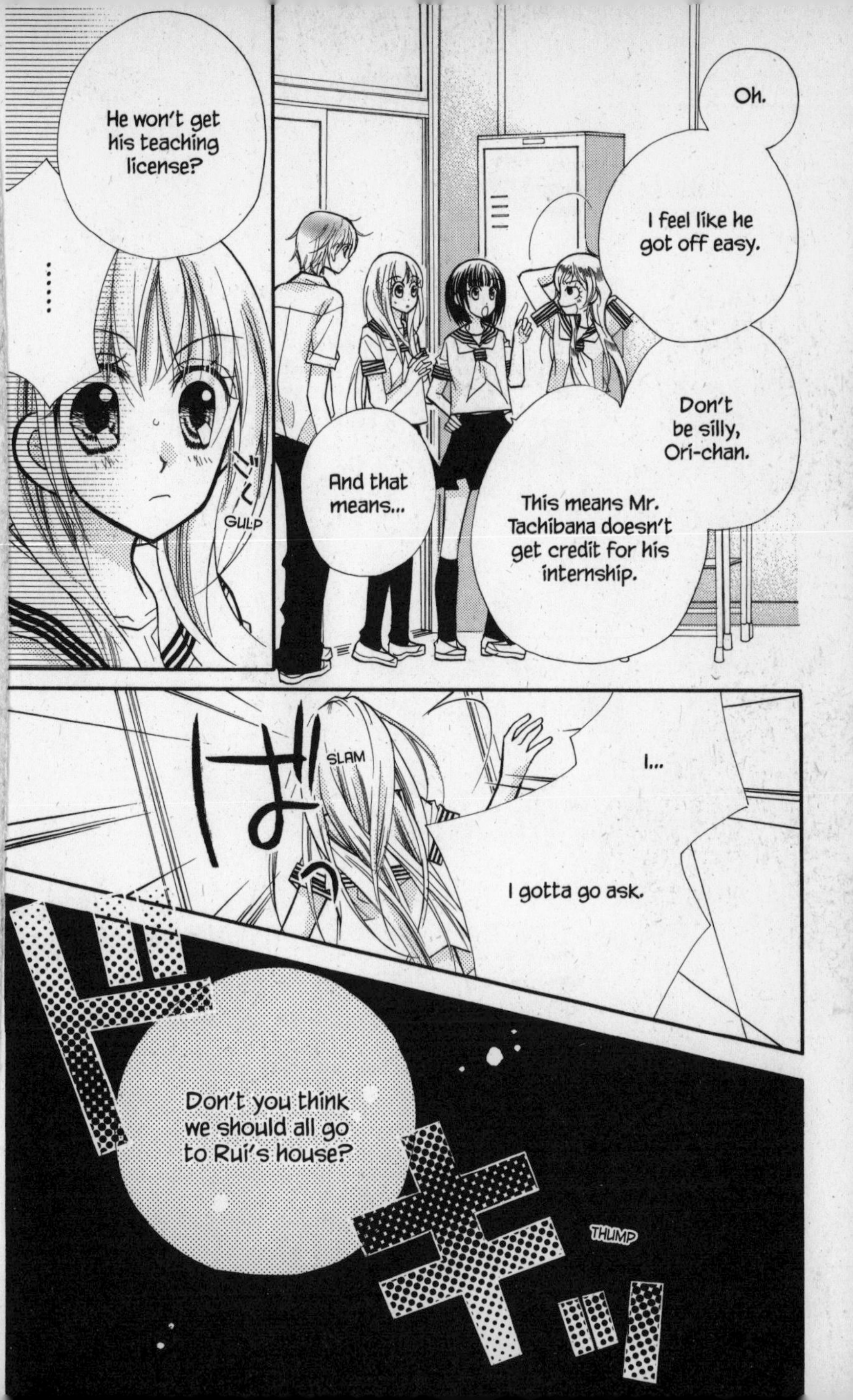
Oh.
I feel like he got off easy.
Don't be silly, Ori-chan.
This means Mr. Tachibana doesn't get credit for his internship.
And that means...
He won't get his teaching license?
......
GULP
SLAM
I...
I gotta go ask.
Don't you think we should all go to Rui's house?
THUMP

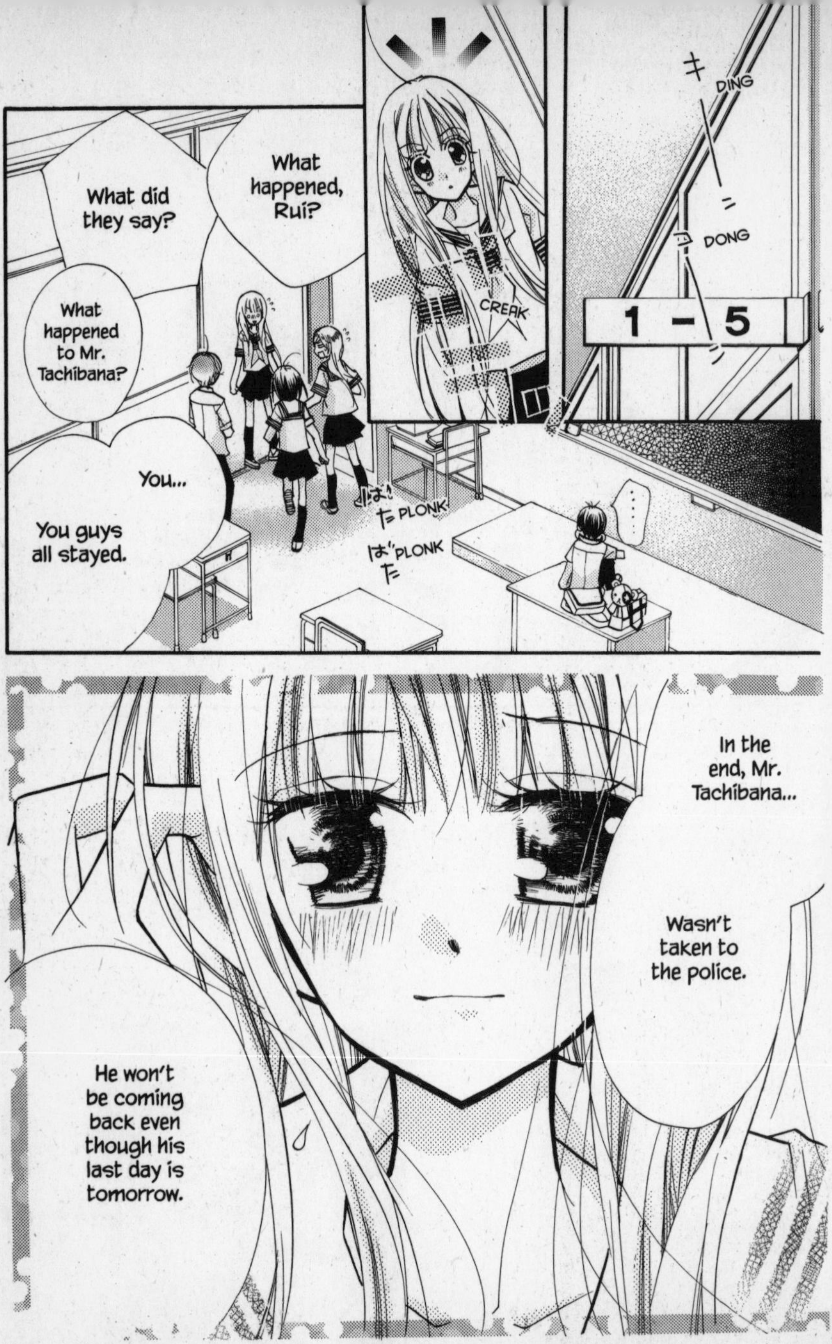
DING
DONG
1 - 5
CREAK
What happened, Rui?
What did they say?
What happened to Mr. Tachibana?
PLONK
PLONK
You...
You guys all stayed.
......
In the end, Mr. Tachibana...
Wasn't taken to the police.
He won't be coming back even though his last day is tomorrow.

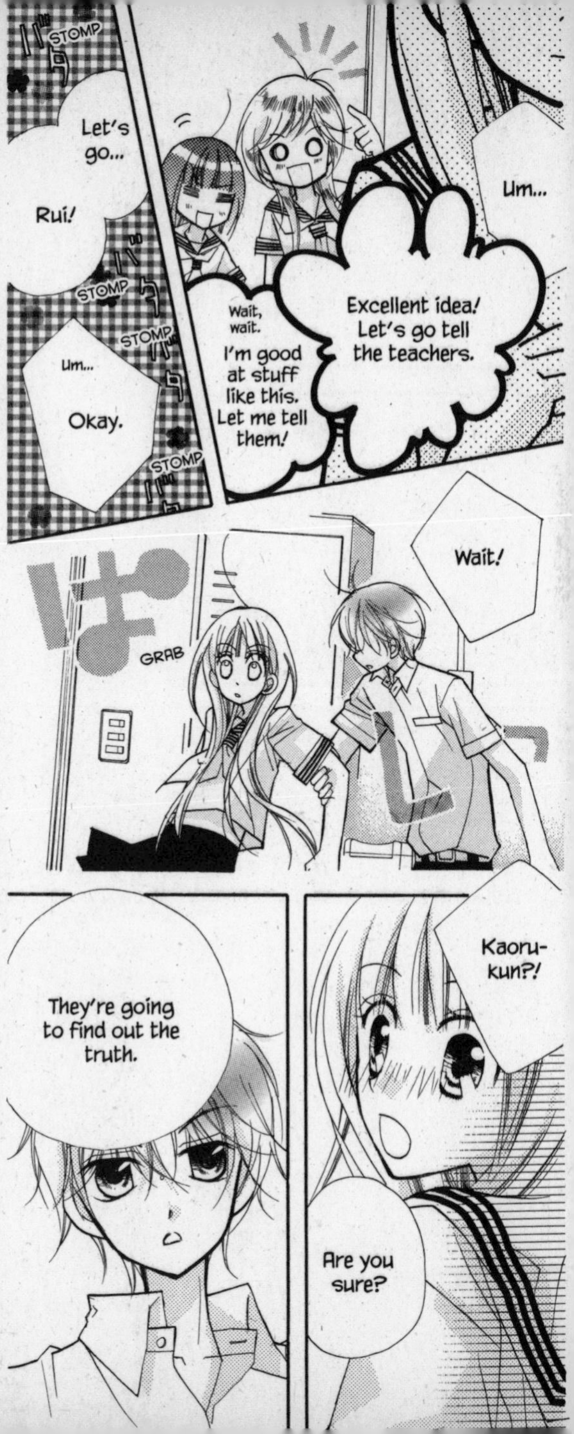
Um...
Excellent idea! Let's go tell the teachers.
Wait, wait.
I'm good at stuff like this. Let me tell them!
Let's go...
Rui!
STOMP
STOMP
STOMP
STOMP
Um...
Okay.
Wait!
GRAB
Kaoru-kun?!
Are you sure?
They're going to find out the truth.

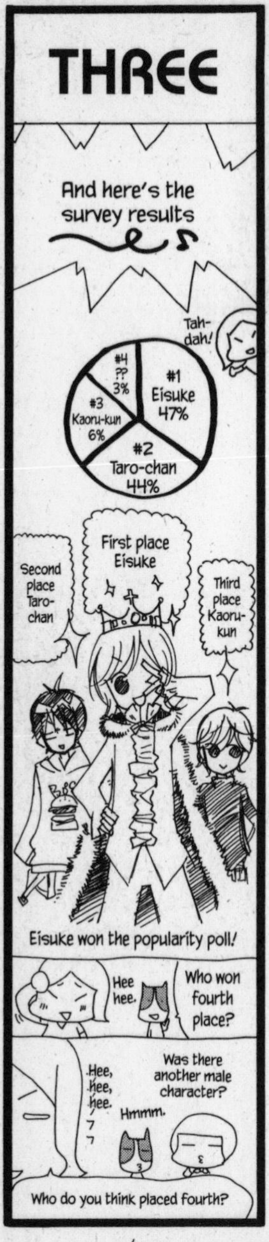
THREE
And here's the survey results
Tah-dah!
#1 Eisuke 47%
#2 Taro-chan 44%
#3 Kaoru-kun 6%
#4 ?? 3%
First place Eisuke
Third place Kaoru-kun
Second place Taro-chan
Eisuke won the popularity poll!
Who won fourth place?
Hee hee.
Was there another male character?
Hmmm.
Hee, hee, hee.
Who do you think placed fourth?

← On to PART FOUR

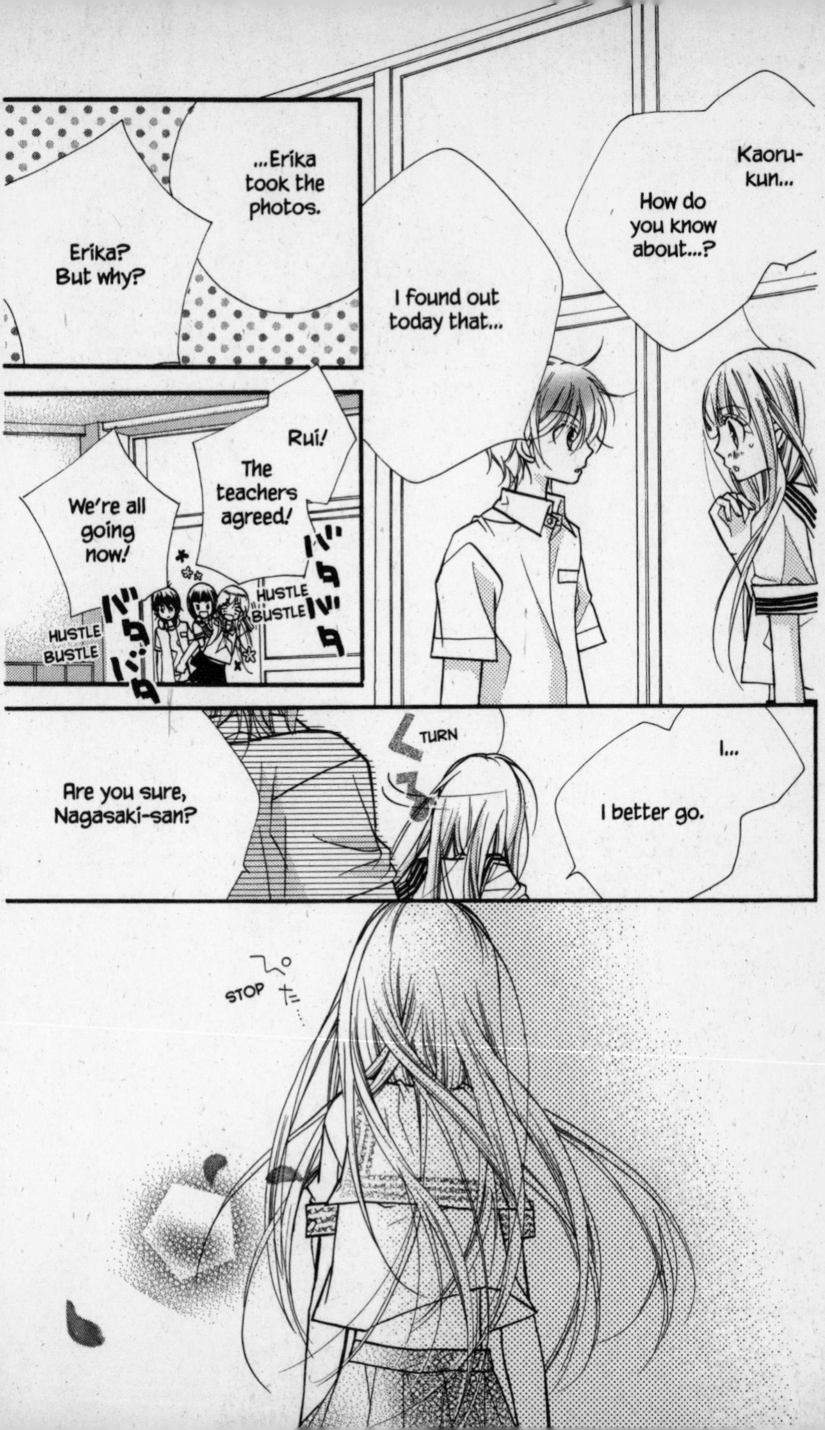
Kaoru-kun...
How do you know about...?
I found out today that...
...Erika took the photos.
Erika? But why?
Rui!
The teachers agreed!
バタバタ
HUSTLE BUSTLE
We're all going now!
バタバタ
HUSTLE BUSTLE
I...
I better go.
TURN
Are you sure, Nagasaki-san?
STOP

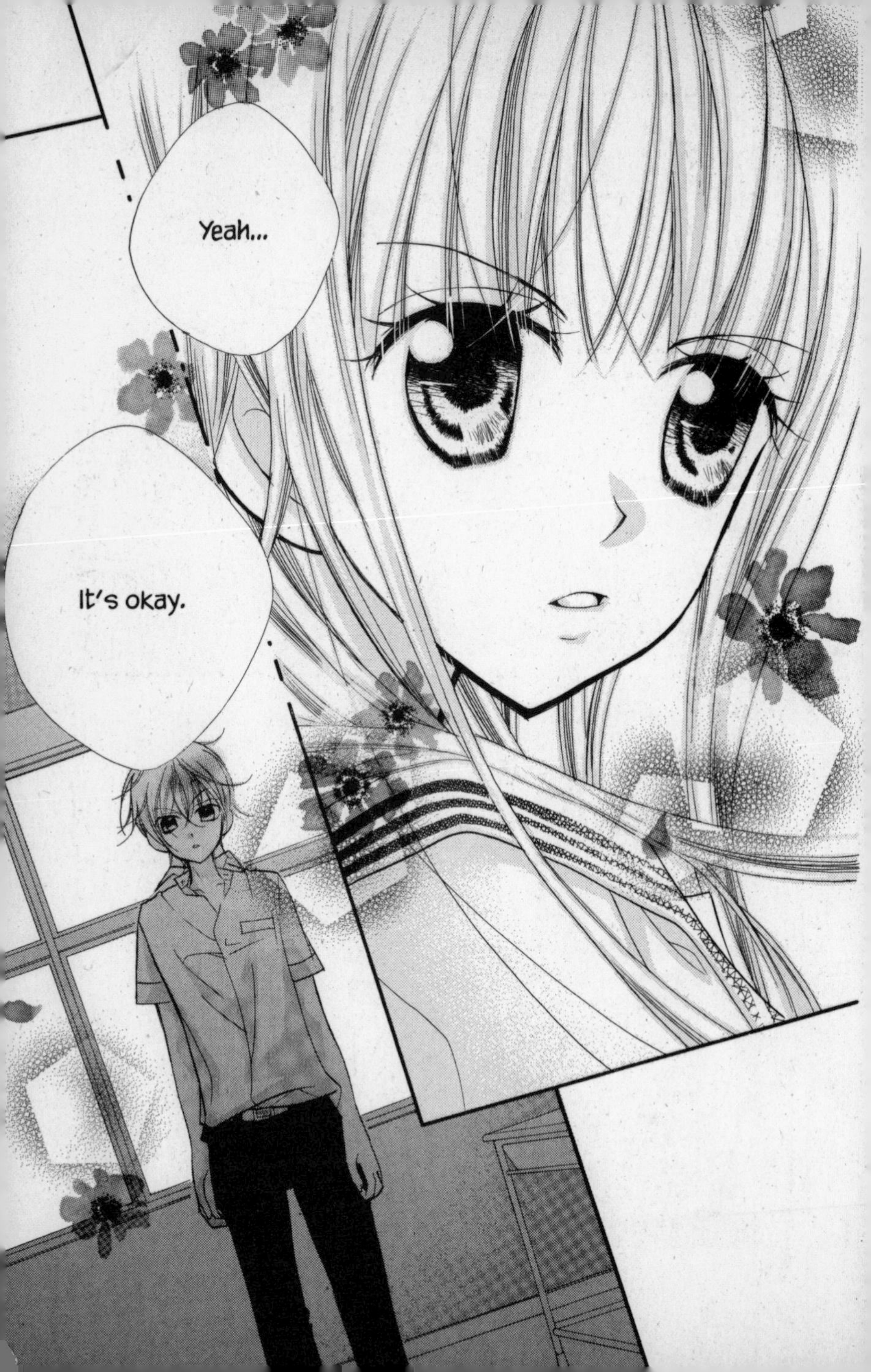
Yeah...
It's okay.

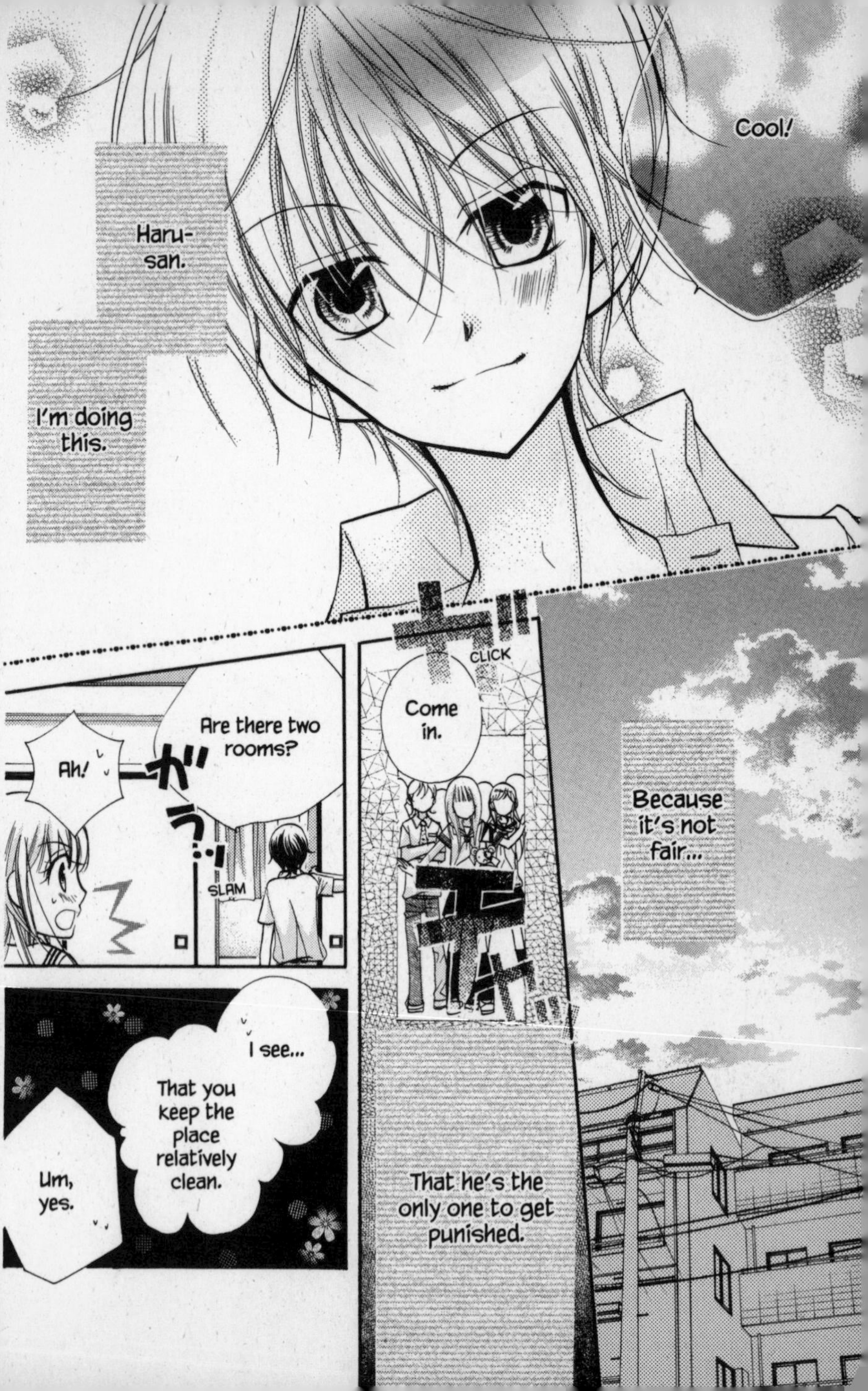
Cool!
Haru-san.
I'm doing this.
Because it's not fair...
That he's the only one to get punished.
CLICK
Come in.
Are there two rooms?
Ah!
SLAM
I see...
That you keep the place relatively clean.
Um, yes.

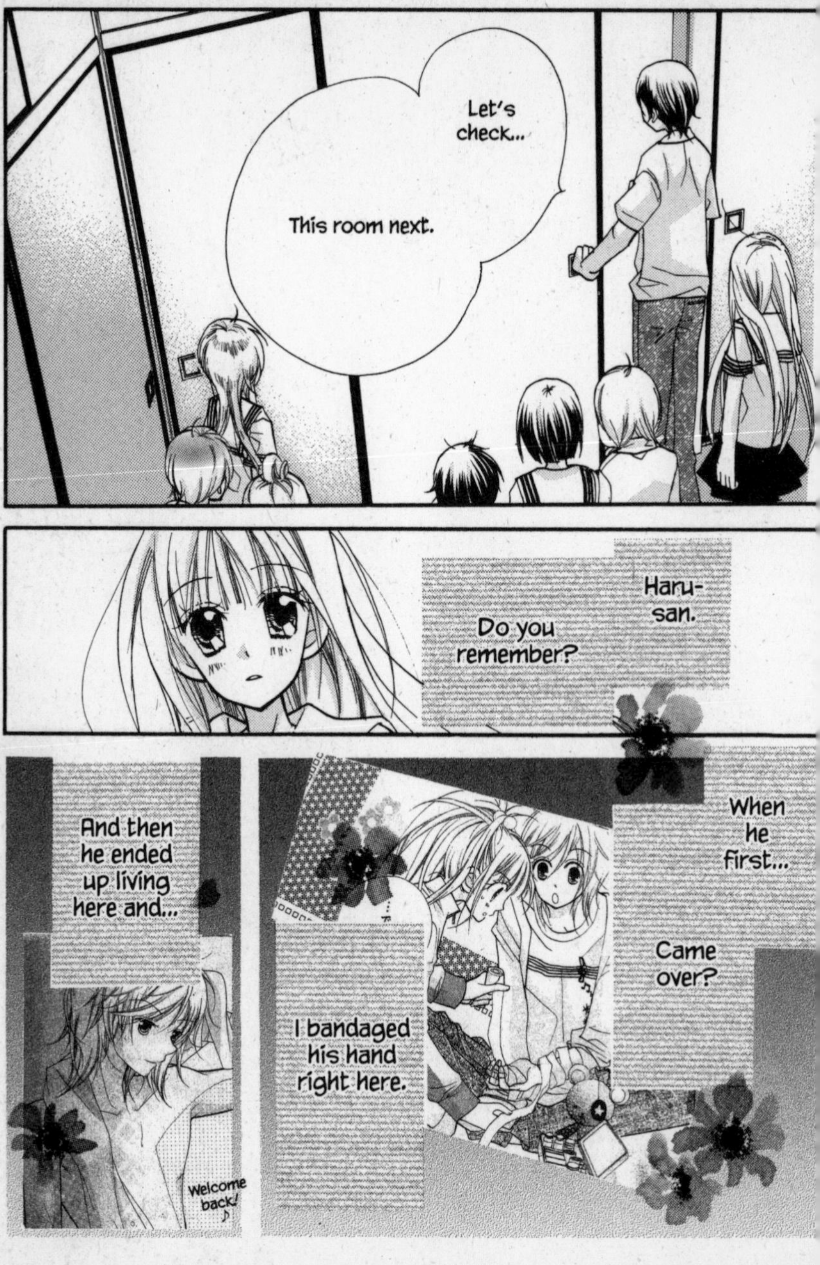
Let's check...
This room next.
Haru-san.
Do you remember?
When he first...
Came over?
I bandaged his hand right here.
And then he ended up living here and...
Welcome back! ♪

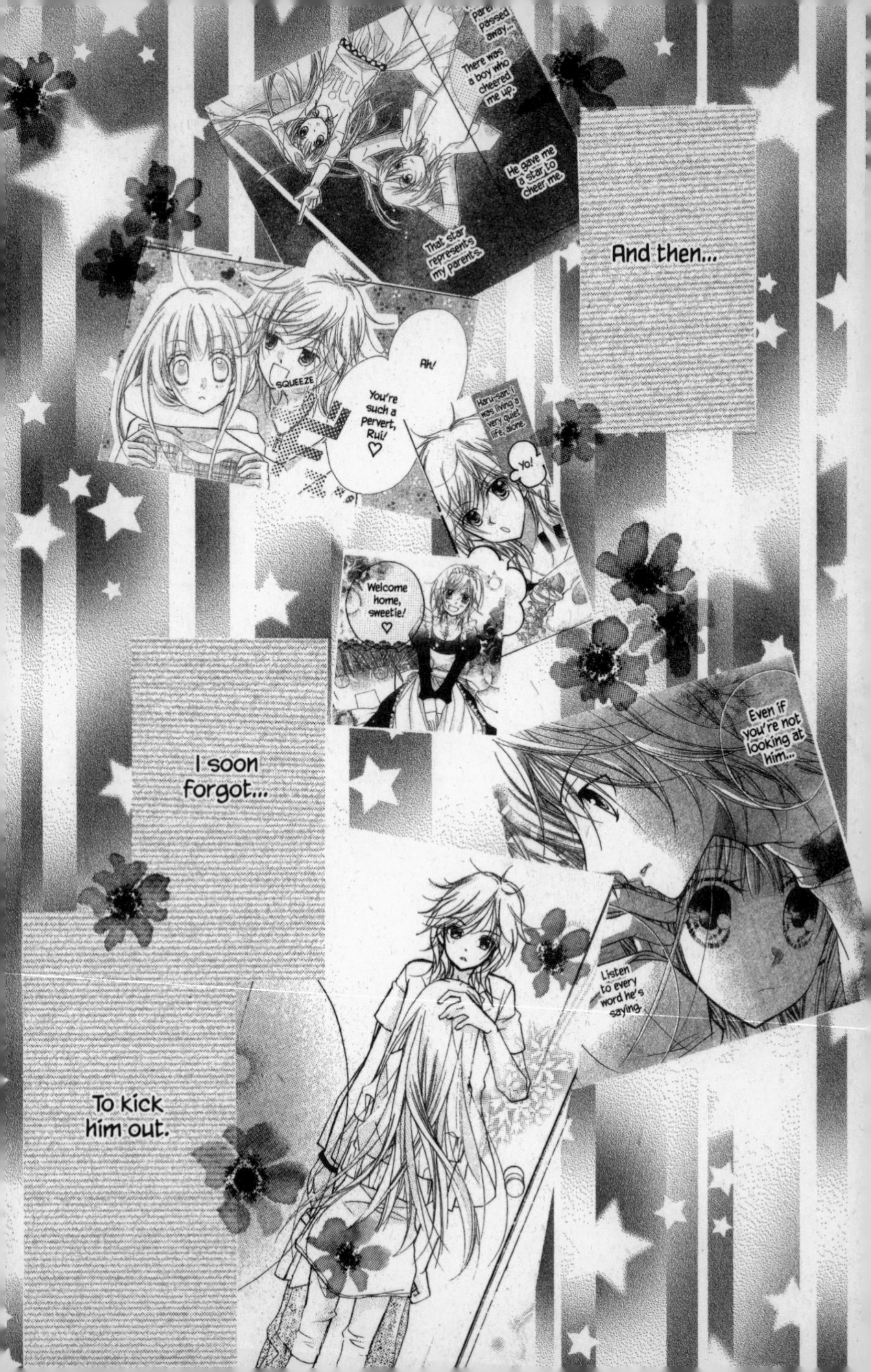

pare... passed away...
There was a boy who cheered me up.
He gave me a star to cheer me.
That star represents my parents.
And then...
Haru-san! I was living a very quiet life, alone.
Yo!
Ah!
You're such a pervert, Rui! ♡
SQUEEZE
Welcome home, sweetie! ♡
I soon forgot...
To kick him out.
Even if you're not looking at him...
Listen to every word he's saying.

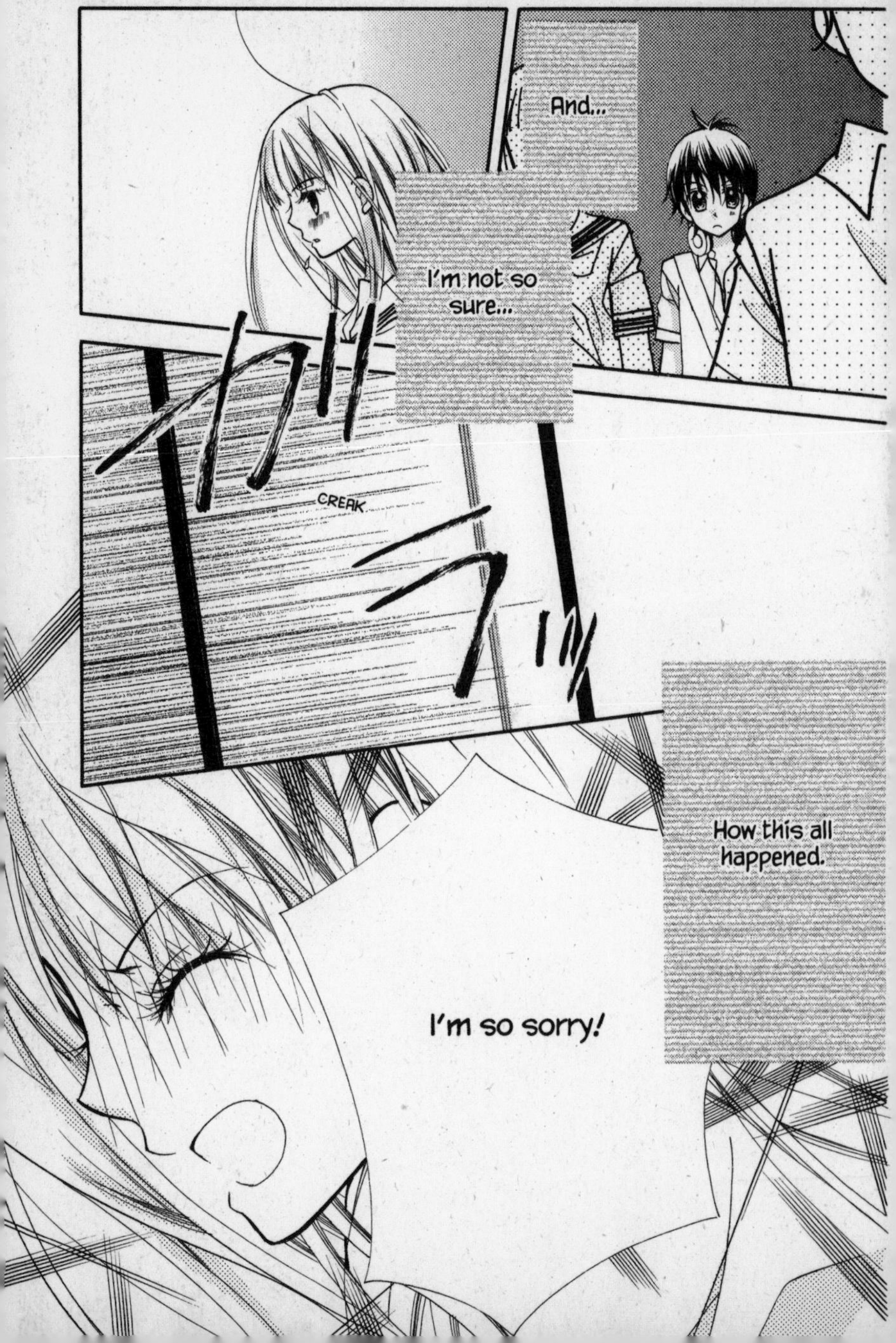
And...
I'm not so sure...
CREAK
How this all happened.
I'm so sorry!

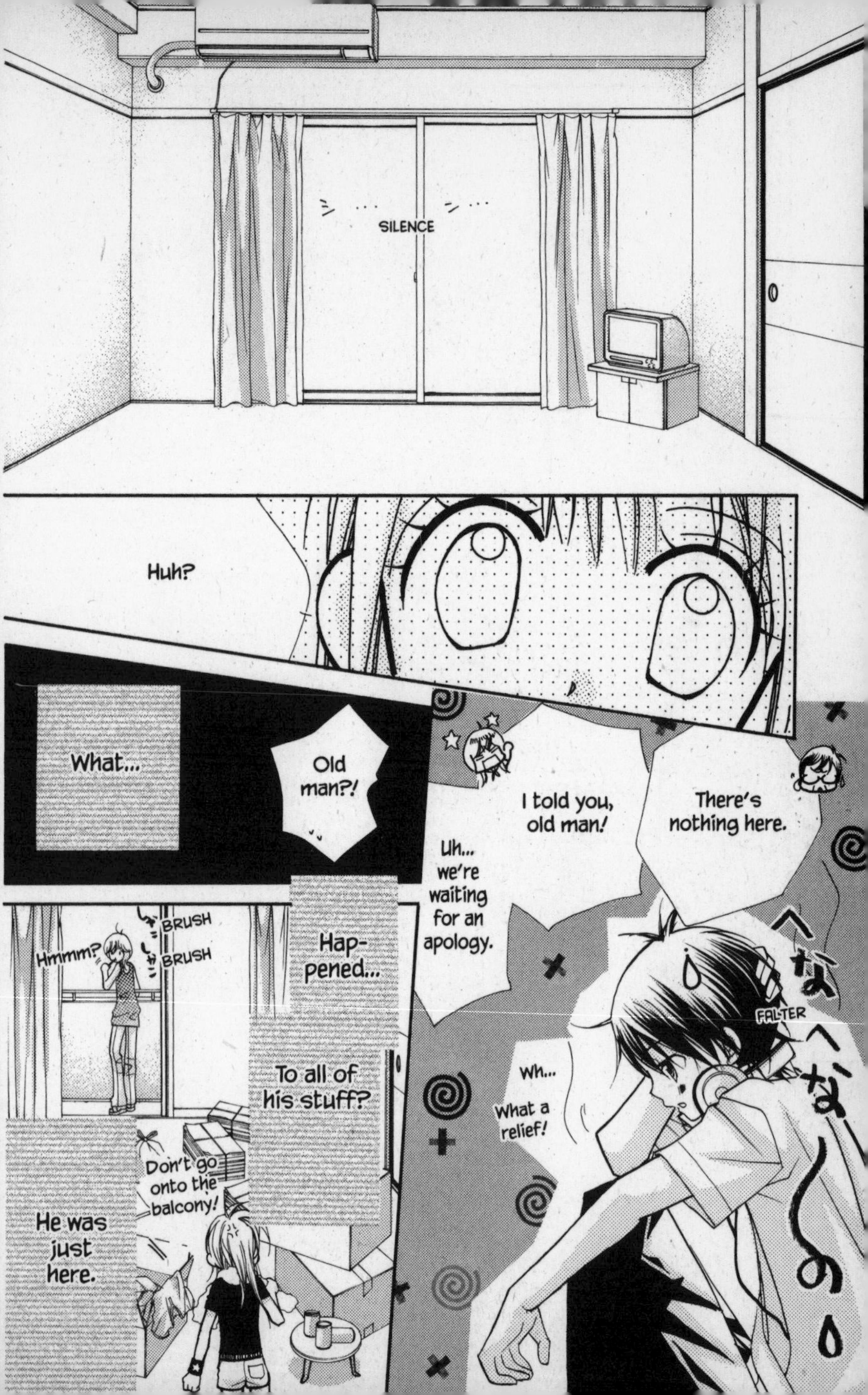
SILENCE
Huh?
There's nothing here.
I told you, old man!
Uh... we're waiting for an apology.
FALTER
Wh...
What a relief!
Old man?!
What...
Hap-pened...
To all of his stuff?
BRUSH
BRUSH
Hmmm?
Don't go onto the balcony!
He was just here.

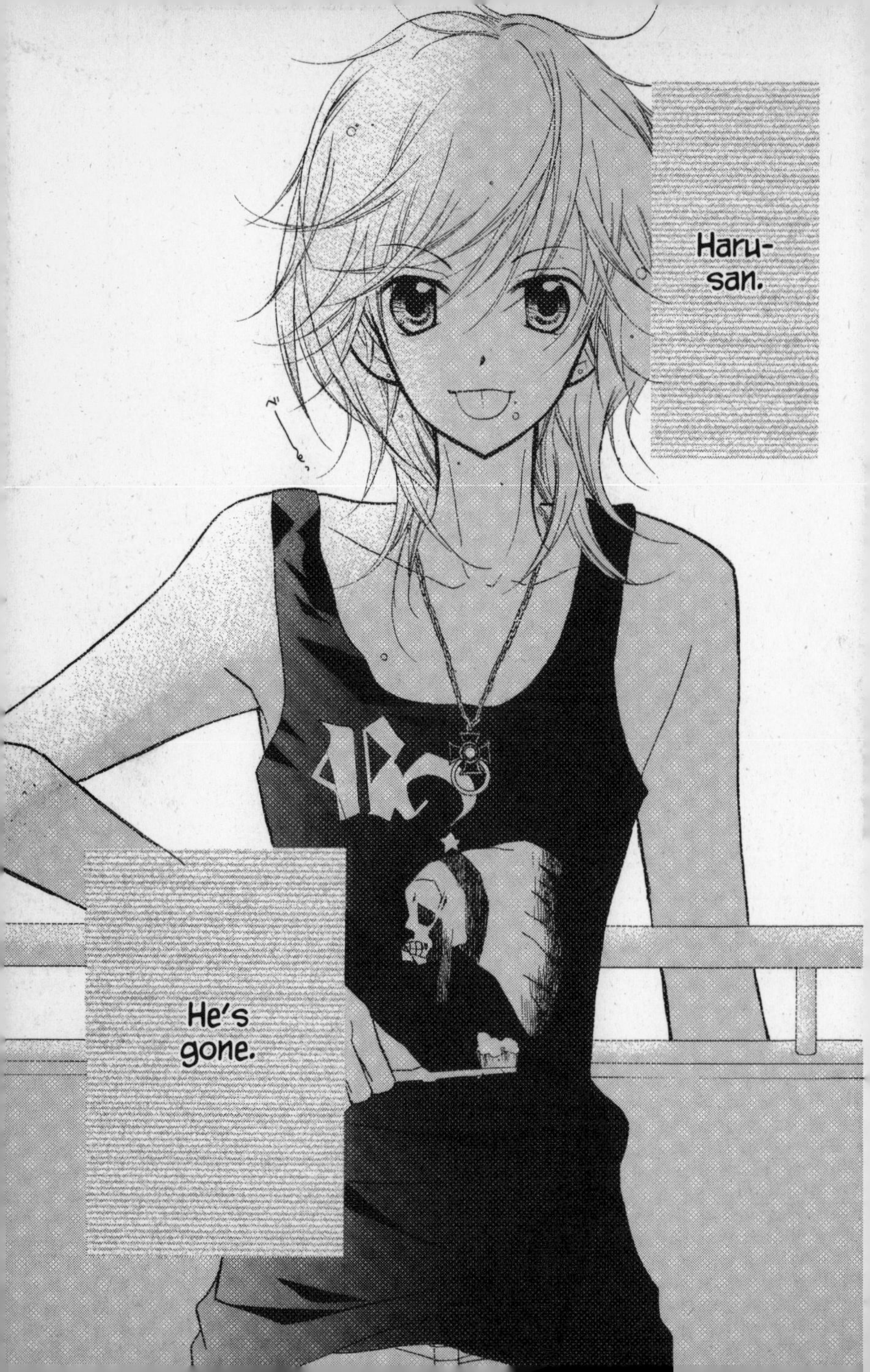
Haru-san.
He's gone.

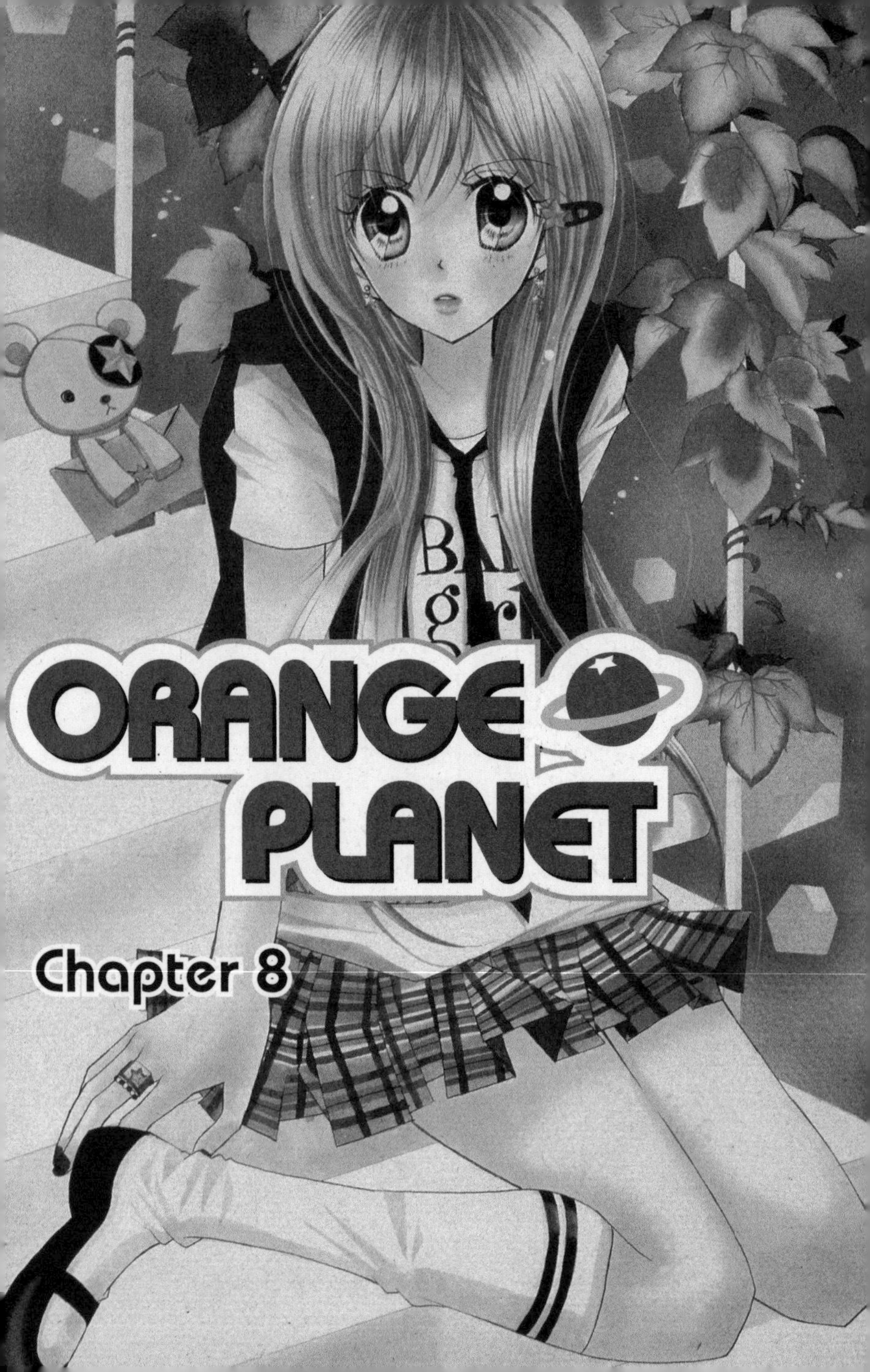
ORANGE PLANET
Chapter 8

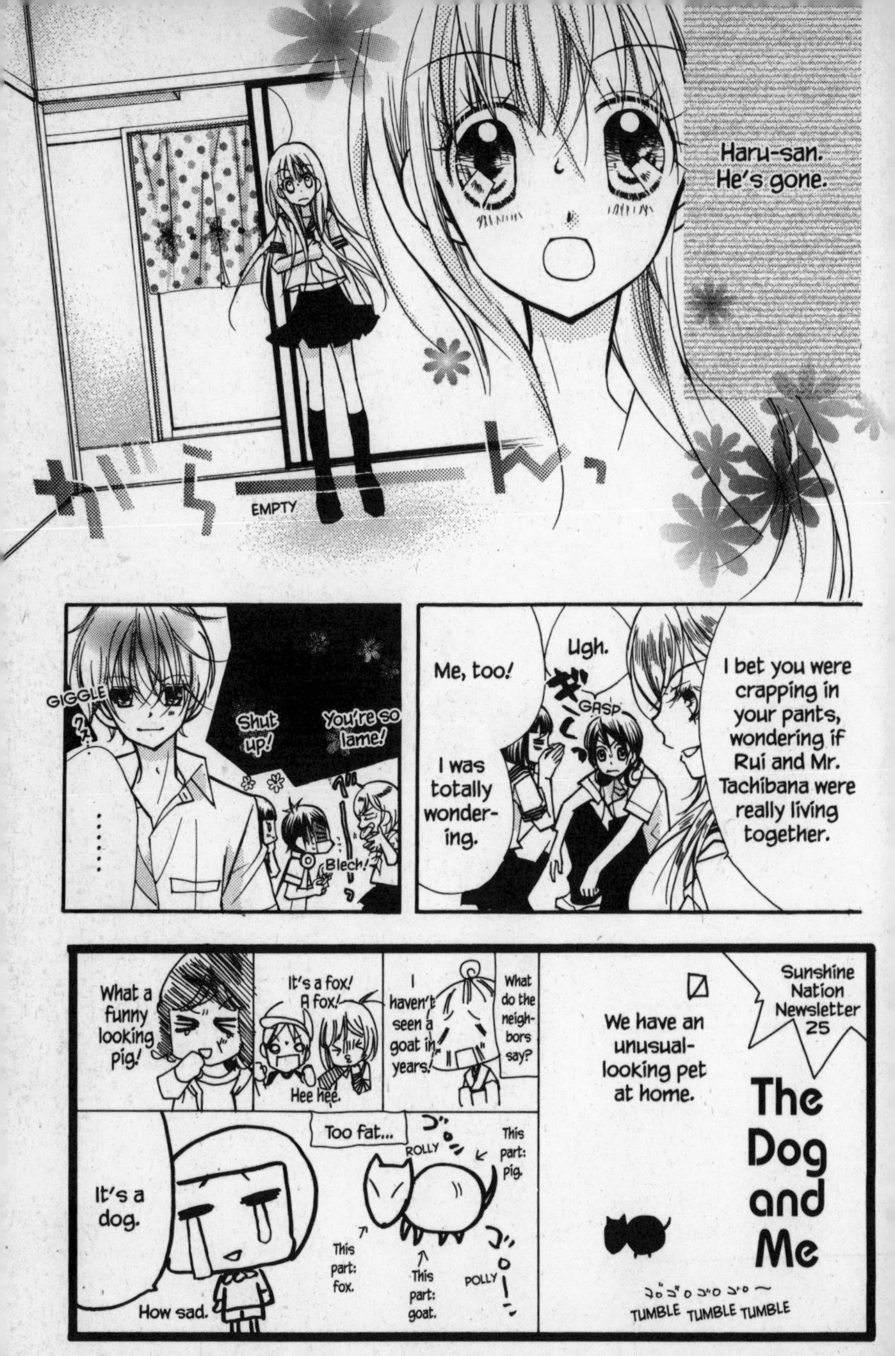
Haru-san. He's gone.
EMPTY
I bet you were crapping in your pants, wondering if Rui and Mr. Tachibana were really living together.
Ugh.
GASP
Me, too!
I was totally wondering.
You're so lame!
Shut up!
Blech!
GIGGLE
Sunshine Nation Newsletter 25
The Dog and Me
We have an unusual-looking pet at home.
TUMBLE TUMBLE TUMBLE
What do the neighbors say?
I haven't seen a goat in years.
It's a fox! A fox!
Hee hee.
What a funny looking pig!
This part: pig.
Too fat...
ROLLY
This part: goat.
This part: fox.
POLLY
It's a dog.
How sad.

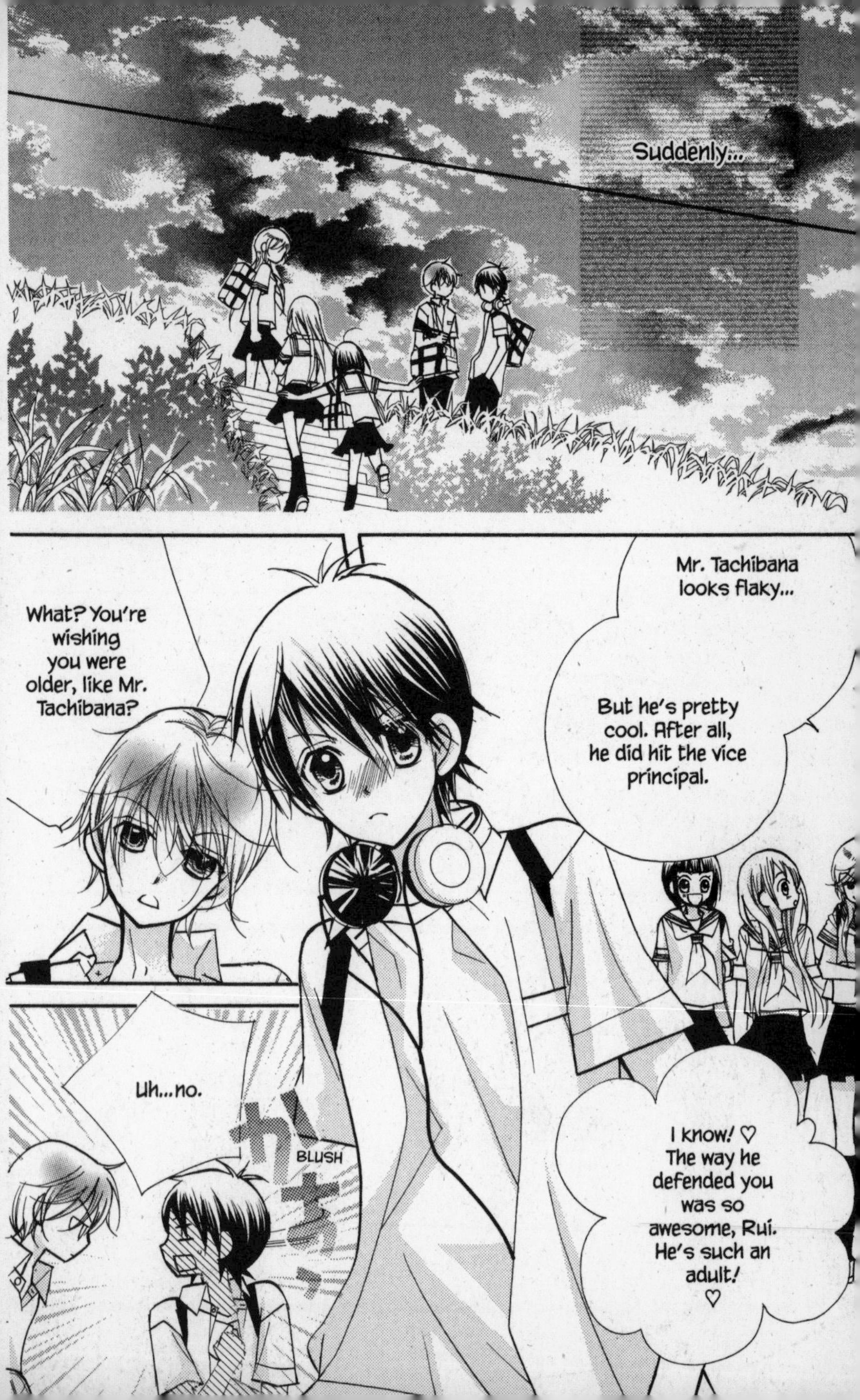
Suddenly...
Mr. Tachibana looks flaky...
But he's pretty cool. After all, he did hit the vice principal.
What? You're wishing you were older, like Mr. Tachibana?
I know! ♡ The way he defended you was so awesome, Rui. He's such an adult! ♡
Uh...no.
BLUSH

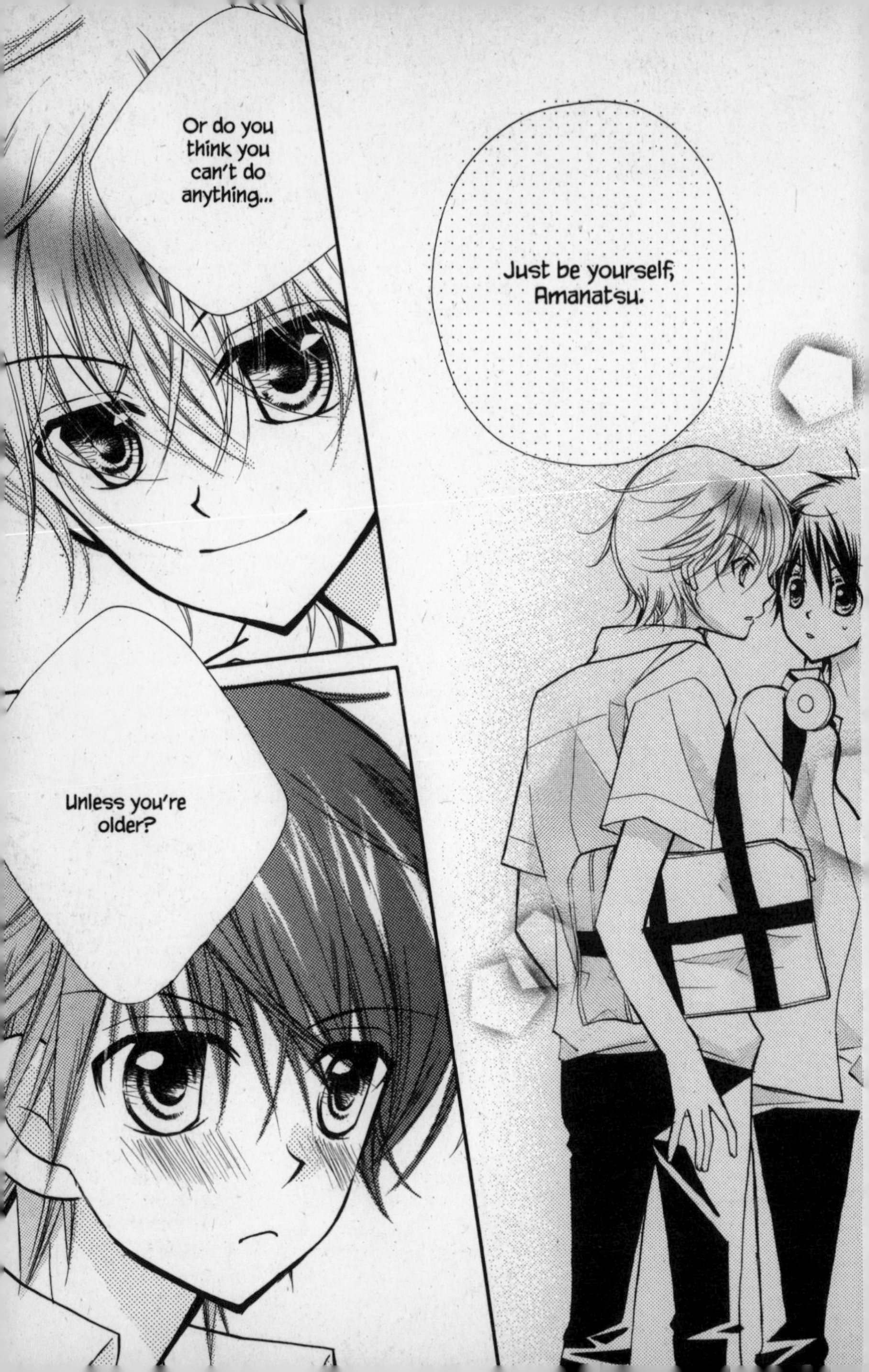
Just be yourself, Amanatsu.
Or do you think you can't do anything...
Unless you're older?

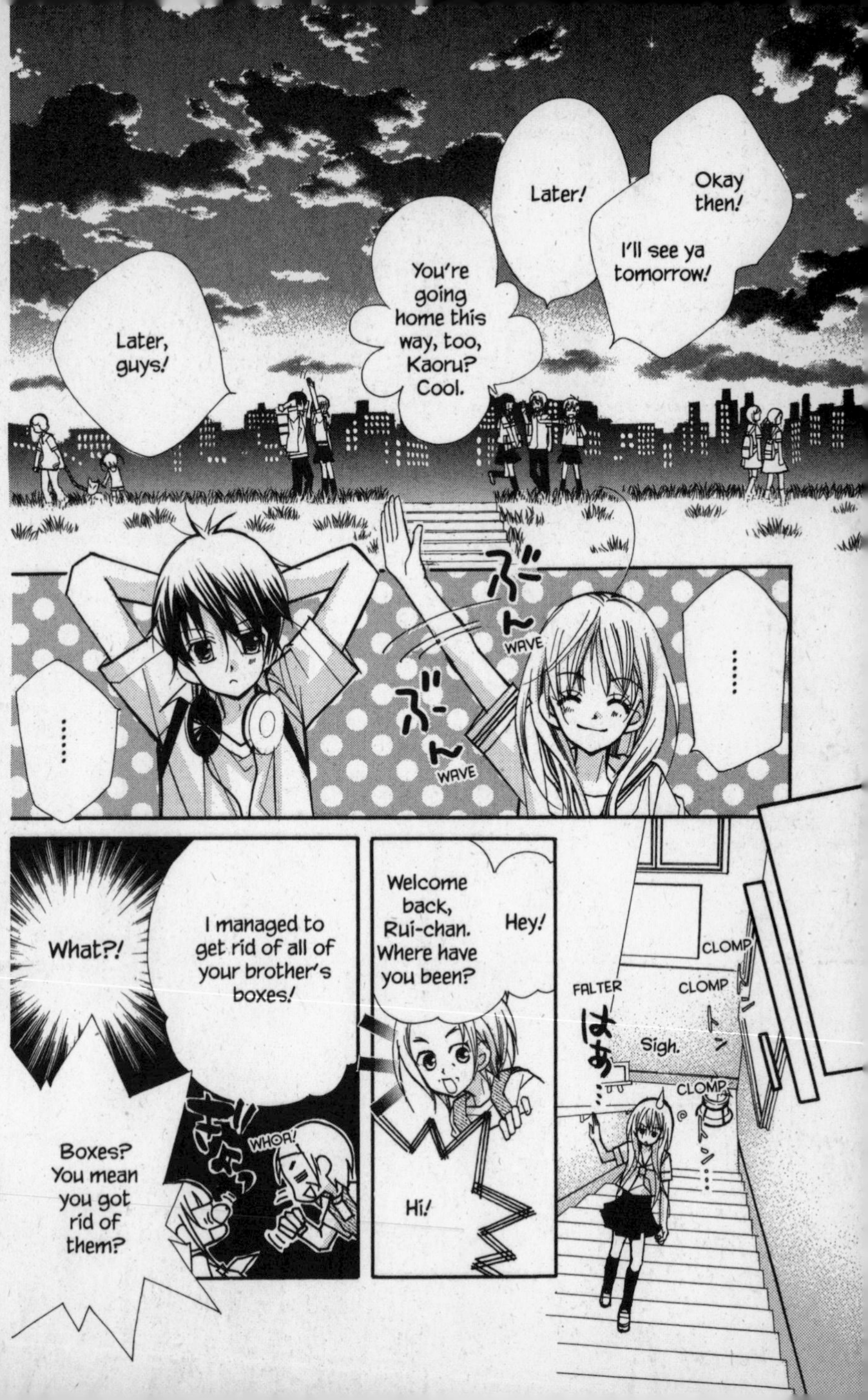

Okay then!
I'll see ya tomorrow!
Later!
You're going home this way, too, Kaoru? Cool.
Later, guys!
……
ぶ～ん
WAVE
ぶ～ん
WAVE
……
CLOMP
CLOMP
FALTER
はぁ…
Sigh.
CLOMP
Hey!
Welcome back, Rui-chan. Where have you been?
Hi!
I managed to get rid of all of your brother's boxes!
What?!
WHOA!
Boxes? You mean you got rid of them?

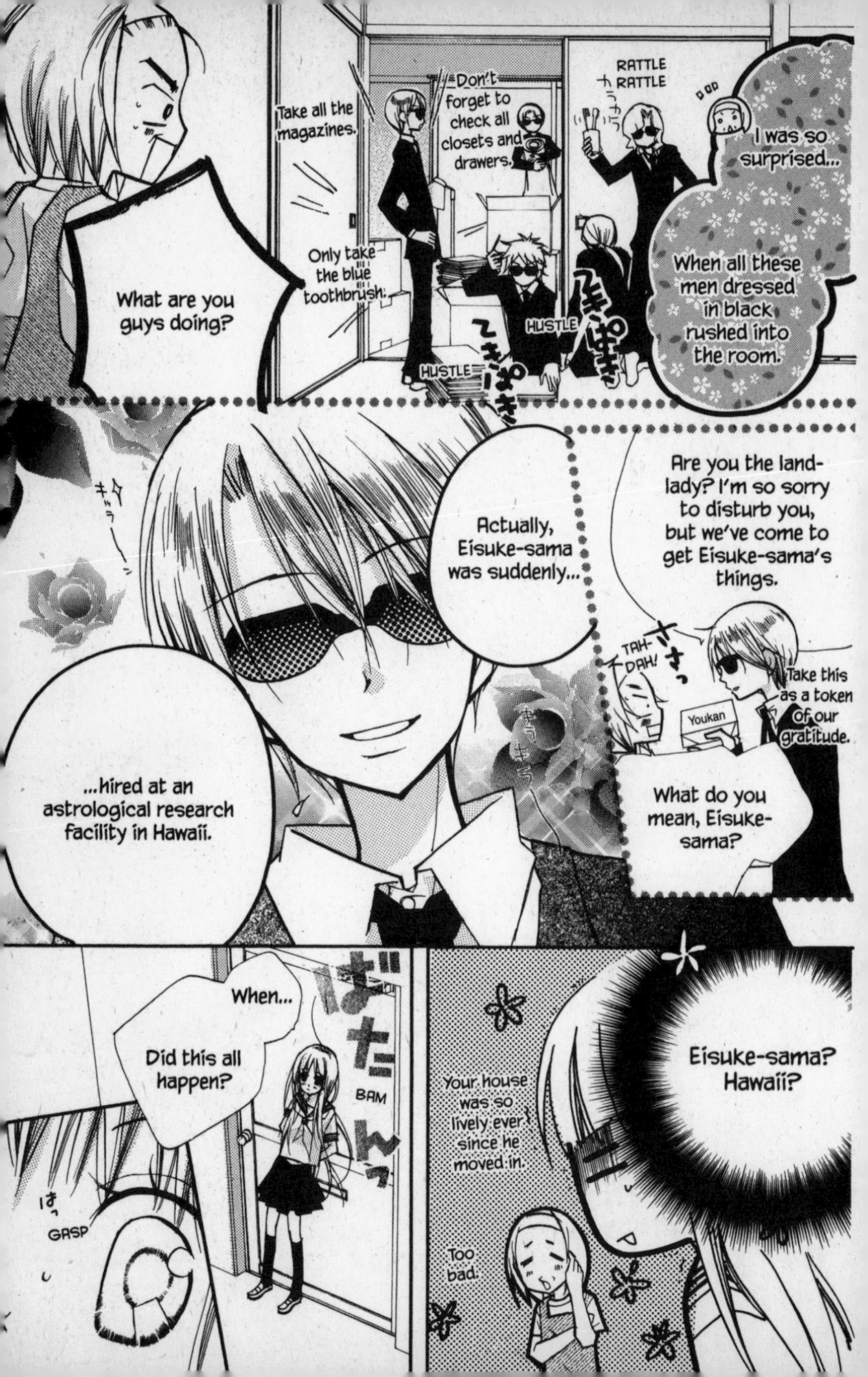
I was so surprised...
When all these men dressed in black rushed into the room.
RATTLE RATTLE
Don't forget to check all closets and drawers.
Take all the magazines.
Only take the blue toothbrush.
HUSTLE
HUSTLE
What are you guys doing?
Are you the land-lady? I'm so sorry to disturb you, but we've come to get Eisuke-sama's things.
TAH-DAH!
Take this as a token of our gratitude.
Youkan
What do you mean, Eisuke-sama?
Actually, Eisuke-sama was suddenly...
...hired at an astrological research facility in Hawaii.
Eisuke-sama? Hawaii?
Your house was so lively ever since he moved in.
Too bad.
BAM
When...
Did this all happen?
GASP

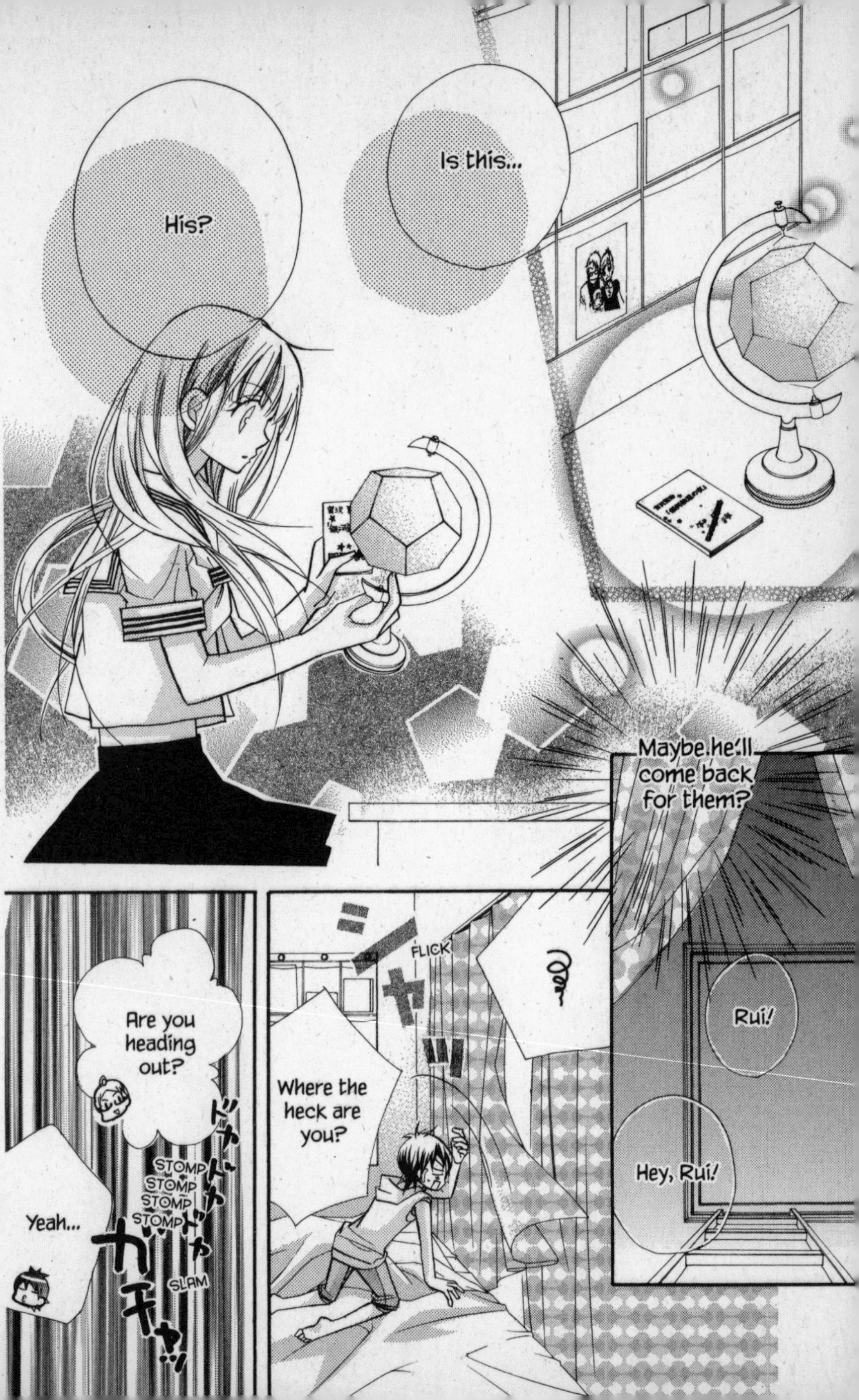
Is this...
His?
Maybe he'll come back for them?
Rui!
Hey, Rui!
FLICK
Where the heck are you?
Are you heading out?
STOMP
STOMP
STOMP
STOMP
Yeah...
SLAM

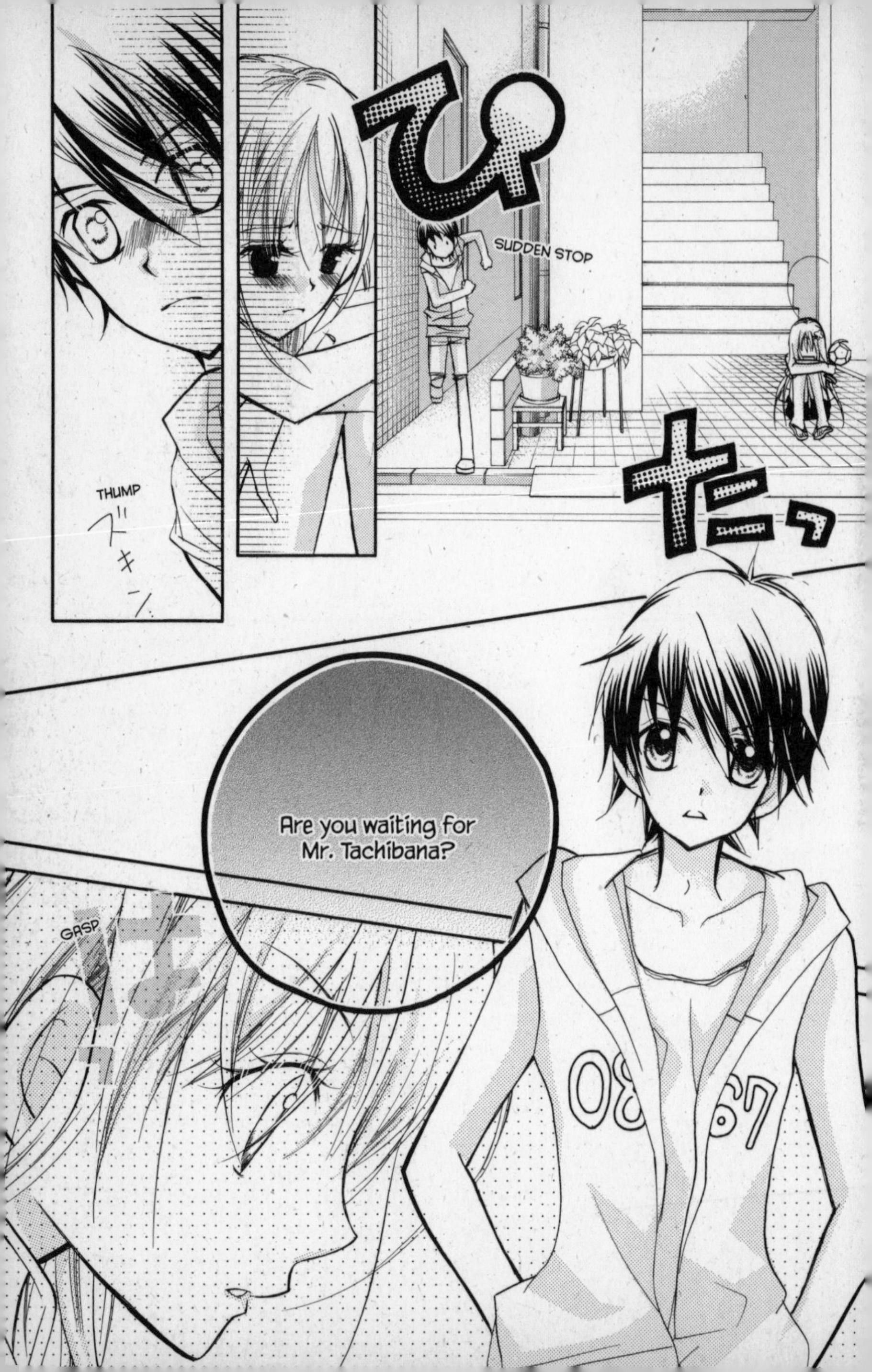
ぴ
SUDDEN STOP
たっ
THUMP
ズキン
Are you waiting for Mr. Tachibana?
GASP

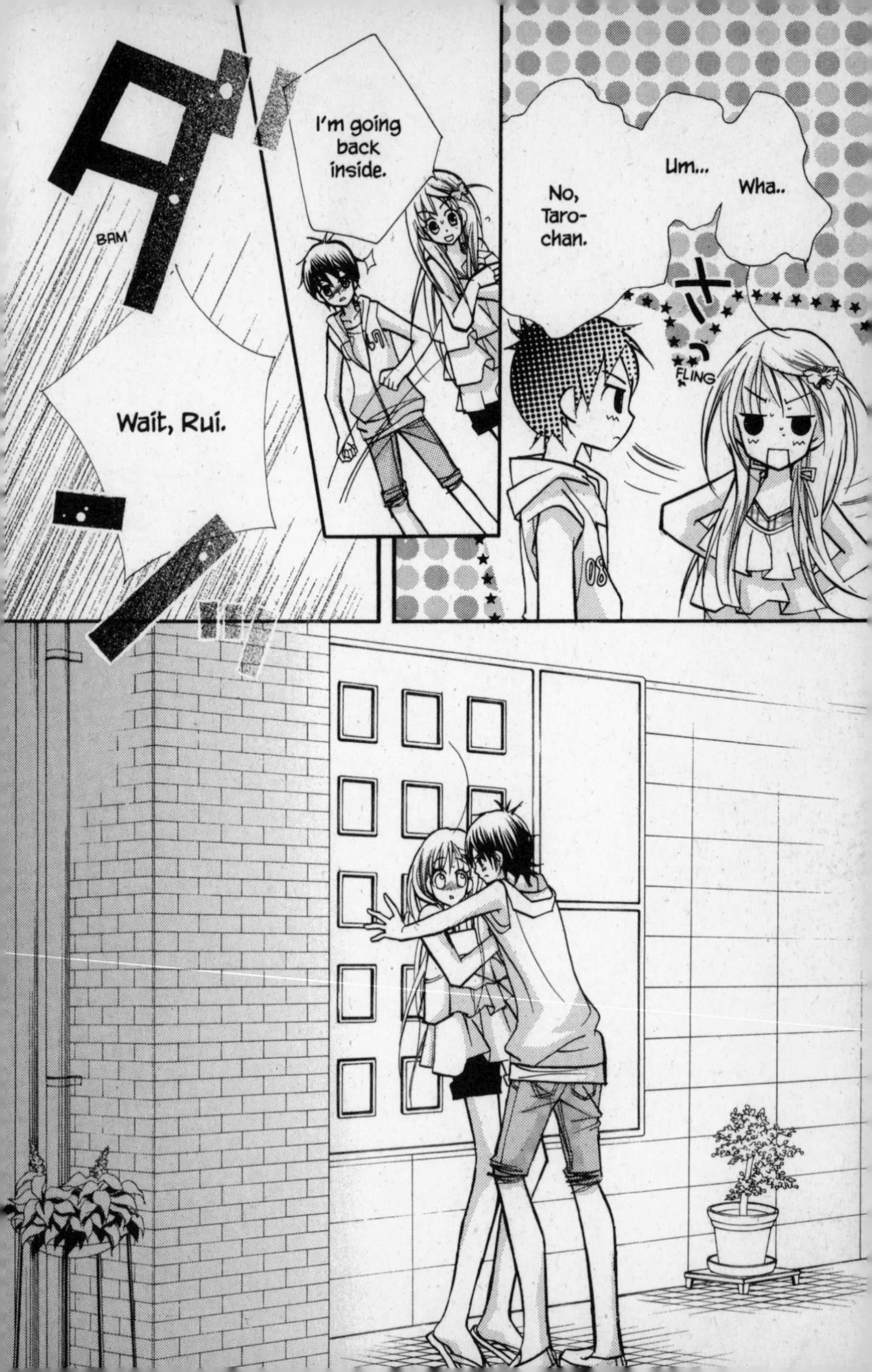
Wha..
Um...
No, Taro-chan.
FLING
I'm going back inside.
BAM
Wait, Rui.

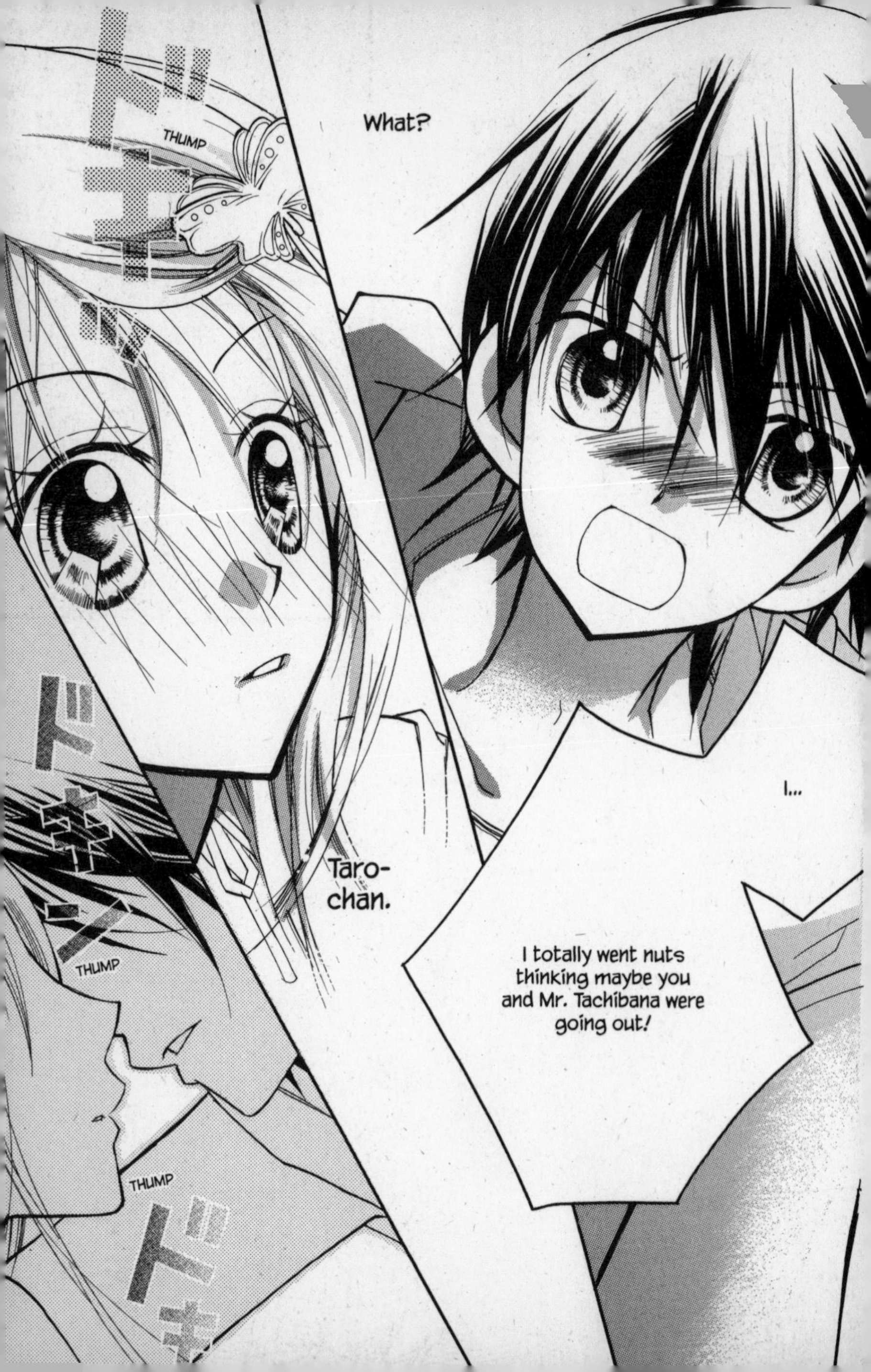
What?
I...
I totally went nuts thinking maybe you and Mr. Tachibana were going out!
THUMP
Taro-chan.
THUMP
THUMP

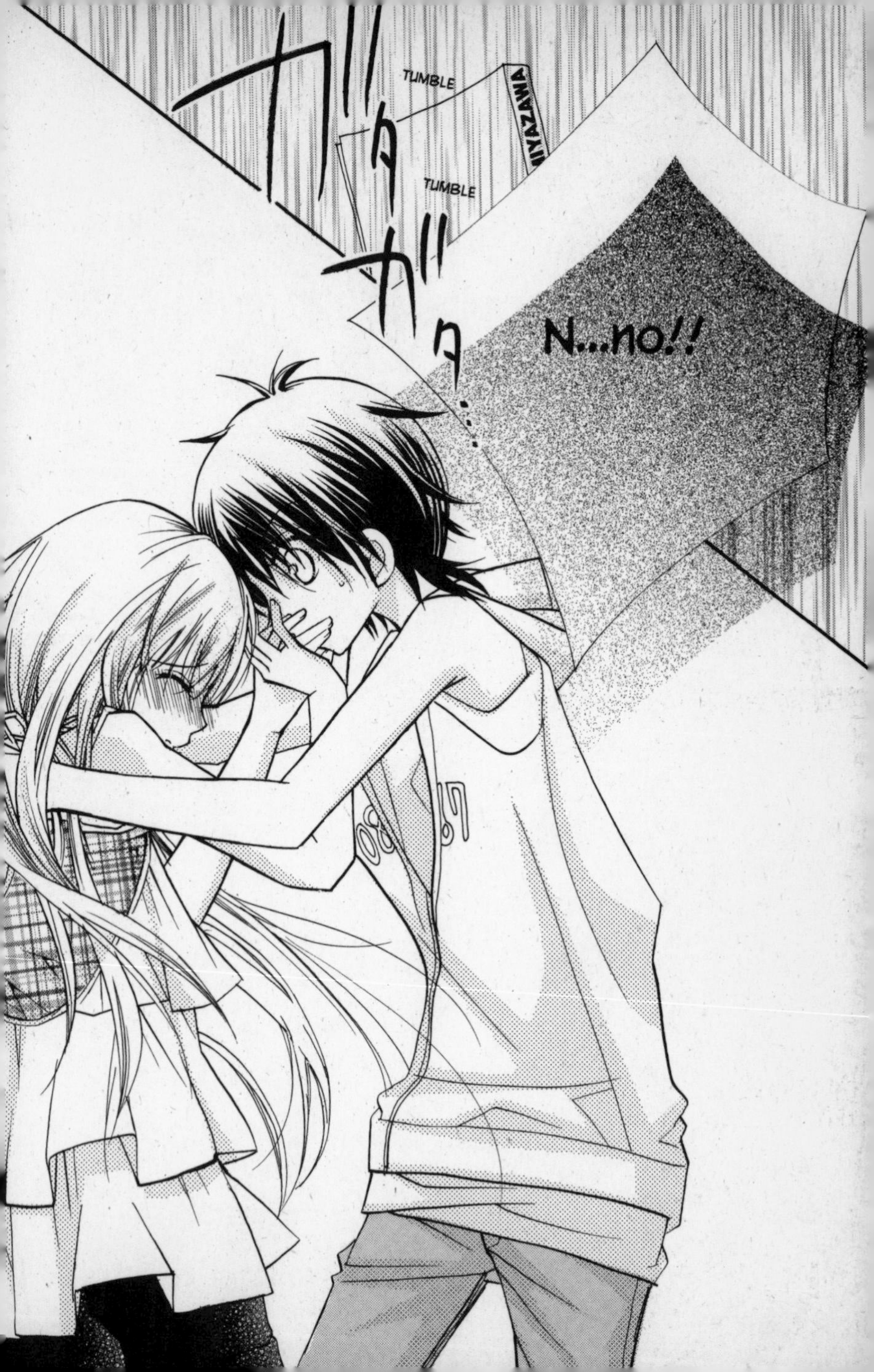
MIYAZAWA
TUMBLE
TUMBLE
N...no!!

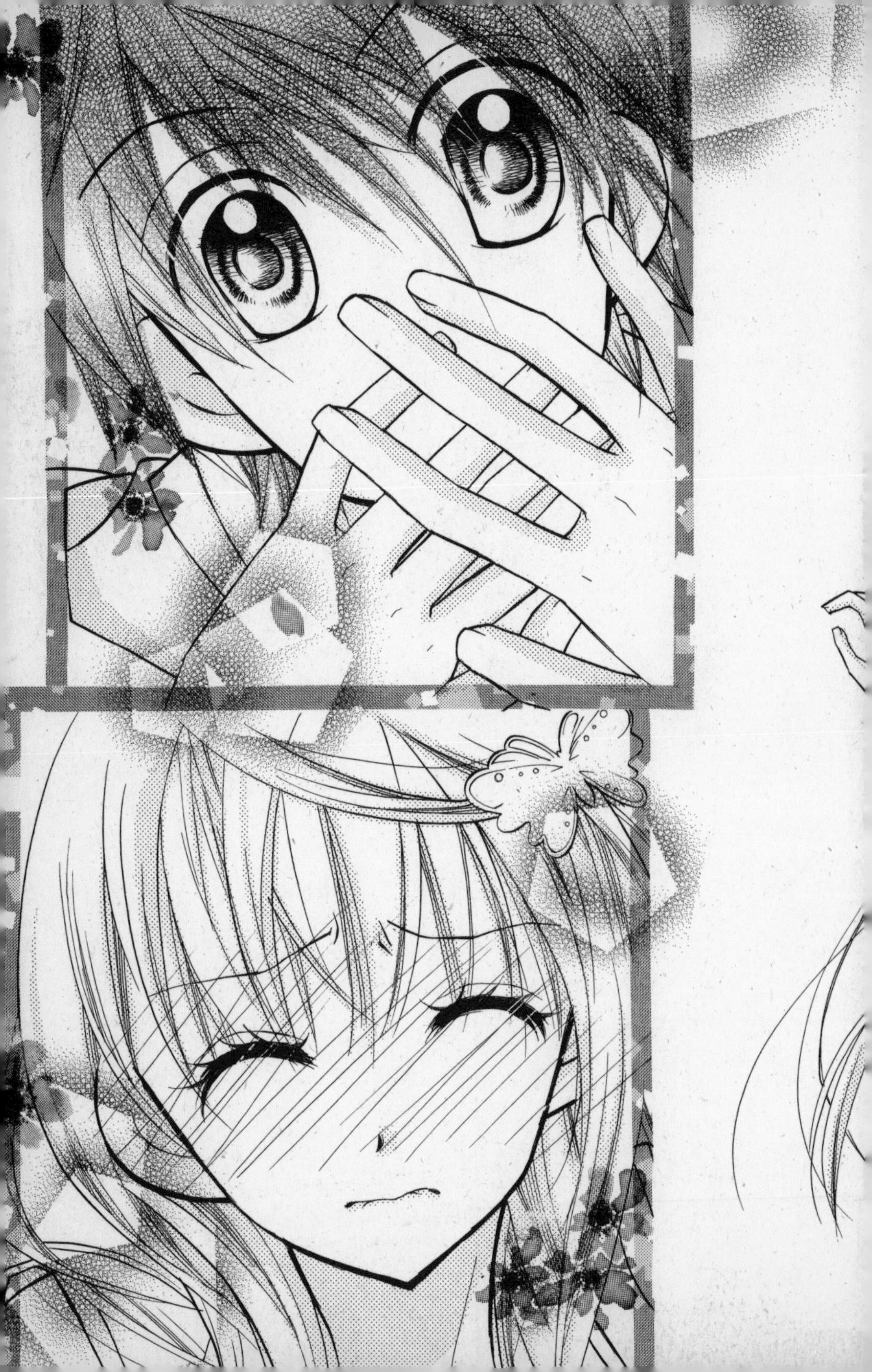

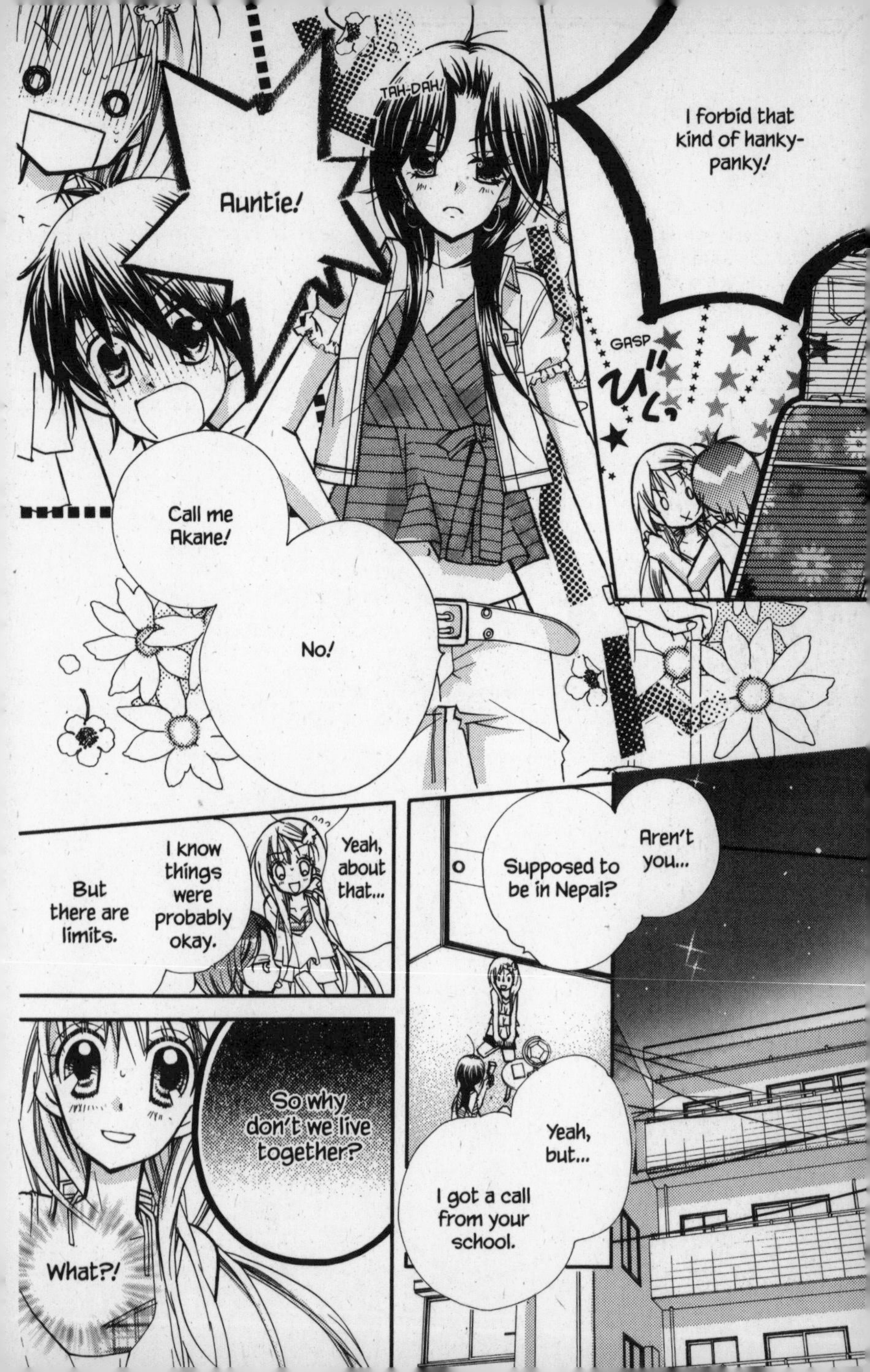
I forbid that kind of hanky-panky!
GASP
びくっ
TAH-DAH!
Auntie!
Call me Akane!
No!
Aren't you...
Supposed to be in Nepal?
Yeah, but...
I got a call from your school.
Yeah, about that...
I know things were probably okay.
But there are limits.
So why don't we live together?
What?!

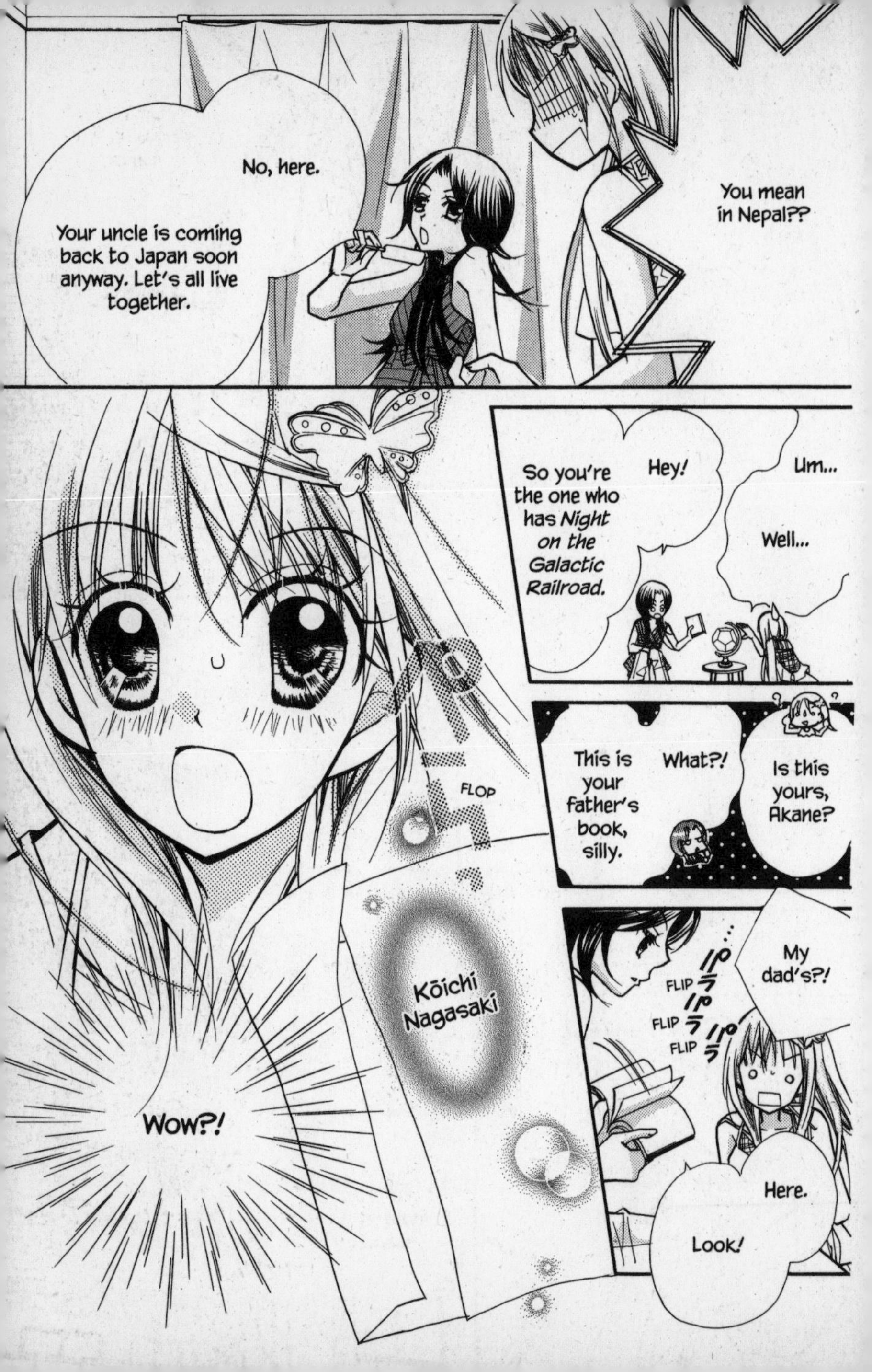
You mean in Nepal??
No, here.
Your uncle is coming back to Japan soon anyway. Let's all live together.
Um...
Well...
Hey!
So you're the one who has *Night on the Galactic Railroad*.
Is this yours, Akane?
What?!
This is your father's book, silly.
My dad's?!
FLIP
FLIP
FLIP
Here.
Look!
FLOP
Kōichi Nagasaki
Wow?!

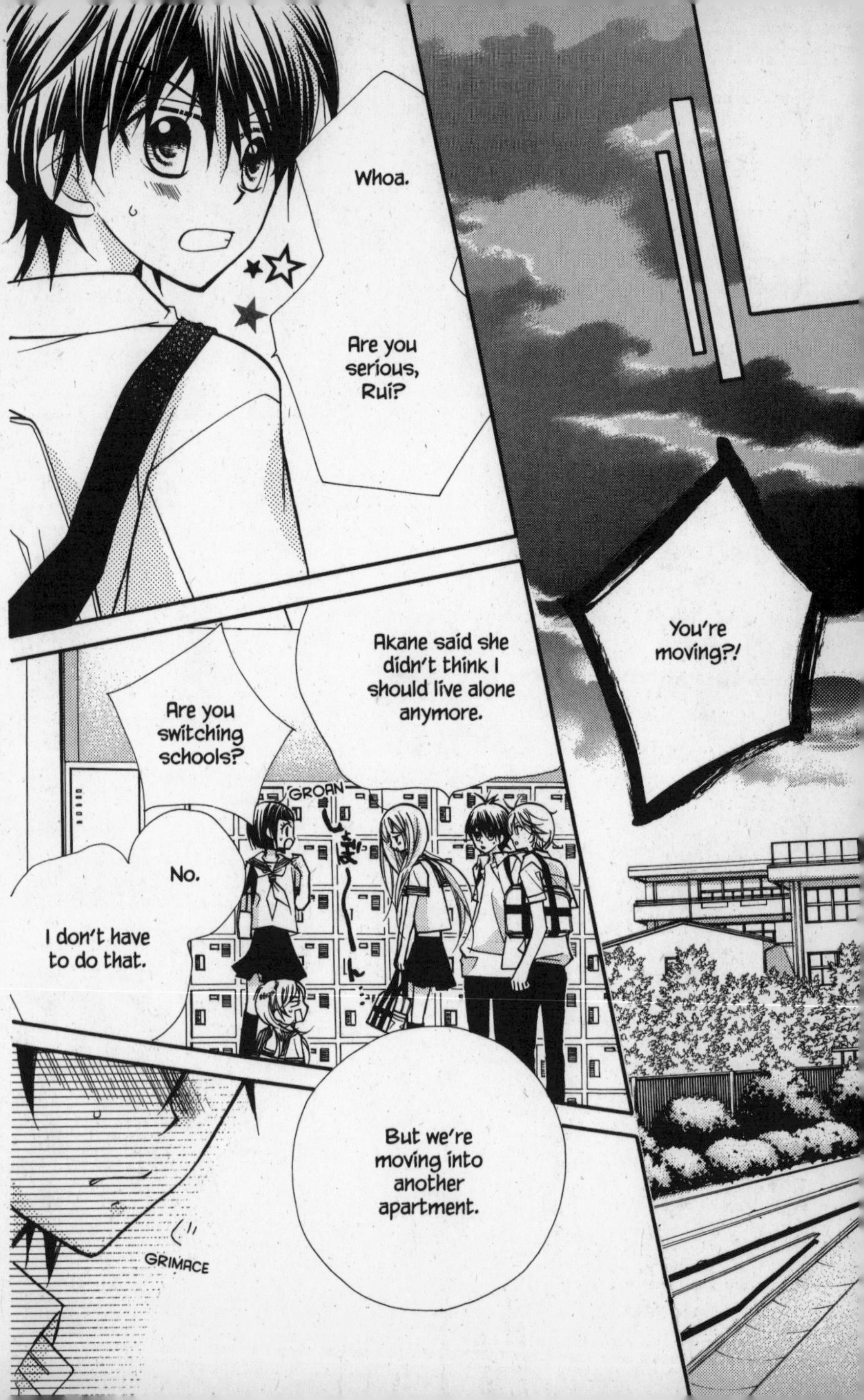
You're moving?!
Whoa.
Are you serious, Rui?
Akane said she didn't think I should live alone anymore.
Are you switching schools?
GROAN
No.
I don't have to do that.
But we're moving into another apartment.
GRIMACE

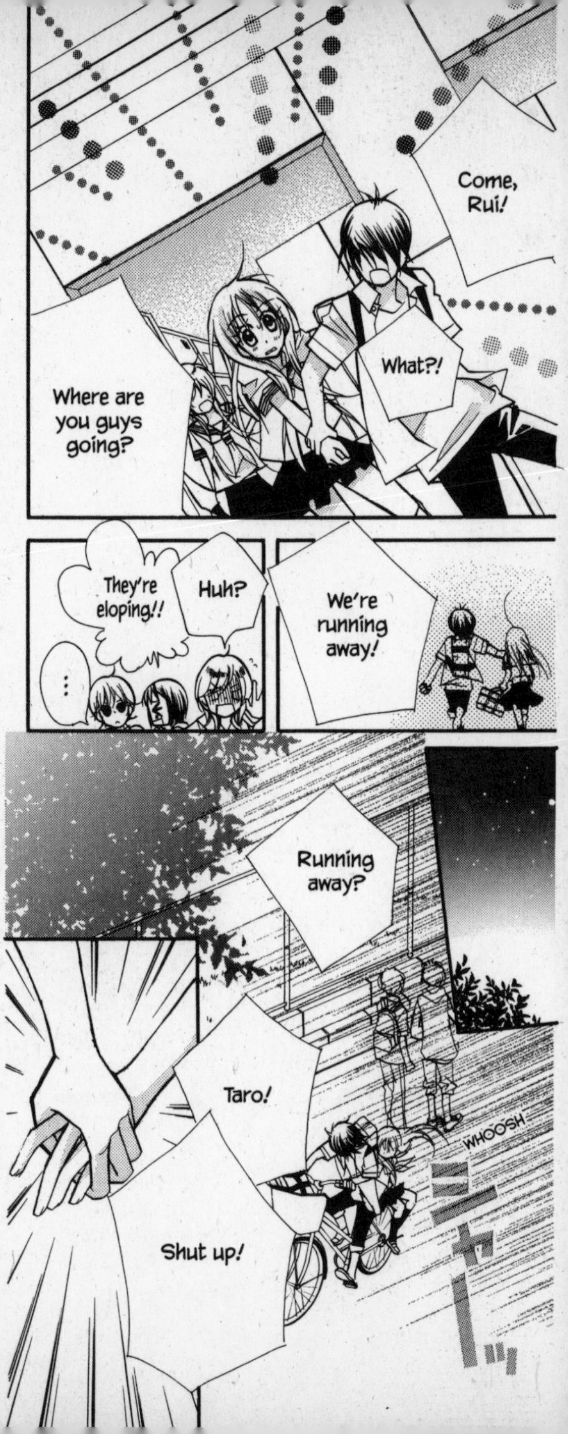
Come, Rui!
What?!
Where are you guys going?
We're running away!
Huh?
They're eloping!!
...
Running away?
Taro!
Shut up!
WHOOSH

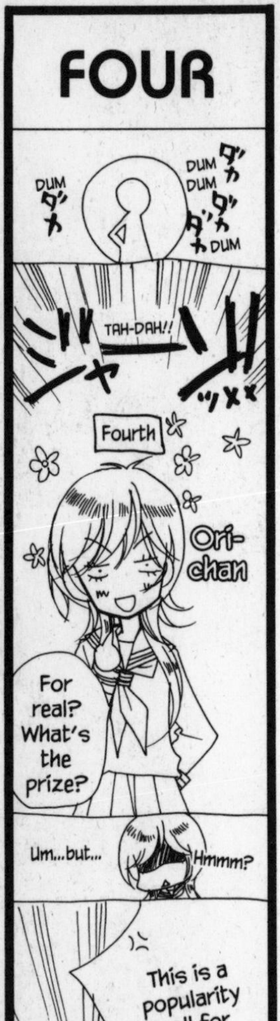
FOUR
DUM
DUM DUM
DUM
TAH-DAH!!
Fourth
Ori-chan
For real? What's the prize?
Hmmm?
Um...but...
This is a popularity poll for boys!!
I'm going to kill y'all!
Ahhhhhh!
True story... (laugh)

On to PART FIVE ←

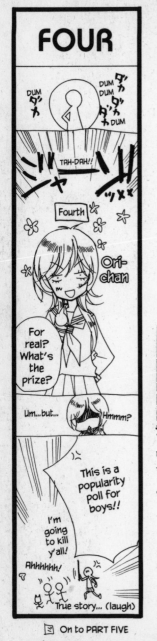

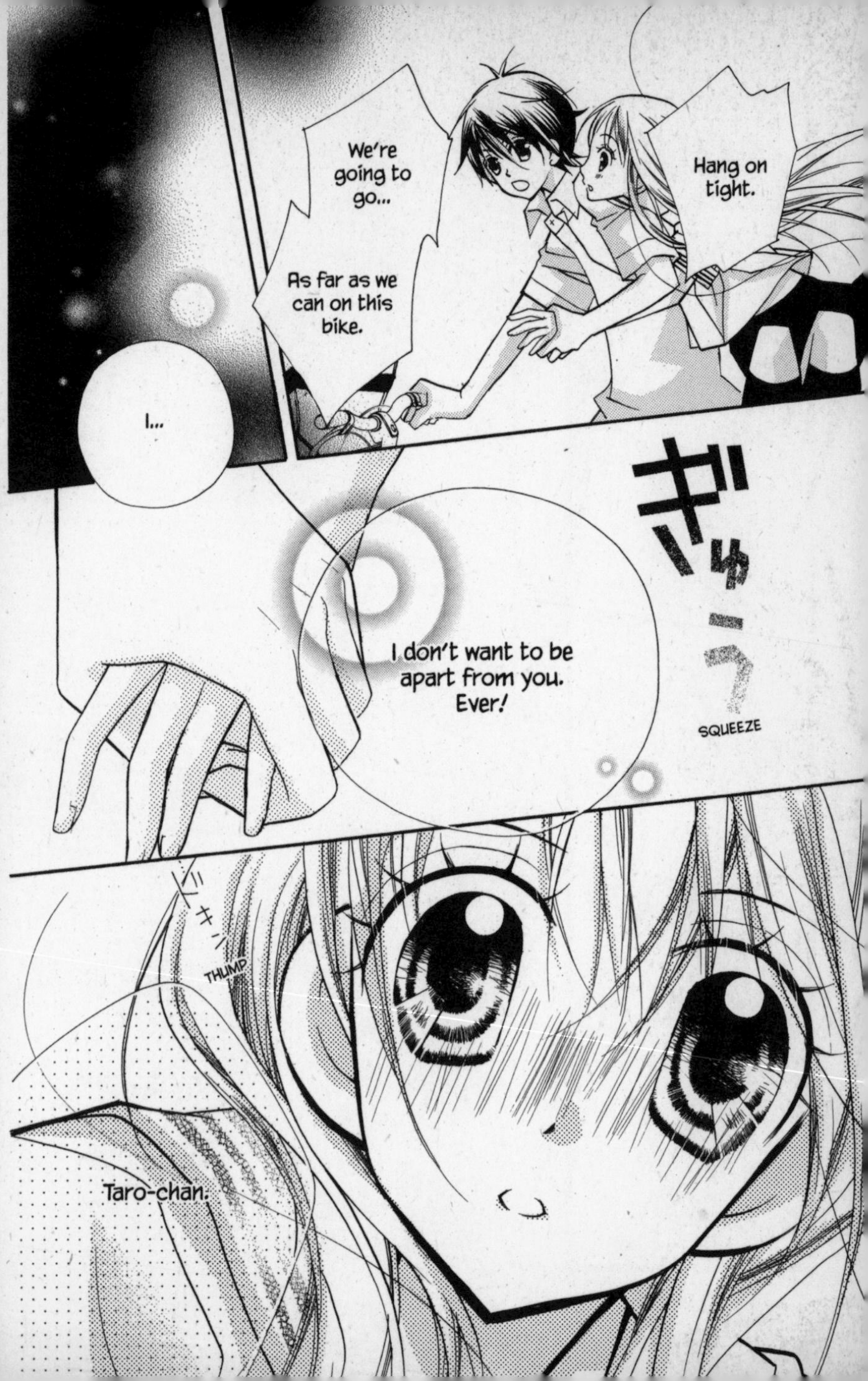
Hang on tight.
We're going to go...
As far as we can on this bike.
I...
ぎゅーっ
SQUEEZE
I don't want to be apart from you. Ever!
ドキッ
THUMP
Taro-chan.

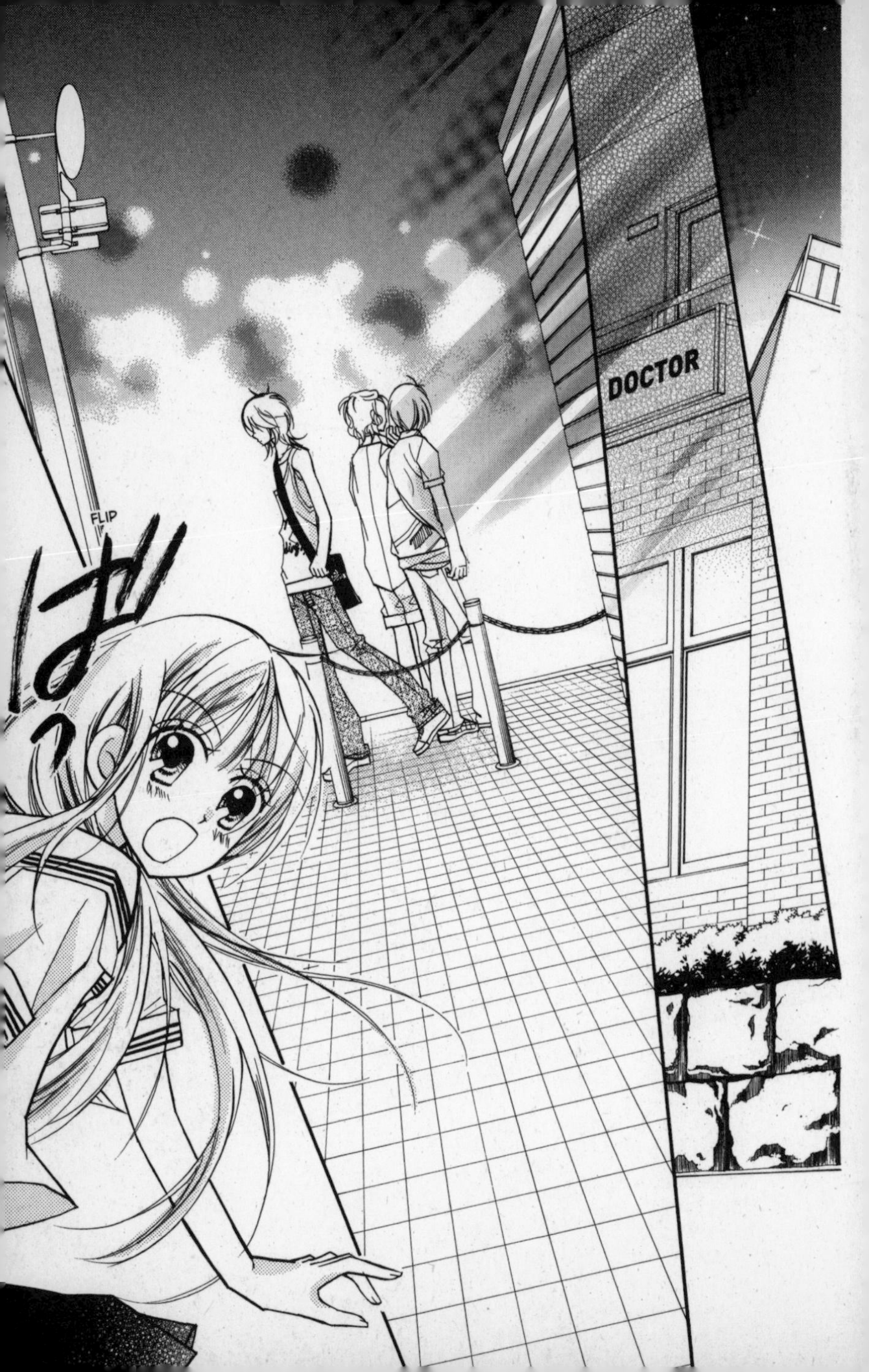
DOCTOR
FLIP
はっ

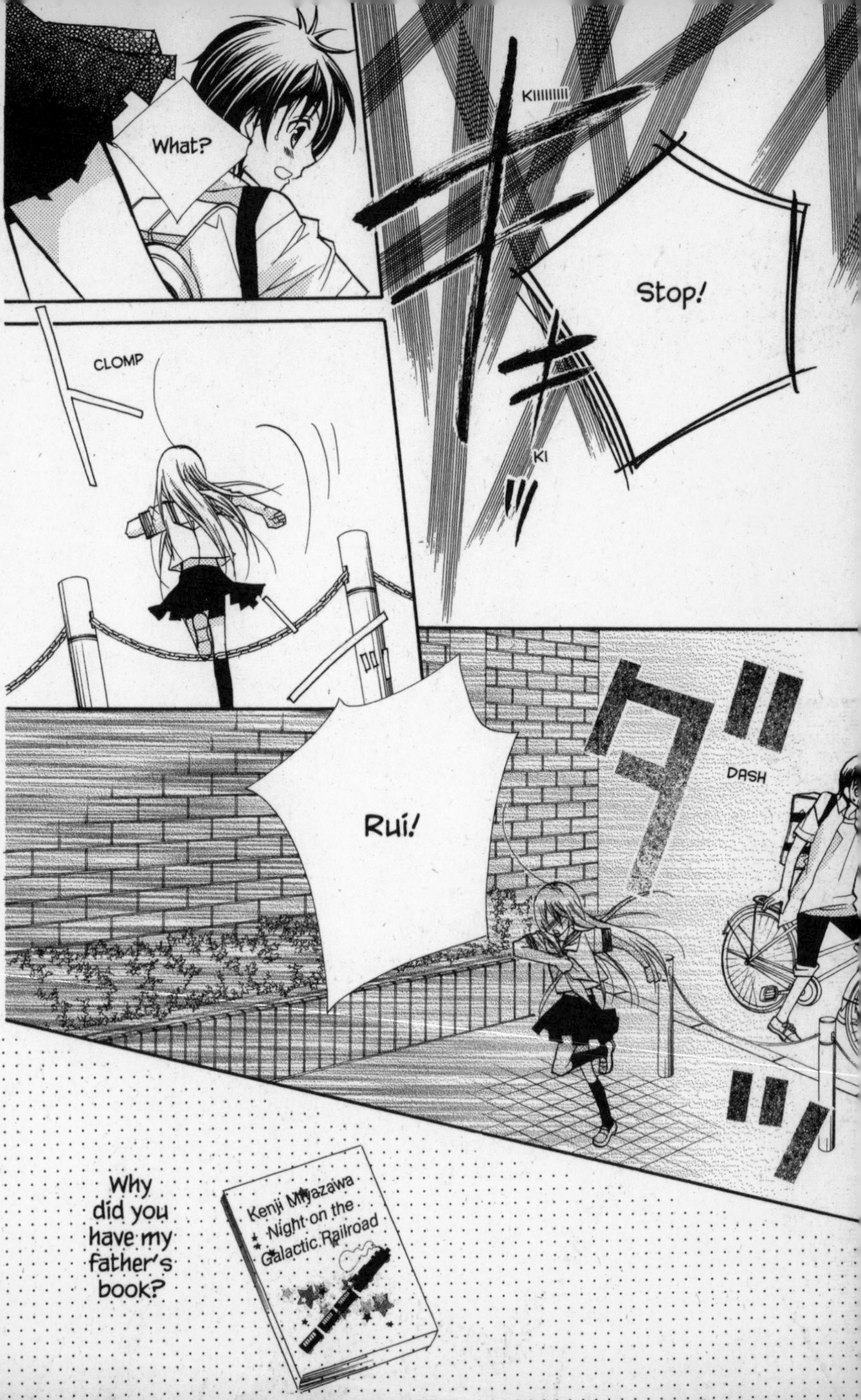
KIIIIIIII
KI
Stop!
What?
CLOMP
DASH
Rui!
Why did you have my father's book?
Kenji Miyazawa
Night on the Galactic Railroad

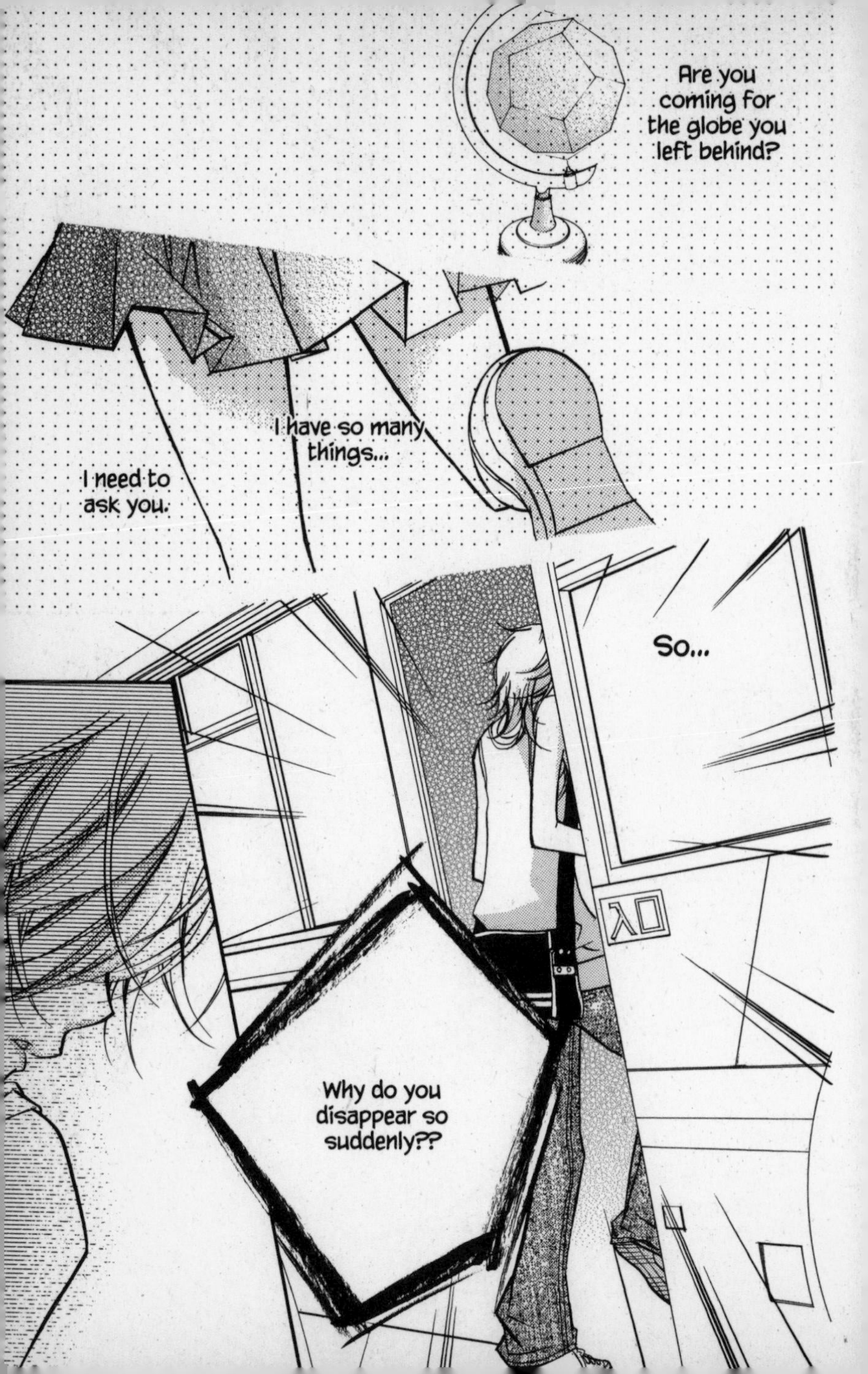
Are you coming for the globe you left behind?
I have so many things...
I need to ask you.
So...
Why do you disappear so suddenly??

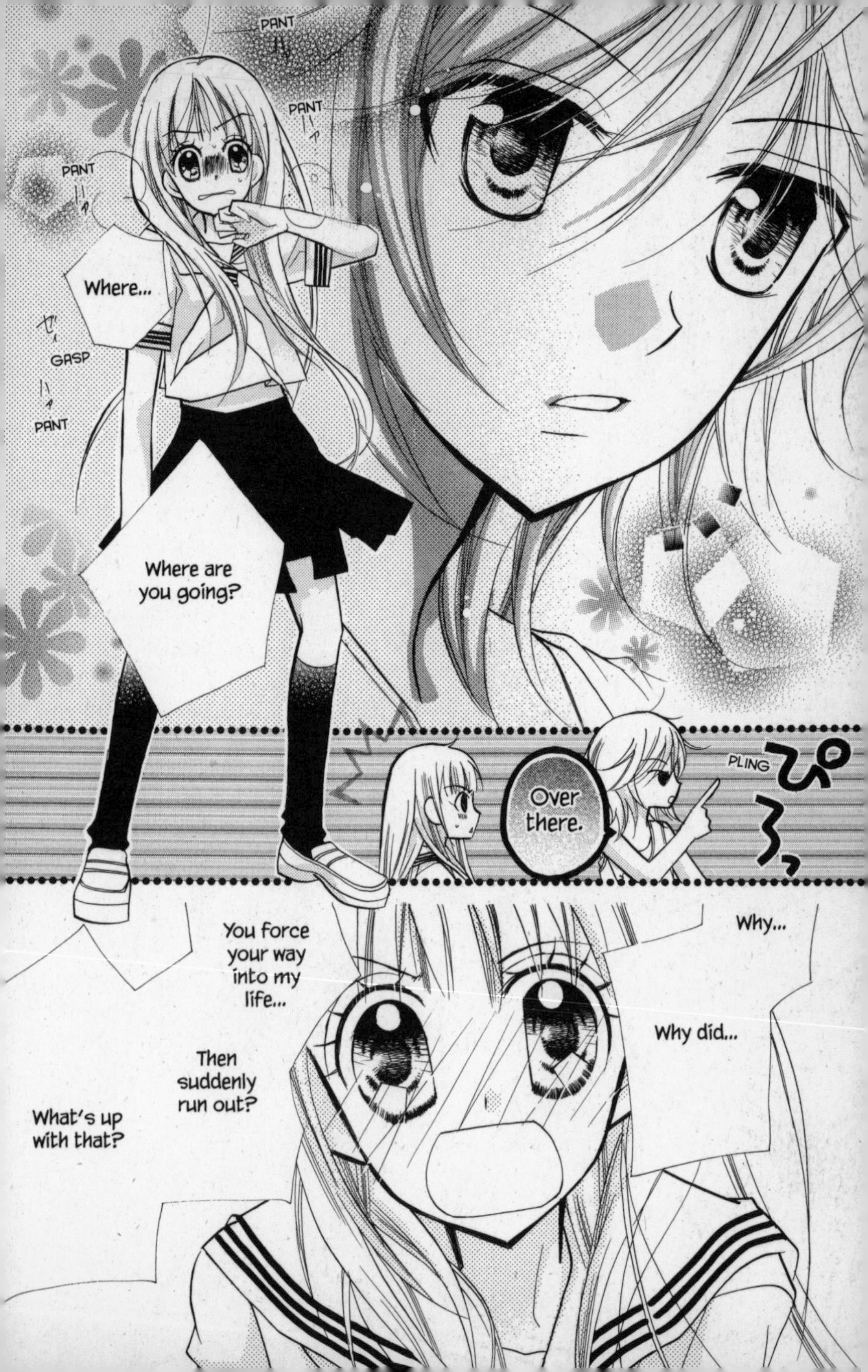
PANT
PANT
PANT
Where...
GASP
PANT
Where are you going?
PLING
ぴろっ
Over there.
Why...
Why did...
You force your way into my life...
Then suddenly run out?
What's up with that?

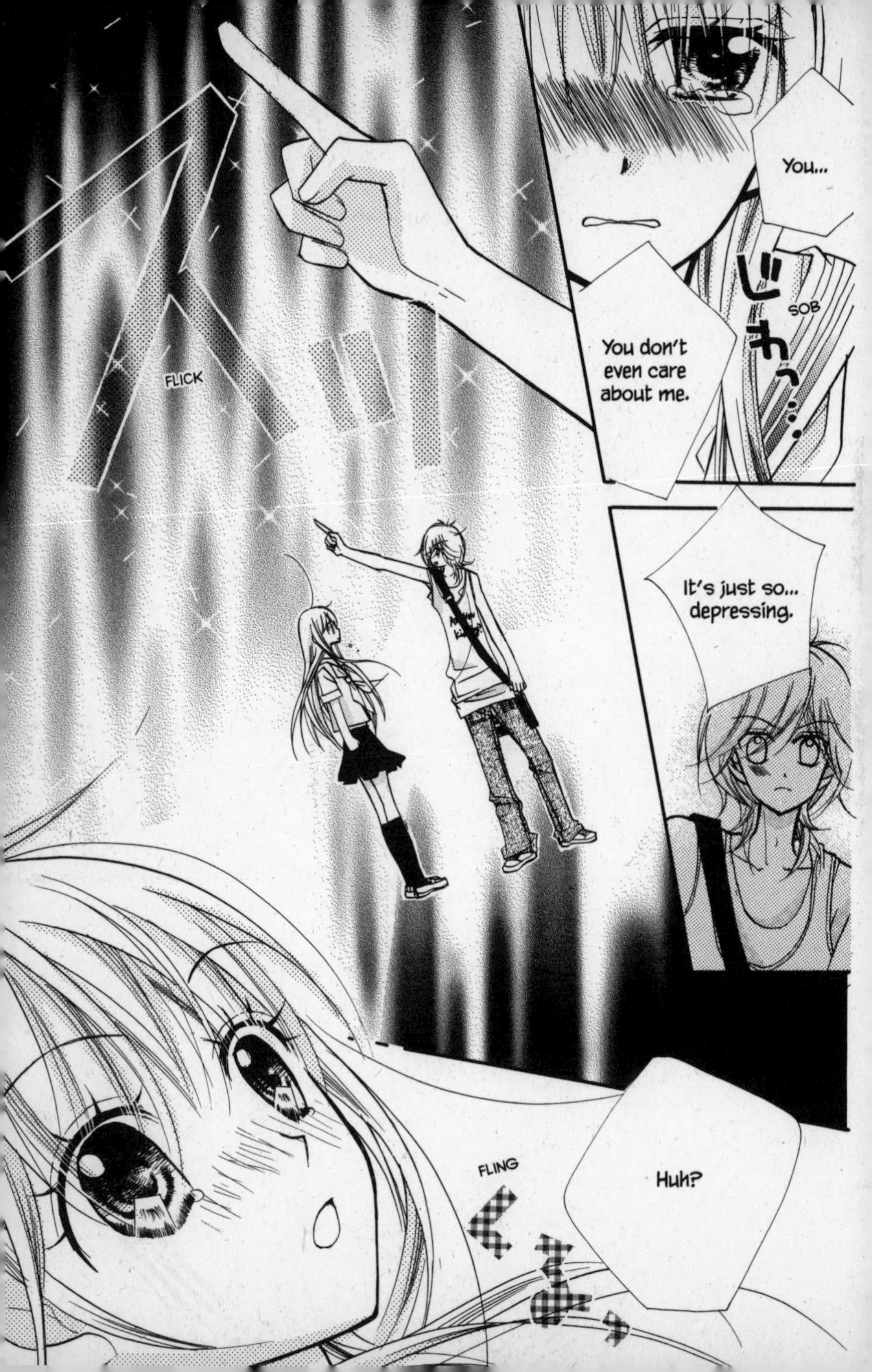
You...
SOB
You don't even care about me.
It's just so... depressing.
FLICK
Huh?
FLING

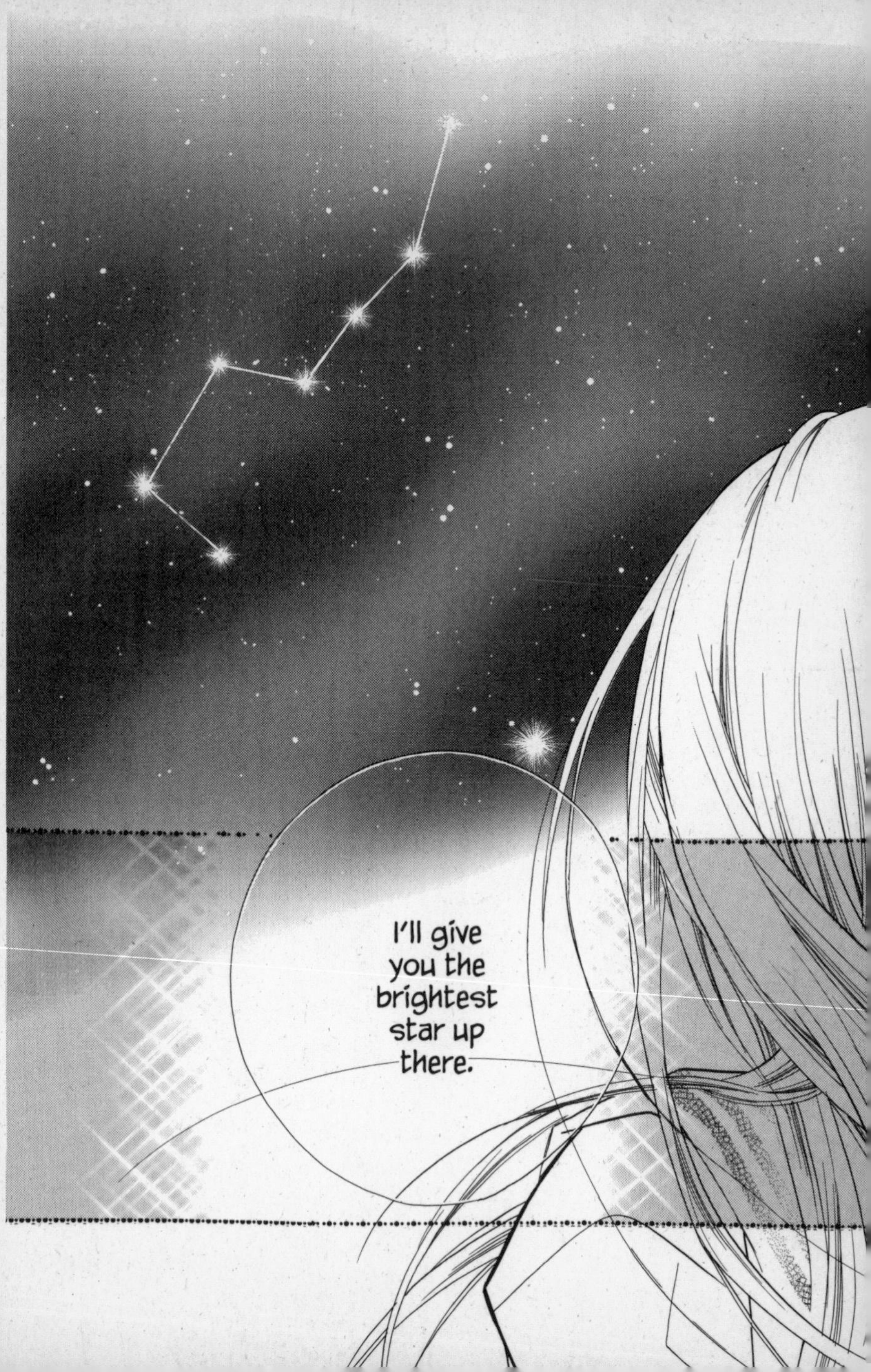
I'll give you the brightest star up there.

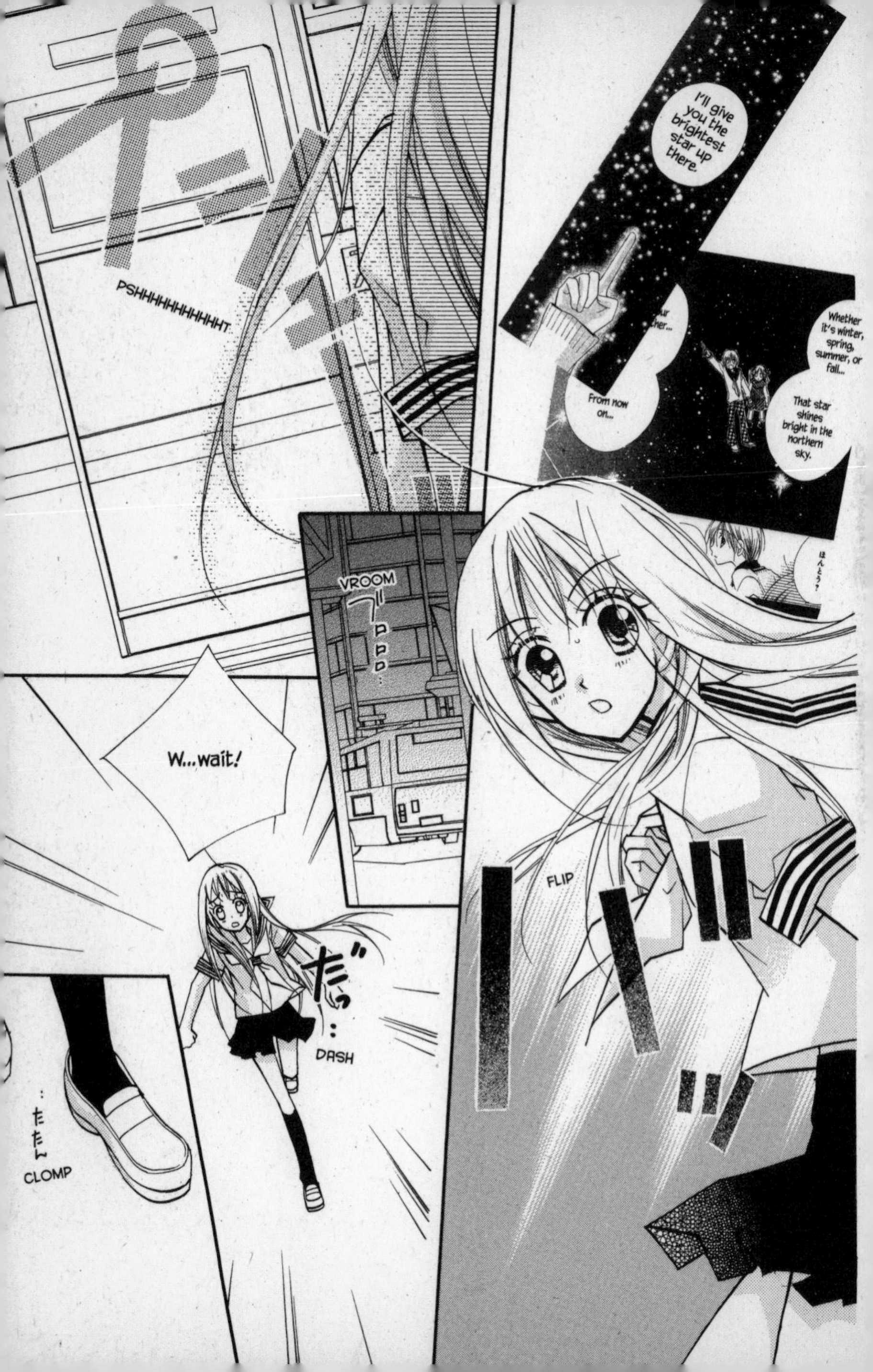
I'll give you the brightest star up there.
Whether it's winter, spring, summer, or fall...
That star shines bright in the northern sky.
From now on...
ほんとう?
PSHHHHHHHHHHHT
VROOM
ブロロロ...
FLIP
W...wait!
だっ...
DASH
たたん...
CLOMP

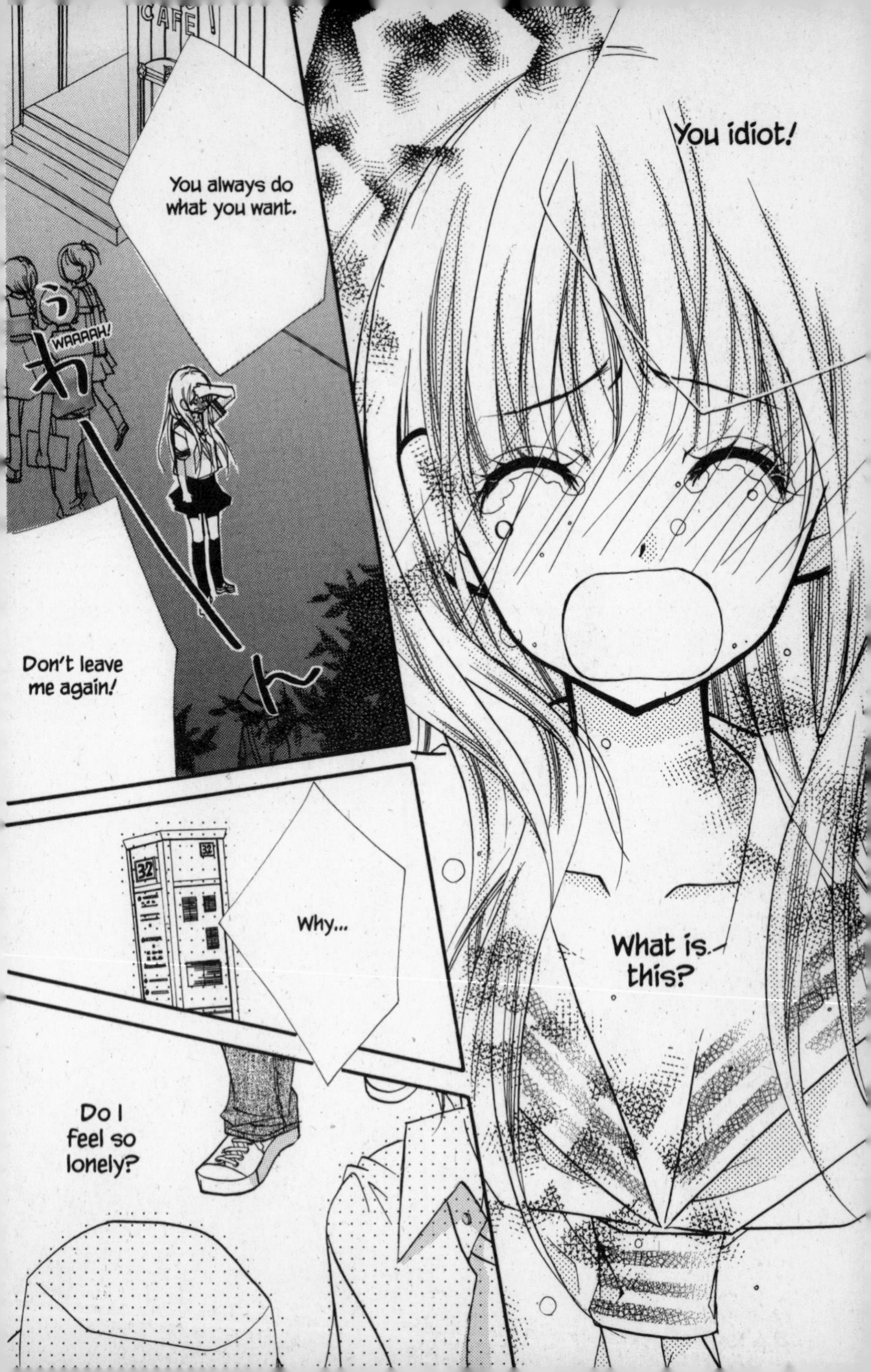
You idiot!
What is this?
You always do what you want.
WAAAAH!
Don't leave me again!
Why...
Do I feel so lonely?

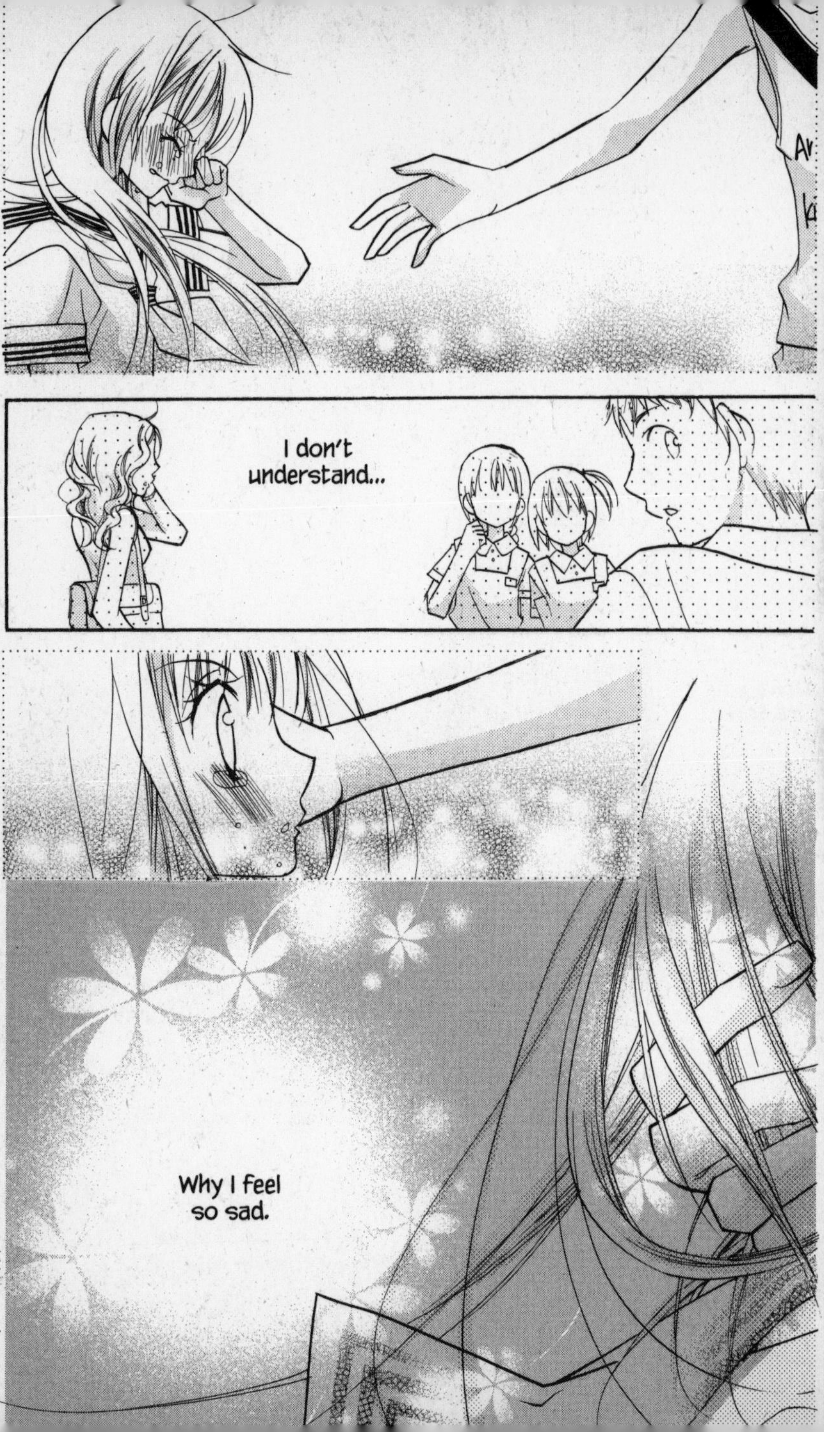
I don't understand...
Why I feel so sad.

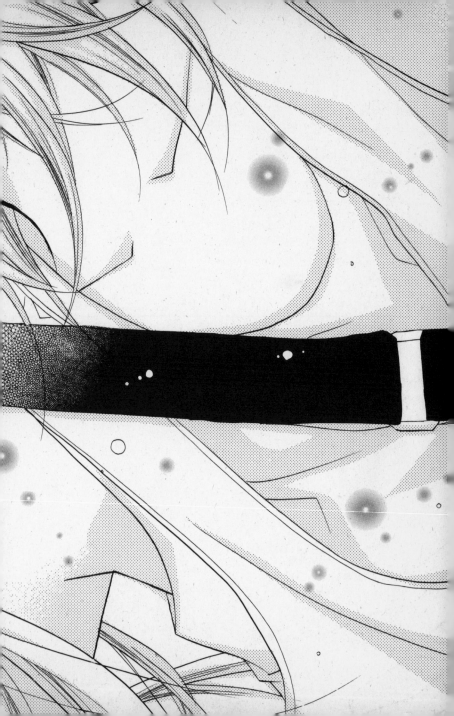

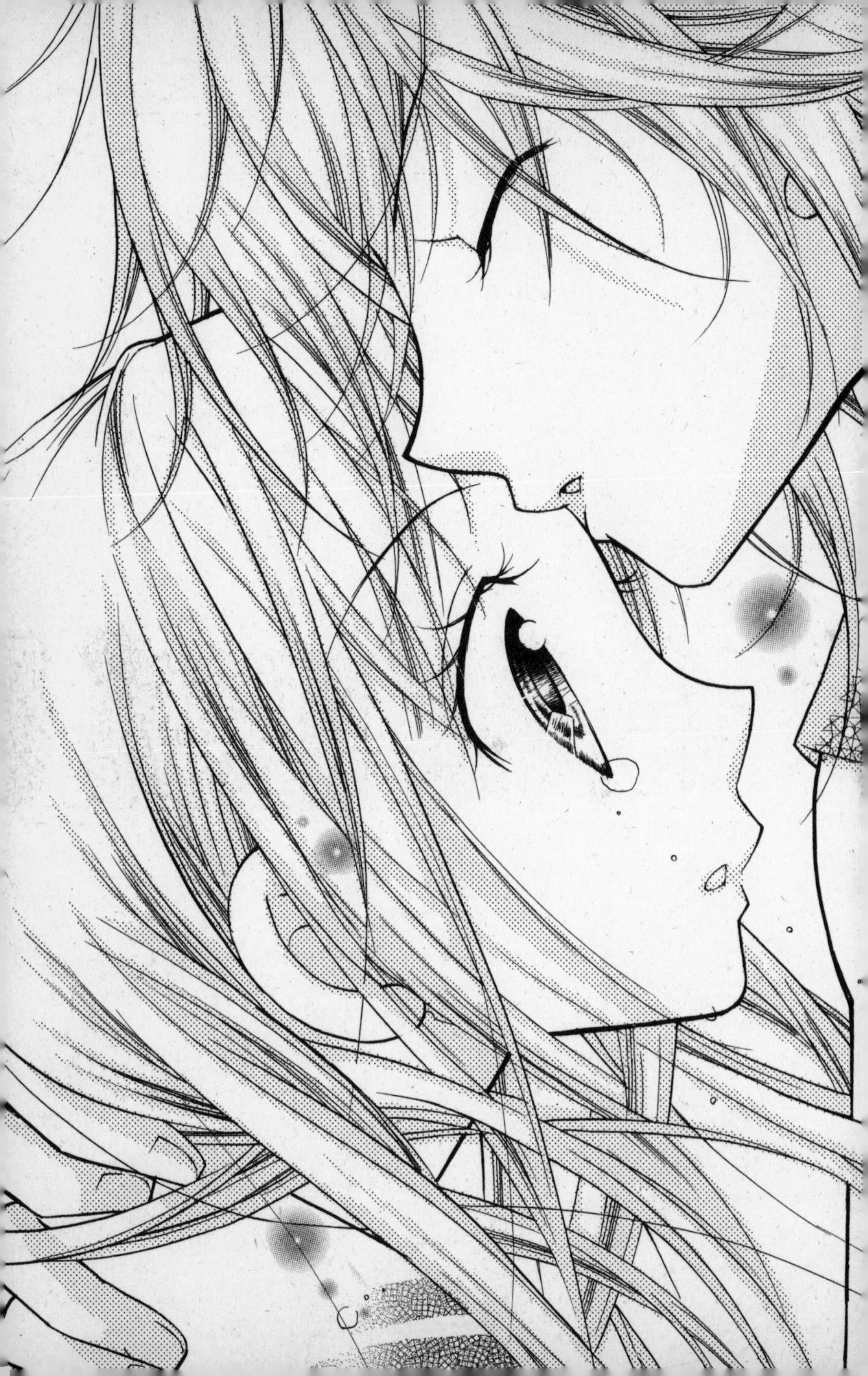

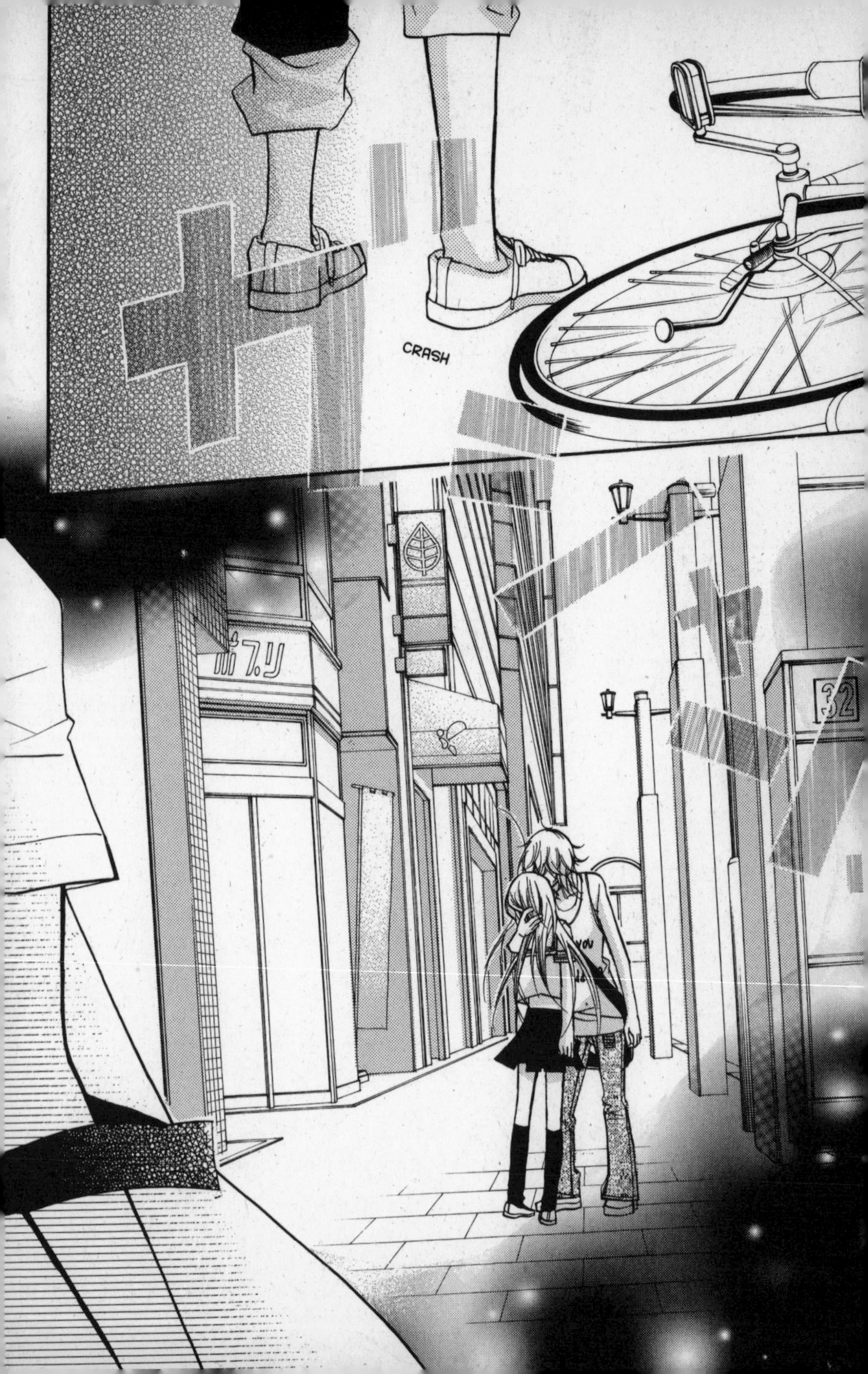
CRASH
ポプリ
32

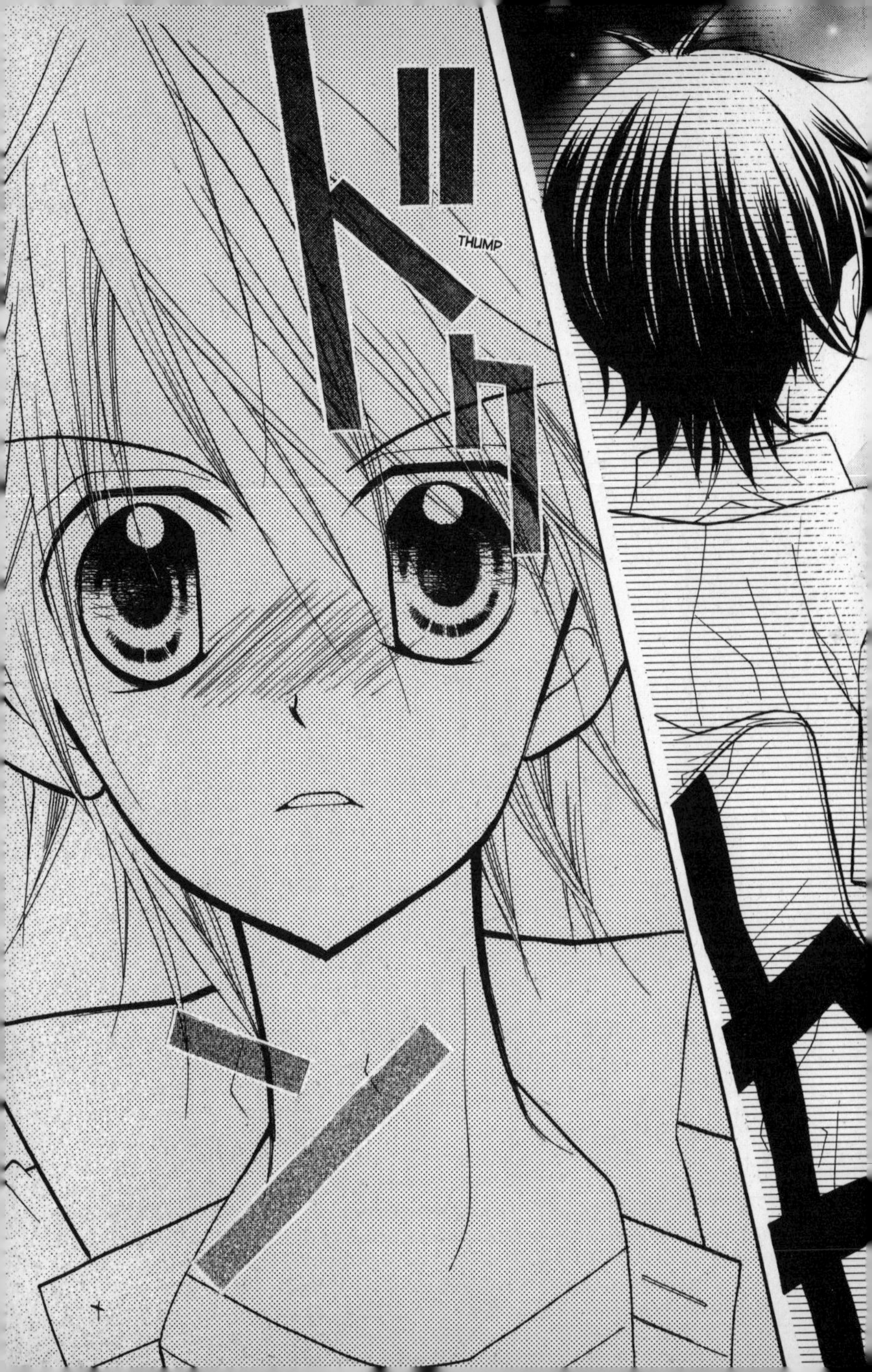
THUMP

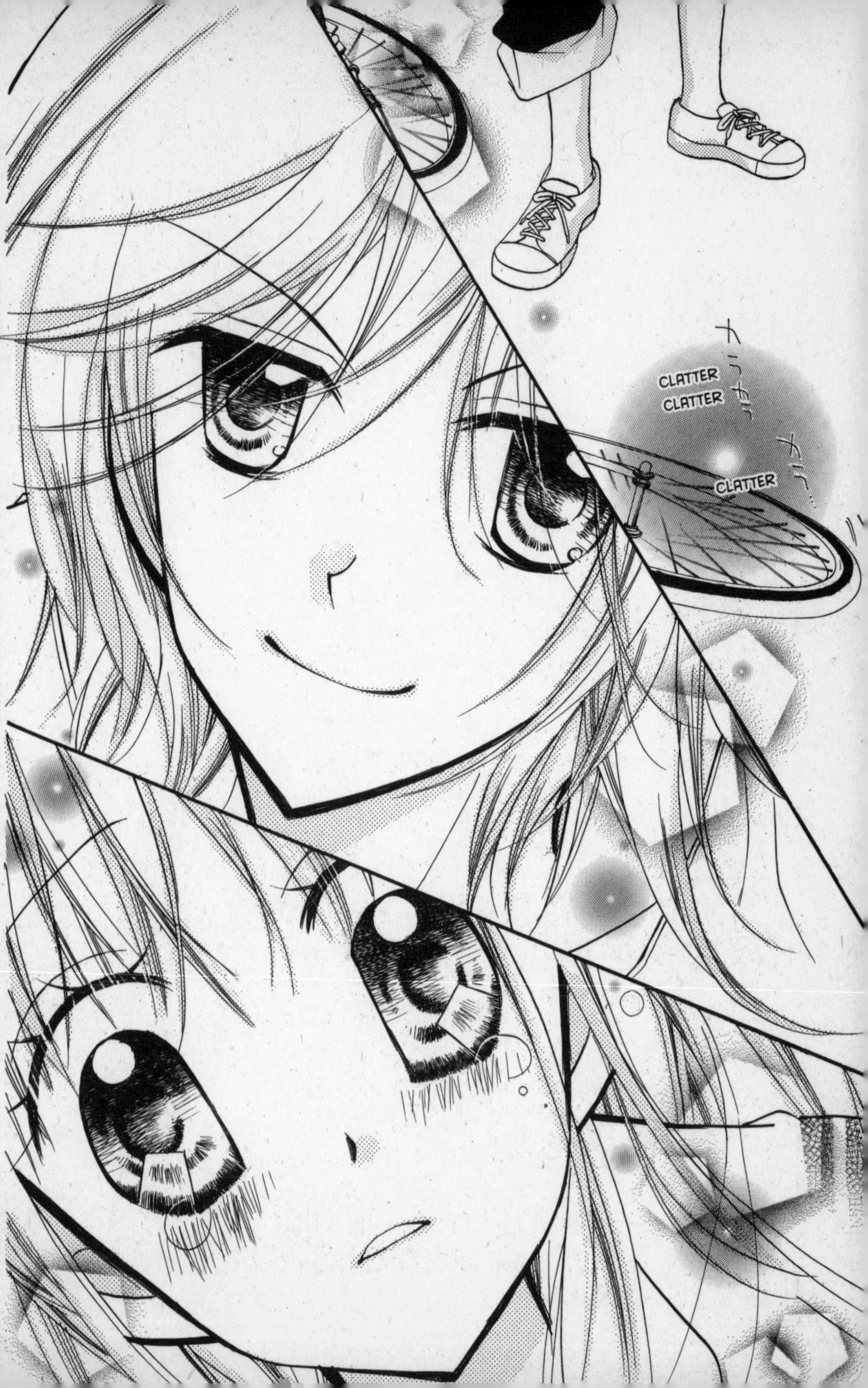
CLATTER
CLATTER
CLATTER

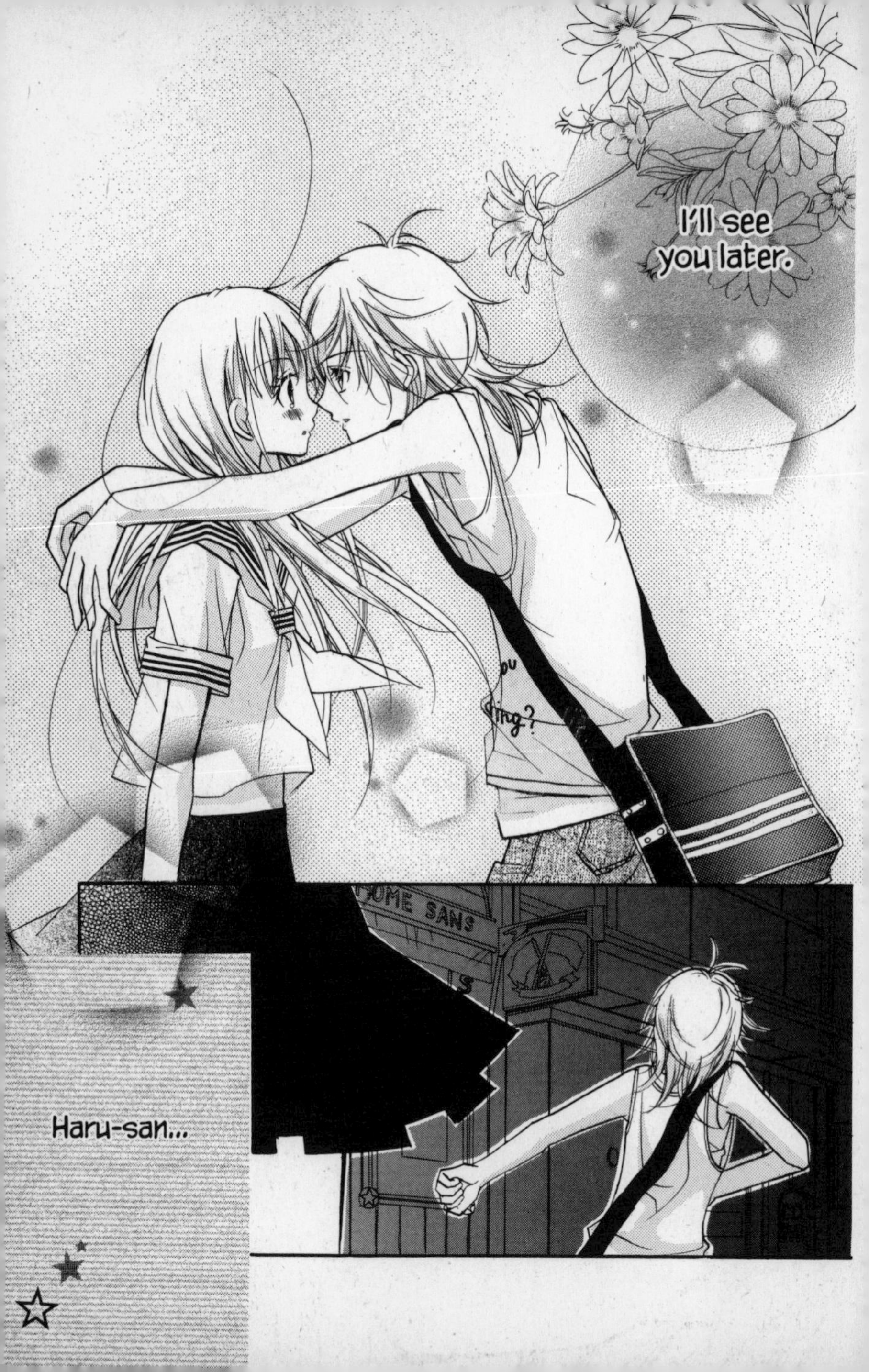
I'll see you later.
Haru-san...

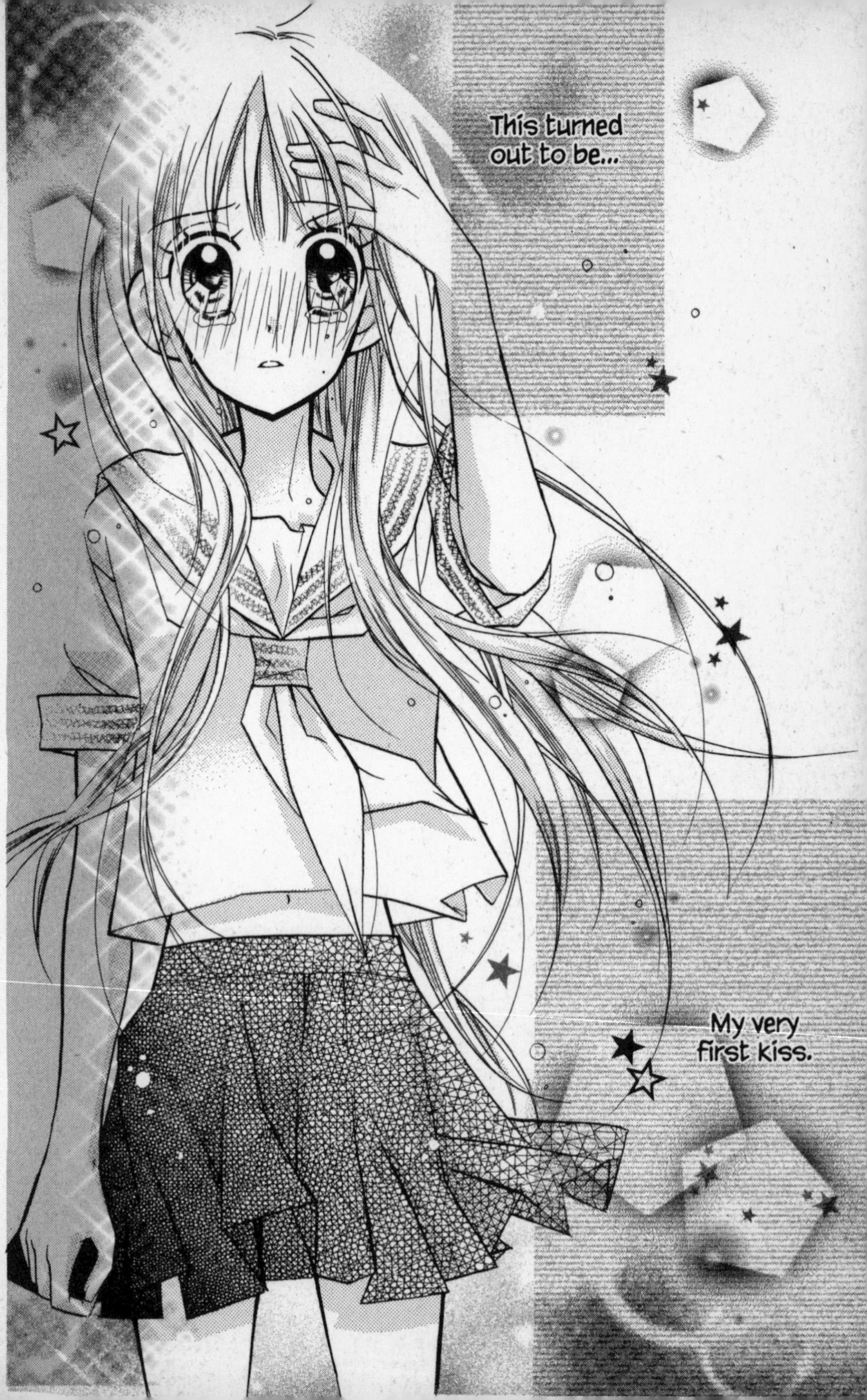
This turned out to be...
My very first kiss.

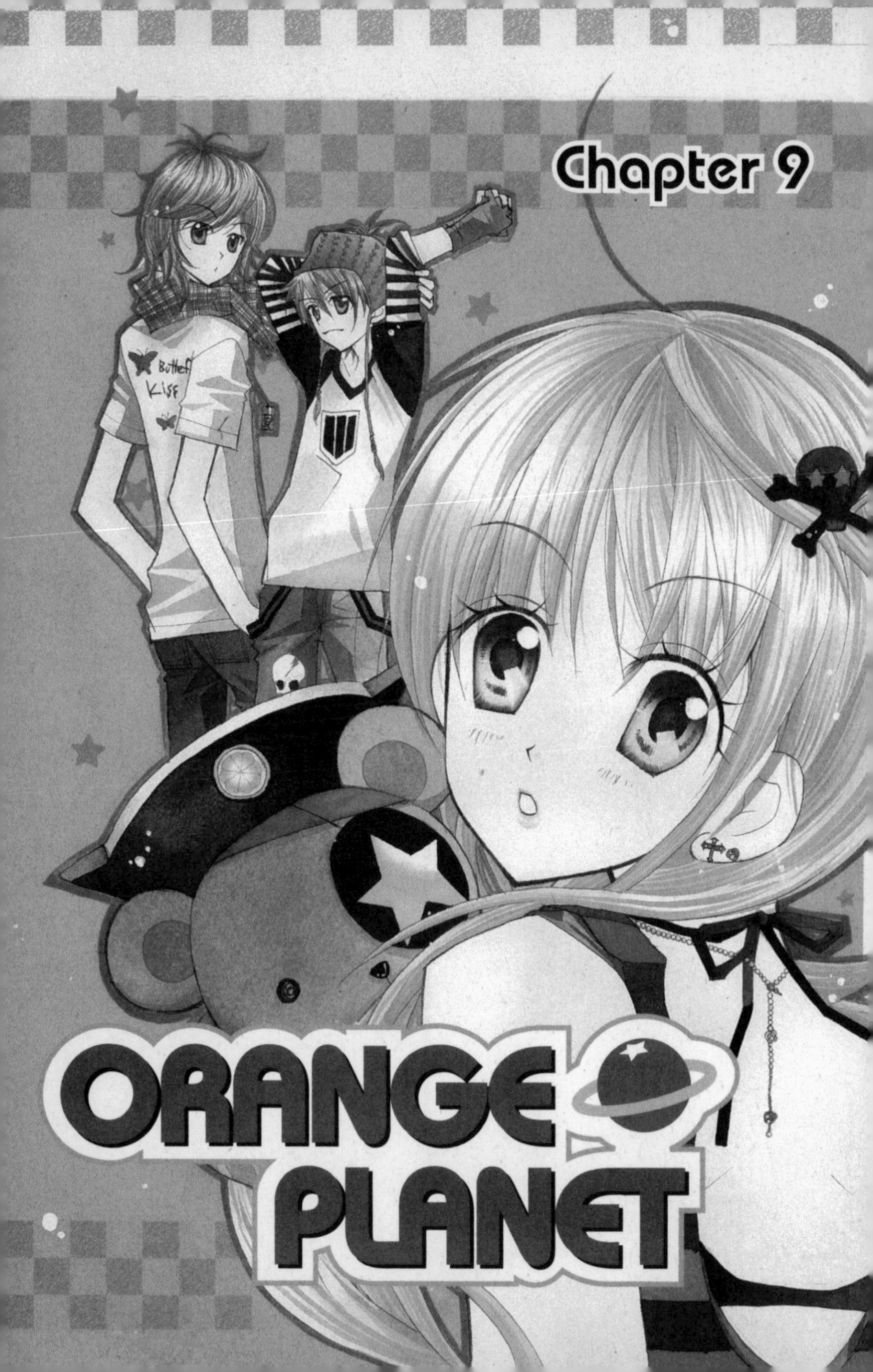
Chapter 9
ORANGE PLANET

In Conclusion...

☑ Thanks for reading my manga so far. There's a lot going on each day, but I'll do my best to have fun and write even better stories.

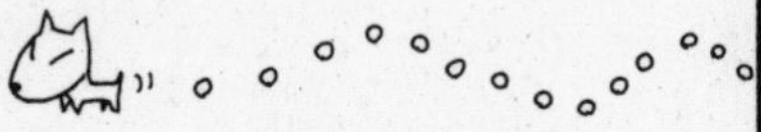

Thanks to everyone who deals with me every day:

Special ☆★☆ Thanks!

- ☑ T. katada
- ☐ S. Hironaka
- ☐ S. kawahara
- ☑ k. Ueyasu
- ☑ M. Fukushima
- ☑ My family
- ☐ My friends

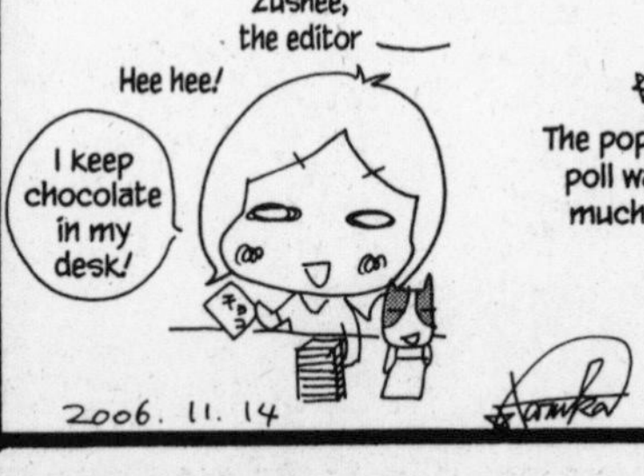
Zushee, the editor
Hee hee!
I keep chocolate in my desk!

The popularity poll was so much fun!

2006. 11. 14

We'll see you again in Volume 3!

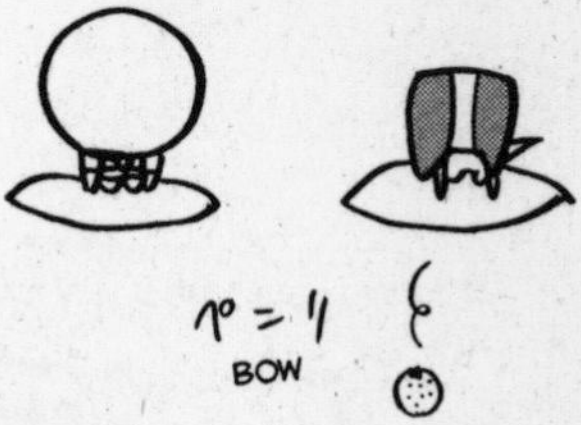
BOW

A secret!

I've got my own Web page.

http://www.roo.to/haruca/

(Started November 2006)

A webmaster friend made my Web page for me. I blog about recent events quite often, so when you have a chance, please check it out.

Thanks, Tsubame-san!

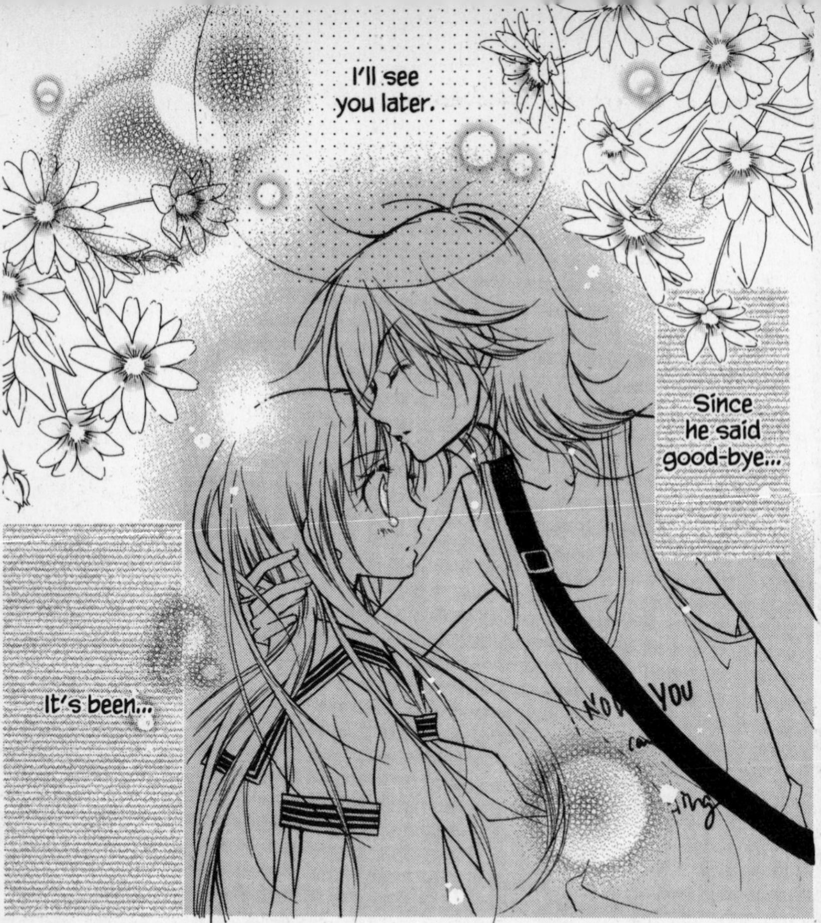
I'll see you later.
Since he said good-bye...
It's been...

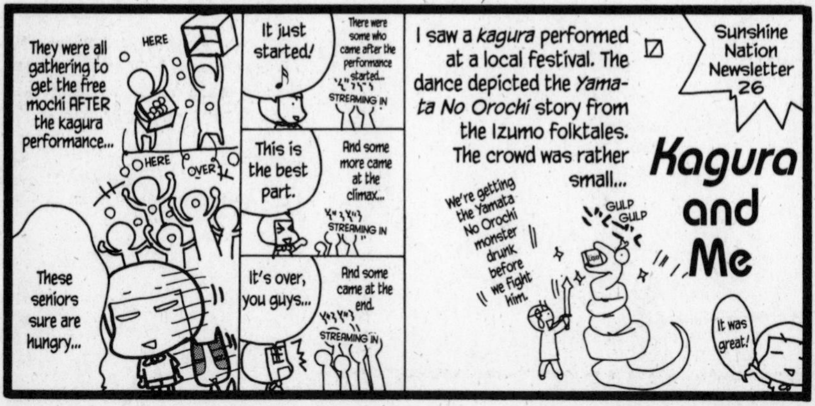
Sunshine Nation Newsletter 26
Kagura and Me
I saw a *kagura* performed at a local festival. The dance depicted the *Yamata No Orochi* story from the Izumo folktales. The crowd was rather small...
We're getting the Yamata No Orochi monster drunk before we fight him.
GULP GULP
It was great!
It just started!
There were some who came after the performance started...
STREAMING IN
This is the best part.
And some more came at the climax...
STREAMING IN
It's over, you guys...
And some came at the end.
STREAMING IN
They were all gathering to get the free mochi AFTER the kagura performance...
HERE
HERE
OVER
These seniors sure are hungry...

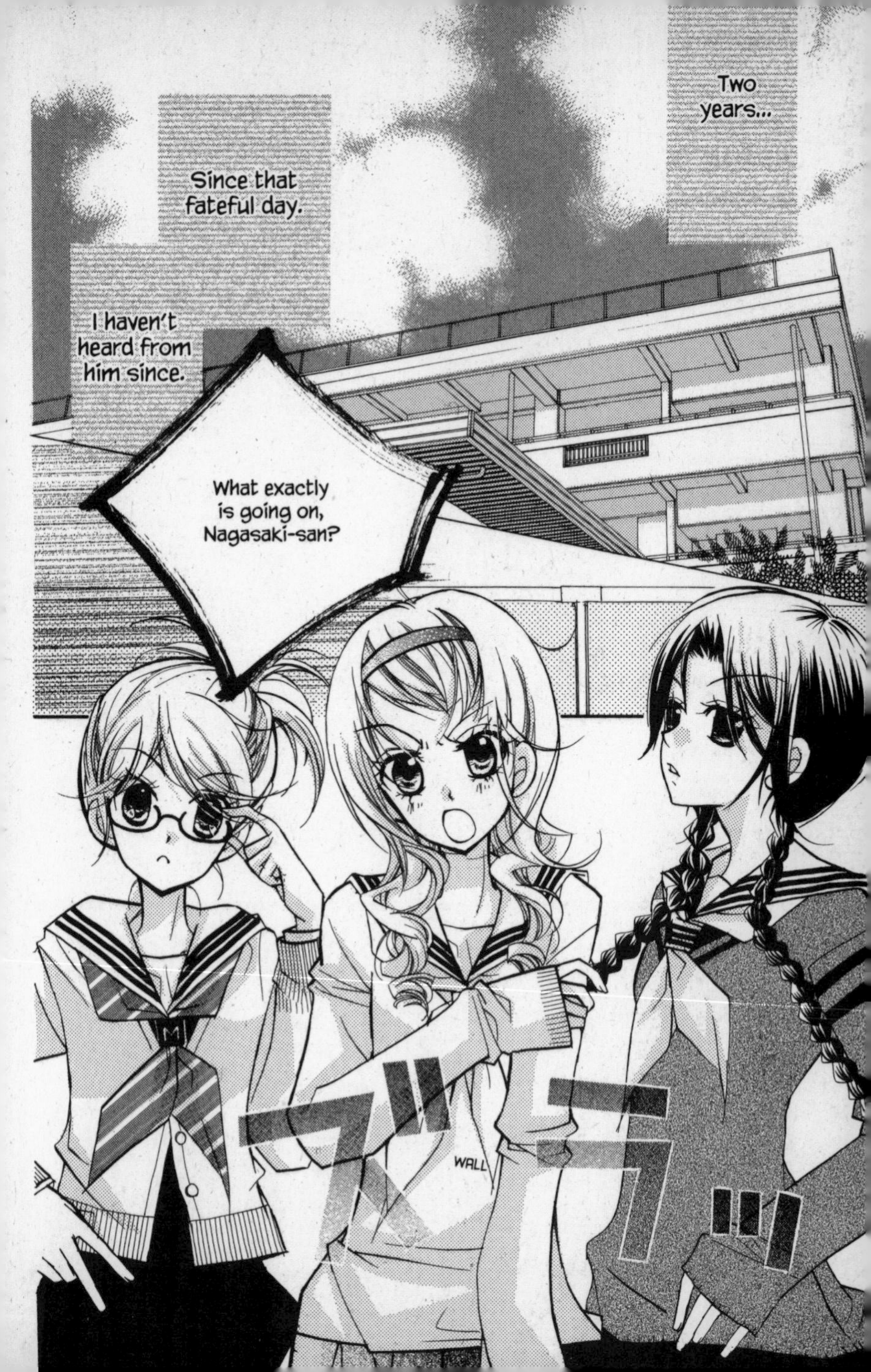
Two years...
Since that fateful day.
I haven't heard from him since.
What exactly is going on, Nagasaki-san?
WALL

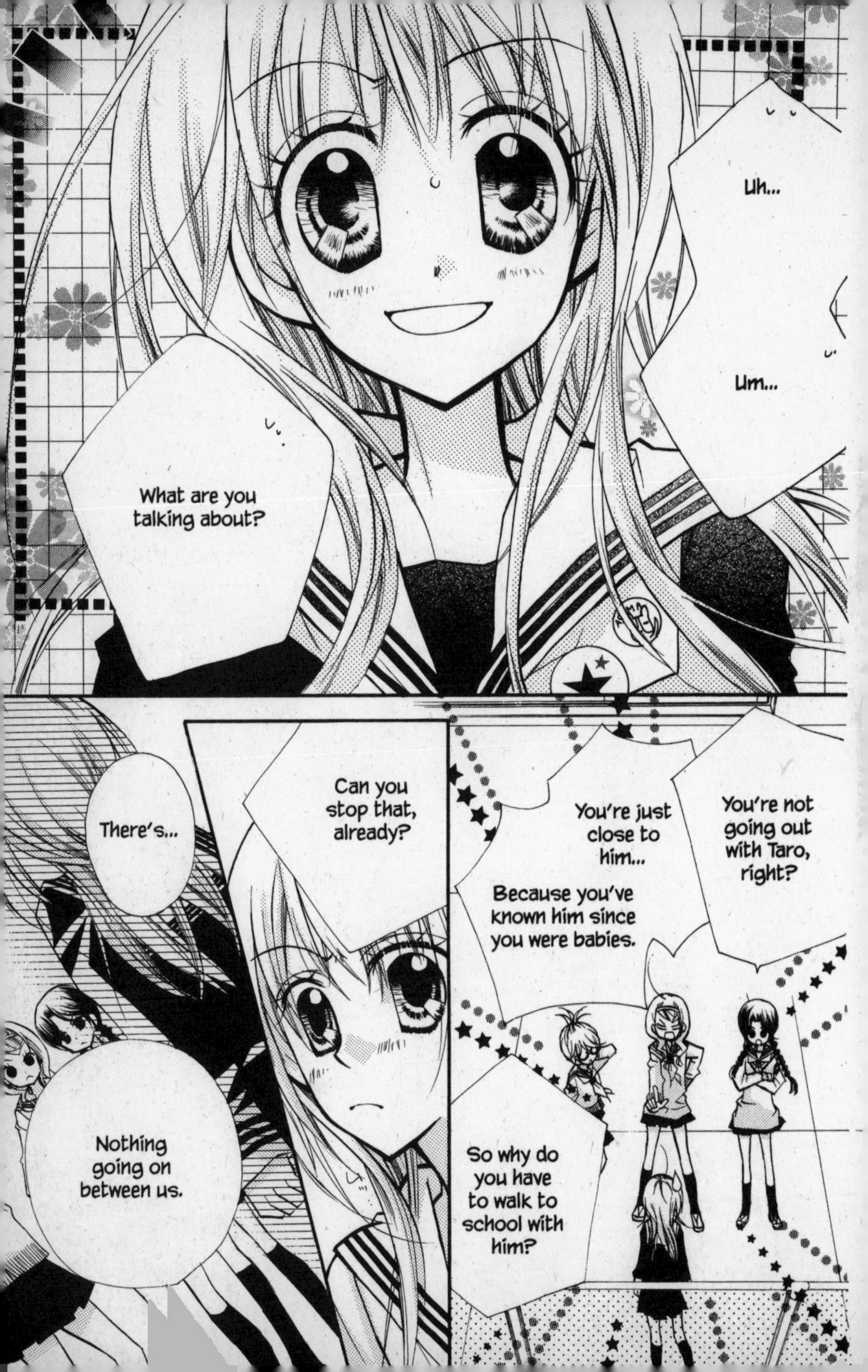
Uh...
Um...
What are you talking about?
You're not going out with Taro, right?
You're just close to him...
Because you've known him since you were babies.
So why do you have to walk to school with him?
Can you stop that, already?
There's...
Nothing going on between us.

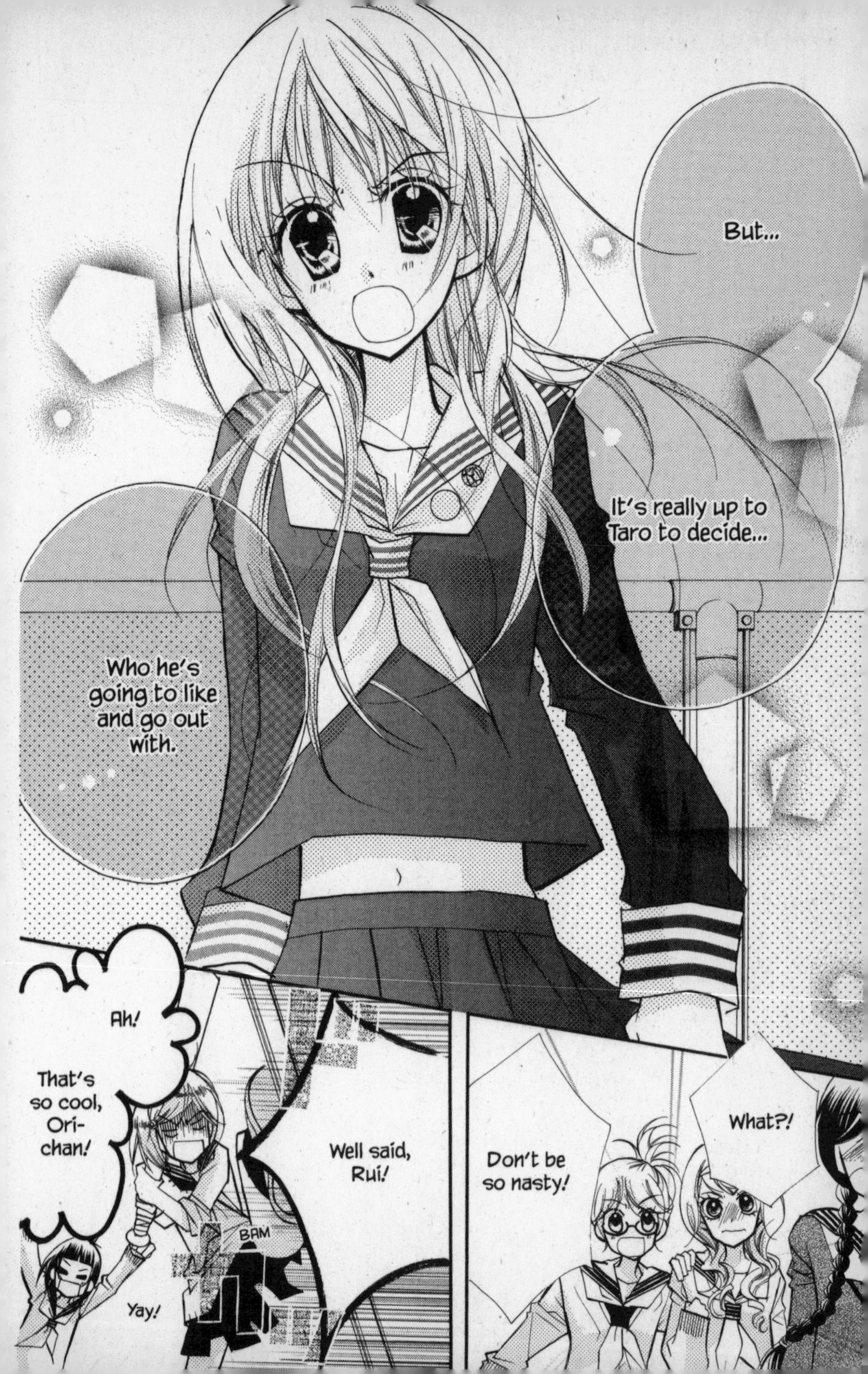
But...
It's really up to Taro to decide...
Who he's going to like and go out with.
What?!
Don't be so nasty!
Well said, Rui!
Ah!
That's so cool, Ori-chan!
BAM
Yay!

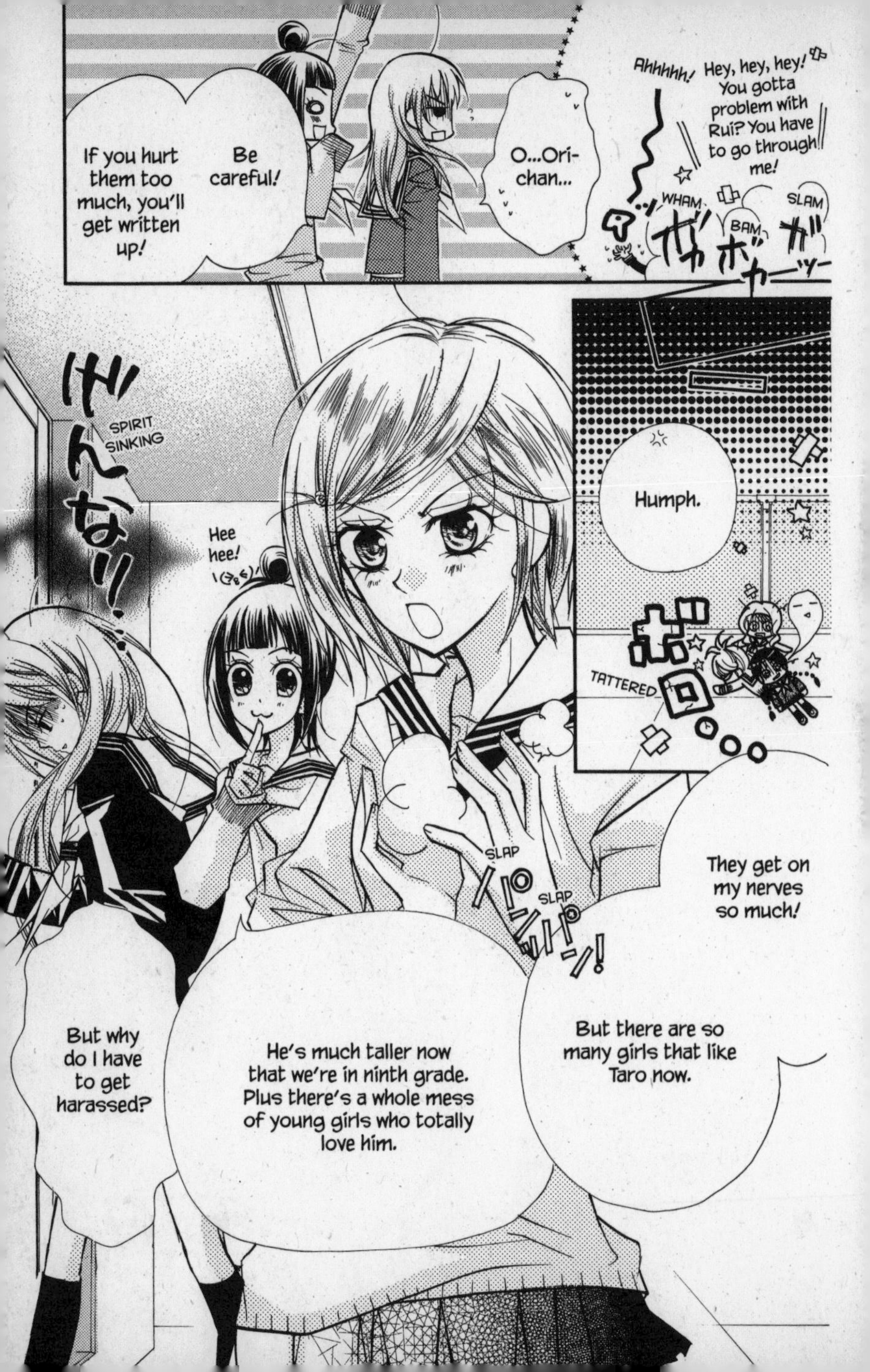
Ahhhhh!
Hey, hey, hey! You gotta problem with Rui? You have to go through me!
WHAM
BAM
SLAM
O...Ori-chan...
Be careful!
If you hurt them too much, you'll get written up!
Humph.
TATTERED
They get on my nerves so much!
SLAP
SLAP
Hee hee!
SPIRIT SINKING
But there are so many girls that like Taro now.
He's much taller now that we're in ninth grade. Plus there's a whole mess of young girls who totally love him.
But why do I have to get harassed?

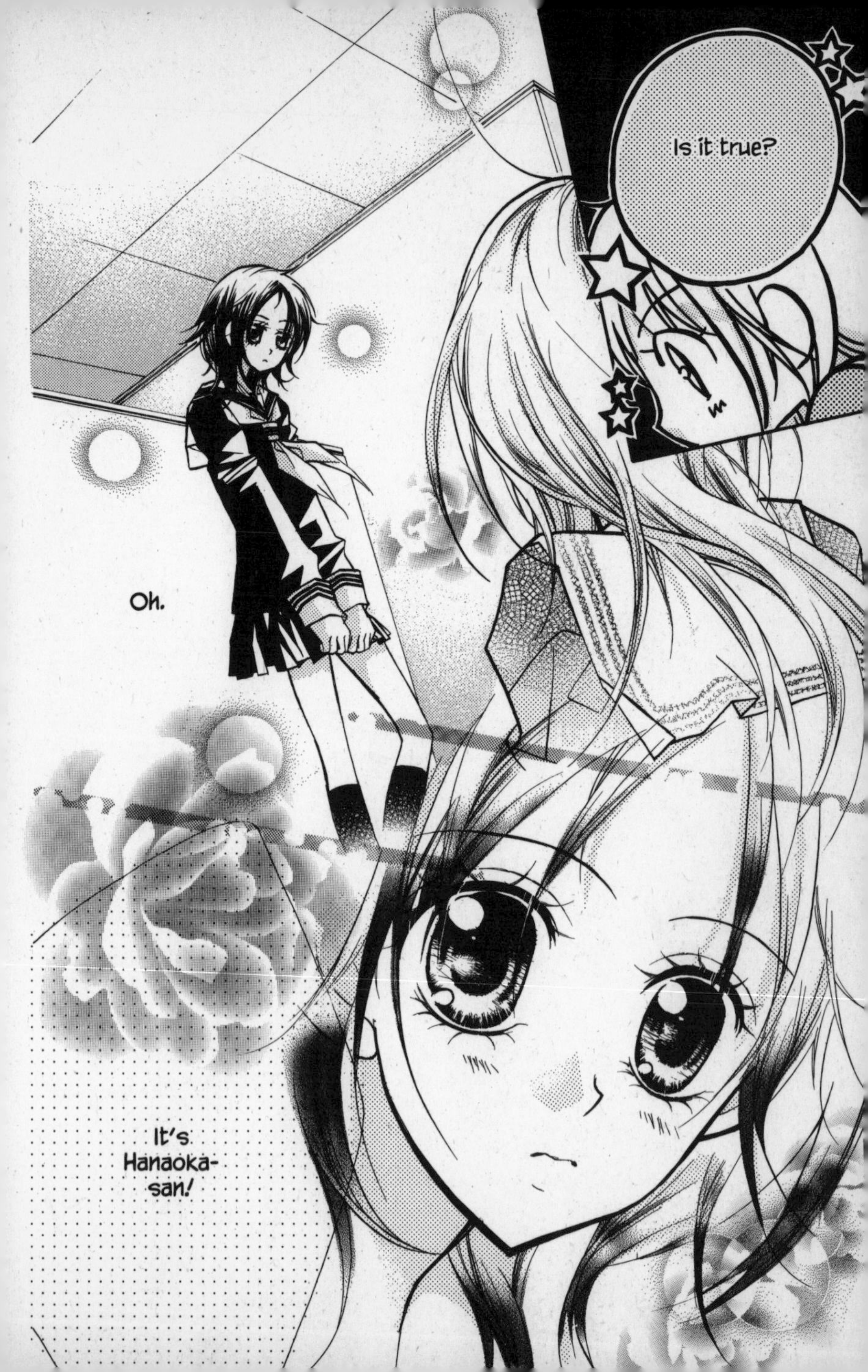
Is it true?
Oh.
It's Hanaoka-san!

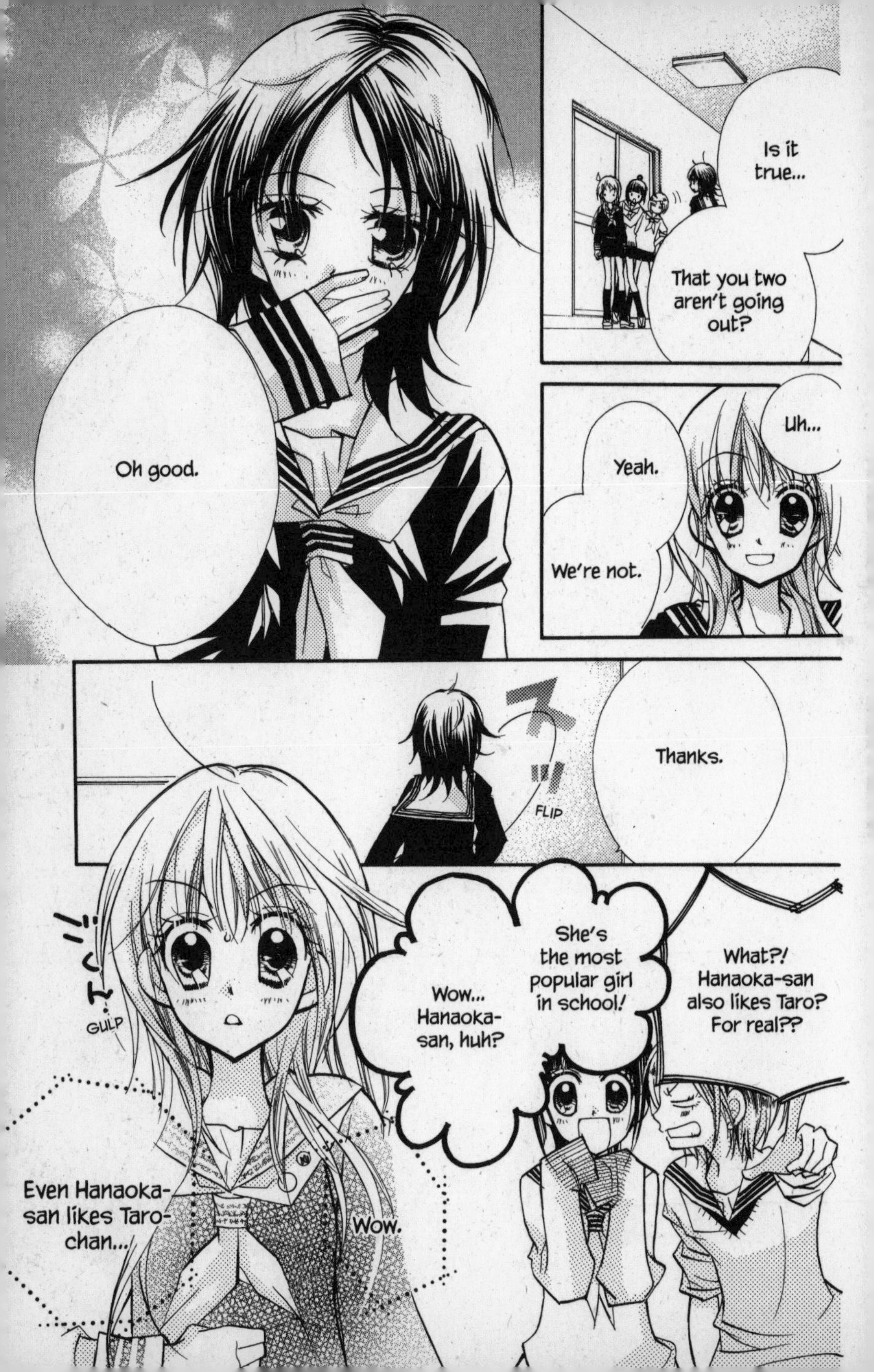
Is it true...
That you two aren't going out?
Uh...
Yeah.
We're not.
Oh good.
Thanks.
FLIP
What?! Hanaoka-san also likes Taro? For real??
She's the most popular girl in school!
Wow... Hanaoka-san, huh?
Wow.
GULP
Even Hanaoka-san likes Taro-chan...

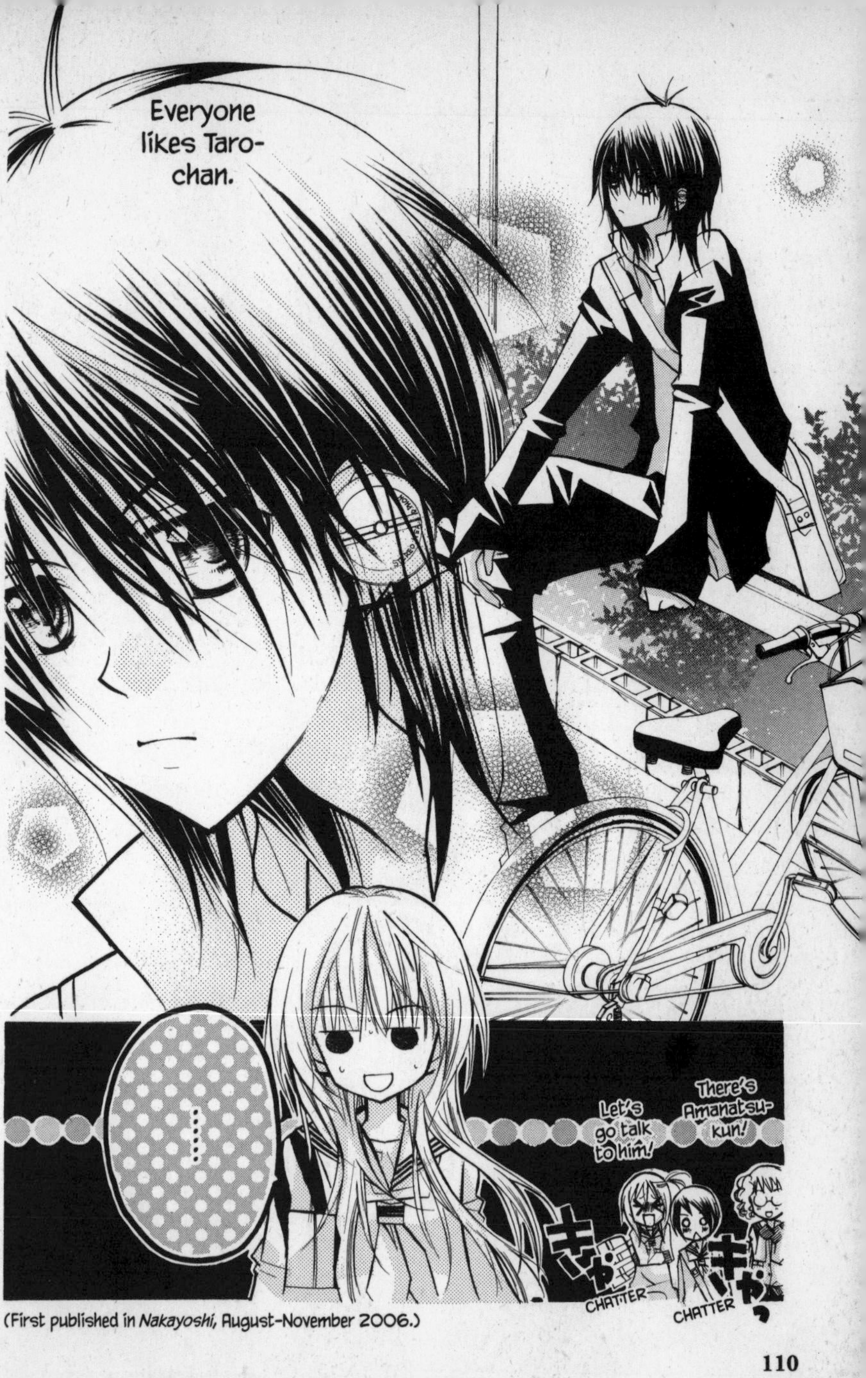
Everyone likes Taro-chan.
There's Amanatsu-kun!
Let's go talk to him!
CHATTER
CHATTER
......!

(First published in *Nakayoshi*, August-November 2006.)

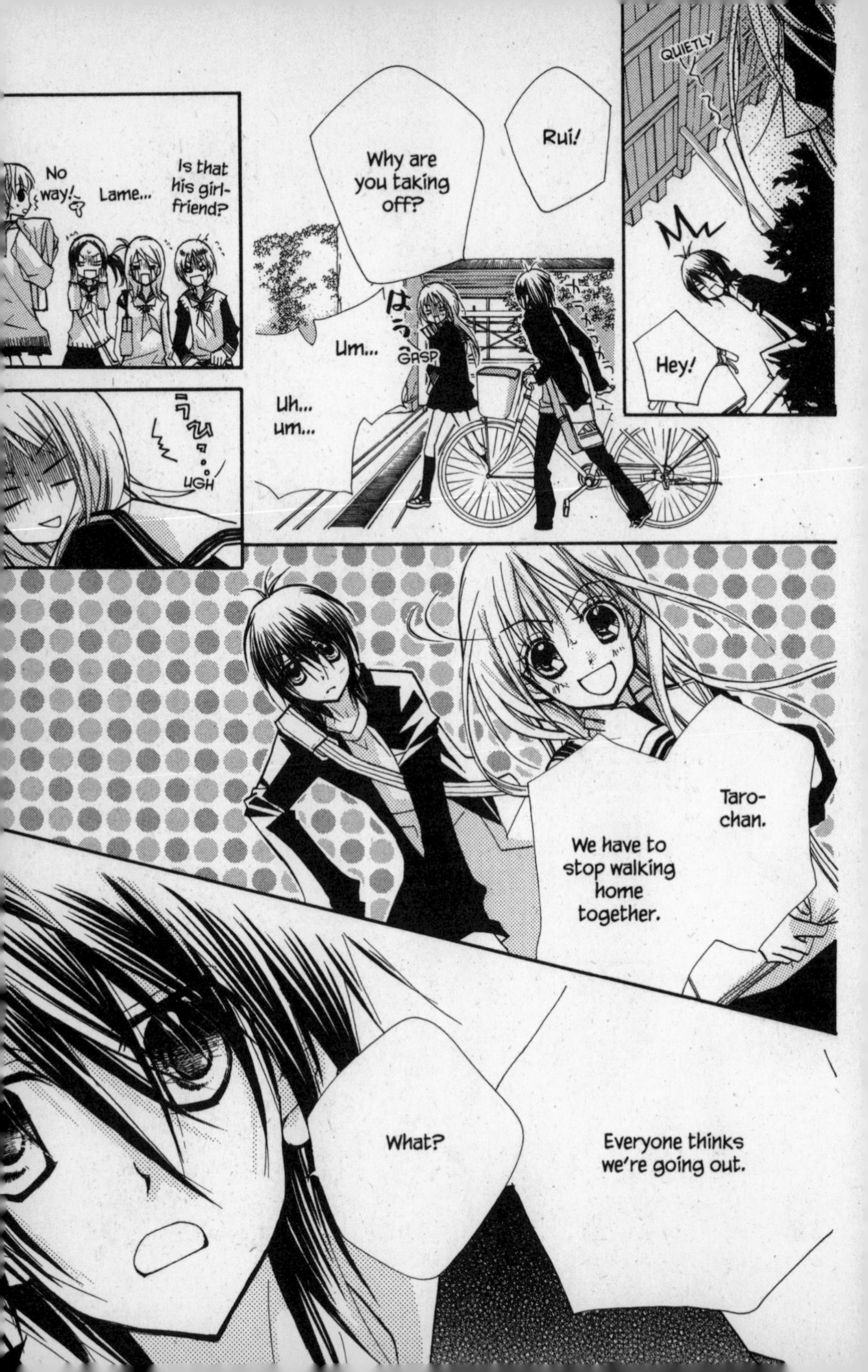

QUIETLY
Hey!
Rui!
Why are you taking off?
GASP
Um...
Uh... um...
Is that his girl-friend?
Lame...
No way!
UGH
Taro-chan.
We have to stop walking home together.
Everyone thinks we're going out.
What?

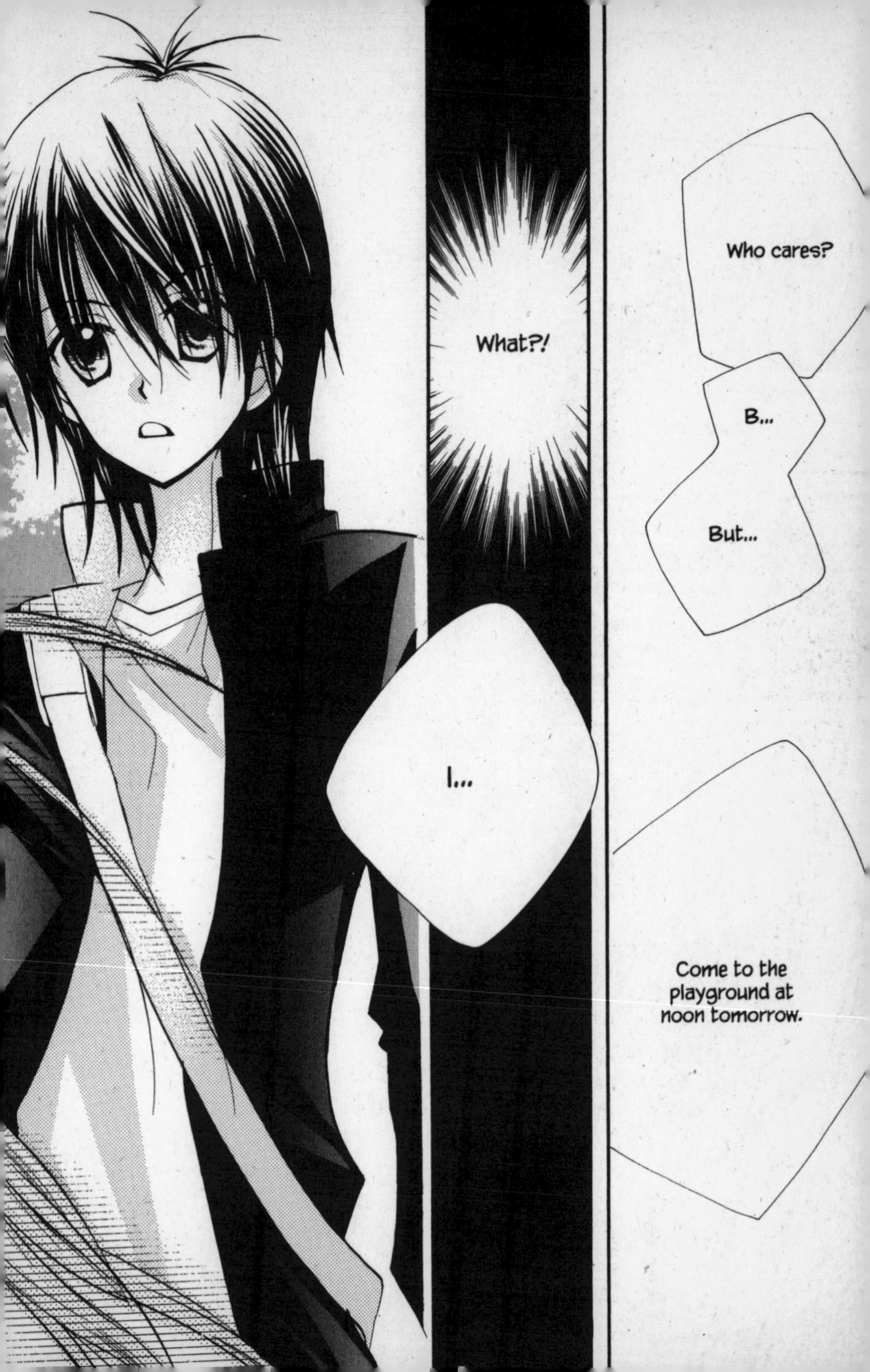
Who cares?
B...
But...
Come to the playground at noon tomorrow.
What?!
I...

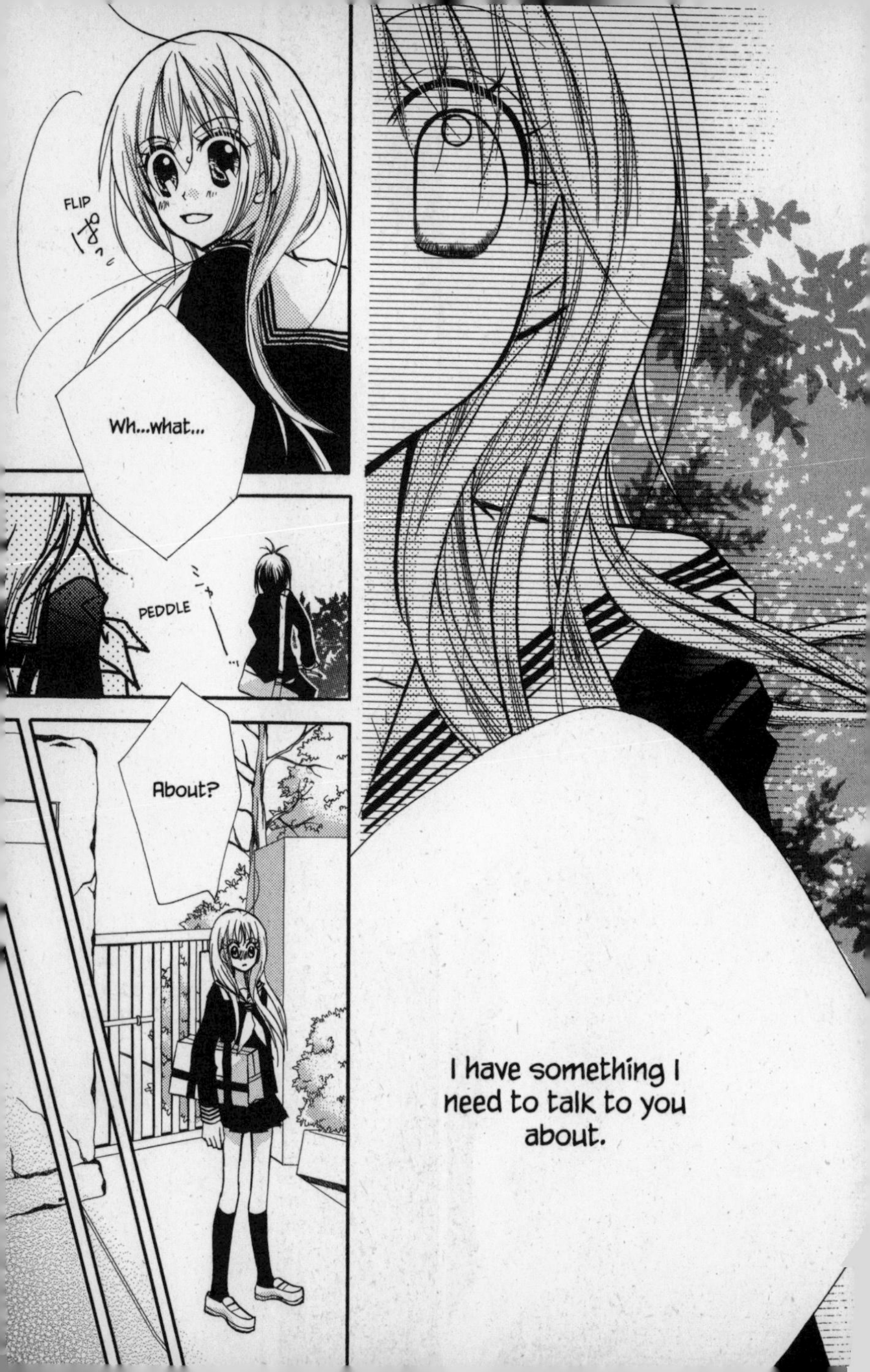
I have something I need to talk to you about.
FLIP
ぱっ
Wh...what...
PEDDLE
About?

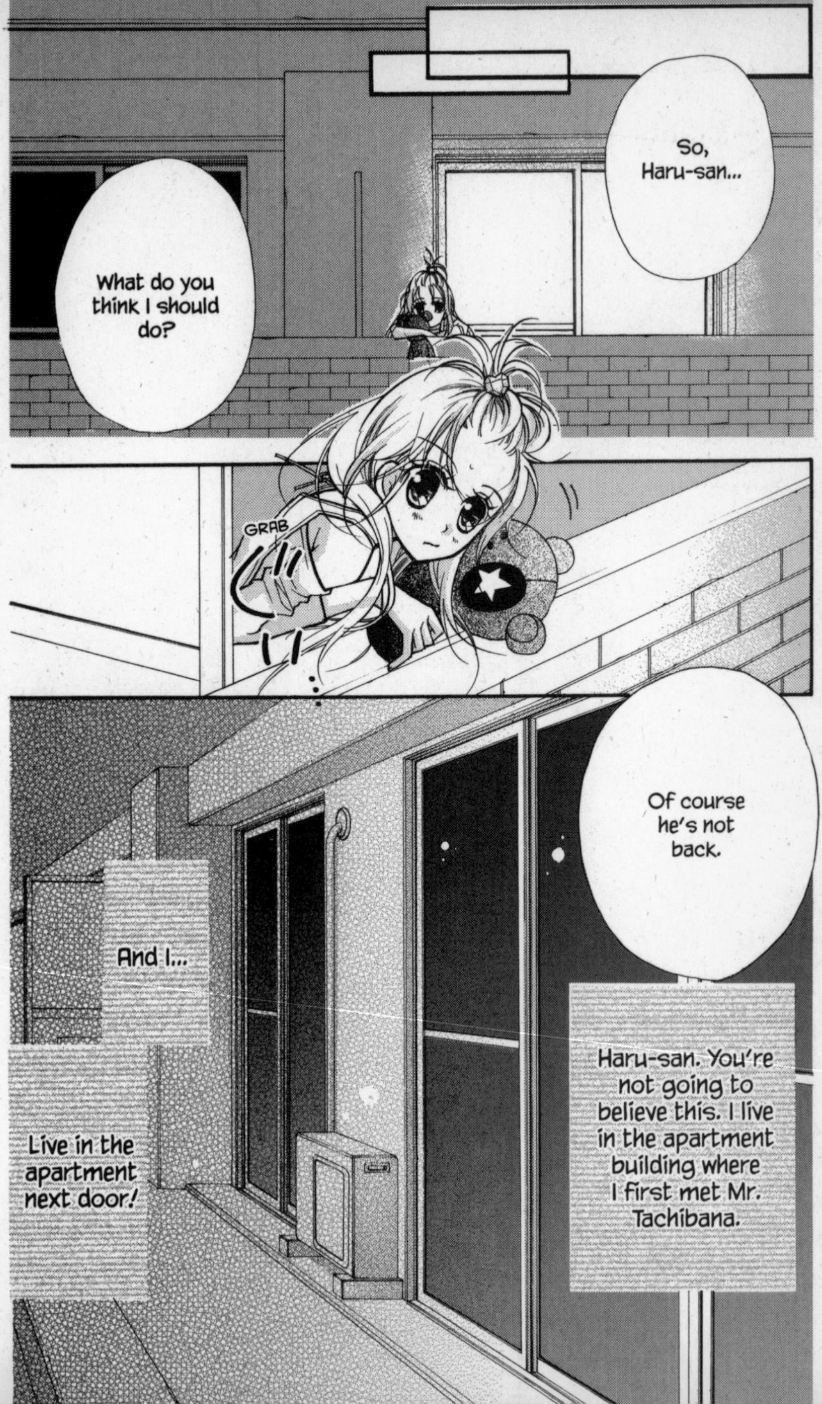
So, Haru-san...
What do you think I should do?
GRAB
Of course he's not back.
Haru-san. You're not going to believe this. I live in the apartment building where I first met Mr. Tachibana.
And I...
Live in the apartment next door!

FIVE

☑ So that's how the popularity poll turned out.

☑ There's going to be some new characters and Taro-chan is going to change as well, so please continue to let me know which male character you like in your letters!

I'll tally everything up for another list!

Haruka Fukushima
c/o Editorial Department,
Nakayoshi
P.O. Box 91 Akasaka Post Office
Tokyo, Japan 107-8652

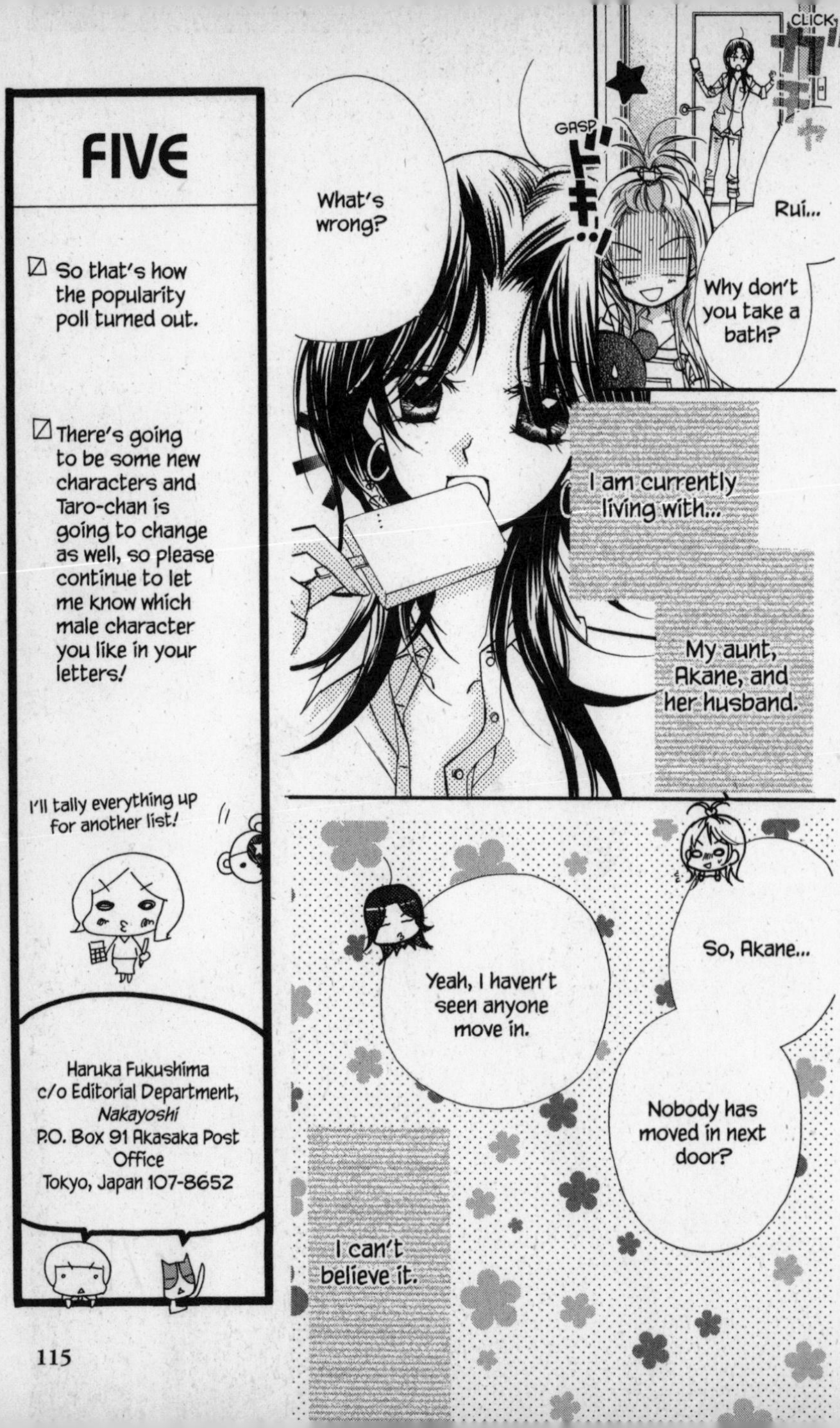
CLICK
Rui...
Why don't you take a bath?
GASP
What's wrong?
I am currently living with...
My aunt, Akane, and her husband.
So, Akane...
Nobody has moved in next door?
Yeah, I haven't seen anyone move in.
I can't believe it.

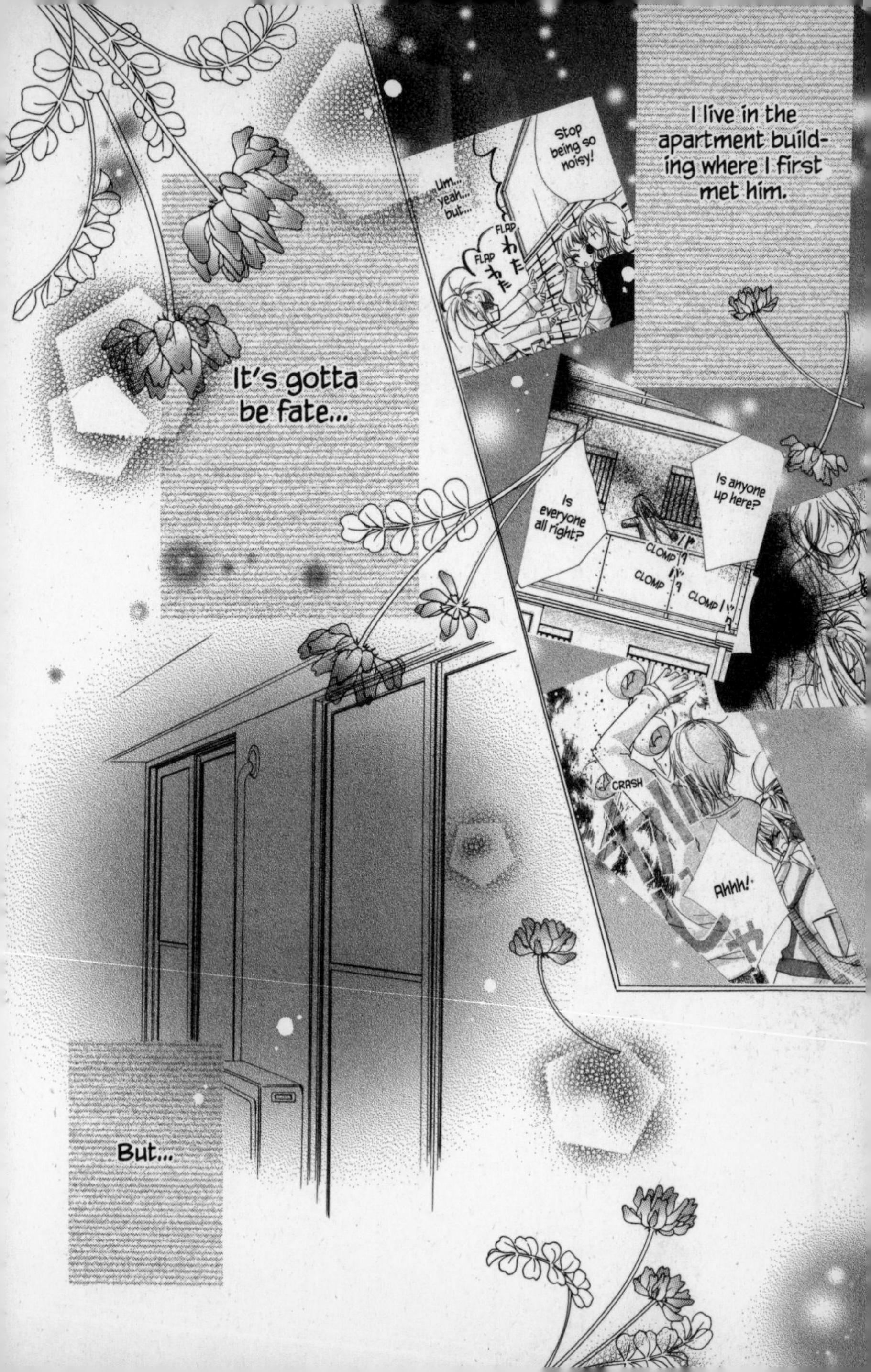

I live in the apartment building where I first met him.
Stop being so noisy!
Um... yeah... but...
FLAP
FLAP
わた わた
It's gotta be fate...
Is anyone up here?
Is everyone all right?
CLOMP
CLOMP
CLOMP
CRASH
Ahhh!
But...

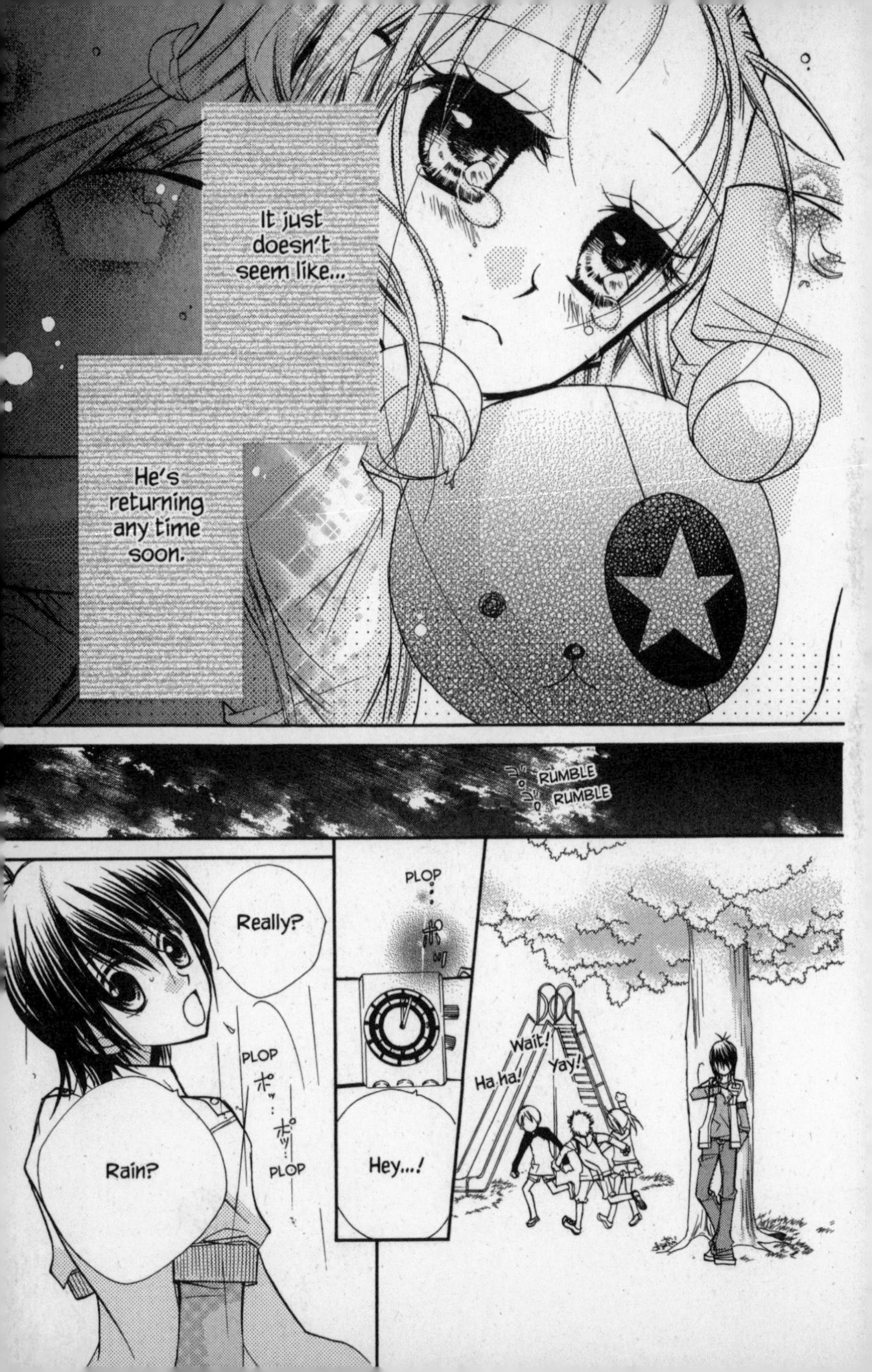
It just doesn't seem like...
He's returning any time soon.
RUMBLE
RUMBLE
Wait!
Yay!
Ha ha!
PLOP
Hey...!
Really?
PLOP
PLOP
Rain?

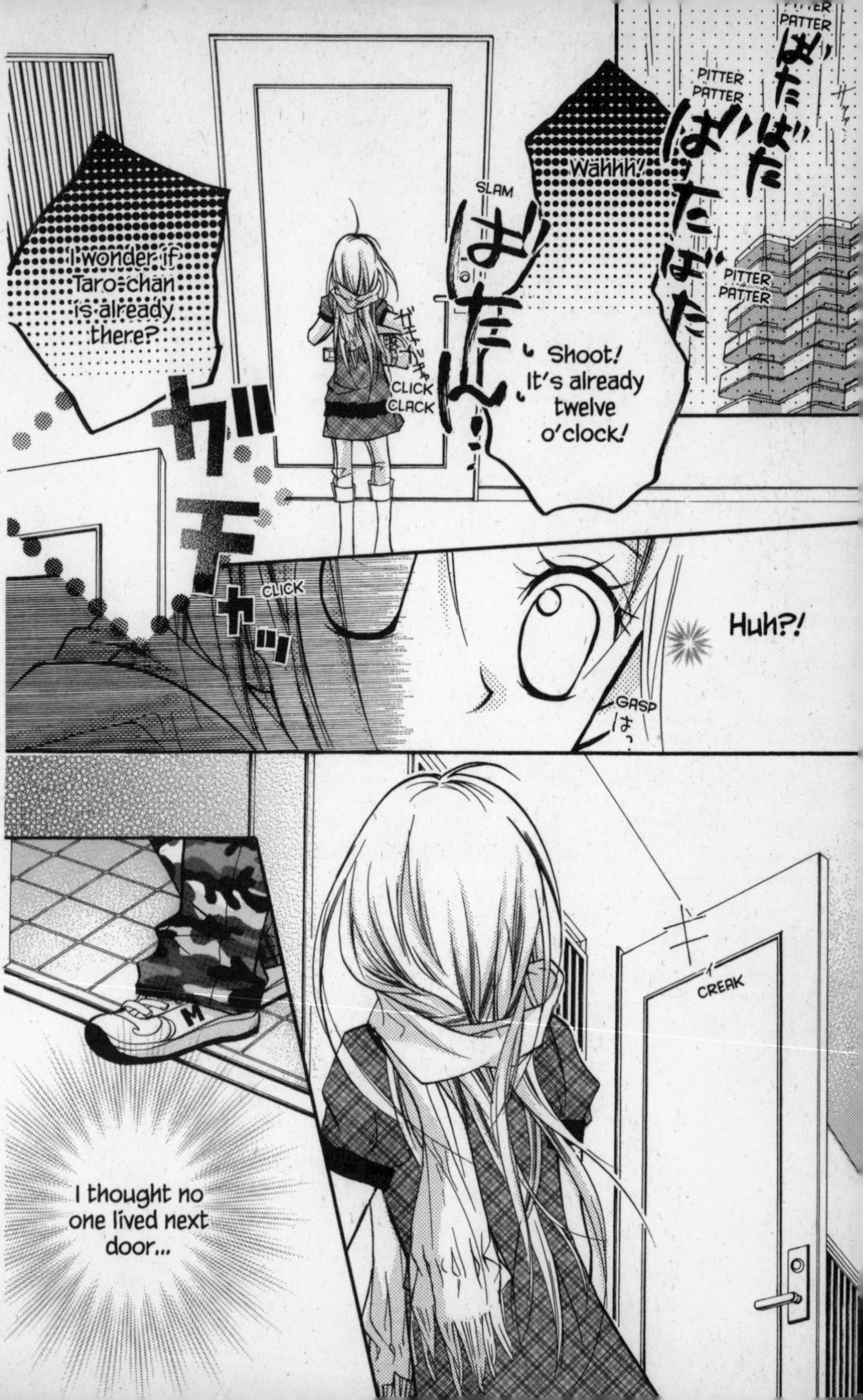
PITTER PATTER
PITTER PATTER
PITTER PATTER
Wahhh!
Shoot! It's already twelve o'clock!
SLAM
CLICK CLACK
I wonder if Taro-chan is already there?
CLICK
Huh?!
GASP
CREAK
I thought no one lived next door...

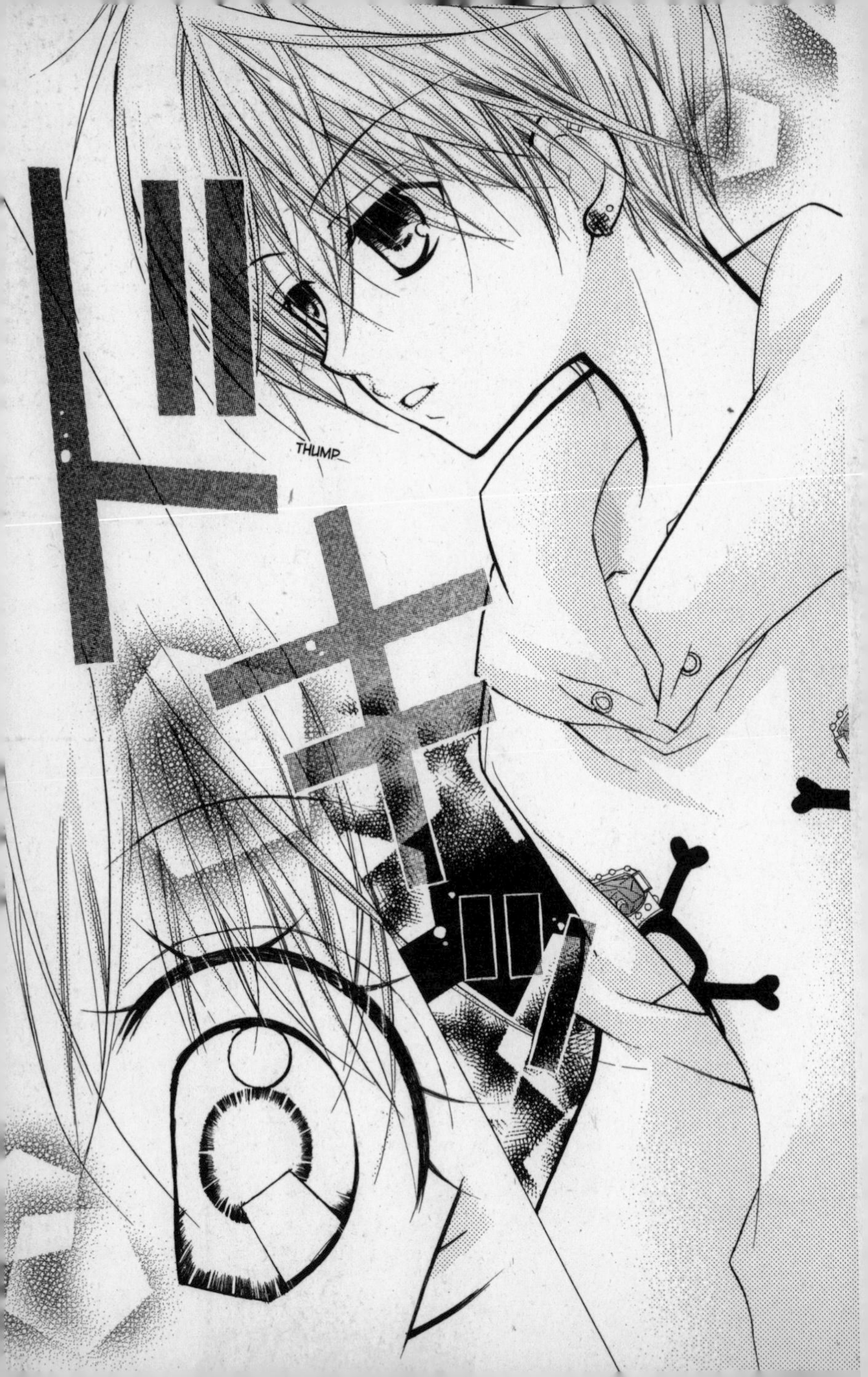
THUMP

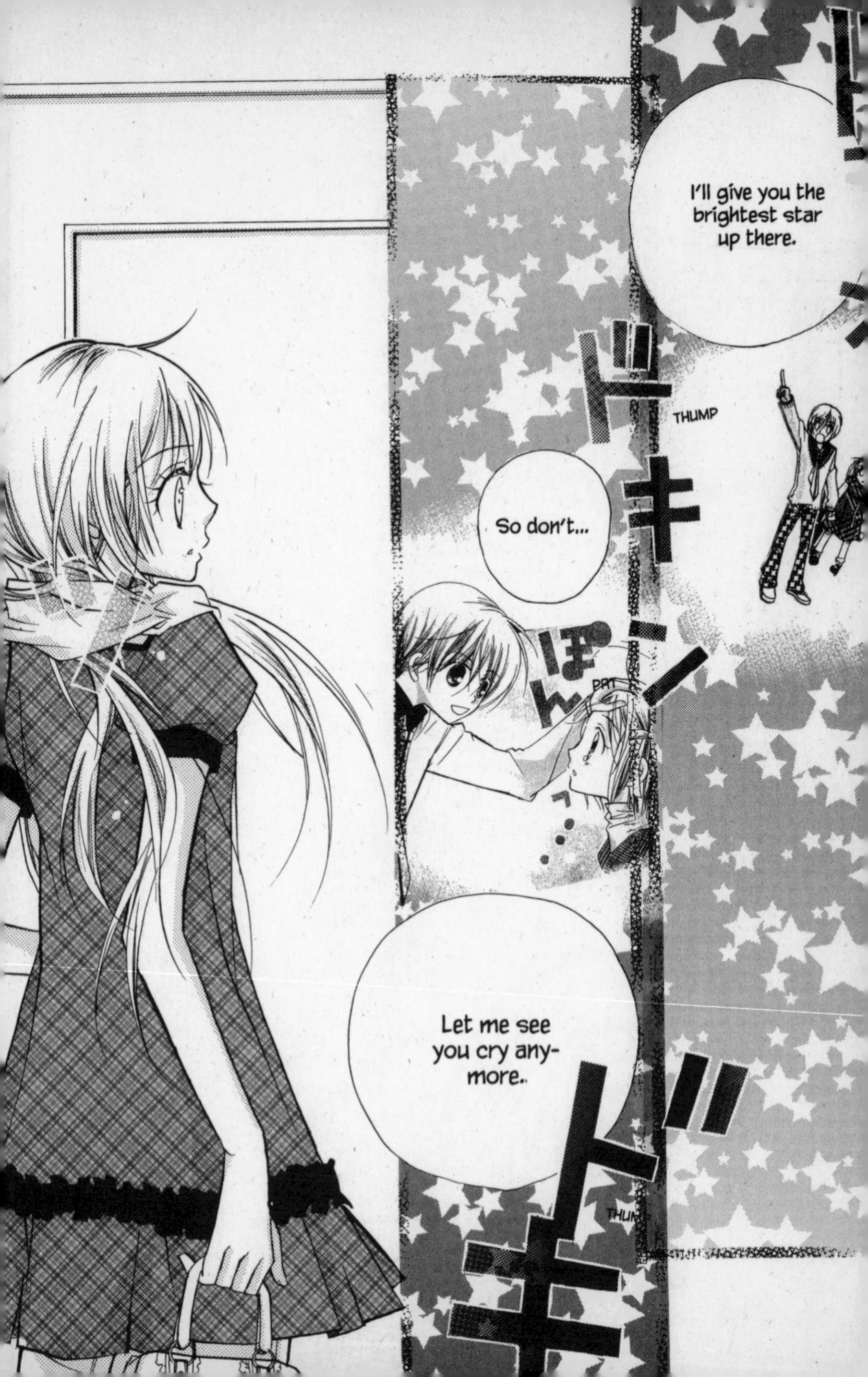
I'll give you the brightest star up there.
THUMP
So don't...
PAT
Let me see you cry any-more..
THUMP

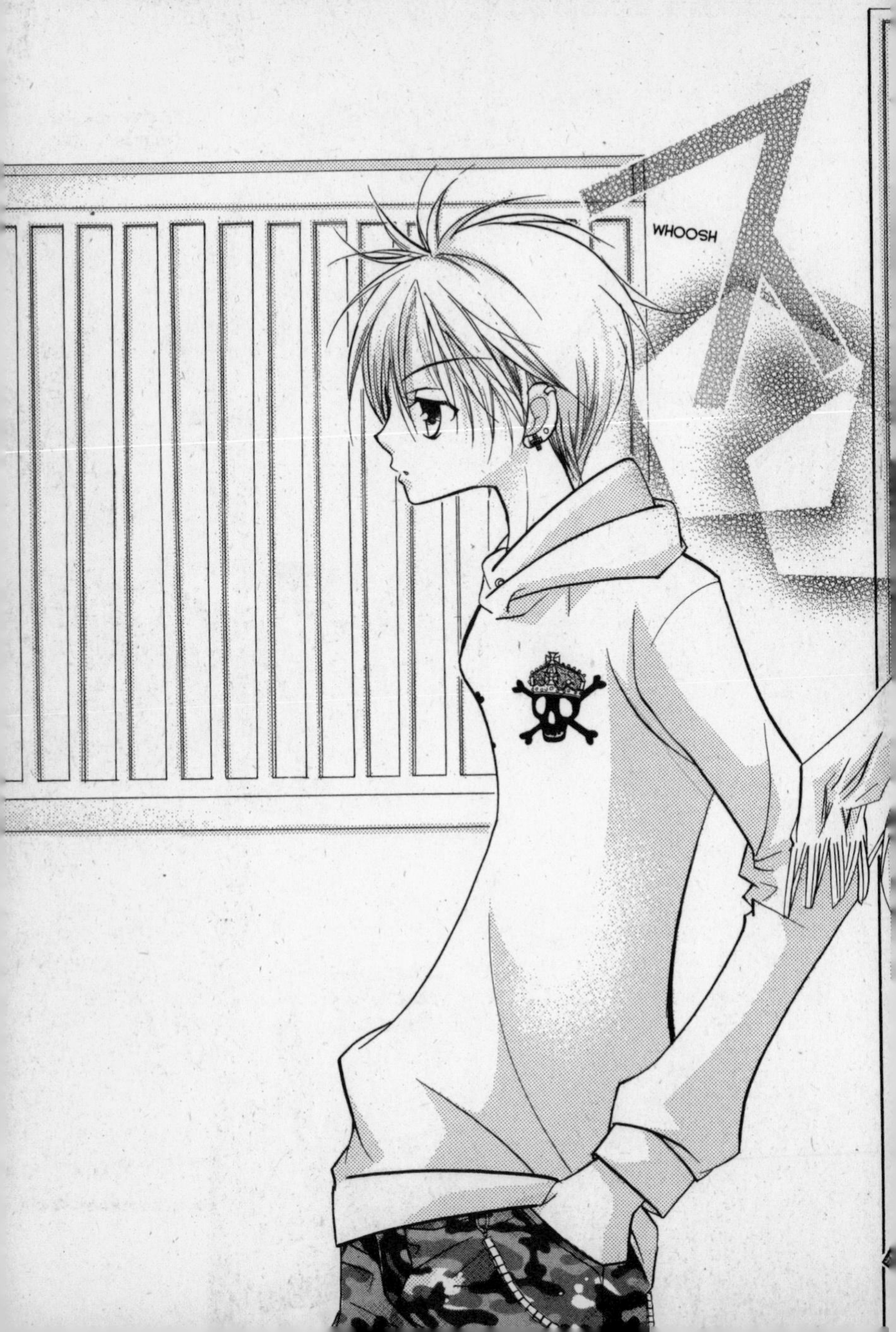
WHOOSH

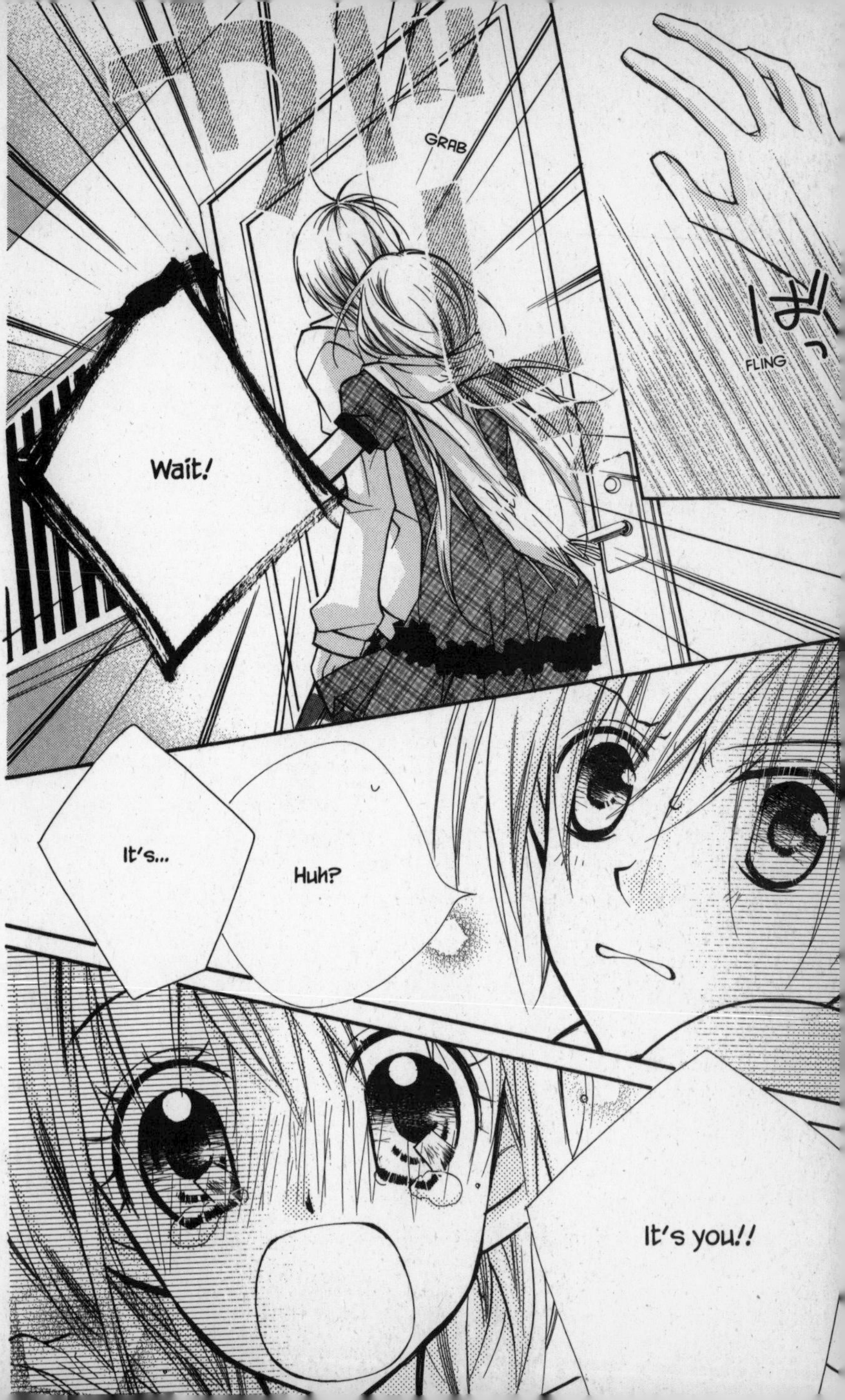
ばっ
FLING
GRAB
Wait!
Huh?
It's...
It's you!!

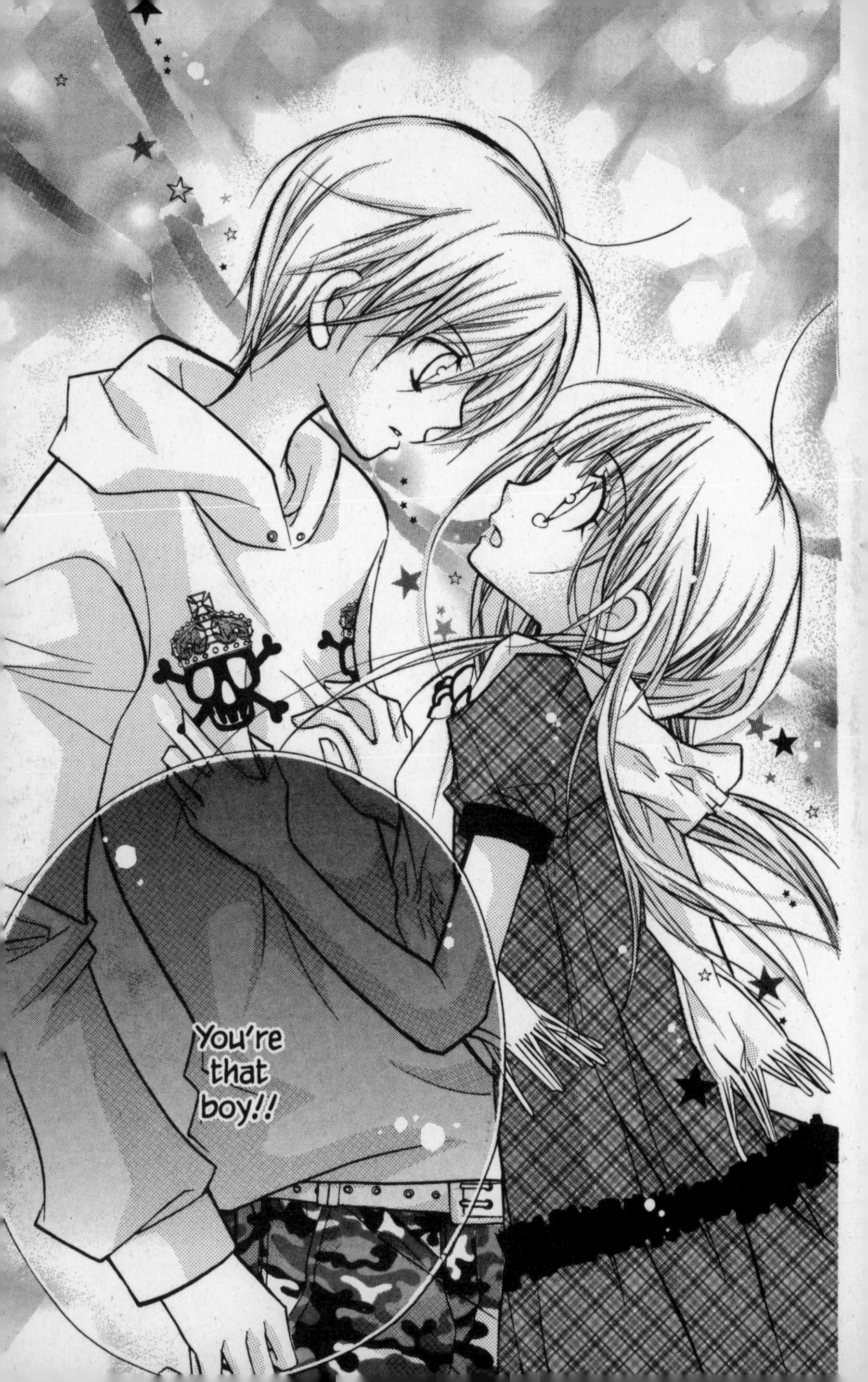
You're that boy!!

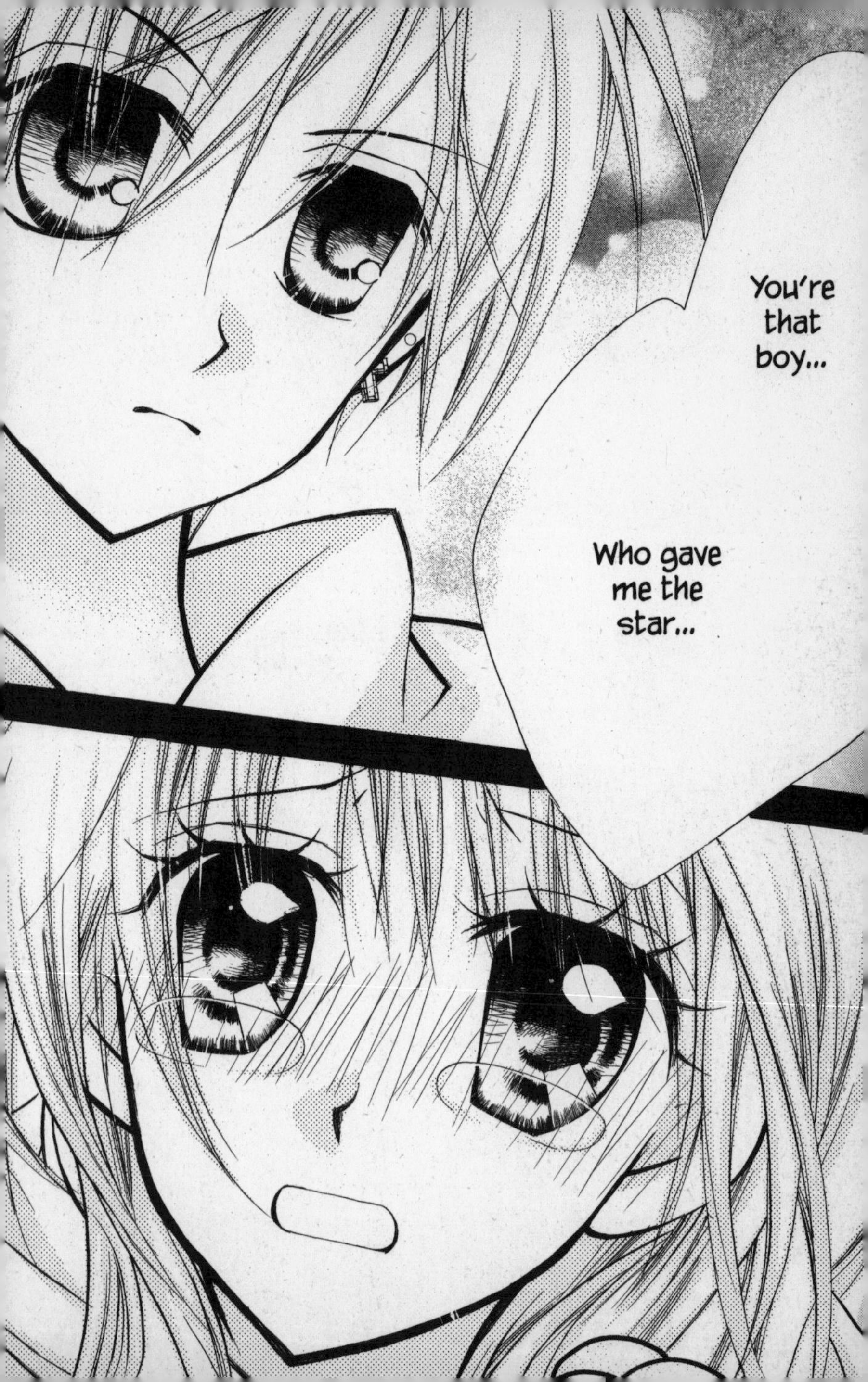
You're that boy...
Who gave me the star...

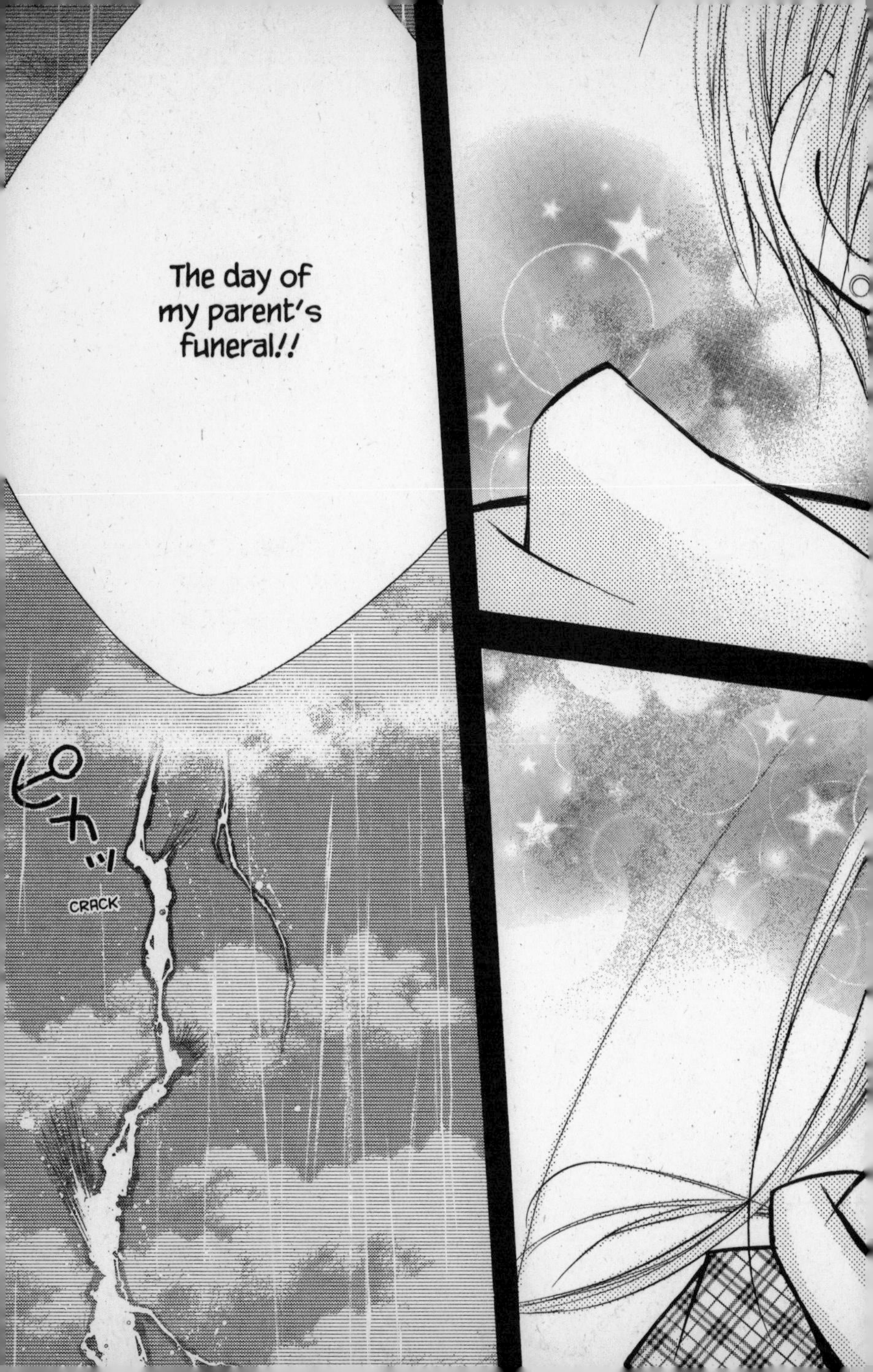
The day of my parent's funeral!!
ピカッ
CRACK

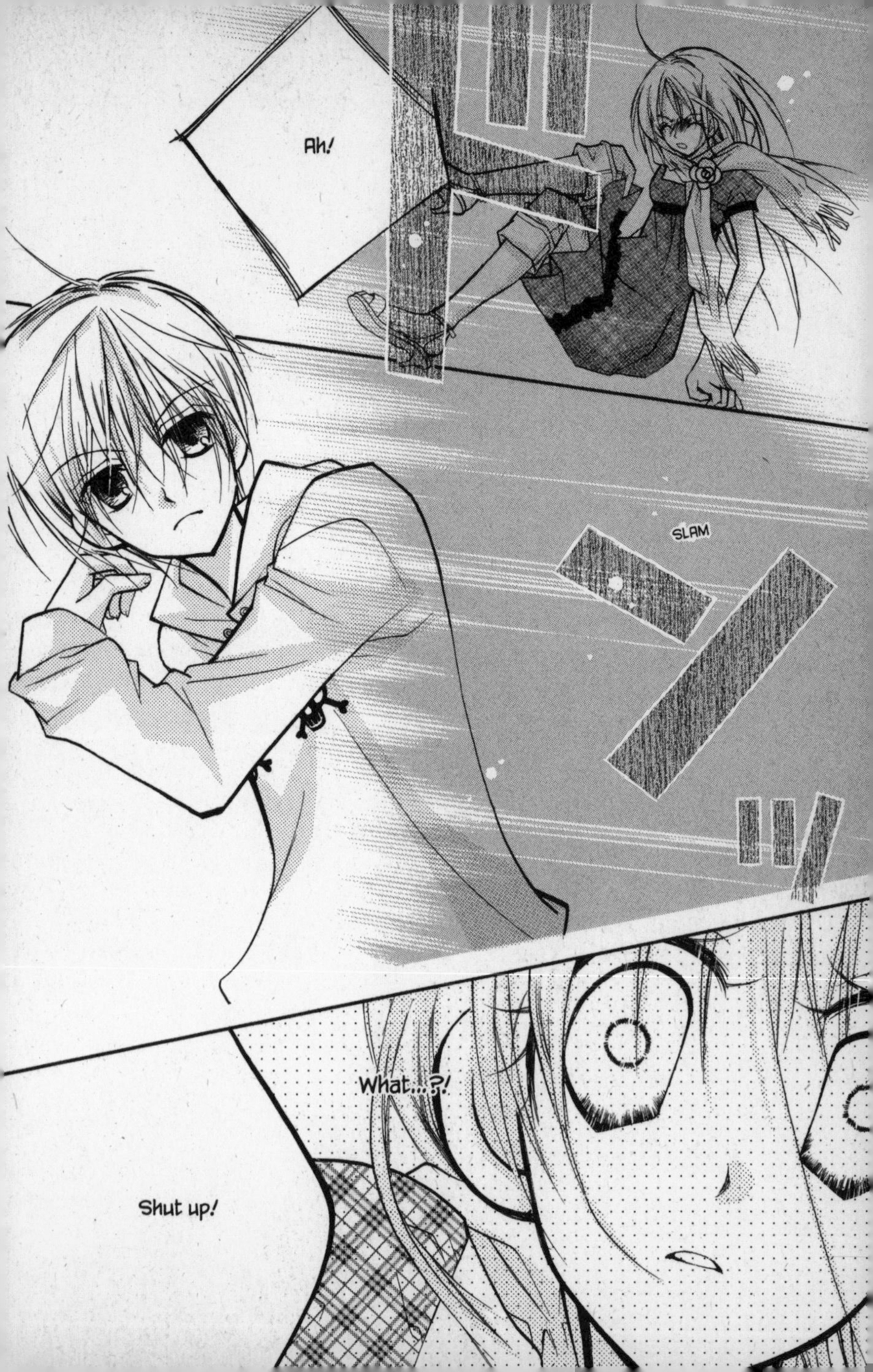
Ah!
SLAM
What...?!
Shut up!

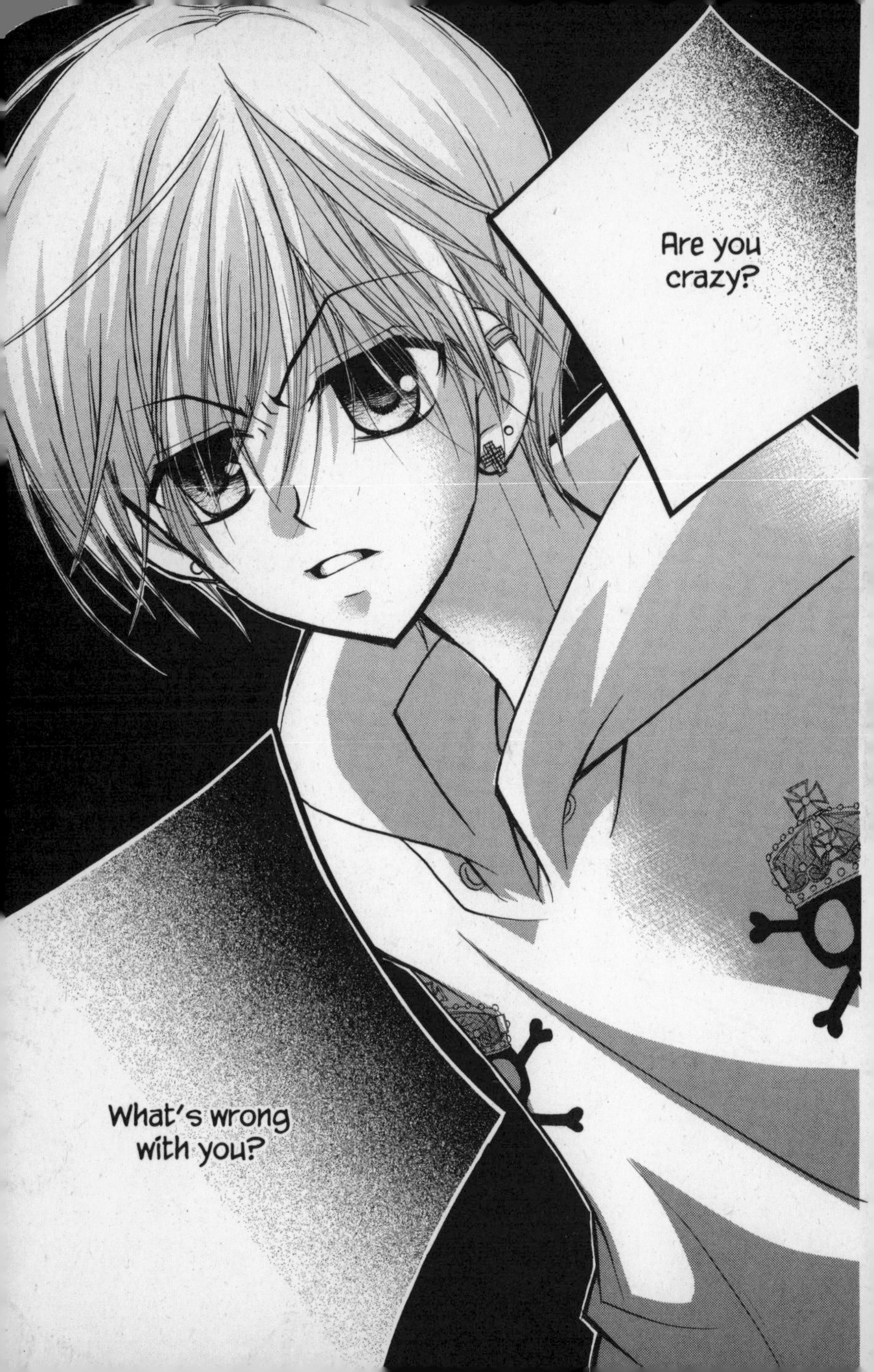
Are you crazy?
What's wrong with you?

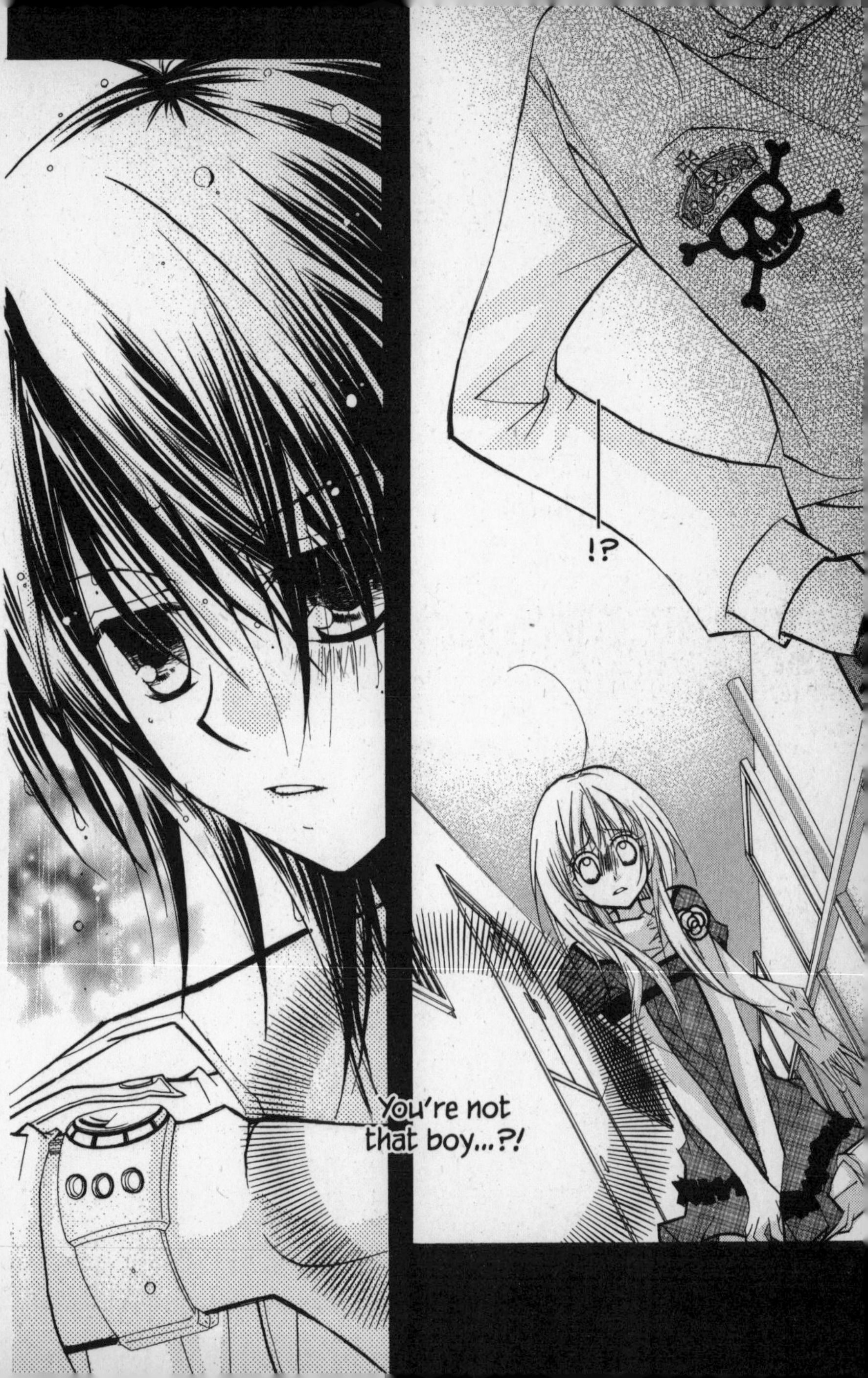
!?
You're not that boy...?!

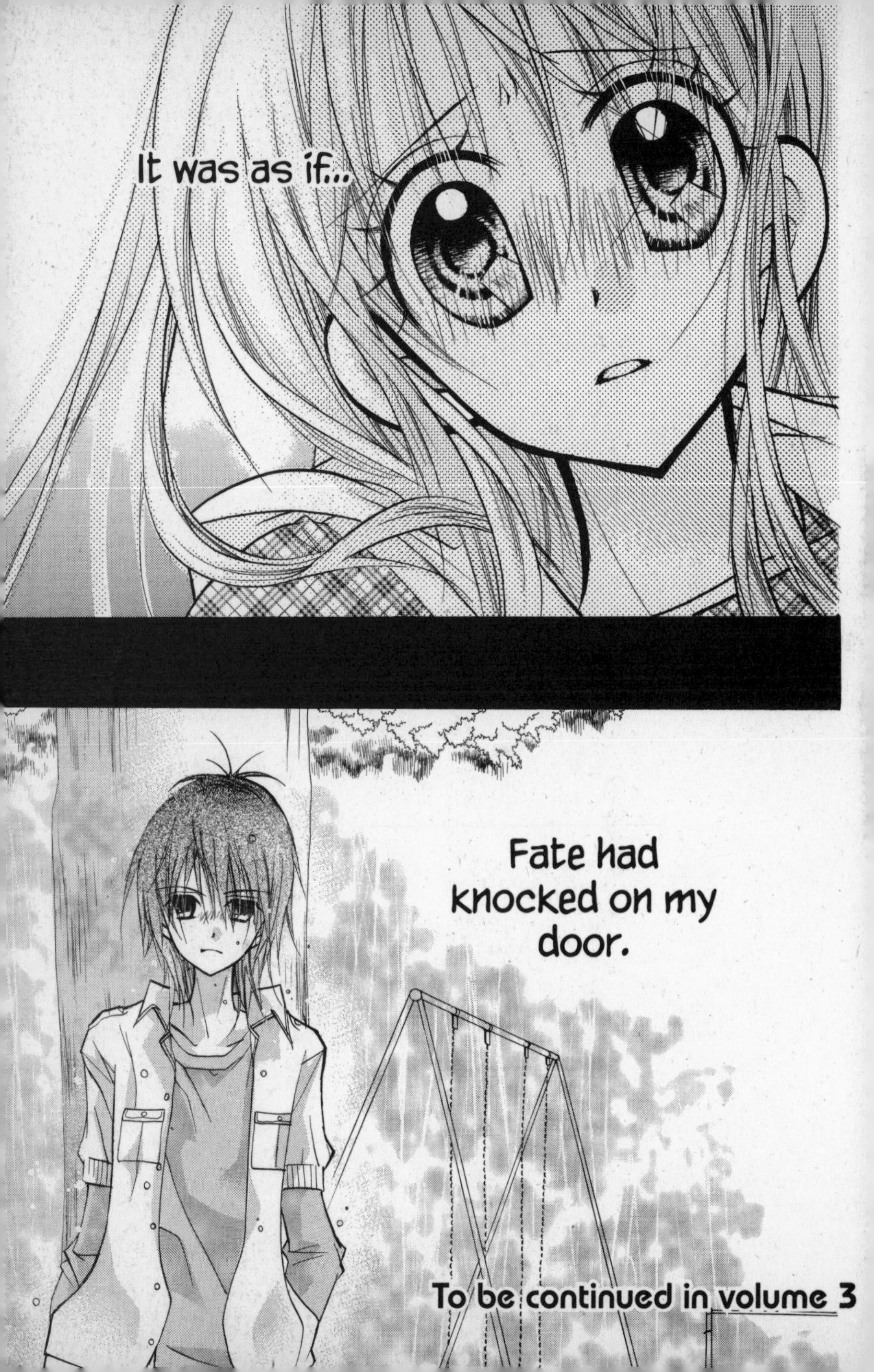
It was as if...
Fate had knocked on my door.
To be continued in volume 3

Special Bonus

Stardust Date

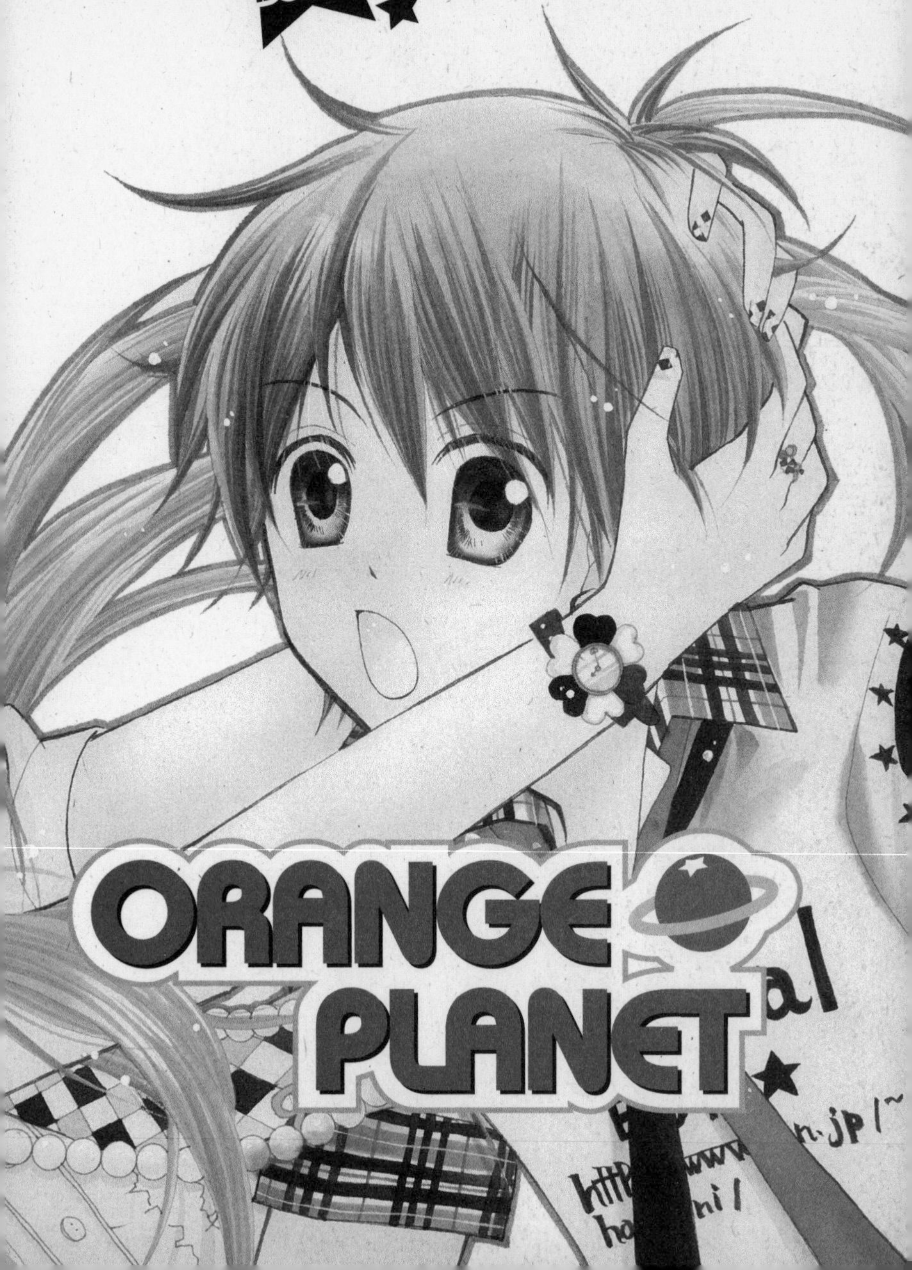
ORANGE PLANET

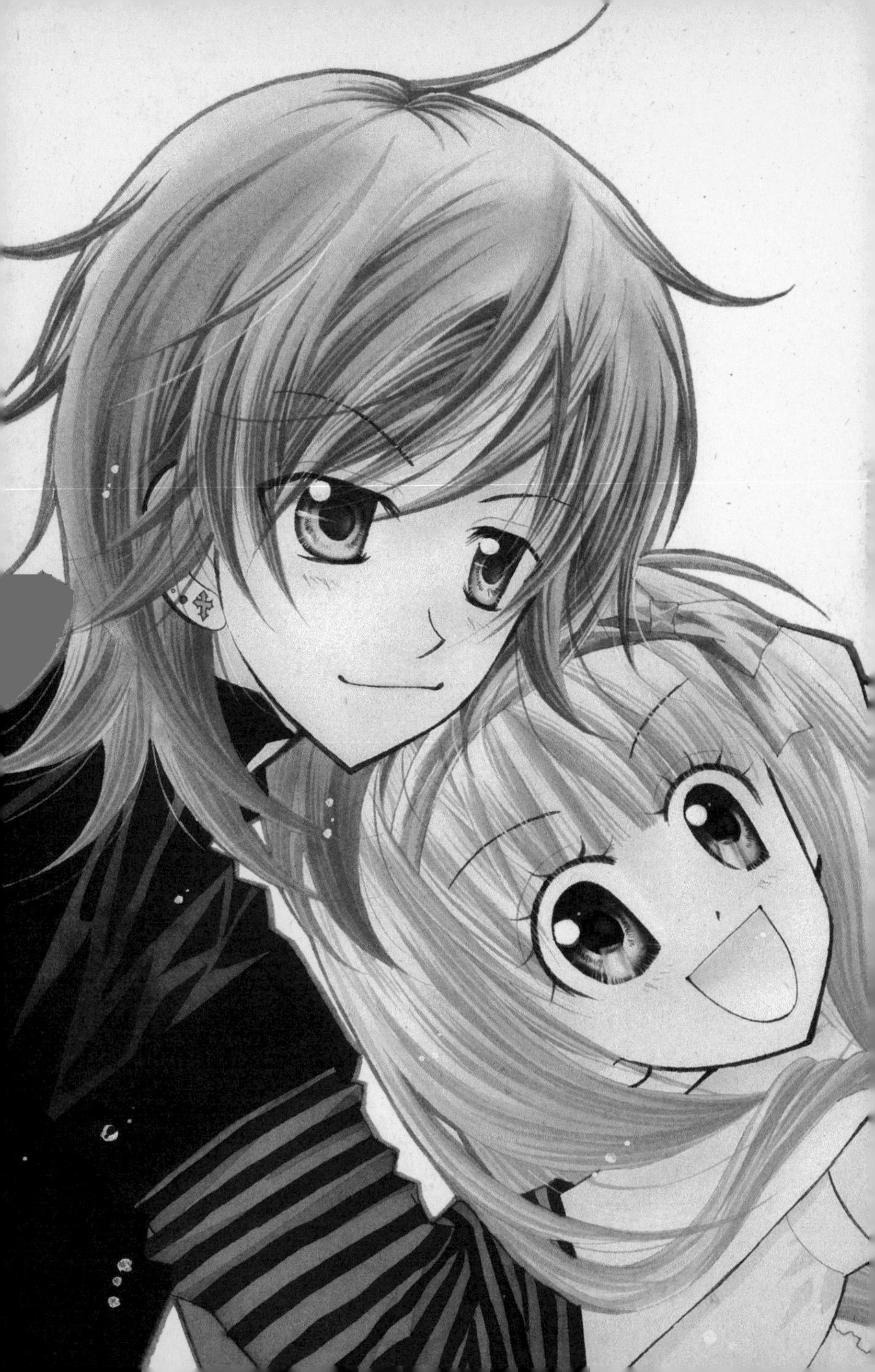

About
Stardust Date...

- It's a short story all about Taro-chan.

For this story...
I put the focus on him. Ahem...

- I wanted to show how cool Taro-chan could be. Tell me what you think!

- I had to remember what my *bunkasai* was like...

I gave out fliers dressed in a doll suit.
Hee hee.
Stir! Stir!
I made tea, nonstop, at the teahouse.
President
Vice President
I laughed so hard when the two (male) class presidents did a show in drag.

There were so many hilarious things. I hope I can incorporate the *bunkasai* into the main story line, too...

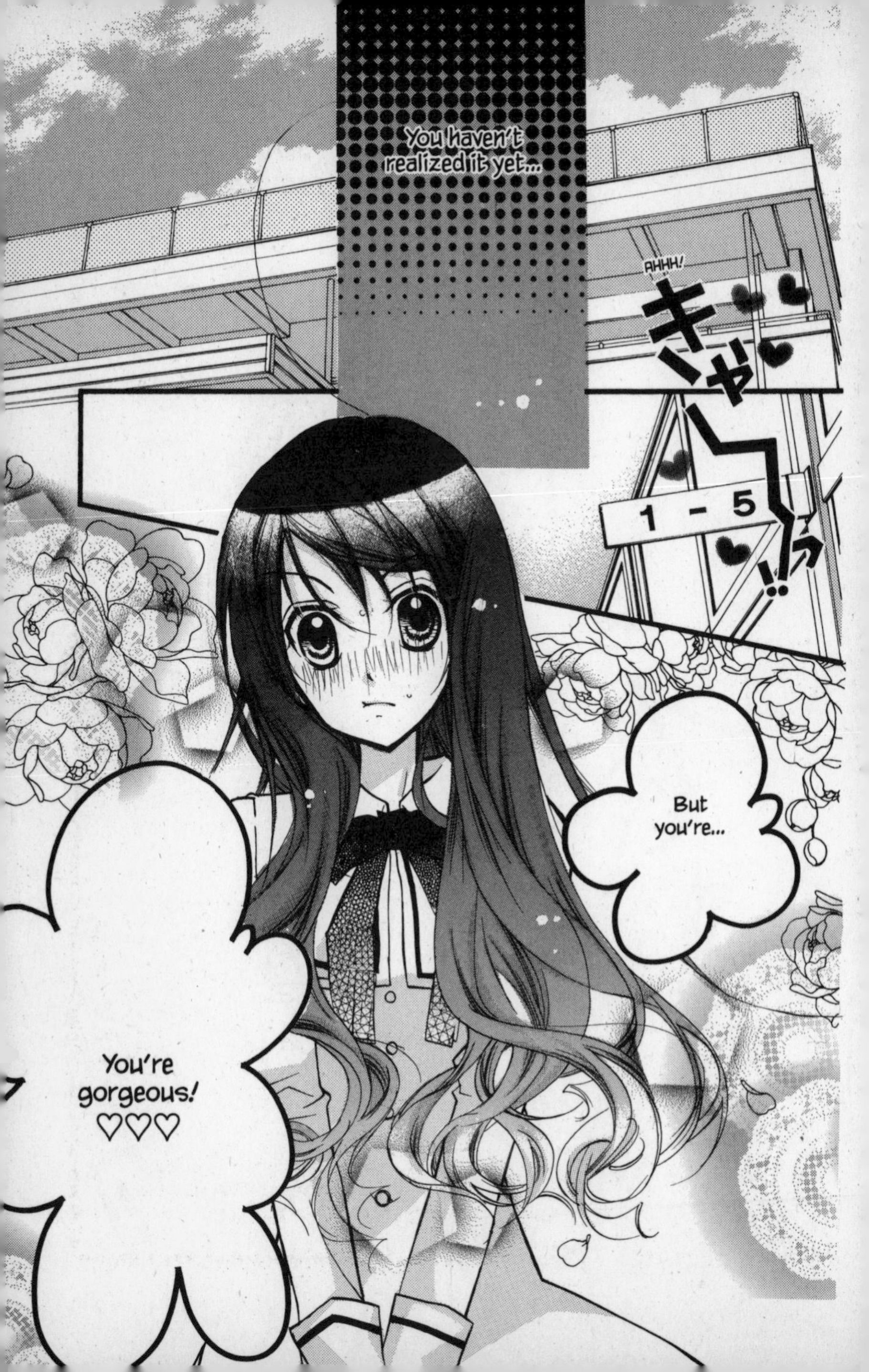
You haven't realized it yet...
AHHH!
キャ〜!!
1 - 5
But you're...
You're gorgeous! ♡♡♡

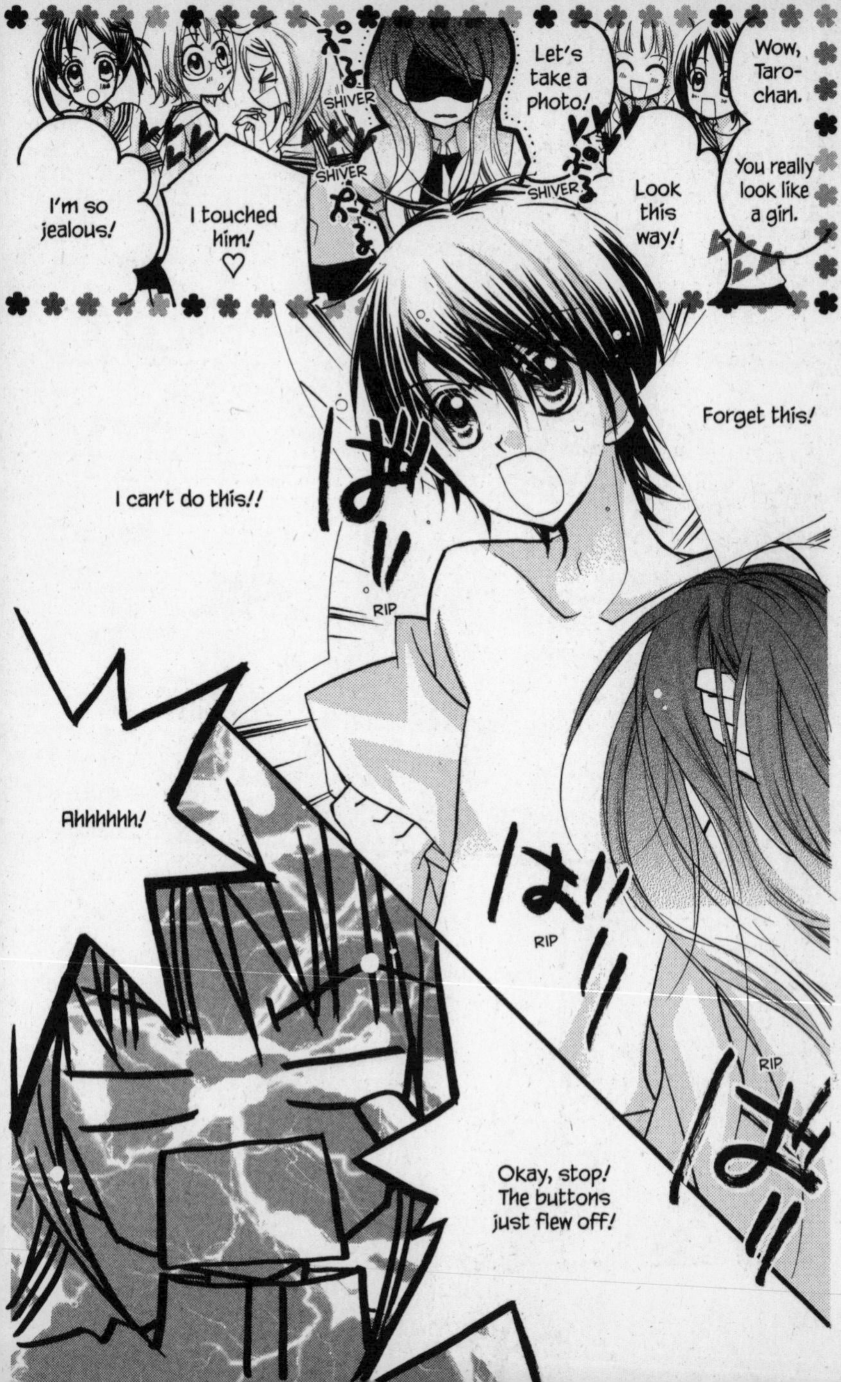
Wow, Taro-chan.
You really look like a girl.
Look this way!
Let's take a photo!
SHIVER
SHIVER
SHIVER
I touched him! ♡
I'm so jealous!
Forget this!
I can't do this!!
RIP
Ahhhhhh!
RIP
RIP
Okay, stop! The buttons just flew off!

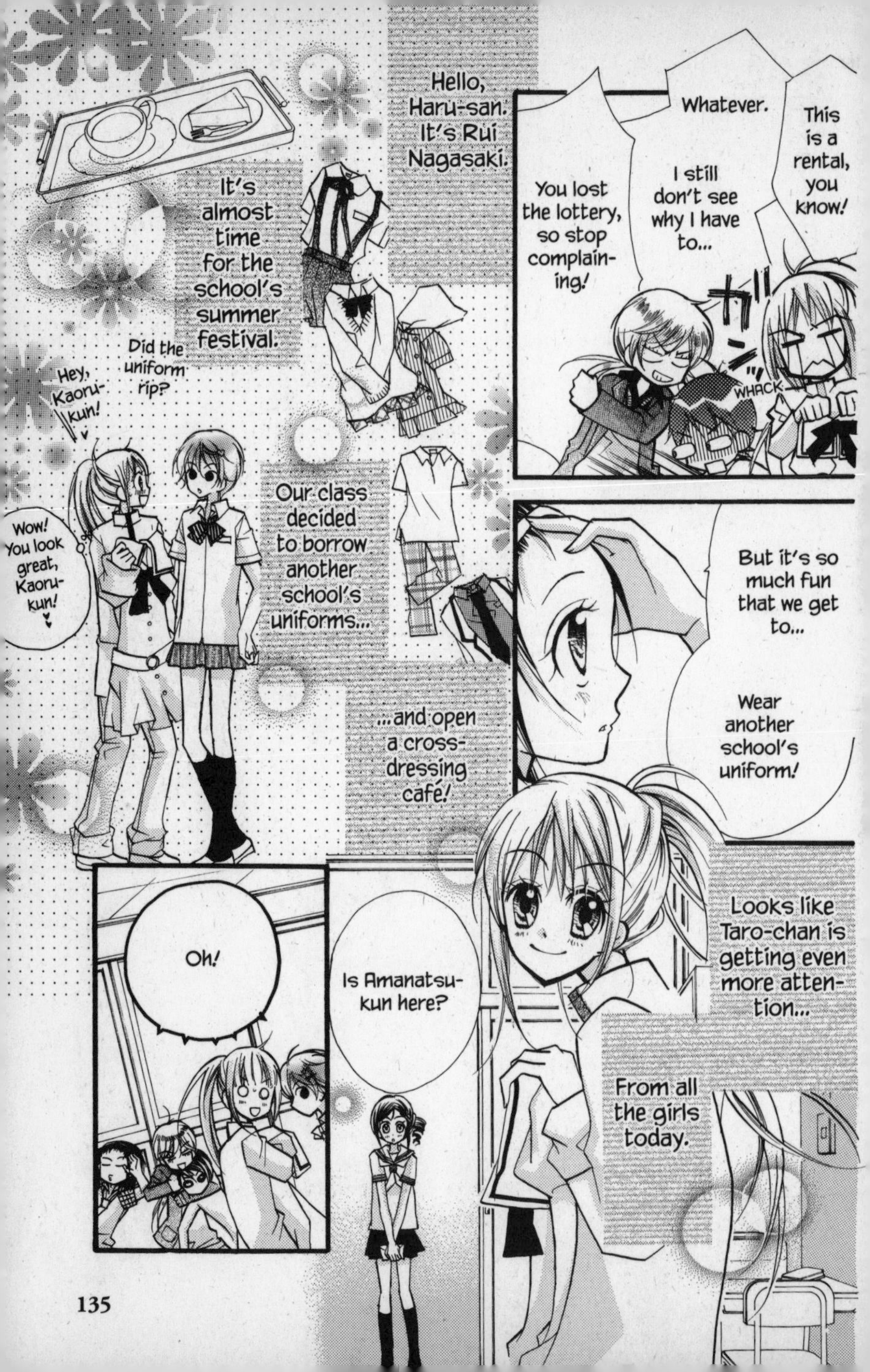
This is a rental, you know!
Whatever.
I still don't see why I have to...
You lost the lottery, so stop complain-ing!
WHACK
But it's so much fun that we get to...
Wear another school's uniform!
Hello, Haru-san. It's Rui Nagasaki.
It's almost time for the school's summer festival.
Did the uniform rip?
Hey, Kaoru-kun!
Our class decided to borrow another school's uniforms...
Wow! You look great, Kaoru-kun!
...and open a cross-dressing café!
Looks like Taro-chan is getting even more atten-tion...
From all the girls today.
Is Amanatsu-kun here?
Oh!

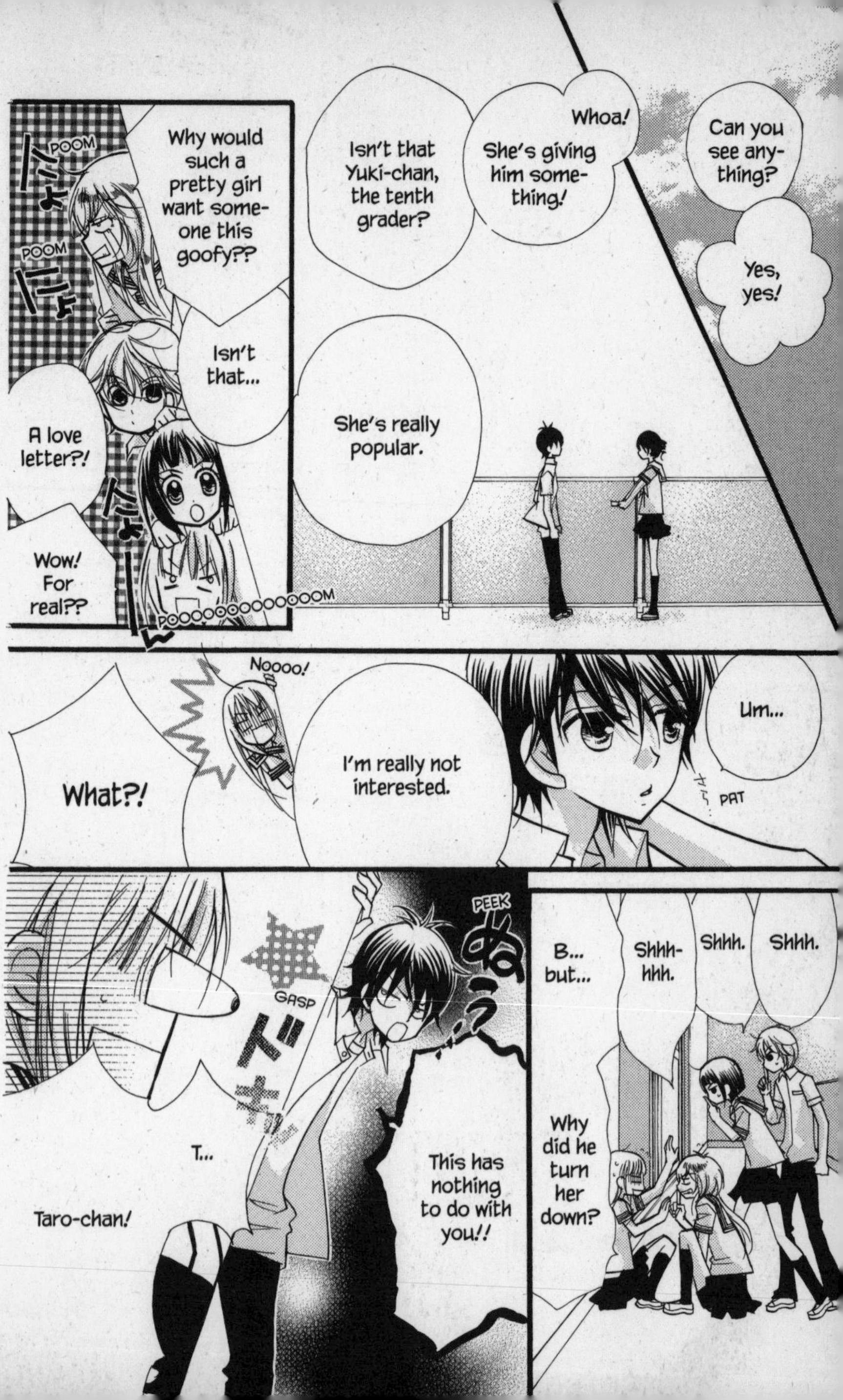
Can you see anything?
Yes, yes!
Whoa!
She's giving him something!
Isn't that Yuki-chan, the tenth grader?
She's really popular.
Why would such a pretty girl want someone this goofy??
POOM
POOM
Isn't that...
A love letter?!
Wow! For real??
POOOOOOOOOOOOOM
Um...
PAT
I'm really not interested.
Noooo!
What?!
Shhh.
Shhh.
Shhh-hhh.
B... but...
Why did he turn her down?
PEEK
GASP
This has nothing to do with you!!
T...
Taro-chan!

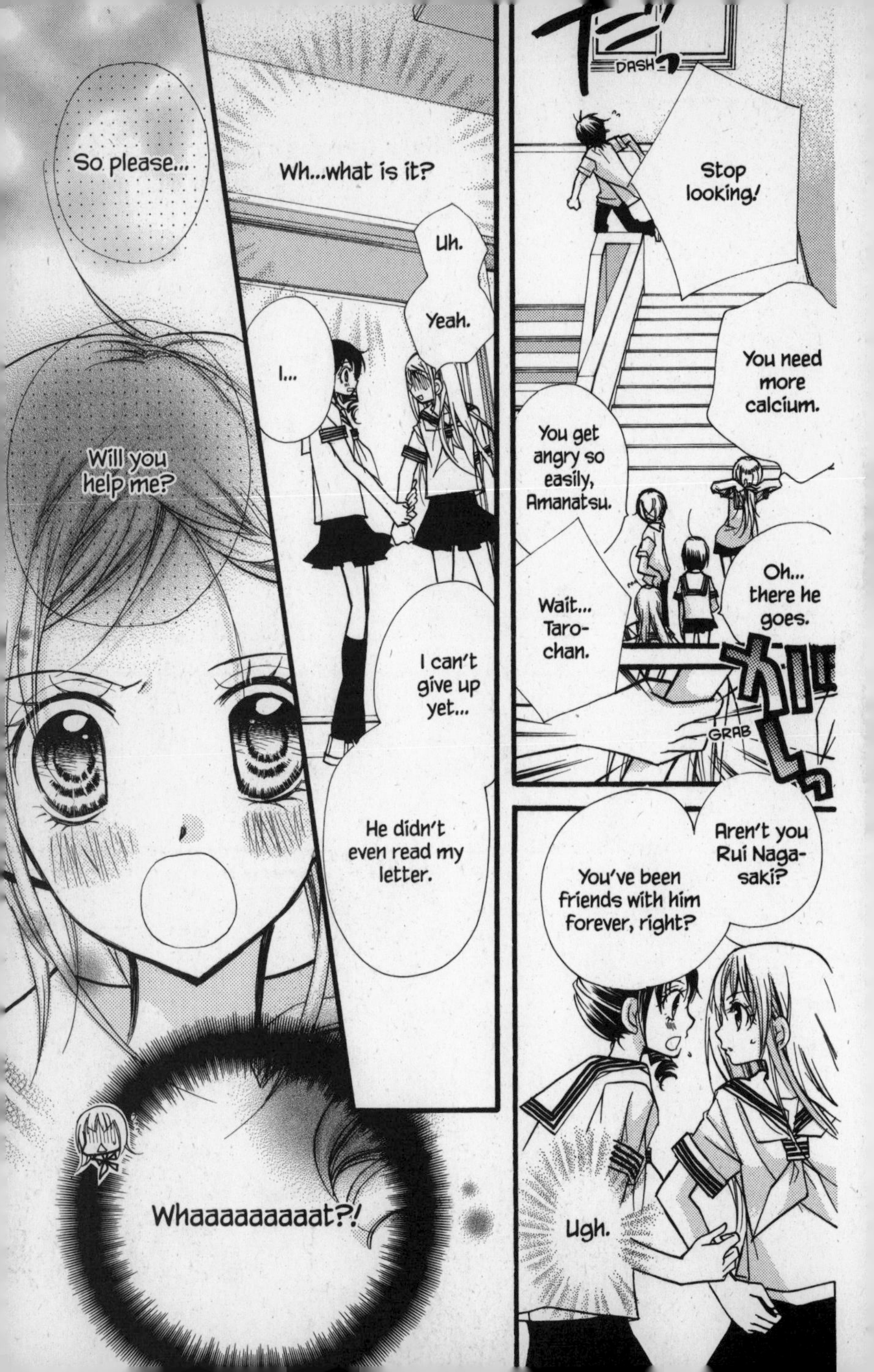
DASH
Stop looking!
You need more calcium.
You get angry so easily, Amanatsu.
Oh... there he goes.
Wait... Taro-chan.
GRAB
Aren't you Rui Nagasaki?
You've been friends with him forever, right?
Ugh.
Wh...what is it?
Uh.
Yeah.
I...
I can't give up yet...
He didn't even read my letter.
So please...
Will you help me?
Whaaaaaaaaat?!

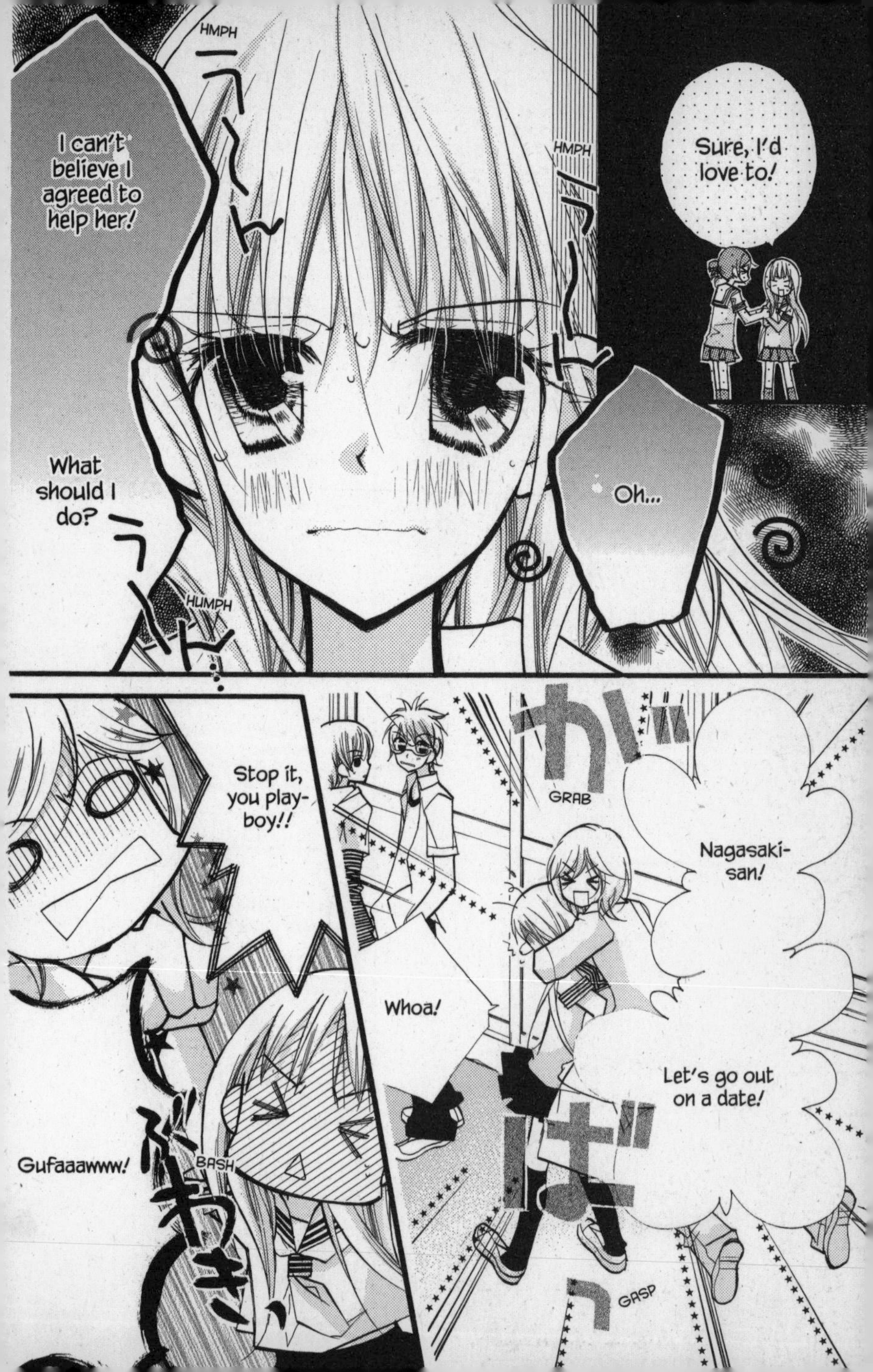
Sure, I'd love to!
Oh...
HMPH
HMPH
I can't believe I agreed to help her!
What should I do?
HUMPH
GRAB
Nagasaki-san!
Let's go out on a date!
Whoa!
GASP
Stop it, you play-boy!!
BASH
Gufaaawww!

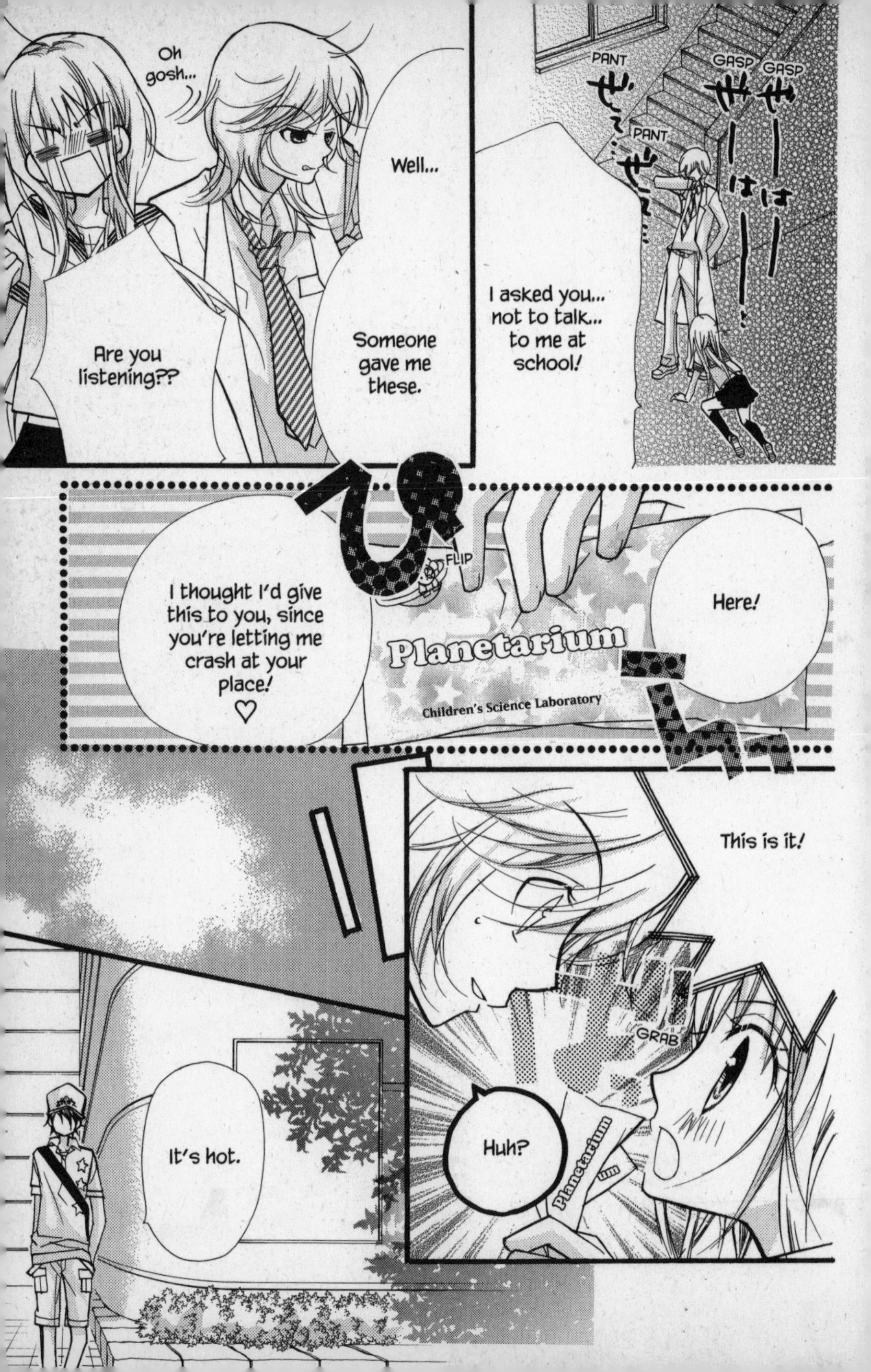
PANT
PANT
GASP GASP
I asked you... not to talk... to me at school!
Well...
Someone gave me these.
Oh gosh...
Are you listening??
Here!
FLIP
Planetarium
Children's Science Laboratory
I thought I'd give this to you, since you're letting me crash at your place! ♡
This is it!
GRAB
Planetarium
Huh?
It's hot.

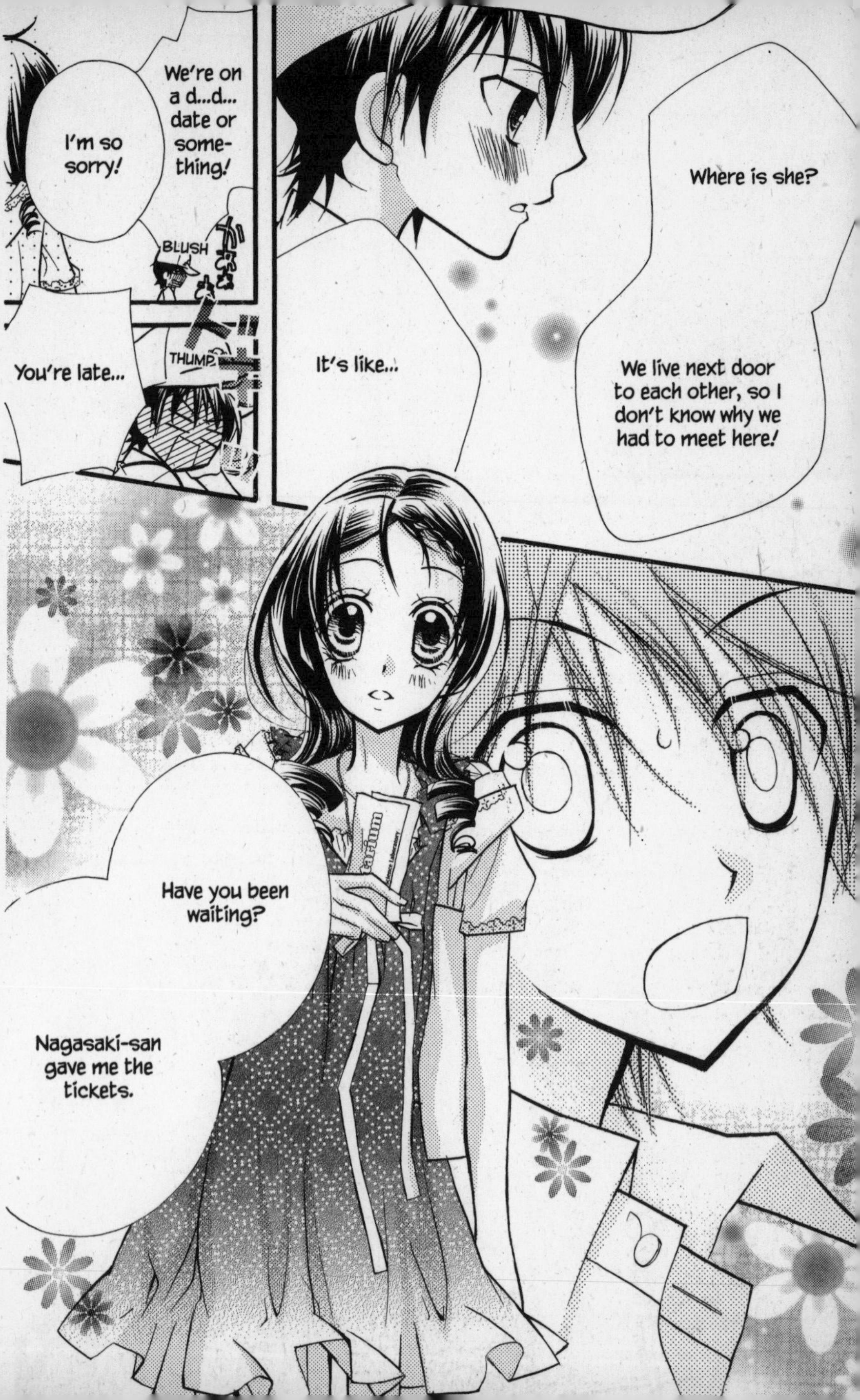
Where is she?
We live next door to each other, so I don't know why we had to meet here!
It's like...
We're on a d...d... date or some-thing!
I'm so sorry!
BLUSH
THUMP
You're late...
Have you been waiting?
Nagasaki-san gave me the tickets.

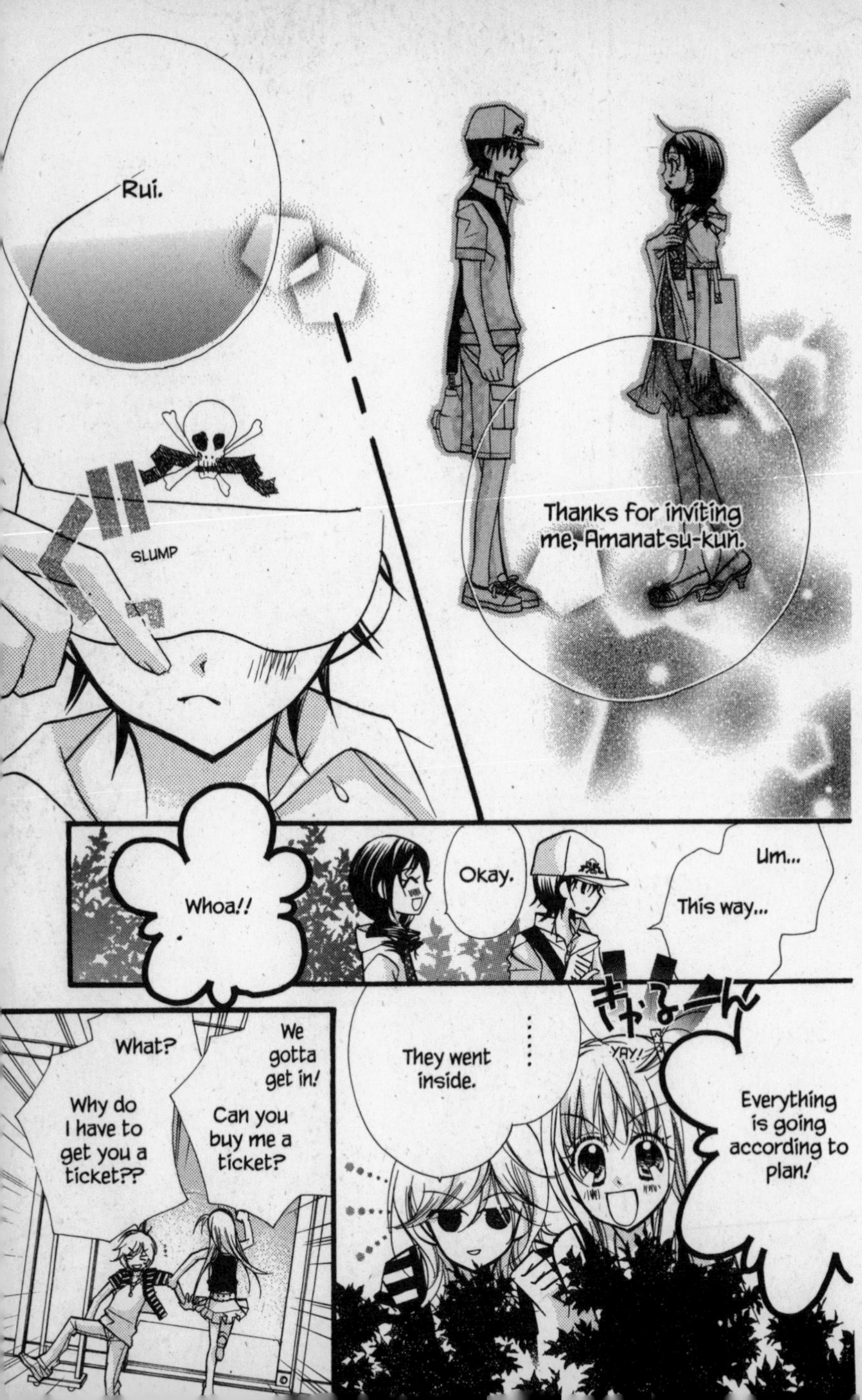
Thanks for inviting me, Amanatsu-kun.
Rui.
SLUMP
Um...
This way...
Okay.
Whoa!!
YAY!
Everything is going according to plan!
......
They went inside.
We gotta get in!
Can you buy me a ticket?
What?
Why do I have to get you a ticket??

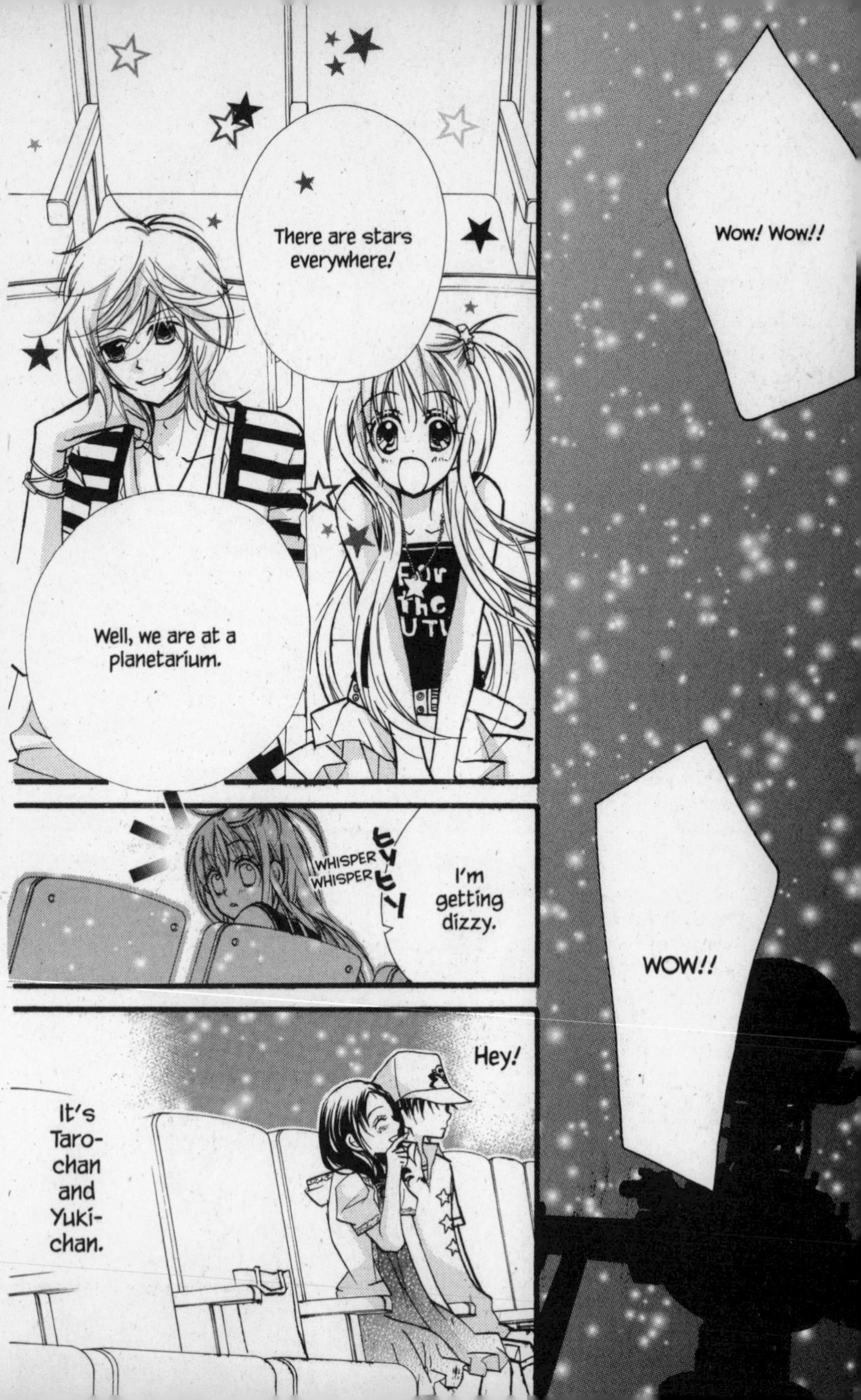
Wow! Wow!!
WOW!!
There are stars everywhere!
Well, we are at a planetarium.
I'm getting dizzy.
ヒソヒソ
WHISPER WHISPER
Hey!
It's Taro-chan and Yuki-chan.

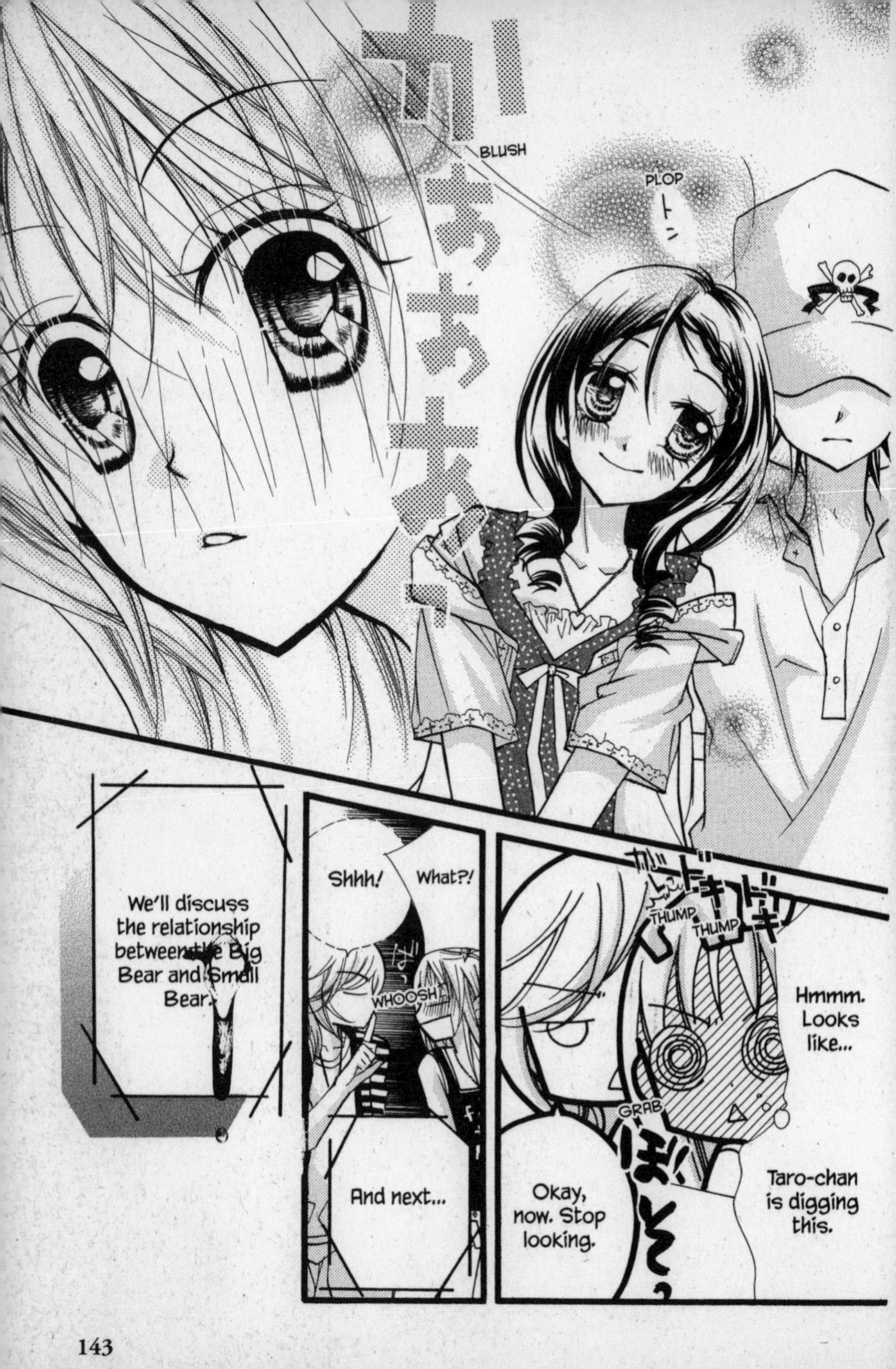
BLUSH
PLOP
THUMP
THUMP
Hmmm. Looks like...
Taro-chan is digging this.
GRAB
Okay, now. Stop looking.
What?!
Shhh!
WHOOSH
And next...
We'll discuss the relationship between the Big Bear and Small Bear.

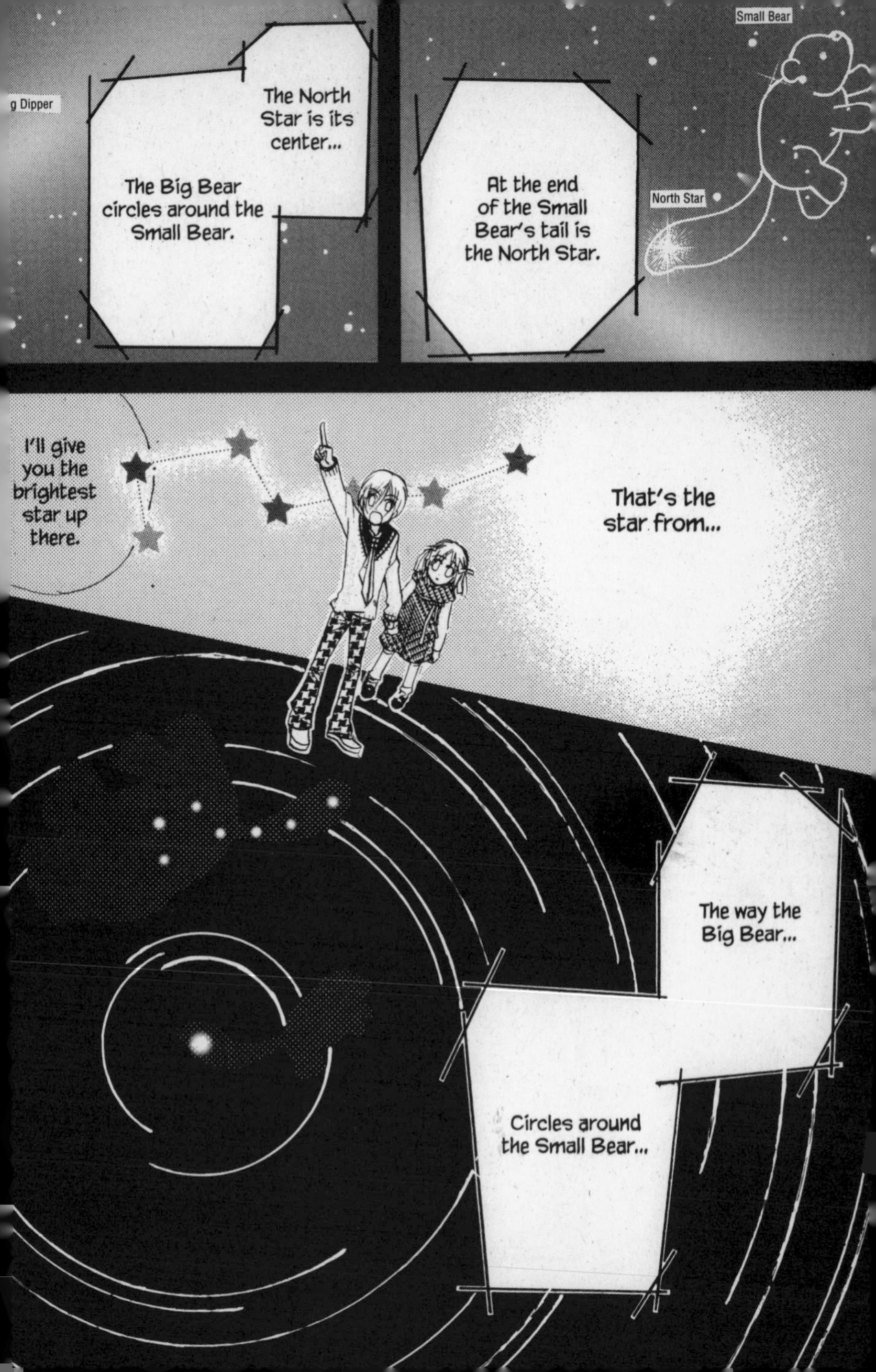
Small Bear
North Star
At the end of the Small Bear's tail is the North Star.
g Dipper
The North Star is its center...
The Big Bear circles around the Small Bear.
That's the star from...
I'll give you the brightest star up there.
The way the Big Bear...
Circles around the Small Bear...

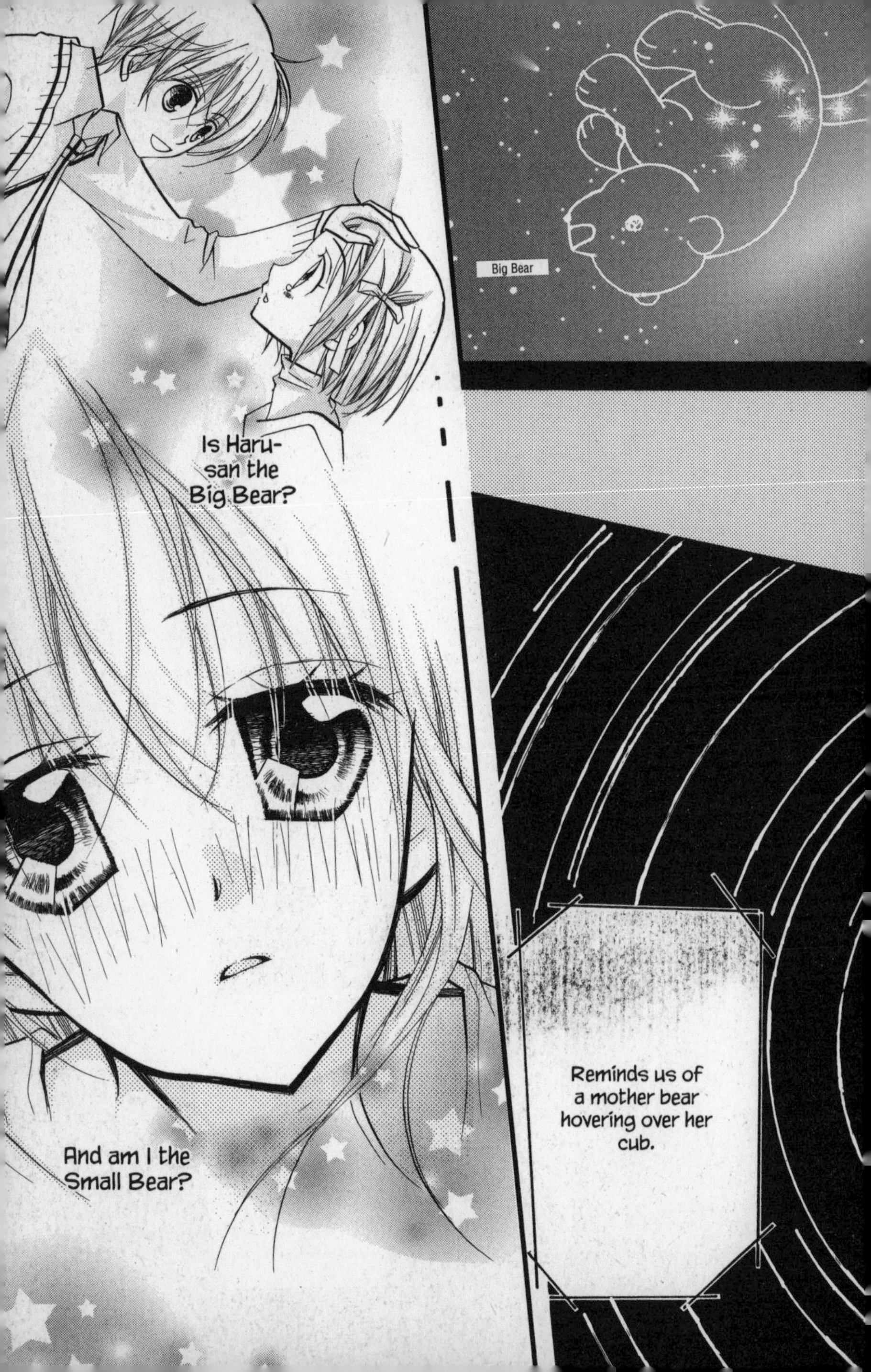
Big Bear
Reminds us of a mother bear hovering over her cub.
Is Haru-san the Big Bear?
And am I the Small Bear?

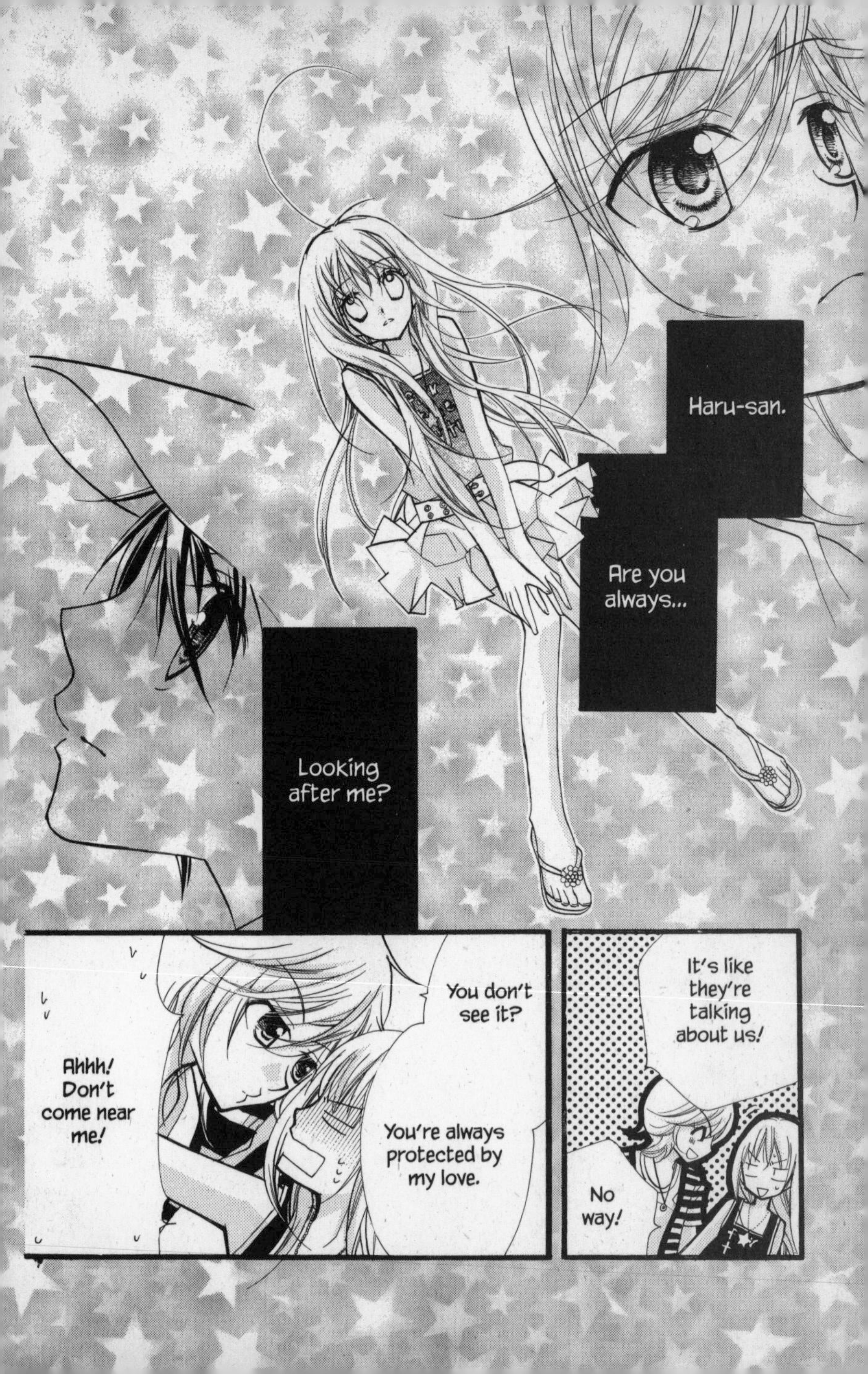
Haru-san.
Are you always...
Looking after me?
It's like they're talking about us!
No way!
You don't see it?
You're always protected by my love.
Ahhh! Don't come near me!

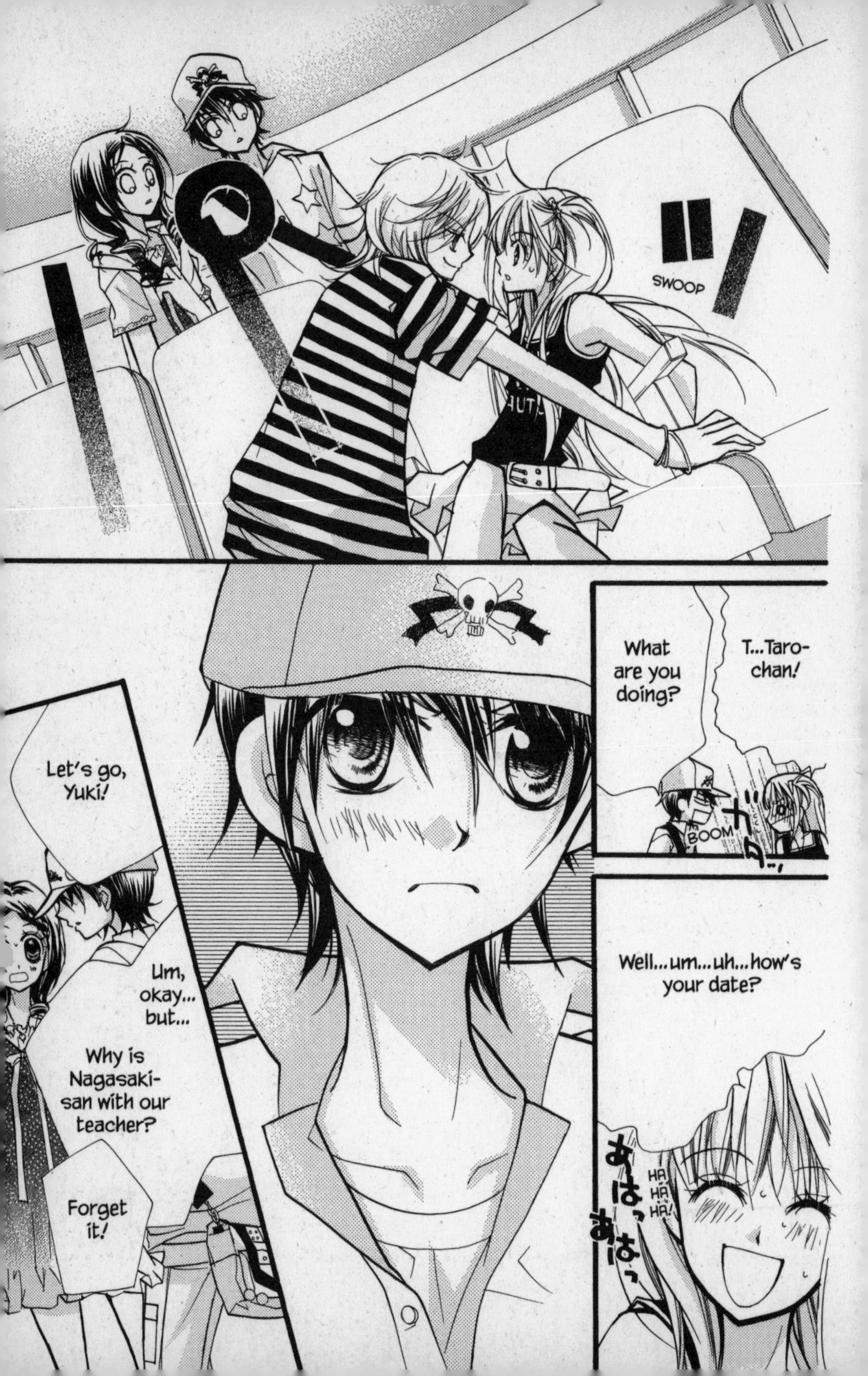
SWOOP
T...Taro-chan!
What are you doing?
BOOM
Well...um...uh...how's your date?
あはっ あはっ
HA HA HA!
Let's go, Yuki!
Um, okay... but...
Why is Nagasaki-san with our teacher?
Forget it!

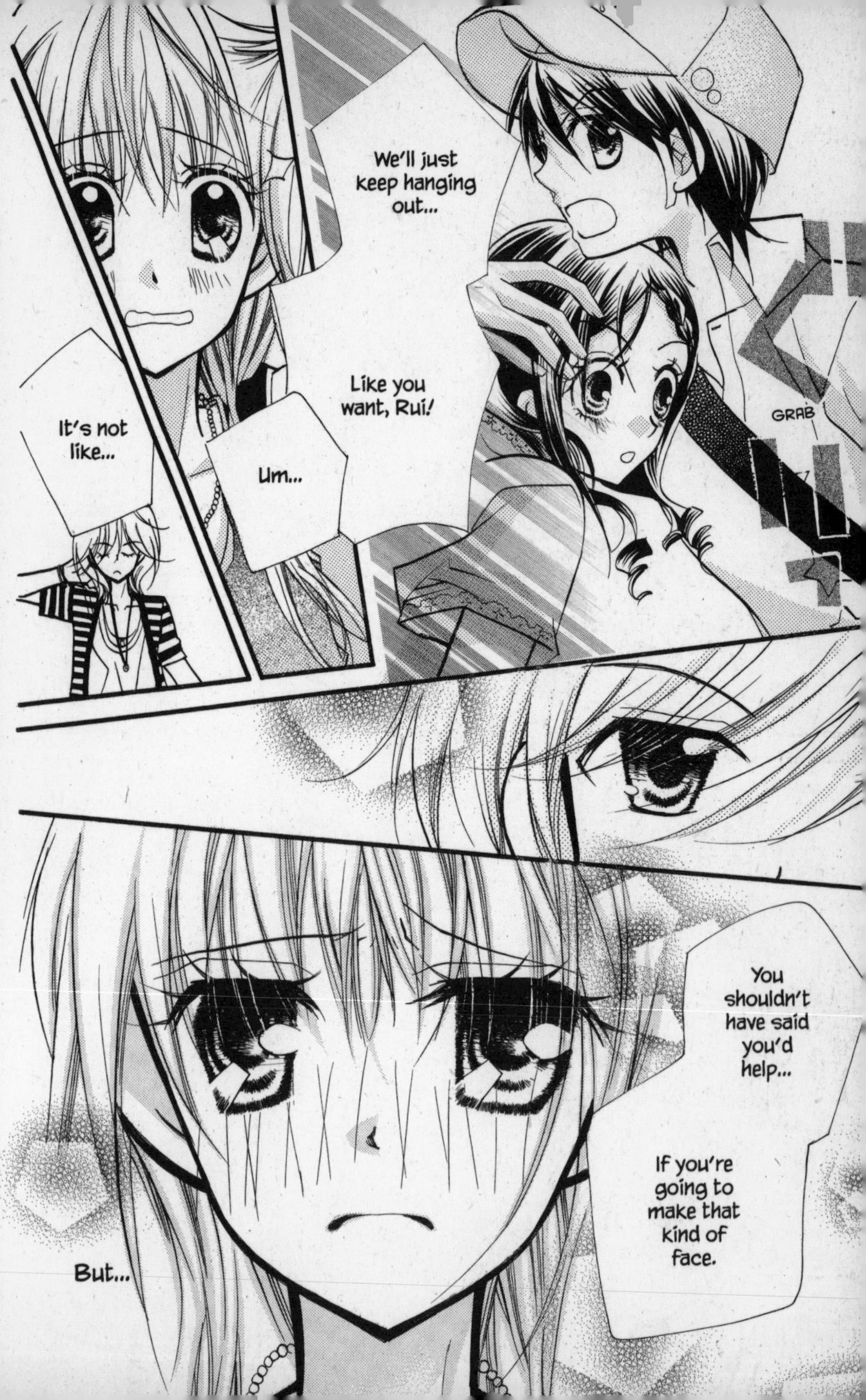
We'll just keep hanging out...
Like you want, Rui!
GRAB
Um...
It's not like...
You shouldn't have said you'd help...
If you're going to make that kind of face.
But...

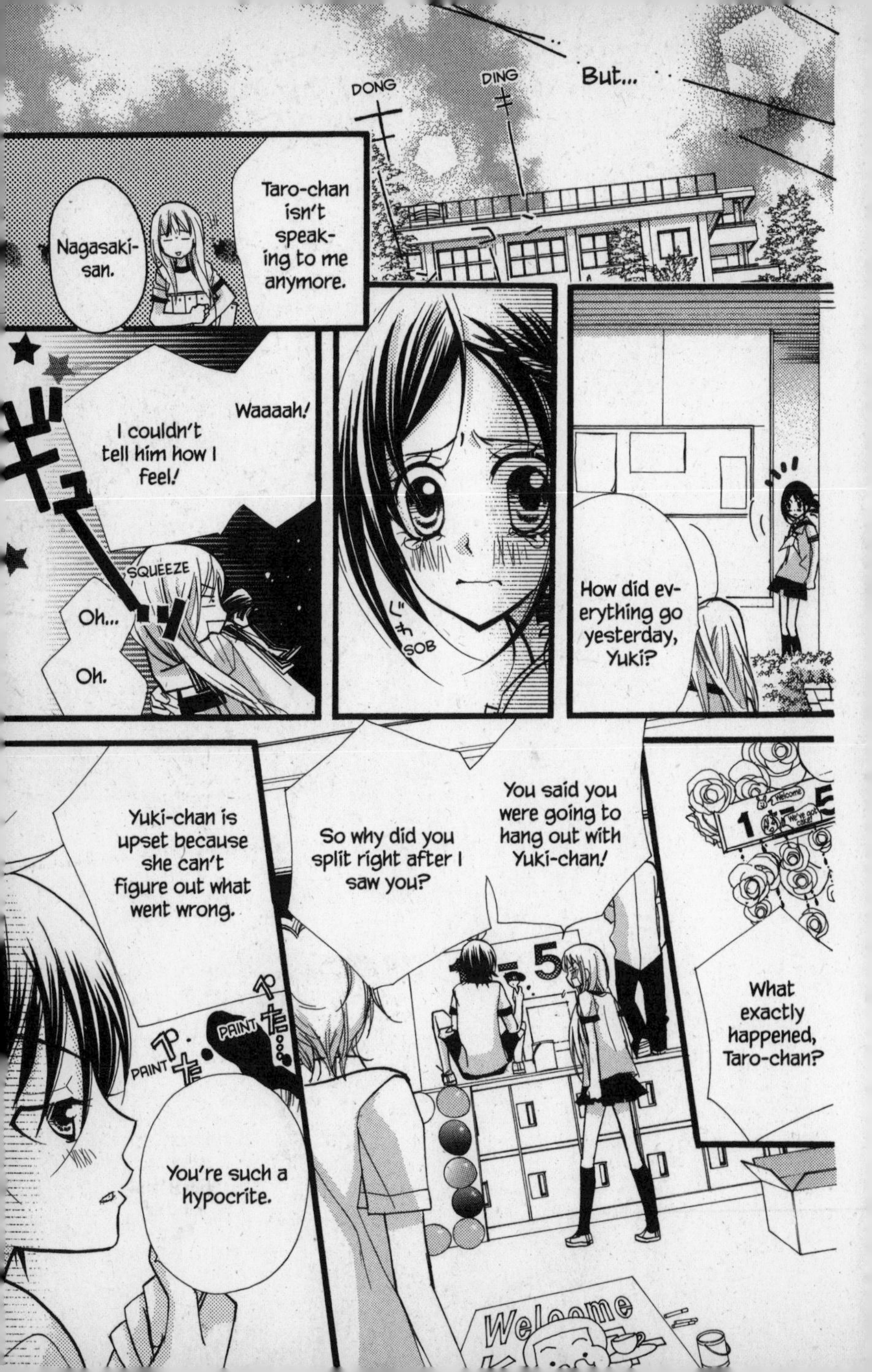
But...
DING
DONG
Taro-chan isn't speak-ing to me anymore.
Nagasaki-san.
How did ev-erything go yesterday, Yuki?
SOB
Waaaah!
I couldn't tell him how I feel!
SQUEEZE
Oh...
Oh.
What exactly happened, Taro-chan?
You said you were going to hang out with Yuki-chan!
So why did you split right after I saw you?
Yuki-chan is upset because she can't figure out what went wrong.
PRINT
PRINT
You're such a hypocrite.
Welcome

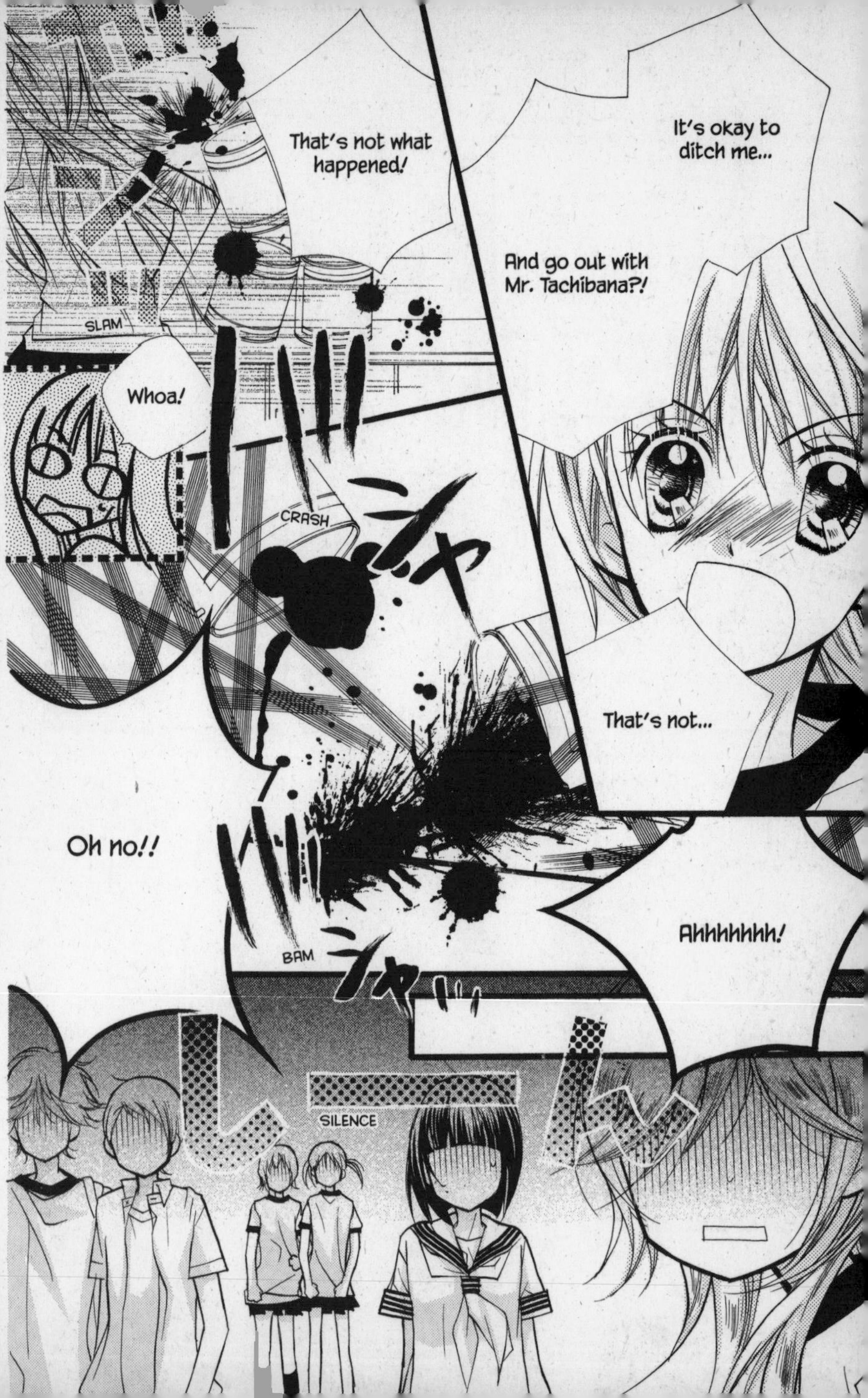
It's okay to ditch me...
And go out with Mr. Tachibana?!
That's not...
That's not what happened!
SLAM
Whoa!
CRASH
Ahhhhhhh!
Oh no!!
BAM
SILENCE

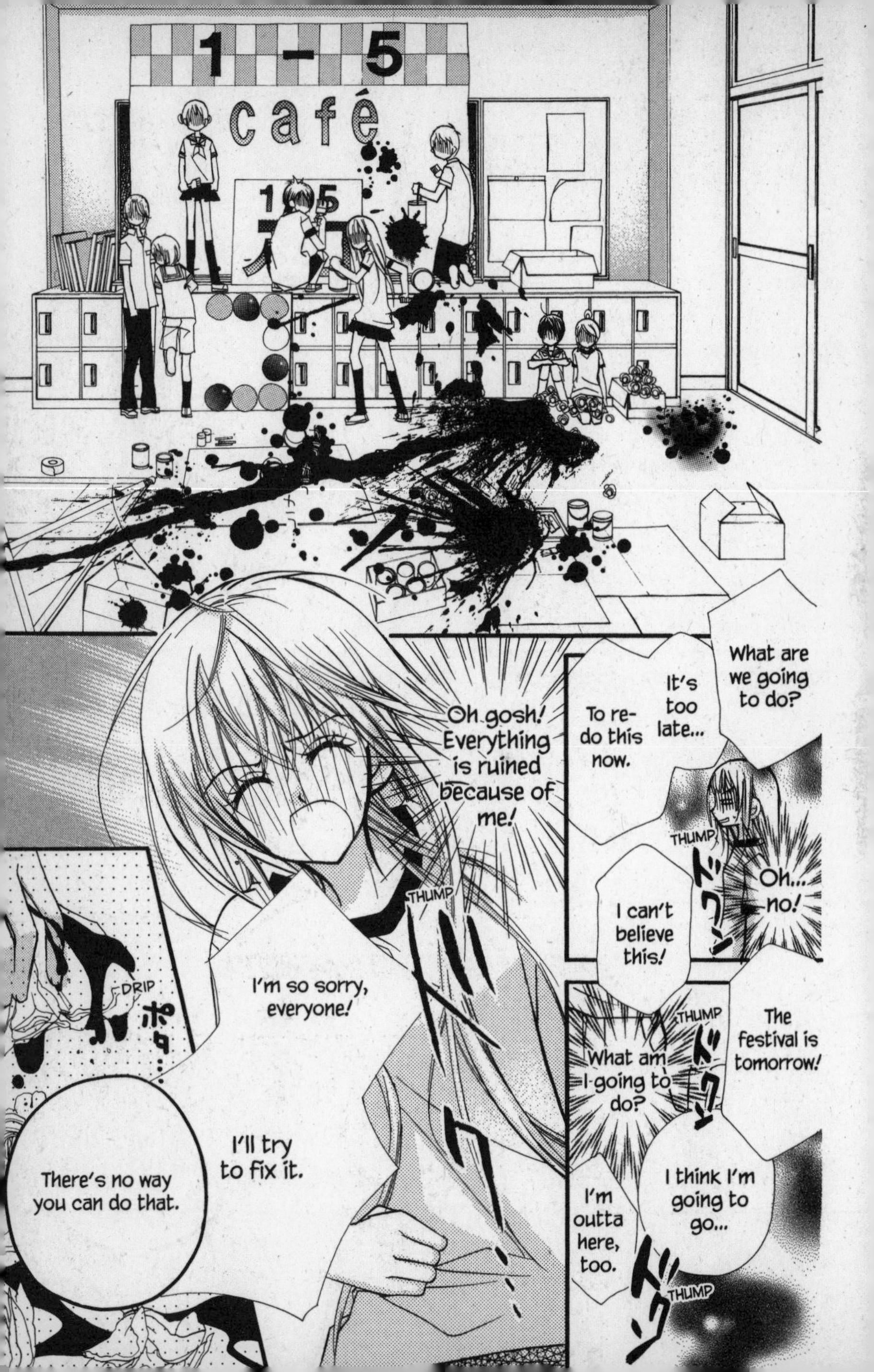
1-5
café
What are we going to do?
It's too late...
To re-do this now.
THUMP
Oh... no!
I can't believe this!
The festival is tomorrow!
THUMP
What am I going to do?
I think I'm going to go...
I'm outta here, too.
THUMP
Oh gosh! Everything is ruined because of me!
THUMP
I'm so sorry, everyone!
I'll try to fix it.
DRIP
ポタ
There's no way you can do that.

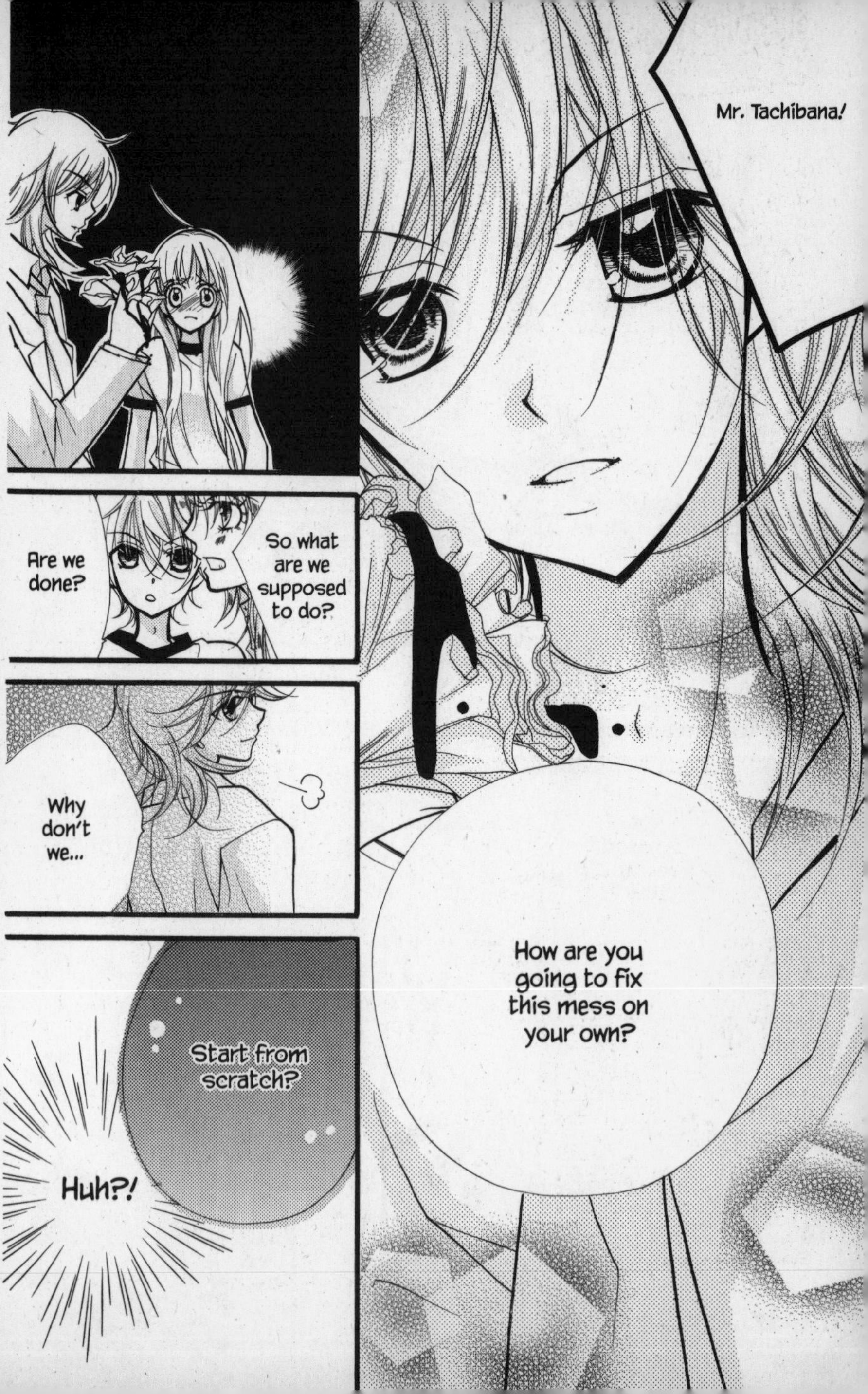
Mr. Tachibana!
How are you going to fix this mess on your own?
So what are we supposed to do?
Are we done?
Why don't we...
Start from scratch?
Huh?!

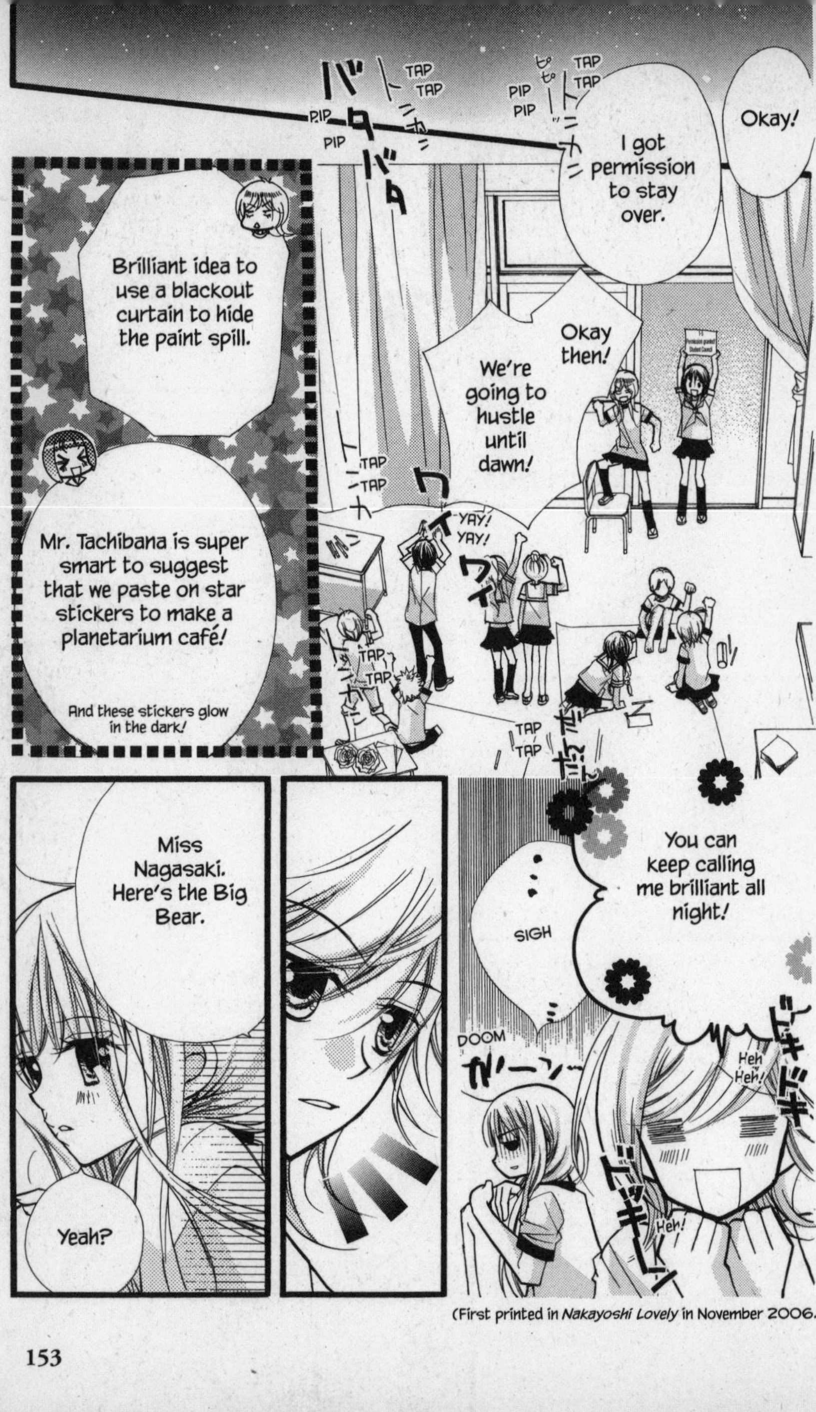
TAP TAP
PIP PIP
TAP TAP
PIP PIP
Okay!
I got permission to stay over.
Okay then!
We're going to hustle until dawn!
TAP TAP
YAY! YAY!
TAP TAP
TAP TAP
Brilliant idea to use a blackout curtain to hide the paint spill.
Mr. Tachibana is super smart to suggest that we paste on star stickers to make a planetarium café!
And these stickers glow in the dark!
You can keep calling me brilliant all night!
...
SIGH
DOOM
Heh Heh!
Heh!
Miss Nagasaki. Here's the Big Bear.
Yeah?

(First printed in *Nakayoshi Lovely* in November 2006.)

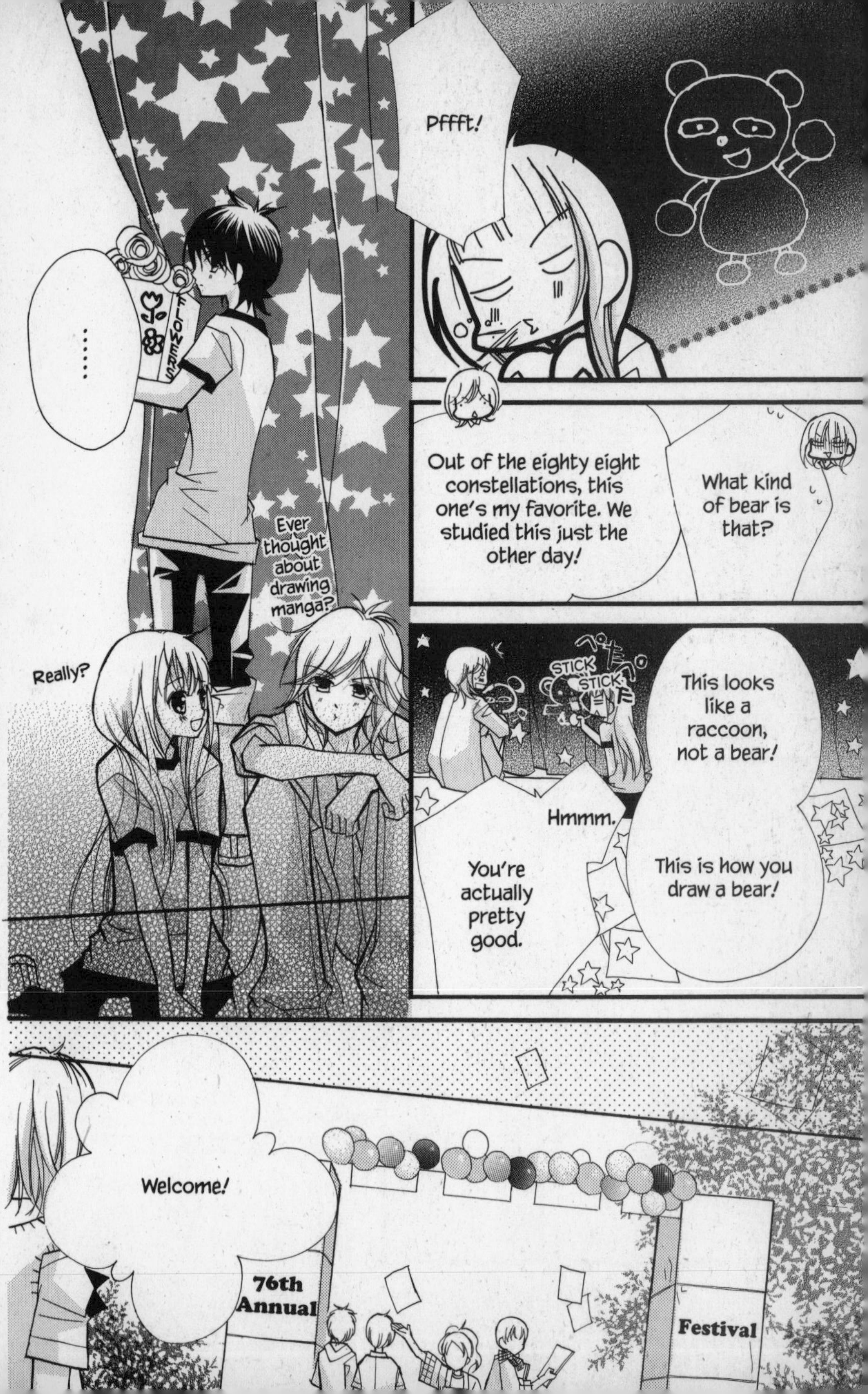
Pffft!
What kind of bear is that?
Out of the eighty eight constellations, this one's my favorite. We studied this just the other day!
STICK STICK
This looks like a raccoon, not a bear!
This is how you draw a bear!
Hmmm.
You're actually pretty good.
FLOWERS
......
Ever thought about drawing manga?
Really?
Welcome!
76th Annual
Festival

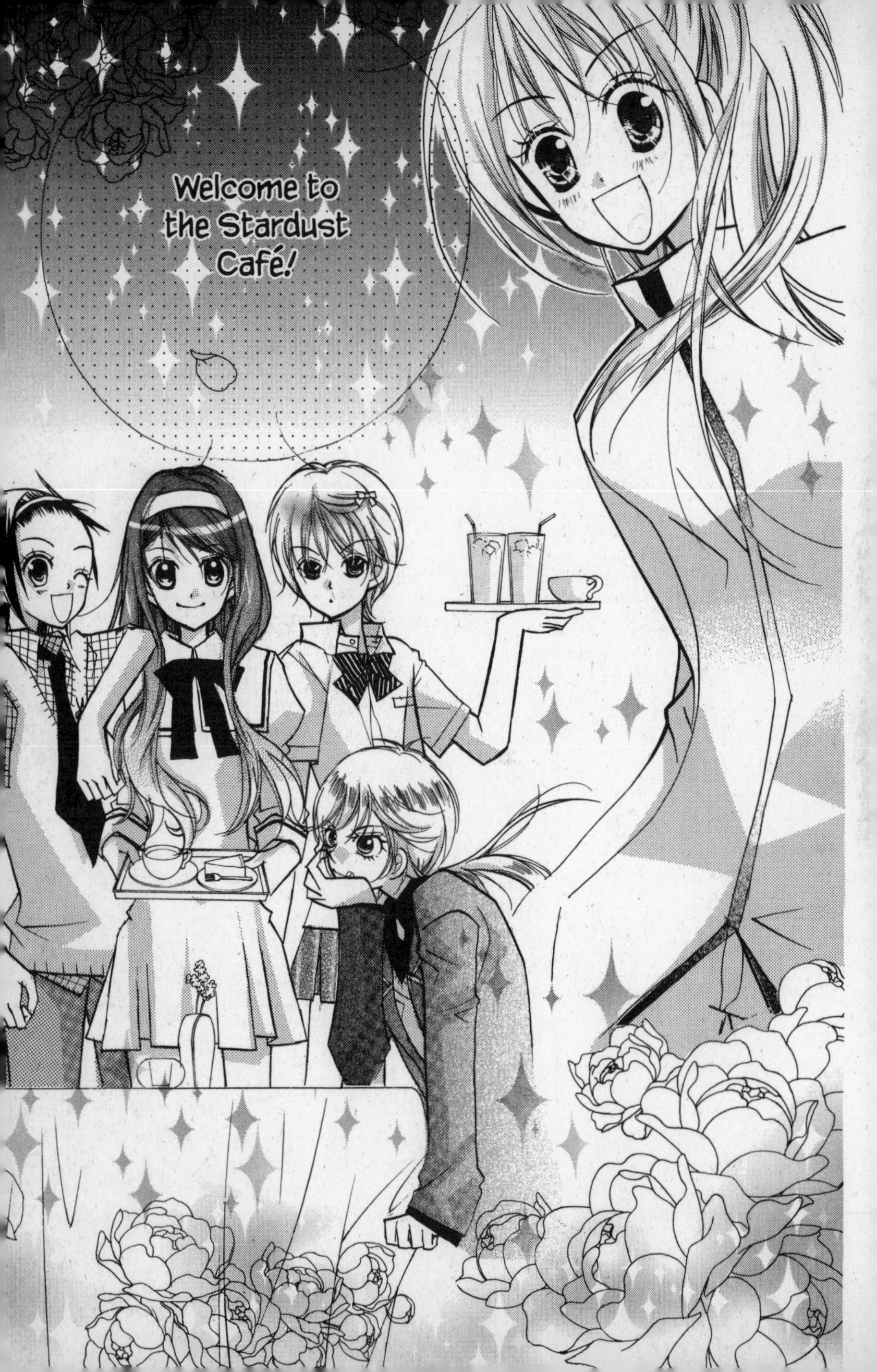
Welcome to the Stardust Café!

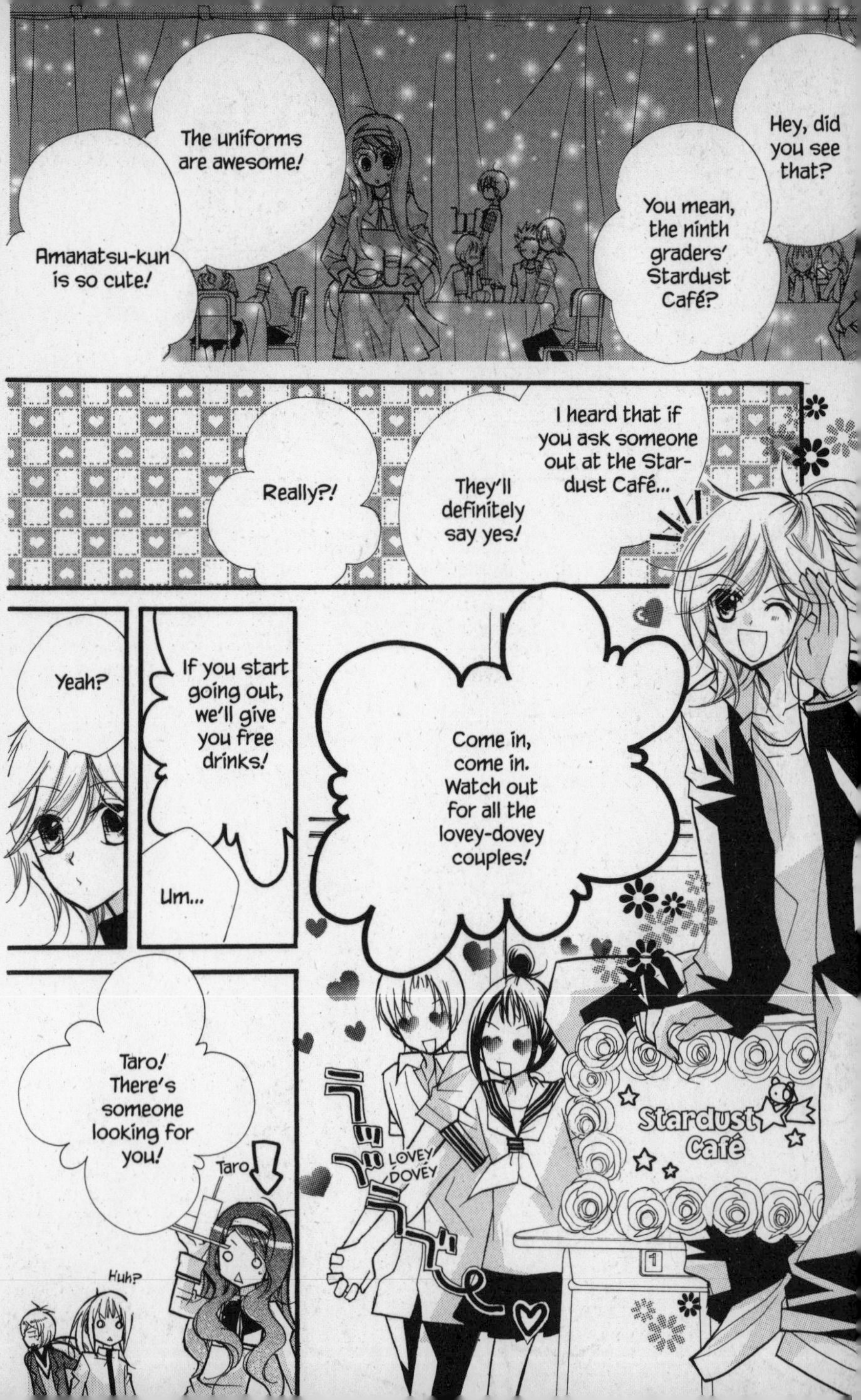
Hey, did you see that?
You mean, the ninth graders' Stardust Café?
The uniforms are awesome!
Amanatsu-kun is so cute!
I heard that if you ask someone out at the Stardust Café...
They'll definitely say yes!
Really?!
Come in, come in. Watch out for all the lovey-dovey couples!
Stardust Café
LOVEY DOVEY
If you start going out, we'll give you free drinks!
Um...
Yeah?
Taro! There's someone looking for you!
Taro
Huh?

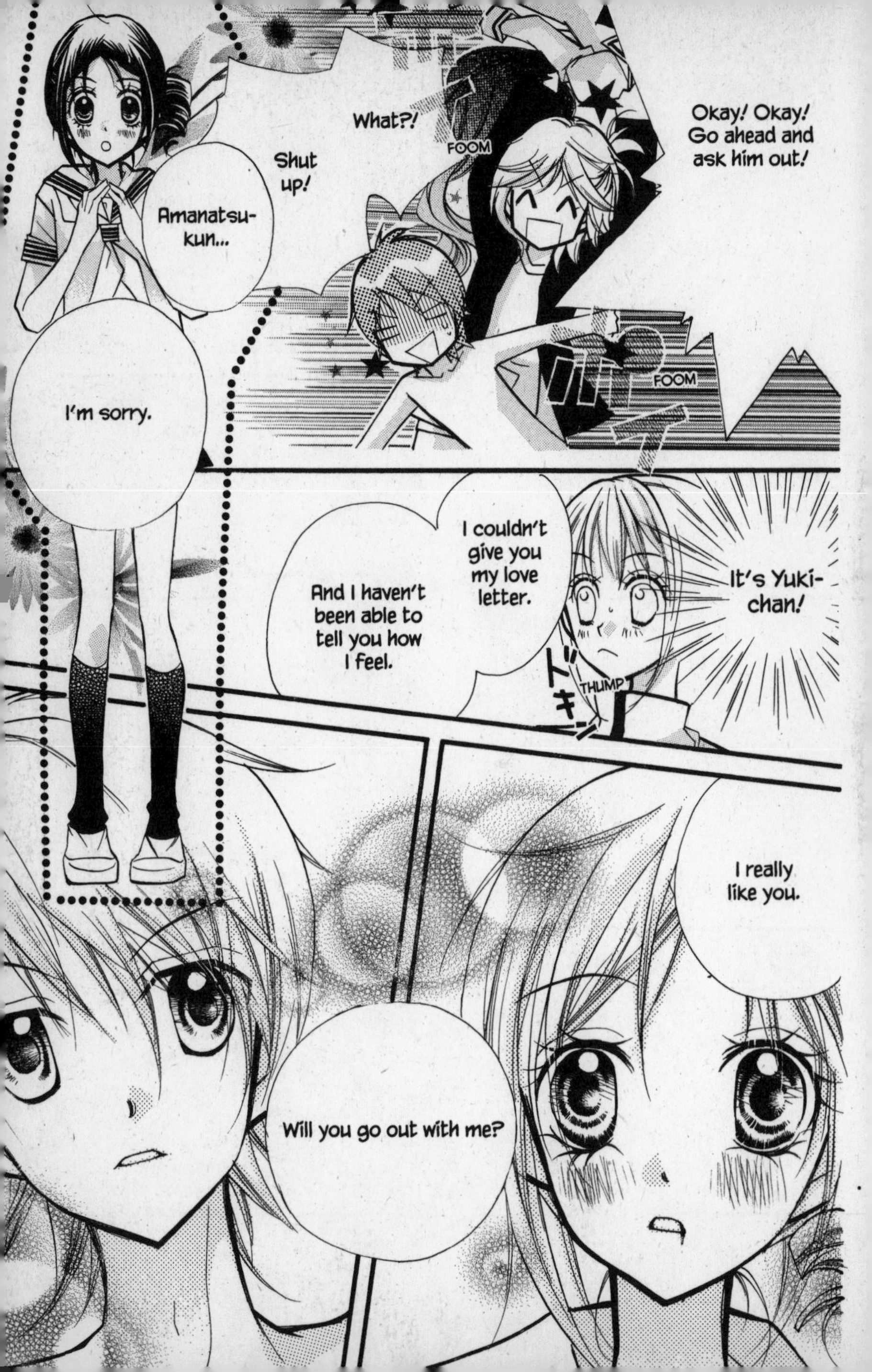
Okay! Okay! Go ahead and ask him out!
FOOM
What?!
Shut up!
FOOM
Amanatsu-kun...
I'm sorry.
It's Yuki-chan!
THUMP
I couldn't give you my love letter.
And I haven't been able to tell you how I feel.
I really like you.
Will you go out with me?

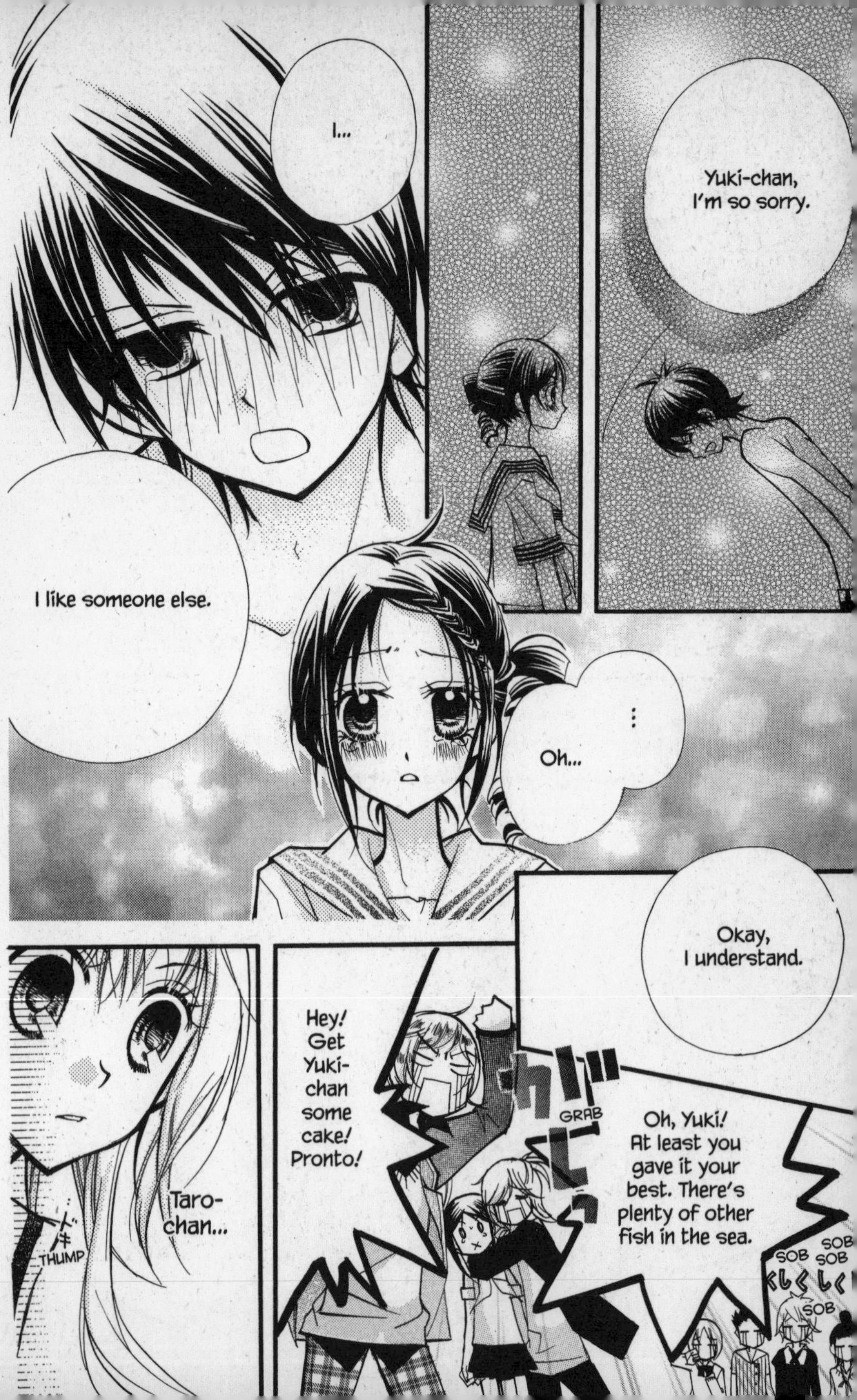
Yuki-chan, I'm so sorry.
I...
I like someone else.
...
Oh...
Okay, I understand.
GRAB
Oh, Yuki! At least you gave it your best. There's plenty of other fish in the sea.
SOB SOB SOB SOB
Hey! Get Yuki-chan some cake! Pronto!
THUMP
Taro-chan...

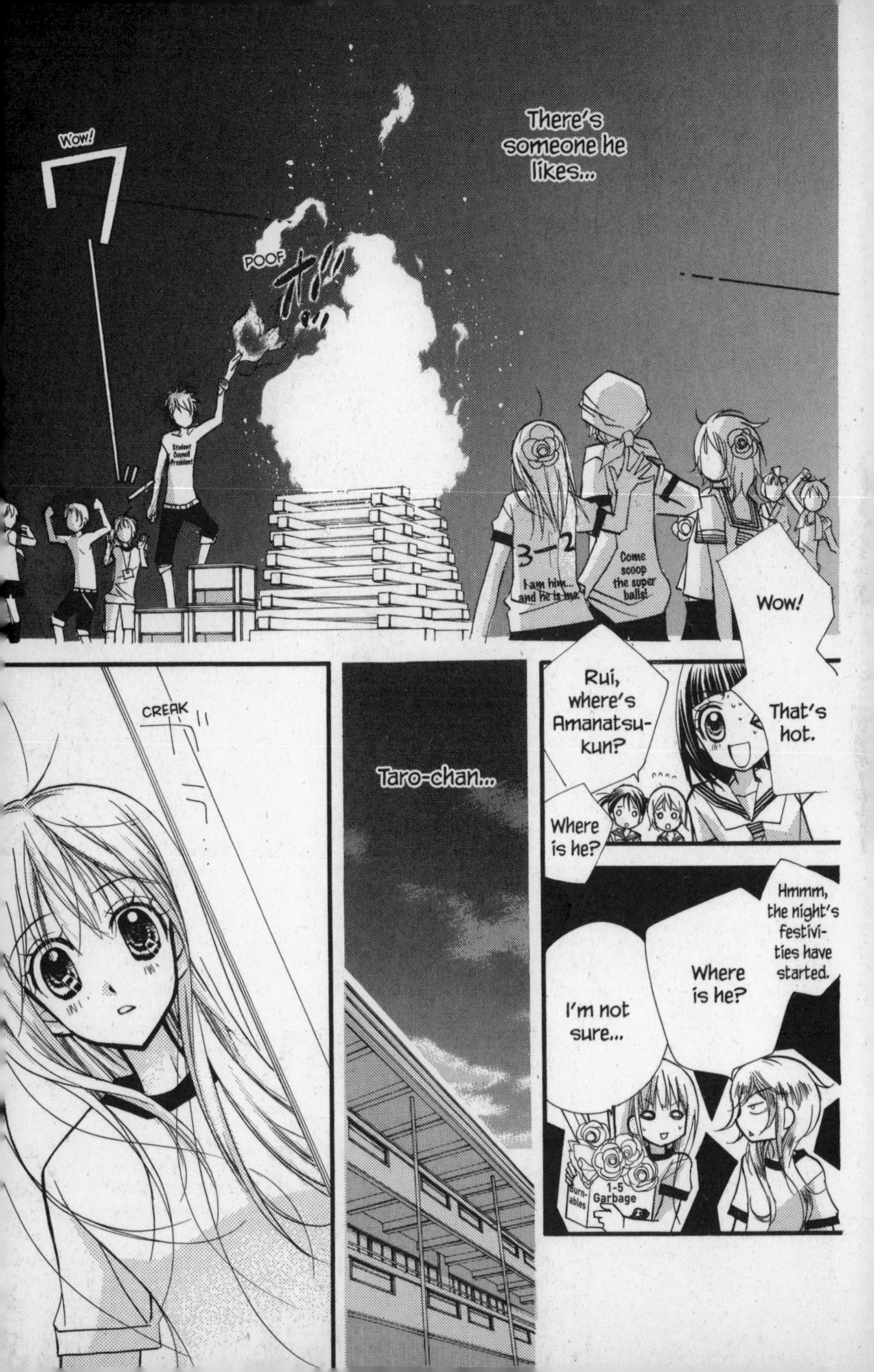
There's someone he likes...
Wow!
Come scoop the super balls!
3-2
I am him... and he is me.
POOF
Student Council President
Wow!
That's hot.
Rui, where's Amanatsu-kun?
Where is he?
Hmmm, the night's festivities have started.
Where is he?
I'm not sure...
1-5 Garbage
Burnables
Taro-chan...
CREAK

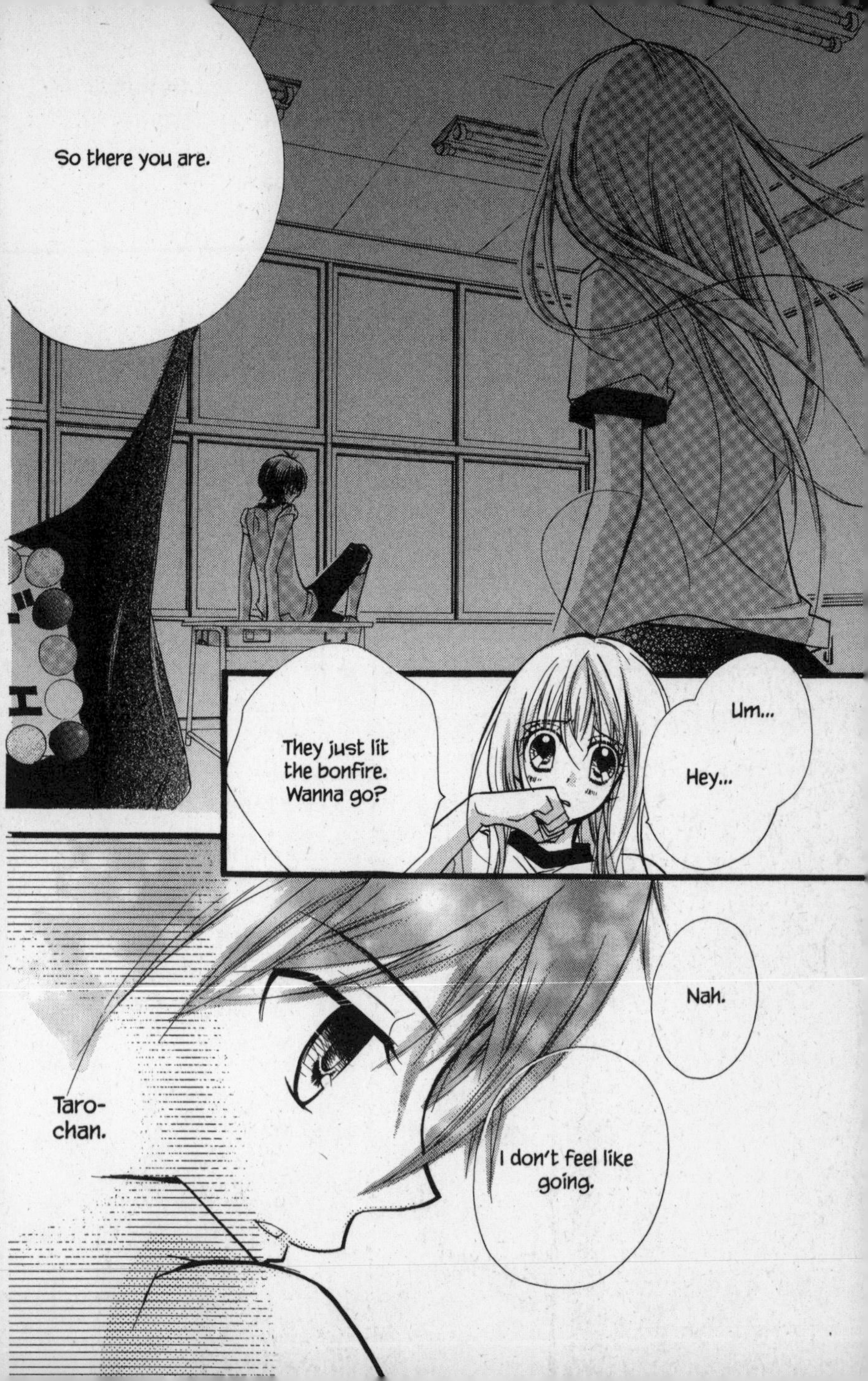
So there you are.
Um...
Hey...
They just lit the bonfire. Wanna go?
Nah.
I don't feel like going.
Taro-chan.

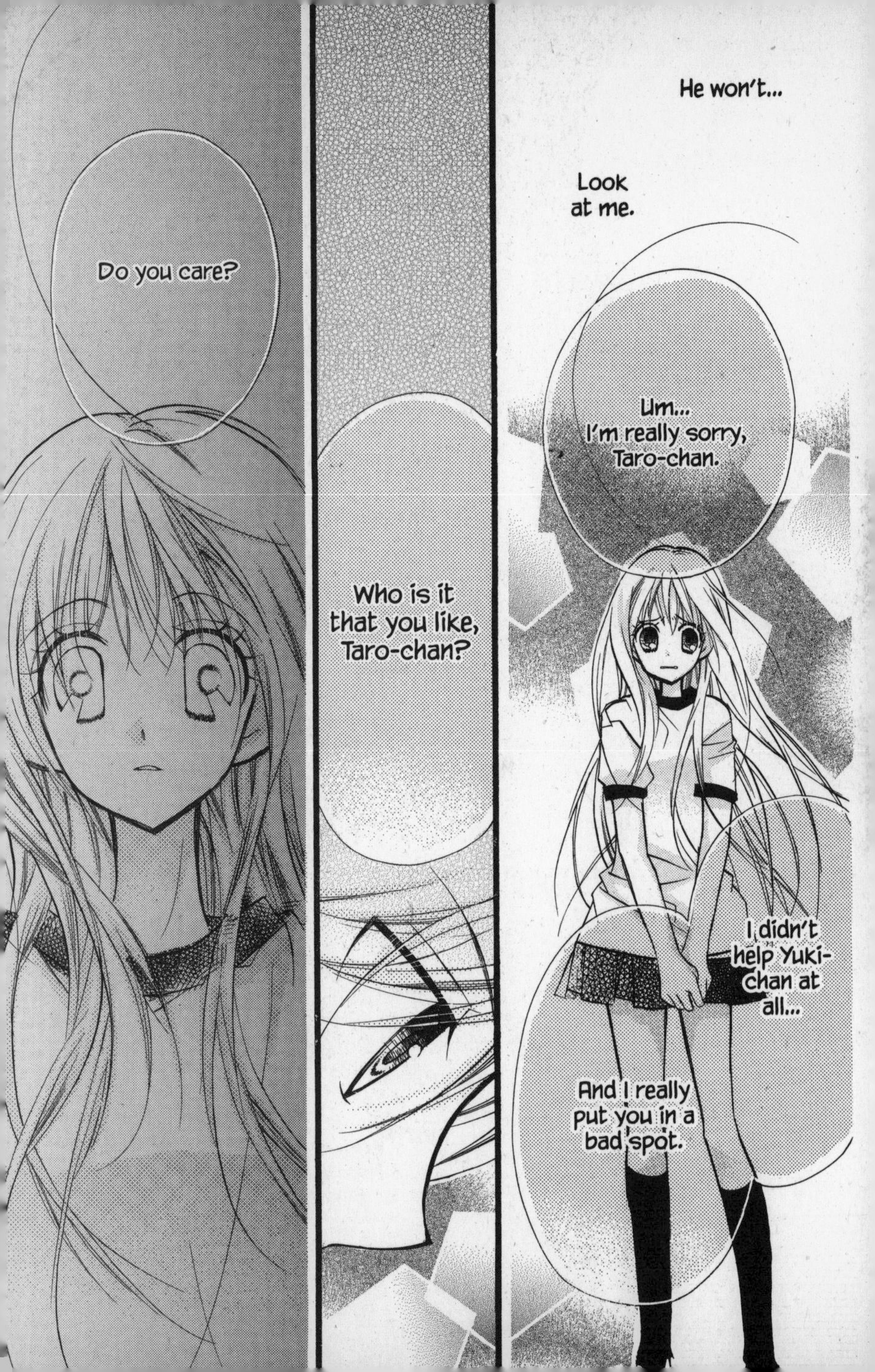
He won't...
Look at me.
Um... I'm really sorry, Taro-chan.
I didn't help Yuki-chan at all...
And I really put you in a bad spot.
Who is it that you like, Taro-chan?
Do you care?

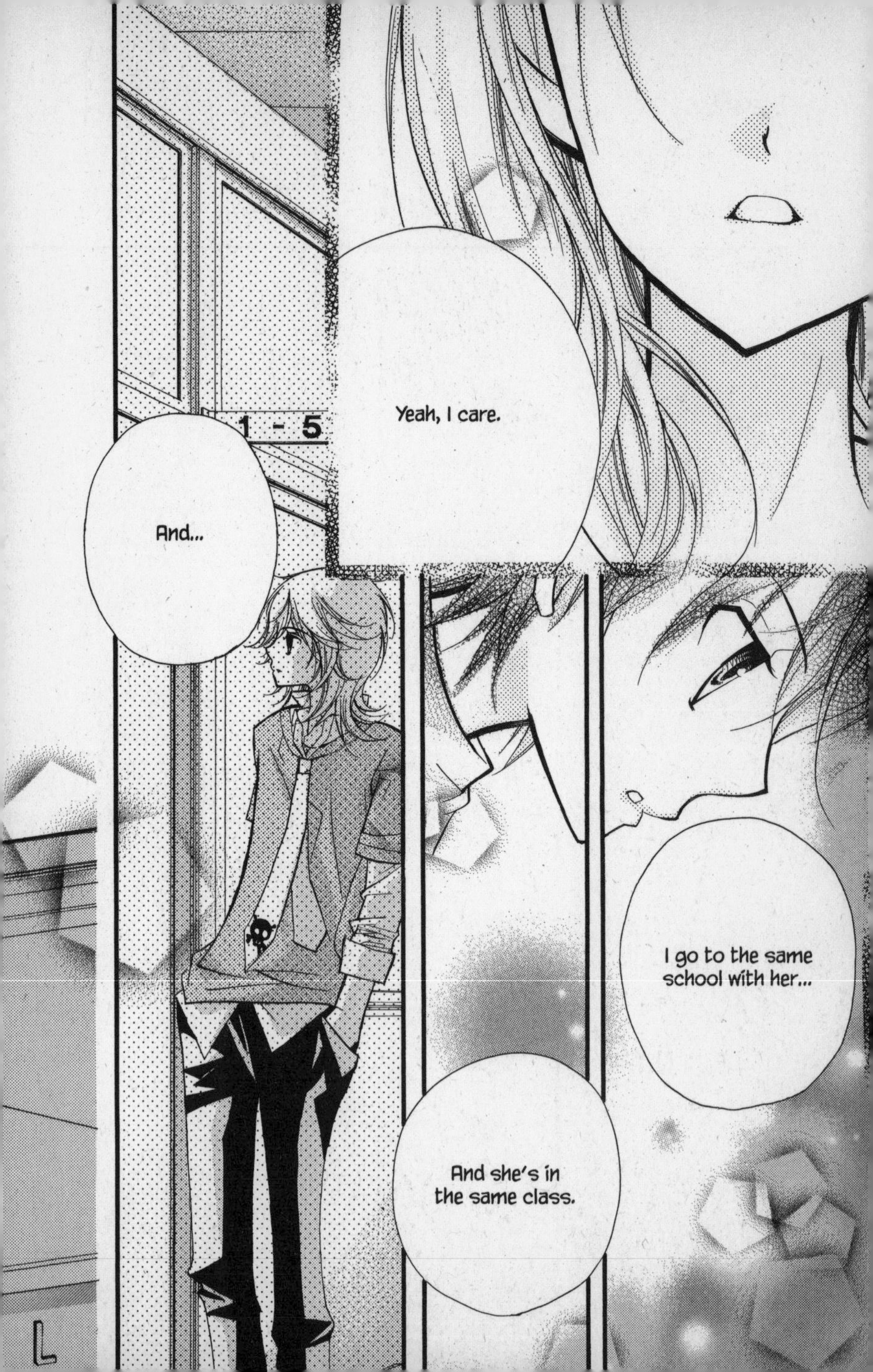
Yeah, I care.
I go to the same school with her...
And she's in the same class.
1 - 5
And...

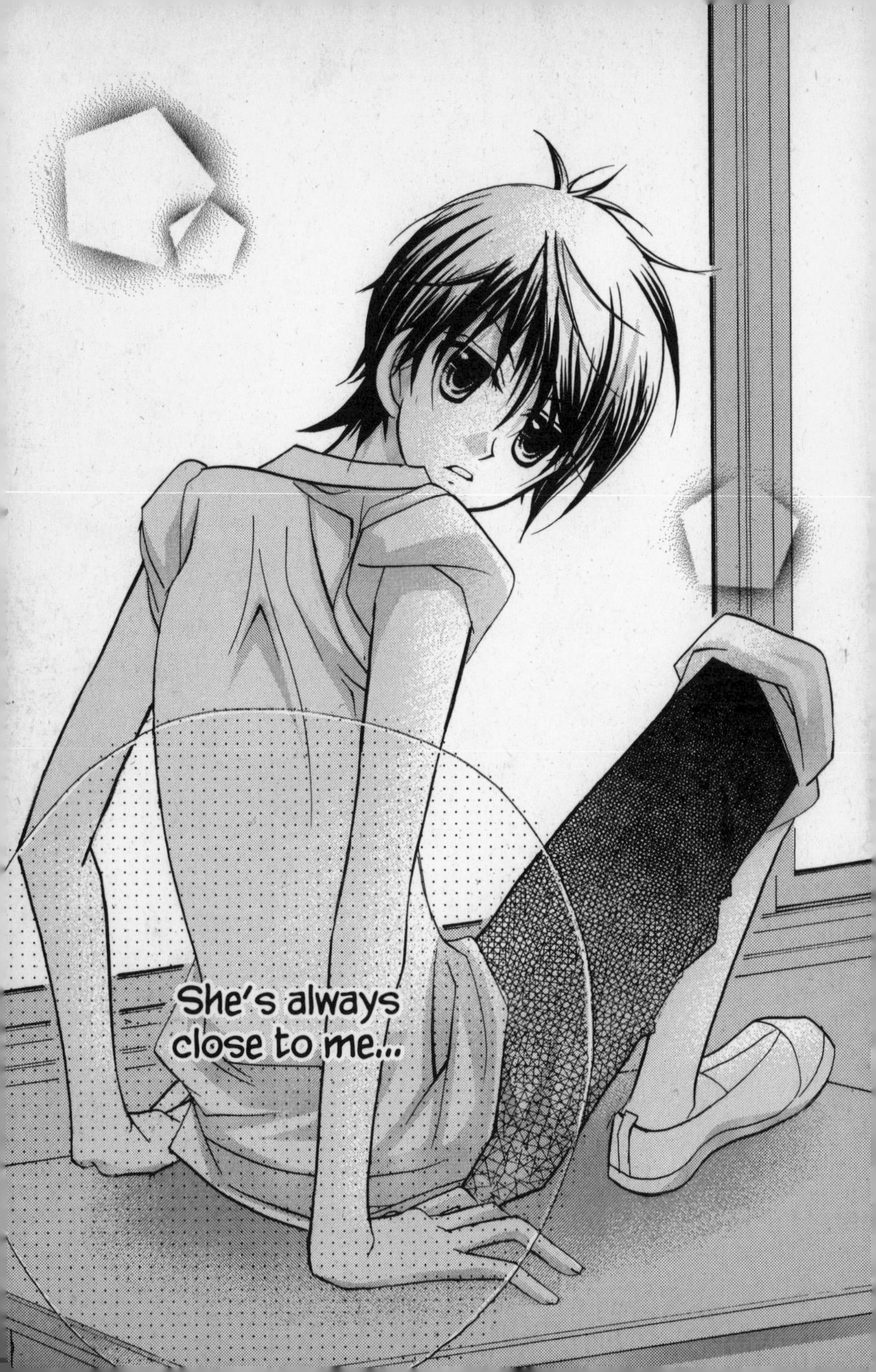
She's always
close to me...

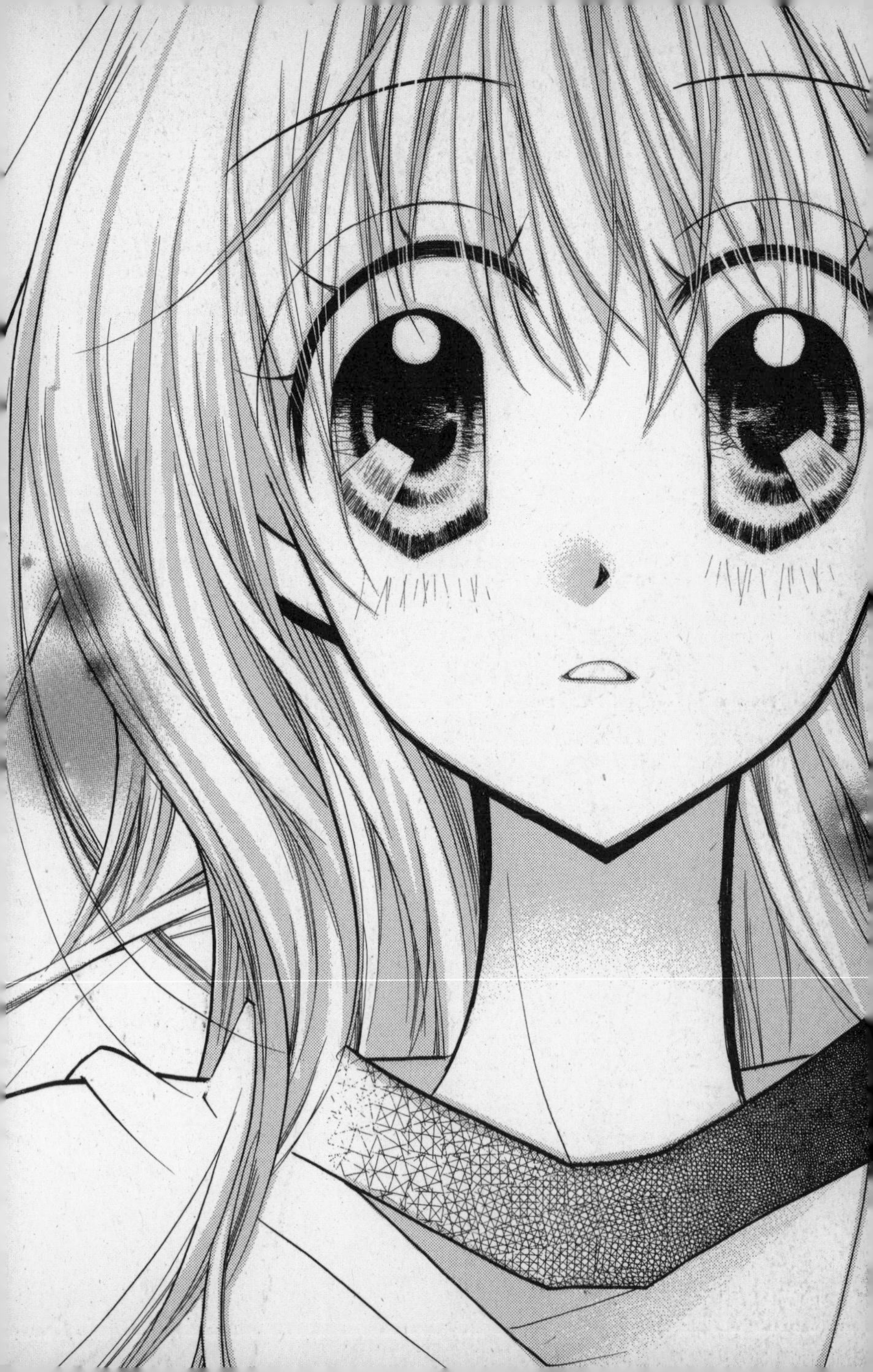

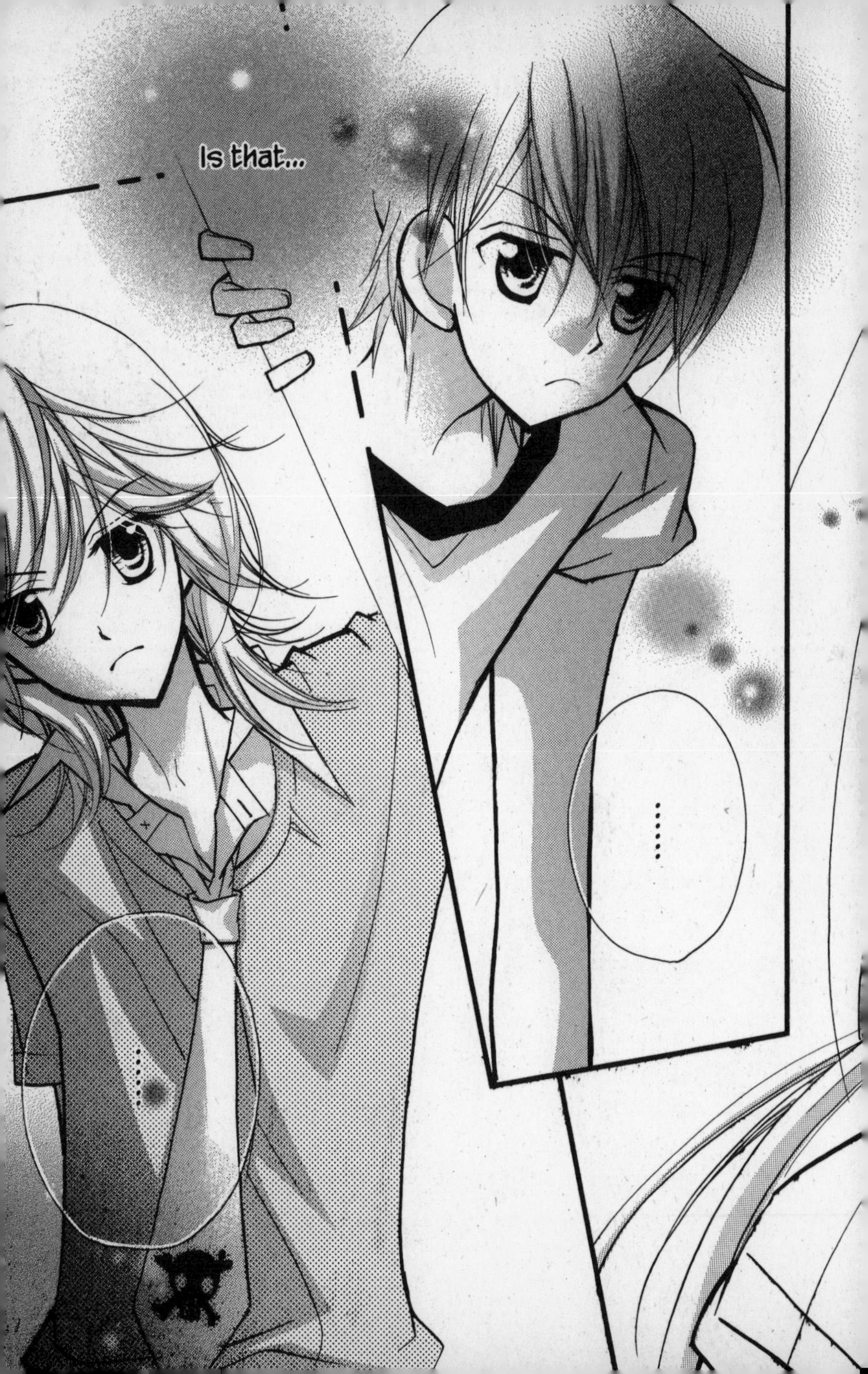
Is that...
......
......

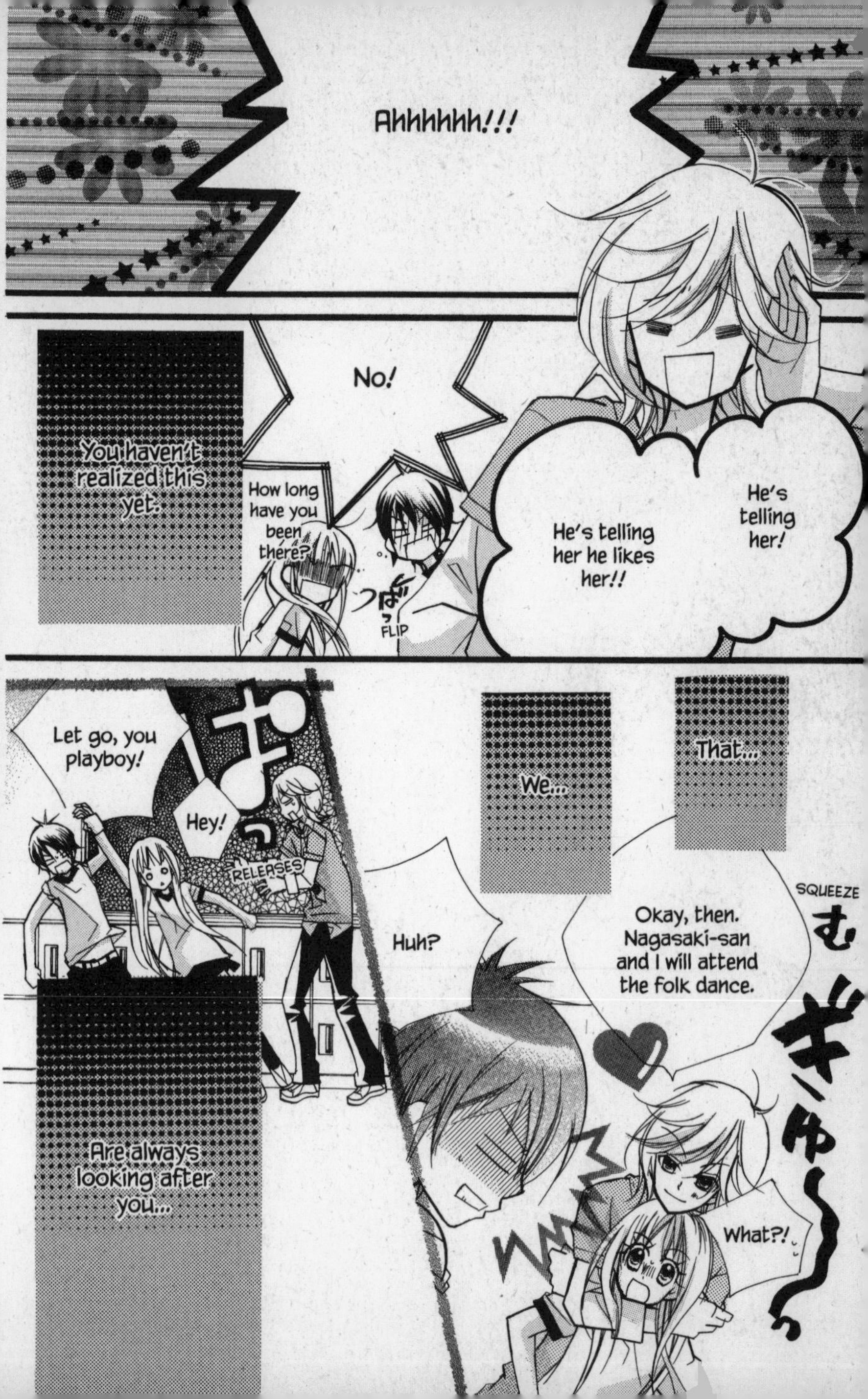
Ahhhhhh!!!
He's telling her!
He's telling her he likes her!!
No!
How long have you been there?
FLIP
You haven't realized this yet.
That...
We...
SQUEEZE
Okay, then. Nagasaki-san and I will attend the folk dance.
What?!
Huh?
Hey!
RELEASES
Let go, you playboy!
Are always looking after you...

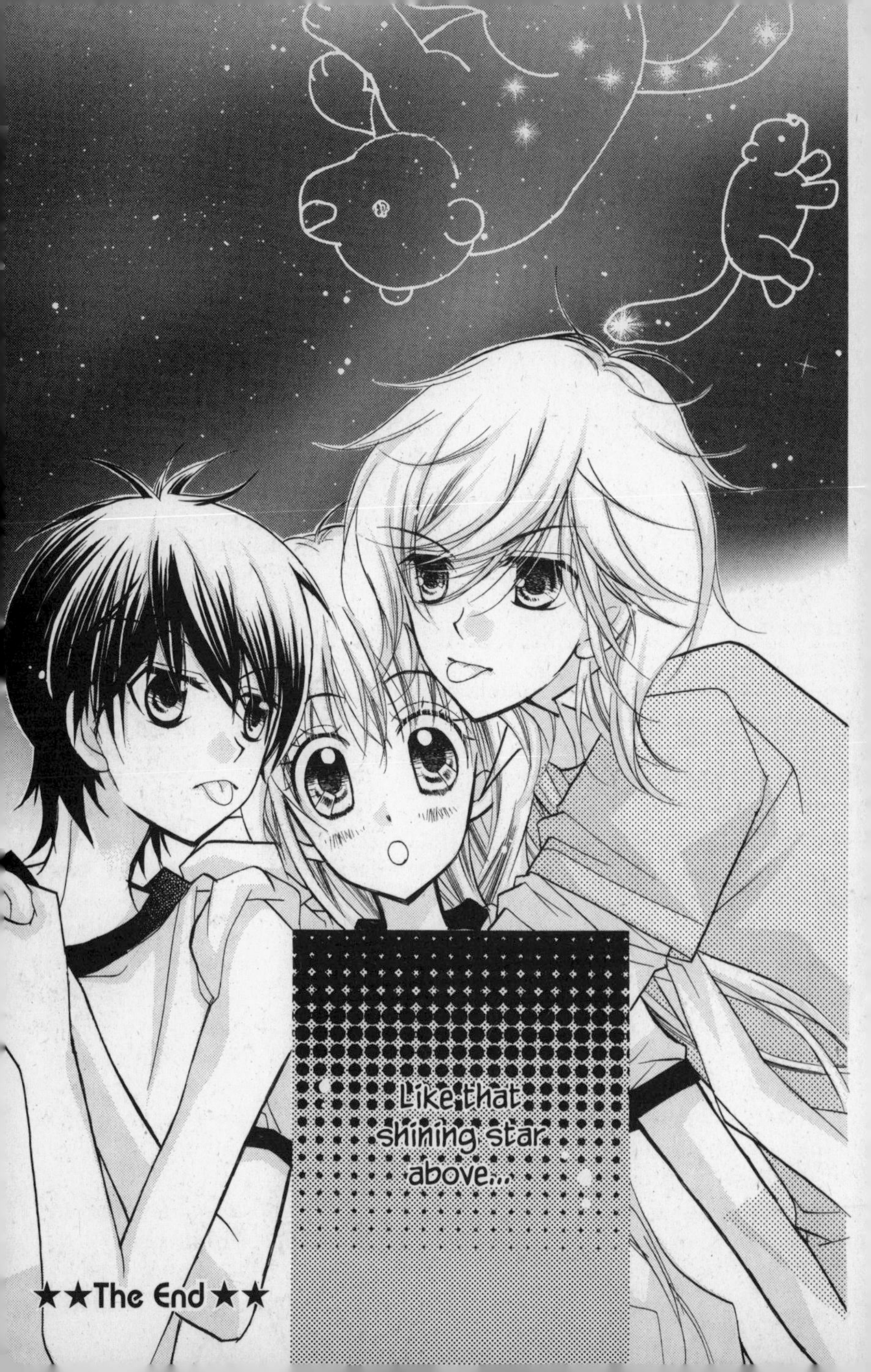
Like that shining star above...
★★The End★★

Translation Notes

Japanese is a tricky language for most Westerners, and translation is often more art than science. For your edification and reading pleasure, here are notes on some of the places where we could have gone in a different direction with our translation of the work, or where a Japanese cultural reference is used.

Necrotic tooth,
page 7
Necrosis refers to the death of body tissue. It happens when there isn't enough blood going to the tissue. In this case, Haruka is complaining that her tooth's nerve endings have died.

Youkan,
page 73
Youkan is a traditional Japanese desert that looks like Jello. It is usually made from sugar, water, and red bean paste.

Kagura,
page 103
Kagura is a traditional Shinto (Japanese religion based on animism) dance that depicts a folktale.

Izumo folktales,
page 103
Folktales that originate from one of the most important Shinto shrines in Japan, located in Shimane Prefecture; they usually center around the first gods who descended upon Japan.

Yamata No Orochi,
page 103
Literally translated as "the eight-forked serpent," the Yamata No Orochi is a folktale about the god named Susano-o, who was expelled from heaven after he tricked his sister, Amaterasu, the sun goddess. When on Earth, he encounters a couple crying by the river. They are sad because they must give up their eighth daughter to an eight-headed monster. Sympathetic, Susano-o gets the monster drunk and then stabs it with a sword, which breaks off in the monster's tail. Susano-o thrusts his hand into the monster and pulls out another sword, which he then gives to his sister as a peace offering.

Mochi, page 103

A staple at festivals, *mochi* is a Japanese desert that's made out of sticky rice. Some are plain, some are grilled, some are stuffed with red bean paste, and some come wrapped in seaweed.

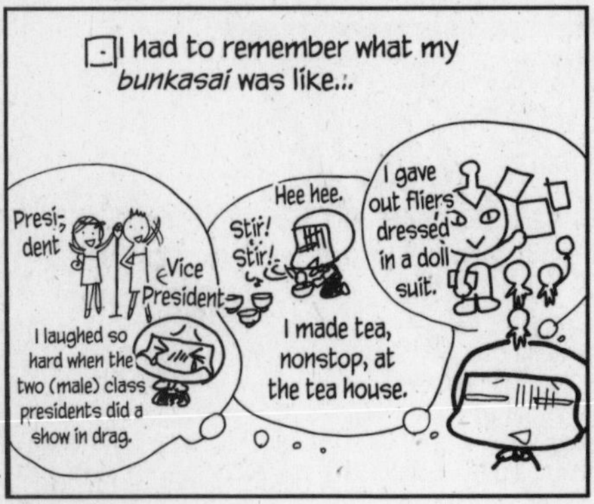
I had to remember what my bunkasai was like...
I gave out fliers dressed in a doll suit.
Hee hee.
Stir! Stir!
I made tea, nonstop, at the tea house.
President
Vice President
I laughed so hard when the two (male) class presidents did a show in drag.

Bunkasai, page 132

All Japanese schools have a *bunkasai*, or cultural festival, once a year. Each class puts on talent shows and plays, puts on a battle of the bands, and set up cafés and other food stalls for everyone's amusement. Many *bunkasai* in Japan end with a bonfire at night; students often do a folk dance around the fire.

Gakuensai, page 135

This term is interchangeable with *bunkasai*. See above for an explanation.

Small Bear and Big Bear, page 143

The Small Bear is a constellation also known as Ursa Minor, or the Little Dipper. The Big Bear, or the Ursa Major, is made up of many stars, but the most distinct set is the Big Dipper, which comprises the tail of the Big Bear.

Burnables, page 159

Recycling in Japan is split into many categories, including flammable and nonflammable garbage.

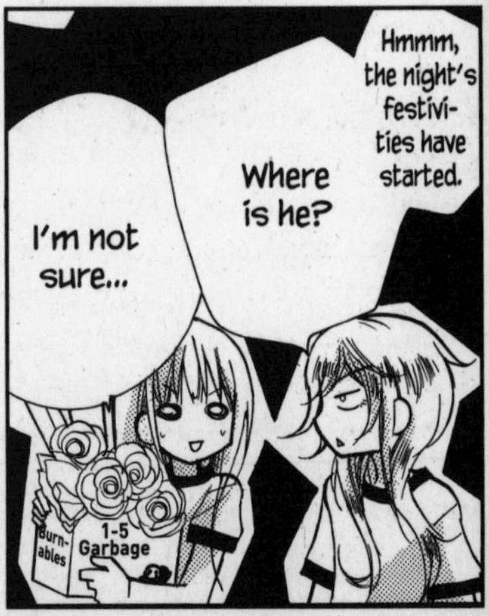
Hmmm, the night's festivities have started.
Where is he?
I'm not sure...
1-5 Garbage
Burnables

TOMARE!

止まれ

[STOP!]

You're going the wrong way!

Manga is a completely different type of reading experience.

To start at the *beginning*,
go to the *end*!

That's right! Authentic manga is read the traditional Japanese way—from right to left. Exactly the *opposite* of how American books are read. It's easy to follow: Just go to the other end of the book, and read each page—and each panel—from right side to left side, starting at the top right. Now you're experiencing manga as it was meant to be!